"*The second edition of Behavioral Family therapy for Psychiatric Disorders is an invaluable resource for clinicians. Mueser and Glynn have provided all the necessary tools for establishing collaborate relationships with families, while teaching them about the management and treatment of psychiatric illness. This book should be on every therapist's bookshelf.*"

> —Arnold A. Lazarus, Ph.D.; Distinguished Professor Emeritus, Graduate School of Applied & Professional Psychology, Rutgers-The State University of New Jersey

"*This is a gem of a book. An absolute must read for all mental health professionals who work with families, it is comprehensive and detailed without being boring. And it provides the information necessary to work with people who are difficult to help. Professionals who have avoided working with the relatives of those with psychiatric disorders, including the serious mental illnesses, will find that difficulties diminish when they adopt the coherent and integrated approach advocated by these authors. Families and consumers of mental health services should also read and benefit from this book. It is a remarkable achievement.*"

> —Dale Johnson, Ph.D.; Professor, Department of Psychology, University of Houston; Past President, National Alliance for the Mentally Ill

"*Behavioral Family Therapy for Psychiatric Disorders: Second Edition is the perfect book for clinicians that want their clients and their families to benefit from evidenced-base care. The book explains why family work is important, teaches clinicians how to do it, and supplies the needed supporting materials. The authors clearly communicate their vast practical experience, allowing motivated clinicians to begin their work many steps ahead. I make it required reading for all trainees.*"

> —William C. Torrey, M.D.; Coordinator of Community Training and Assistant Professor of Psychiatry, Dartmouth Medical School; Medical Director of West Central Services, Lebanon, New Hampshire

"*The challenges faced by families with severe mental illness are many and varied. Mueser and Glynn have crafted a book that is sensitive to these challenges, both from the perspective of persons with mental illness and their family members. This volume is a comprehensive summary of the assessment and intervention strategies that will empower families to address the burden of schizophrenia and other mental illness. In its second edition it advances these efforts with a detailed and thoughtful summary of current research on behavioral family therapy. A must read for all practitioners, the book is also accessible to consumers, their families, and others interested in expanding their knowledge about mental illness and the family.*"

> —Patrick W. Corrigan, Psy. D., Executive Director, Center for Psychiatric Rehabilitation; Associate Professor of Psychiatry, Pritzker School of Medicine of the University of Chicago

"*Behavioral Family Therapy for Psychiatric Disorders: Second Edition*, is a superb description of how help family members communicate with severely disturbed psychiatric patients. It is clearly articulated, well written, informative, and data oriented. The book is replete with excellent examples that should enable both students and active professionals to have greater impact on the families of psychiatric patients. In short, Mueser and Glynn's book should be on the shelf of all professionals who work with the families of psychiatric patients."

—Michel Hersen, Ph.D., A.B.P.P., Professor and Dean, School of Professional Psychology, Pacific University

"*One of the major impacts of mental illness is the disconnections it causes for family members. Behavioral Family Therapy: Second Edition improves these often severely bruised connections by providing all family members knowledge of mental illness and recovery, as well as communication and problem-solving skills, within a supportive, educational process.*

I especially liked the focus on the family as a whole. Siblings, for example, have often been neglected or ignored by the mental health system. Yet they have very profound reactions to the onset of mental illness in a brother or sister. The authors show great sensitivity to the struggles of consumers and each of their family members by clearly describing what is happening, how to develop coping mechanisms, what it takes to rebuild family life and find the meaning in their experiences.

This book should be read by every mental health professional that is working with people with mental illness and their families.

—LeRoy Spaniol, Ph.D., Executive Publisher, *The Psychiatric Rehabilitation Journal*

"*Well-organized, clearly presented, and easy to read, this wonderful text can be used not only to learn about behavioral family therapy, but also as a manual in clinical practice. Each stage of treatment is clearly described and excellent examples are provided at every step. The guidelines allow the therapist flexibility in working with specific families. This makes it a valuable resource for those working with both inpatients and outpatients with schizophrenia, including those who are experiencing their first episode of psychosis for whom an individual family approach is preferred.*"

—Jean Addington, Ph.D., Adjunct Associate Professor, University of Calgary; Coordinator of the Calgary Early Psychosis Program

Behavioral Family Therapy for Psychiatric Disorders

Second Edition

Kim T. Mueser

Shirley M. Glynn

New Harbinger Publications, Inc.

Distributed in the U.S.A. by Publishers Group West; in Canada by Raincoast Books; in Great Britain by Airlift Book Company, Ltd.; in South Africa by Real Books, Ltd.; in Australia by Boobook; and in New Zealand by Tandem Press.

Copyright © 1999 by Kim T. Mueser and Shirley M. Glynn
          New Harbinger Publications, Inc.
          5674 Shattuck Avenue
          Oakland, CA 94609

Cover design by Poulson/Gluck Design
Text design by Michele Waters

Library of Congress Catalog Card Number: 98-68758
ISBN 1-57224-143-8 Paperback

The first edition of this book was published by Allyn and Bacon in 1995.

New Harbinger Publications' Website address: www.newharbinger.com

01   00   99

10   9   8   7   6   5   4   3   2   1

First printing

To our parents, Sonja and Roland (KTM) and Philip and Shirley (SMG), for their love and support over the years.

To my family, Rachel, Jacob, Anna, and Ben (KTM).

And to the courageous families with whom we have worked who have let us into their lives and shown strength in the face of many obstacles.

CONTENTS

FOREWORD

Biobehavioral therapies are the treatments for mental disorders in the 21ˢᵗ century. *Behavioral Family Therapy*, integrated with judicious types and doses of psychotropic medications, is one of the 'cutting edge' *biobehavioral therapies* that has been empirically documented to be effective for a variety of mental disorders—schizophrenia, bipolar disorder, and major depression (Miklowitz & Goldstein, 1997; Falloon et al., 1999). When combined with appropriate psychotropic medications, patients and relatives who participate in behavioral family therapy can expect to gain mastery and control over heretofore baffling mental illnesses, experience fewer relapses and rehospitalizations, attain higher levels of social and occupational functioning, and enjoy a better quality of life.

As a therapist's manual, *Behavioral Family Therapy* stands out from many others that are now emerging for use by practitioners. In the first place, the manual is highly practical and operationalized so that most clinicians can use the techniques that the authors describe. If it is true, as Albert Einstein is reputed to have said, that "God is in the details," then Mueser and Glynn have produced a heavenly book. Secondly, through almost two decades of their direct clinical experience, Mueser and Glynn have shared with clinicians 'tried and tested' methods that have survived the test of time. Thirdly, the procedures that the authors present in their manual are readily adapted to a wide variety of clinical populations, therapists, and settings. In fact, many of the principles and procedures in *Behavioral Family Therapy* were first validated in improving the quality of distressed marriages (Liberman et al., 1980). Thus, the educational techniques for improving communication and problem-solving skills are 'generic' and helpful for everyone—whether or not a mental disorder is present.

Finally, the authors have crafted a manual with interventions that are linked to the phases of mental disorders. For example, they provide methods for engaging the family as partners in the treatment enterprise—a step that should be taken when the patient is in his or her *acute* phase of mental disorder. During acute episodes of psychosis or depression, family members tend to be at the height of their motivation for engagement with the treatment team, and Mueser and Glynn show how to capitalize on this heightened motivation. Training the family and patient conjointly in communication and problem-solving skills comes later, when the patient has entered the *stable* phase of disorder and can assimilate the more rigorous learning of skills encompassed by this stage of behavioral family therapy. Also distinctive in the Mueser and Glynn manual is the integration of assessment with intervention. They show clearly how to go about soliciting information from relatives which is then utilized for individualizing the educational process for each family.

It is particularly gratifying to see a second generation of experienced scientist-clinicians—such as Kim Mueser and Shirley Glynn—take the methods that were developed in the 1970's and early 1980's by myself and my colleagues—and elevate them to a higher level of flexibility, adaptability, and utility for clinicians. Seeking ways to use *flexible levels of intervention* to meet the varied needs of families, patients, clinicians and mental health programs, Mueser and Glynn have organized and written a superb book or treatment manual that should be close at hand for everyday use by all mental health professionals who wish to amplify their impact by constructively involving families in their work. For a double-barreled repertoire, clinicians will also want to use the companion book for family members and patients, the very fine guidebook, *Coping with Schizophrenia* (Mueser and Gingerich, 1994).

Robert Paul Liberman, M.D.
Professor of Psychiatry, UCLA School of Medicine;
Director, UCLA Center for Research on Treatment and
Rehabilitation of Psychosis

PREFACE

Serious psychiatric disorders have a devastating effect on the family. However, despite the profound impact of mental illness on clients and their relatives, families can learn how to cope effectively with the disorder and ensure that the personal needs of all members are met. This book is designed to help mental health professionals foster a positive, supportive, and mutually collaborative relationship to assist families with a psychiatric client.

For many individuals with a psychiatric disorder, family ties are the most important social relationships in their lives. However, symptomatic behaviors that are unpredictable, frustrating, and even frightening often lead to tension and conflict in the family. Stressful family relationships can worsen the course of psychiatric disorders and increase the burden of caring for the client on relatives. There is a pressing need for clinical interventions aimed at improving the quality of life of all the individuals in families with a psychiatric client.

Behavioral Family Therapy (BFT) is a family treatment model that combines educational and social learning approaches to enhance the functioning of the family and improve the course of the psychiatric disorder. The BFT model posits that families, working together with professionals, have the capacity to monitor and manage serious psychiatric disorders, thereby promoting clients' independence, improving their social functioning, and reducing relapses and rehospitalizations. The BFT approach to psychiatric disorders is similar to comprehensive treatments for debilitating physical illnesses, such as diabetes or heart disease, wherein the family is engaged to support the patient in making substantial lifestyle changes (e.g., diet, exercise, medication) and in dealing with stress more effectively.

In order for family members to participate successfully in the management of a psychiatric disorder, they need basic information about the nature of the disorder, such as its characteristic symptoms, the effects of medication and psychological treatments, and its long-term course. Furthermore, because stress often leads to a breakdown in communication between family members, families also benefit from improving their ability to communicate more effectively, and from learning strategies for resolving problems and achieving personal and family goals. The BFT model addresses each of these needs in a structured yet flexible format that is applicable to a wide range of psychiatric disorders and family constellations. This book has been written to provide professionals with the necessary background and theoretical rationale for BFT, as well as to describe in detail the clinical application of the model.

Chapter 1 ("Families as Members of the Treatment Team") provides a historical review of the relationship between mental health professionals and families of the mentally ill and describes the theoretical underpinnings of the BFT model, who may benefit from BFT, and who is qualified to provide the treatment. Chapter 2 ("An Overview of Behavioral Family Therapy") summarizes the BFT model, addresses logistical issues about conducting the therapy, and discusses overarching clinical practices guiding the provision of BFT. In chapter 3 ("Engaging the Family") we describe strategies for engaging families in the therapeutic process and creating positive expectations for participation in therapy. Chapter 4 ("Assessment of the Family") covers assessment, which, as with other behavior therapies, is the cornerstone of BFT. Chapters 5 ("Education about Psychiatric Disorders"), 6 ("Communication Skills Training"), and 7 ("Problem-Solving Training") describe the clinical methods that are the core of BFT. In chapter 8 ("Special Problems") we give suggestions for addressing specific problems that pose a threat to optimal family functioning, such as substance abuse, persistent psychotic symptoms, violence, chronic anxiety, disorganization, and negative symptoms or secondary depression. Chapter 9 ("Termination and Strategies for Maintenance") provides a guide for assessing the readiness of a family to terminate therapy, preparing family members for the end of treatment, developing strategies to ensure the maintenance of treatment gains (such as continued "booster" sessions or participation in a multiple-family support group), and anticipating future needs of participants. Chapter 10 ("Research on Behavioral Family Therapy") provides a review of research on BFT for schizophrenia, major affective disorders, and anxiety disorders.

One of our primary goals in writing this book has been to make it as "user friendly" as possible. To this end, throughout the book we have provided numerous clinical vignettes (based on real families) and excerpts from actual treatment sessions to illustrate specific points and BFT strategies. We have also provided an extensive list of resources (organizations and books) at the end of chapter 5 to help therapists and families learn more about specific psychiatric disorders and their management. Finally, the appendixes contain blank copies of the assessment and homework forms which therapists can use when working with their families. The appendixes also contain handouts identifying the different steps of the communication and problem solving techniques taught in BFT, as well as educational handouts describing various psychiatric disorders, medications, the stress-vulnerability model, the role of families, and the effects of alcohol and drugs on people with a psychiatric disorder. Copyright permission has been granted for therapists to make copies of all the material contained in the appendixes.

BFT for psychiatric disorders is a broad-based model that is most often applied by psychologists, psychiatrists, nurses, social workers, and case managers. Our experience with BFT suggests that the model is particularly beneficial to families with a member who has schizophrenia-spectrum disorder, bipolar disorder, major depression, chronic post-traumatic stress disorder, or obsessive-compulsive disorder. In addition to these disorders, the BFT model can also be applied to help families cope with other disorders, such as other chronic anxiety disorders (e.g., generalized anxiety disorder, agoraphobia, panic disorder), personality disorders (e.g., borderline personality disorder), and eating disorders (e.g., bulimia).

As reviewed in chapter 10, empirical research supports the clinical effectiveness of the BFT model. We are encouraged that the provision of BFT, embedded in a comprehensive treatment model with components such as pharmacotherapy, case management, rehabilitation, supported employment, and individual counseling, can substantially improve the quality of life for these clients and their relatives. BFT represents a viable approach for establishing a collaborative relationship between professionals and families that builds on all available resources for the care of psychiatric disorders.

ACKNOWLEDGMENTS

We are grateful to many individuals who have influenced our thinking about families and mental illness and who have contributed in various ways to the writing of this book. Among the most important people we have learned from, Robert P. Liberman, M.D., Ian R.H. Falloon, M.D., Christine McGill, M.S.W., Ph.D., and the late Gayla Blackwell, R.N., M.S.W. stand out as mentors and role models.

Our colleagues have provided us with much support and assistance in explicating the BFT model for psychiatric disorders. We wish to thank the following colleagues for the help they have given us: Julie Agresta, M.S.S., Patricia Auciello, M.A., Edward Bailey, M.A., Alan S. Bellack, Ph.D., Robin E. Clark, Ph.D., Emil Coccaro, M.D., Robert E. Drake, M.D., Ph.D., Spencer Eth., M.D., Edna B. Foa, Ph.D., Lindy Fox, M.A., Blanche Freund, Ph.D., Susan L. Gingerich, M.S.W., Sylvia Gratz, D.O., James D. Herbert, Ph.D., Samuel J. Keith, M.D., Michael J. Kozak, Ph.D., Tim Kuehnel, Ph.D., Marc LaPorta, Ph.D., Douglas L. Levinson, M.D., Stephen Marder, M.D., William McFarlane, M.D., Douglas L. Noordsy, M.D., Maggie Pfeiffer, M.S.W., Eugenia T. Randolph, Ph.D., Steven L. Sayers, Ph.D., Nina R. Schooler, Ph.D., George M. Simpson, M.D., Deborah Spungeon, M.A., William Torrey, M.D., and Joye Weisel-Barth, Ph.D.

In addition to the collegial support we have received, we appreciate the opportunity to have worked with so many fine family therapists, whose skills are evident throughout this book, including: Susan Balder, M.S.W., Hillary Baumgarten, R.N., Laurie Boxer, Ph.D., Michele Cascardi, Ph.D., Kathleen Cleary, M.S.N., Deborah Clemment, M.A., Judith Crothers, Ph.D., Harry Cunningham, M.A., Ester Deblnger, Ph.D., Martin Franklin, Ph.D., Michele Hamilton, M.S.N., Mark Heller, M.S.W., Deborah Olivieri, R.N., Susan Rappaport, M.S.N., Carole K. Rosenthal, Ph.D., Margaret Sayers, Ph.D., Vivian Schirn, M.A., Edward Schlaeger, M.S.W., Marleen Urbaitis, Ph.D., Eileen Wade, Ph.D., and Marcella Walters, M.S.W.

We owe thanks to several people who have proved invaluable to us in the production of the second edition of this book: Kathy Luger, Pauline Morrisette, Somi Park, Peggy Bowman, and Peter Glynn.

Finally, we are indebted to the many families with whom we have worked over the years, whose strength, determination, and love have taught us so much about how families can cope and live with a psychiatric disorder.

CHAPTER 1

FAMILIES AS MEMBERS OF THE TREATMENT TEAM

Comparable to a serious physical illness, the experience of having a serious psychiatric illness profoundly changes the life of the person with the disorder and those who care for him or her. At a most basic level, the need to interact consistently with a mental health treatment system and to adhere to a set of recommendations and medication regimens can be complicated and distressing for both clients and relatives. Just as important, psychiatric symptoms such as hallucinations, delusions, unremitting depressions, or obsessive thoughts are by their very nature usually extremely disturbing, often creating additional anxiety in both the ill individual and the family. Functional impairments accruing from these symptoms, such as an inability to hold a job, social withdrawal, and a failure or inability to plan for the future, can further stress the family system. As in the case of those with chronic but episodic physical disorders such as multiple sclerosis, both the client and the family are also confronted with the prospect that active management of the illness, including adherence to an optimal treatment plan, can greatly improve the prognosis of the disorder, but even under the best circumstances, occasional exacerbations are to be expected. Simply put, the client and family must hope and work for the best times while preparing for the worst times.

Family participation in a treatment plan to improve the outcome of a serious physical illness is commonplace. A visit to any hospital will likely reveal "heart healthy" cooking classes for caregivers of cardiac patients, support sessions on sexual dysfunction and other disabilities for partners of diabetic and cancer patients, and intensive social work involvement with families of people who have had a stroke. Implicit in these services is the recognition not only that patients bear an enormous responsibility for participating in their own rehabilitation but also that family members, who are often the primary support persons for these patients, can add immeasurably to these efforts. Provision of these services is also an acknowledgment that a serious physical illness usually causes an upheaval in a family, not just in a patient. Old hopes, dreams, and habits are surrendered (at least temporarily—and sometimes permanently) for new fears, reduced expectations, and lifestyle changes.

Although the similarities seem clear, the role of family participation in the treatment plans of individuals with a serious psychiatric illness is much more complicated than in the case of those with a serious physical illness. Throughout much of this century, families were viewed by professionals as either incidental to the development and course of psychiatric disorders, which were presumed to be strictly biological in nature, or they were actually thought to play a key role in their cause (Sullivan, 1927; Fromm-Reichmann, 1948; Bateson et al., 1956; Bowen, 1961). As the latter viewpoint gained acceptance among psychiatrists, psychologists, and social workers from the 1940s through the 1960s, the predominant attitude of professionals toward families of the seriously psychiatrically ill gravitated from one of indifference to one of suspicion and blame, grounded in the belief that a pathological family was at the root of every mental disorder.

While etiological theories of the family's role in mental illness enjoyed considerable popularity for several decades, support for these theories began to wane as evidence accumulated from research in the 1960s and 1970s that challenged their validity. Research on familial factors in mental illness using data from studies of twins or adopted-away offspring repeatedly documented that family members with an ill relative have an increased genetic vulnerability to similar disorders that could not be readily explained by a shared environment (Rosenthal & Kety, 1968; Gottesman & Shields, 1972; Gershon et al., 1976; Bertelsen et al., 1977). Similarly, advances in the pharmacological treatment of psychiatric disorders, such as the discovery of antipsychotic medications, antidepressant medications, and lithium, raised further questions about the plausibility of purely psychological theories of these disorders (Meltzer, 1987).

A second major challenge to models of family etiology of psychiatric disorder was the dismal failure of family interventions based on these theories (reviewed by Massie & Beels, 1972). These family therapy approaches usually focused on conveying to relatives the role they were believed to have played in the development of the psychiatric disorder. Understandably, family members often reacted negatively to these well-intentioned efforts, which rarely had any clinical benefits. The unintended outcome of many of the early family interventions was that family therapy had a destructive effect on the family unit by alienating relatives from an active participation in the psychiatric treatment plan of their ill family member (Appleton, 1974; Terkelsen, 1983).

Grounded in a biological reformulation of the etiology of serious psychiatric illnesses over the past twenty years, a paradigmatic shift has occurred in the relationship between mental health professionals and the families of persons with a psychiatric disorder. Theories of the family as the cause of psychiatric disorders are now widely accepted as obsolete. A new model has emerged that views family members as an important resource to the client and the professional, similar to that offered by families of patients with biologically based disorders. Clients with a serious psychiatric illness are now understood to also be dealing with a biologically based illness that is exacerbated by environmental stress. The realization that the family can contribute to the treatment of psychiatric disorder has not been limited to those clients with the most severe disorders, requiring periodic hospitalization, but has extended to those with other disorders as well, including those that rarely require inpatient hospitalization, such as most anxiety disorders and many cases of major depression. Under the best circumstances, the family can be integral to helping all of these clients manage stress and reduce biological vulnerability through adherence to a medication regimen. Under less than ideal circumstances, when their own needs are not being met, families can be an unfortunate source of stress on clients. Interventions designed to increase medication compliance and improve stress management are thus optimal for clients and families.

This alternative intervention model represents a crucial shift in thinking. The new paradigm has forced professionals to confront the biological reality of most serious psychiatric disorders, challenging long-held assumptions that disturbed family relationships are at the root of these disorders. The new attitude adopted by mental health professionals eschews blaming and pathologizing the family and instead seeks to understand and empathize with the distress relatives experience when attempting to cope with an ill family member. Above all, the new model recognizes that the concern of relatives for their loved one and their high degree of contact with the ill family member represent an important opportunity for collaboration with the professional in the treatment of the disorder.

By joining with professionals as members of the client's extended treatment team, the family has become recognized as an invaluable resource, and its role has grown in the management and rehabilitation of psychiatric disorders, just as with physical health disorders. The acceptance of this new model of the family as members of the treatment team is reflected in the recent proliferation of books for family members about psychiatric disorders (e.g., Backlar, 1994; Bourne, 1996; Copeland, 1994; Klein & Wender, 1993; Matsakis, 1996; Mueser & Gingerich, 1994; Torrey, 1995; Whybrow, 1997), as well as books for professionals about the families of the mentally ill (e.g., Atkinson & Coia, 1995; Marsh, 1992, 1998; Marsh & Magee, 1997). Behavioral Family Therapy (BFT) was developed to help family members, including the client, actively join with professionals in the treatment of psychiatric disorder.

Behavioral Family Therapy (BFT) for Psychiatric Disorders

In order for family members to become active participants in the client's treatment, they must acquire general knowledge about the disorder and be able to solve common problems and achieve goals related to it. Relatives need to learn basic information about their family member's psychiatric disorder, such as the diagnosis, its symptoms, the presumed biological causes, and the medications used to treat it. Helping relatives understand the nature of the family member's disorder is crucial for reducing the tendency of some relatives to blame the client for symptoms. Given the episodic course of many of the major psychiatric disorders, family members need to be able to recognize the characteristic symptoms in order to monitor the course of the disorder and to take steps to prevent "full-blown" relapses. Finally, they need to be educated about the effects of psychotropic medications on psychiatric disorders as well as their side effects. This information can help family members take a more active role in the treatment, allowing them to recognize possible side effects, facilitate the client's compliance with medication, and alert the treatment team when noncompliance arises. Providing basic information to the family about the psychiatric disorder is an important component of the BFT model.

Although teaching family members about the disorder is a necessary ingredient in effective family interventions, families also benefit from learning how to communicate better with one another and how to pursue goals and solve problems together. Most families with a psychiatric client experience some difficulties communicating with each other and with their ill family member. For example, they may avoid dealing with problems involving the client, or tend to be overly demanding, or try to argue the client out of delusions, hallucinations, or phobic behaviors. In a similar vein, relatives may hesitate or fail to pursue important personal goals or may set unrealistic goals for the client, leading to a high level of stress in the family. Improving the communication skills of relatives can help them learn how to encourage and reinforce small steps made by their loved one toward greater independence and responsibility. Good communication between family members is at the heart of establishing nurturing, supportive family relationships, which are conducive to the growth of everyone involved. Helping families learn how to set realistic, attainable goals and to solve problems using strategies designed to minimize stress and facilitate finding effective solutions can enable them to deal more effectively with the inevitable stress associated with coping with a psychiatric disorder.

The major focus of BFT is threefold: helping families develop a basic knowledge of their relative's disorder; improving communication skills; and fostering the ability to solve problems and achieve goals. In short, the emphasis is on improving the knowledge and skills of family members rather than on resolving specific conflicts or achieving specific goals. The assumption of this approach is that providing relevant information about the psychiatric disorder and enhancing the interactive skills of all family members will strengthen the foundation of the family unit, eventually enabling them to monitor the course of the disorder, to set personal and family goals, and to solve problems without the continuing aid of a therapist. In this way, the goal of BFT is to fortify the family's resources to the point at which the therapist is no longer necessary to help family members monitor the disorder and resolve interpersonal conflicts. By working directly on the skills of family members rather than attempting to solve their problems, the therapist avoids fostering the family dependence on him or her. BFT assumes that most families are capable of solving their own problems when they have developed sufficient skills. Thus, the main role of the therapist in BFT is to teach the family about the disorder and to help them develop more effective strategies for interpersonal communication and problem solving. Solving problems per se is not the therapist's job in this approach.

A final goal of BFT is to enable every family member to achieve a satisfactory quality of life, rather than focusing solely on the client. Although knowledge about the disorder and skills for communicating and solving problems together are necessary ingredients for a fruitful collaboration between families and professionals, relatives also need to learn how to attend to their own desires and goals and how to live their own lives. It is important for relatives to learn how to balance their own needs with those of the client, instead of devoting all of their energy and attention to the client, so that a supportive environment can be created for the entire family. By attending to the needs and goals of all family members, BFT differs from family therapy models for psychiatric disorders with a more predominantly psychoeducational focus, such as interventions for schizophrenia developed by Anderson et al. (1986), Leff and his colleagues (Leff et al., 1982, 1985; Kuipers et al., 1992), Glick and his colleagues (Glick et al., 1985; Haas et al., 1988), and McFarlane (1990; McFarlane et al., 1993).

The importance of addressing the needs of the entire family in BFT is shared by strategic and systems family therapy models (e.g., Minuchin, 1974; Selvini-Palazzoli et al., 1989), which also focus on enhancing the functioning of the family as a unit. A critical difference between BFT and these other family models, however, is that the alternatives deny or downplay the actual existence of biologically based psychiatric disorders, instead conceptualizing "symptoms" in a family member as the result of "scapegoating" or efforts to retain the structural unity and homeostasis of the family. BFT, on the other hand, accepts the biological basis of specific psychiatric disorders, but views the family as having an important potential influence on the course and outcome of the disorder.

The primary aims of BFT are to teach family members the requisite information about psychiatric disorders and to improve their communication and problem-solving skills using social learning methods that have been amply documented to enhance social competence in both clients and the general population. The purpose of this book is to provide a guide to therapists for conducting BFT with families of psychiatric clients, including how to engage clients and relatives in treatment, assess the individual and collective needs of the family, and provide educational material, communication skills, and training in solving problems.

Before describing the BFT method, we provide the reader with necessary background information about the role of the family in caring for psychiatric clients. We first discuss the role of the deinstitutionalization movement in shifting the long-term management of serious psychiatric disorders from state hospitals to the community and directly onto the shoulders of many families. The negative impact of this increased responsibility on families is considered, as are the effects of a major psychiatric disorder on the quality of family and marital relationships. The importance of the family consumer movement, which arose to advocate for badly needed reforms in community-based treatment of serious psychiatric disorders, is considered. We also review evidence indicating that a stressful family environment and interpersonal conflict can worsen the course of psychiatric disorder, increasing the client's vulnerability to relapses and rehospitalizations. These findings are integrated in an interactive model that incorporates our current knowledge about the burden of psychiatric disorder on the family, family and client coping, and the possible outcomes of the client's disorder. We then provide a brief overview of the BFT model (chapter 2 contains a more in-depth overview), followed by a discussion of its history. Finally, we address the question of who may benefit from BFT and the qualifications needed by therapists to conduct this treatment.

The Unmet Service Needs of People with Serious Psychiatric Illnesses

The focus of treatment for serious psychiatric illness has changed dramatically in the past forty years. The genesis and impact of the deinstitutionalization movement has been well documented (e.g., Grob, 1994; A.B. Johnson, 1990). In the era preceding deinstitutionalization, the primary function of the state hospital was to provide custodial care to psychiatric clients with the tacit assumption that serious psychiatric disorders were essentially untreatable. In the late 1950s and early 1960s, the discovery of psychotropic medications generated more hope for recovery. These medications resulted in dramatic improvements in symptomatology for many institutionalized clients who were previously thought to be untreatable, thus obviating the need for long-term inpatient treatment. However, while the notion of community-based care is laudable, it is also fraught with challenges, many of which have not been met.

One of the most central questions raised by deinstitutionalization and community care is: where will the client live? Estimates of the proportion of clients with a serious psychiatric illness who live with their parents, siblings, or spouses are high, ranging from 25 percent to 65 percent (Brown & Birtwistle, 1998; Carpentier et al., 1992; Goldman, 1984; Mueser et al., in press). In addition, many psychiatric clients live independently or in supervised residences but maintain ongoing contact with family members. Many of the most seriously mentally ill clients reside in nursing homes (Goldman, 1984), and an increasing number of clients are homeless (Drake et al., 1991; Rosenheck et al., 1997; Susser et al., 1989) or in jails (Jordan et al., 1996; Lamb & Weinberger, 1998; Teplin, 1984; Torrey et al., 1992).

Despite the beneficial effects of medications on schizophrenia, major affective disorders, and anxiety disorders, drugs alone rarely eliminate all the symptoms of a disorder, and clients still experience difficulties in assuming major social roles. Relapse rates for major psychiatric disorders tend to be high, even with optimal pharmacological treatment, with rates often exceeding 25 percent over one year, 50 percent over two years, and 75 percent over three years or more following an acute symptom episode (Andersson et al., 1998; Barlow, 1988; Coryell et al., 1998; Davis, 1976; Goodwin & Jamison, 1990; Moncrieff, 1995; Shea et al., 1992). Furthermore, clients are frequently noncompliant with their medication, undermining the medication's prophylactic effects (Blackwell, 1976; Fenton et al., 1997; Garavan et al., 1998; Gerber & Nehemkis, 1986; Schou, 1997). Not surprisingly, as state hospitals became depopulated, the number of admissions to hospitals for the treatment of acute symptom exacerbations increased proportionately, with readmissions constituting 60 to 70 percent of all hospital admissions (Sharfstein, 1984; Talbott, 1984). The overly optimistic expectations for the effects of psychotropic drugs that set the stage for deinstitutionalization have been tempered by the realization that medication is not a panacea for mental disorder, but rather needs to be complemented with psychosocial interventions and system supports to maximize client outcomes.

The chronic and episodic nature of most serious psychiatric illnesses necessitates ongoing, consistent intervention. When treatment was centralized in state hospitals, it was clear who was responsible for the provision and coordination of clients' care. As care became more community based, ambiguity emerged as to who would assume responsibility for specific facets of their treatment. The diffusion of responsibility for managing the treatment of psychiatric clients in the community disrupted the continuity of care, often resulting in disastrous effects on the course of their disorder. Many clients' families were left "holding the bag," attempting to coordinate mental health services in a complex, fragmented system that was historically resistant to or suspicious of their attempts to help. In essence, many families have been forced to become de facto case managers for their ill relative.

The prospect of treating psychiatric disorders at a lower cost in the community than in the hospital was an important impetus toward deinstitutionalization. In retrospect, however, this expectation appears to have been naive. Clients living in the community require a multifaceted, coordinated array of treatments in order to achieve the best possible outcome, suggesting that effective community-based treatment may sometimes be more expensive than hospital treatment (Häfner & an der Heiden, 1989; Kirk & Therrien, 1975). Nevertheless, psychiatric treatment in the community has been notoriously underfunded since the passage of the Community Mental Health Centers Act in 1963 (Torrey et al., 1988; Talbott, 1990). Model programs such as assertive community treatment (ACT), which was developed by Stein and Test (1980) and involves outreach and comprehensive community-oriented treatment teams, can be more effective, both clinically and economically, for clients with severe psychiatric disorders than hospital-based treatment (Mueser, Bond, et al., 1998). However, the core services required to ensure positive outcomes are often not available in the community, including high-quality pharmacological management, psychosocial rehabilitation, and integrated case management. The result is that relatives often have to spend their own money to buy these services for their ill family member or the client receives substandard treatment.

Families have reacted to their difficulty in getting services and straight answers from professionals with frustration and distrust, which sometimes culminate in high levels of stress at home for the entire family. This dissatisfaction with the mental health system and the treatment they received from professionals led families to organize collectively and to advocate forcefully for changes in the system to better meet the needs of ill family members, as well as their own needs (Hatfield & Lefley, 1987, 1993; Lefley & Johnson, 1990). Organizations such as the National Alliance for the Mentally Ill (NAMI) have played an important role in improving the relationship between professionals and families of the mentally ill by helping to eradicate outmoded theories of the family as the psychogenic cause of psychiatric disturbance and advocating for a higher standard of psychiatric care.

Despite the shortcomings of deinstitutionalization, few have advocated a return to asylums, and there is a consensus that most clients are better off living in the community. Another benefit of the community mental health movement was that professionals have come to recognize the positive role families can play in improving the course of the disorder. In the early years following deinstitutionalization, professionals were unsure of how to work with families of the mentally ill, viewing relatives alternately as a nuisance or irrelevant to the treatment of the client. As families became more vocal in advocating for their own needs as well as those of the client, it became increasingly apparent that they could be potentially important allies of the professional. At the same time, professionals have become enlightened about the difficulties experienced by family members and the need to help them cope more effectively with psychiatric disorder, a primary mission of BFT. We next consider the impact of psychiatric disorder on the well-being and quality of life of family members.

Burden of Psychiatric Disorder on the Family

The negative effect of severe psychiatric disorder on the functioning of other family members has been amply documented in surveys (Creer & Wing, 1974; Hatfield, 1978; Stueve et al., 1997) and poignant personal accounts (Berger & Berger, 1991; Deveson, 1991; Moorman, 1992; Swados, 1991; Vine, 1982). Family members often are faced with learning how to cope with a wide array of problems, including poor self-care skills, aggressive or inappropriate behavior, medication noncompliance, pronounced social withdrawal, suicidality, pervasive anxiety or depression, mood swings, substance abuse, hypomanic or manic behavior, ritualizing behaviors and excessive rumination, and hallucinations and delusions (Cooper, 1996; Jones et al., 1995; Runions & Prudo, 1983). The sheer unpredictability of maintaining a close relationship with a psychiatric client often has a profoundly negative effect on relatives. Research on both animals and humans has shown that aversive events that are not *predictable* have a more damaging effect and are more likely to cause anxiety than equally aversive events that are predictable but not *controllable* (e.g., Mineka et al.,1984). The erratic behavior of many psychiatric clients, combined with the lack of accurate information families often have about the disorder, is stressful and renders family members susceptible to anxiety, depression, and anger.

The distress experienced by relatives who are living with or in close contact with a mentally ill family member can be appreciated by reviewing a survey conducted by Spanoil (1987) of 140 NAMI family members. Table 1.1 summarizes the percentage of relatives who experienced each of several negative emotions related to their family member's disorder. It can be seen from this table that anxiety, frustration, and worry are the most common symptoms of distress experienced by relatives, followed closely by a "sense of burden" and depression. Indeed, distress and burden are pervasive in relatives with a mentally ill family member. Gibbons et al. (1984) reported that there was evidence of hardship, such as emotional or physical ill health, in 90 percent of households containing a relative with a psychiatric disorder. Coyne et al. (1987) reported that more than 40 percent of those living with a depressed client had sufficiently severe stress to meet standardized critera for referral for therapeutic treatment.

TABLE 1.1
COMMON SYMPTOMS OF PSYCHOLOGICAL DISTRESS
EXPERIENCED BY FAMILY MEMBERS
WITH A SERIOUSLY MENTALLY ILL FAMILY MEMBER

Symptom	%
Anxiety	58
Frustration	58
Worry	56
Sense of Burden	55
Depression	48
Grief	47
Anger	42
Shame/Embarrassment	21
Guilt	18

Adapted from Spaniol (1987)

The distinction between objective burden, subjective burden, and personal distress can be useful in understanding the impact of psychiatric disorder on involved relatives (Hoenig & Hamilton, 1966). *Objective burden* refers to the disruptions that the disorder imposes on the routine of the family and its economic resources. *Subjective burden* pertains to the discomfort or distress experienced by the relative that is directly attributed to the psychiatric disorder in the family. *Personal distress* is the overall experience of negative emotions in family members, irrespective of their origin. As might be expected, indices of objective and subjective burden tend to be moderately associated with each other (Coyne et al., 1987; Potasznik & Nelson, 1984; Provencher & Mueser, 1997; Thompson & Doll, 1982), and there is a strong relationship between the experience of burden and levels of personal distress (Coyne et al., 1987; Jackson, et al., 1990; Lefley, 1996).

The economic costs of psychiatric disorder are considerable for many families, especially in the United States, where the fragmentary and poorly funded mental health system often requires them to contribute to the cost of housing or to purchase services for their relative to make up for gaps in available funding (Franks, 1990). For example, Lefley (1987) reported in a survey of NAMI members that a mean of $44,080 was spent by the relatives over the course of the family member's disorder. Economic hardship is particularly burdensome in families where the primary wage earner develops the psychiatric disorder (Clausen & Yarrow, 1955; Noh & Avison, 1988), or where the psychiatric client has a comorbid substance abuse problem (Clark & Drake, 1994).

TABLE 1.2
FACTORS ASSOCIATED WITH INCREASED BURDEN ON RELATIVES

Male client
Female relative
Single parent home
Children in the home
Client living at home
Severity of "negative" symptoms
Duration of disorder
Lack of social support
Stressful life events

The burden and distress experienced by family members with an ill family member is mediated by a number of factors related to the living situation, the characteristics of the family, and the client and his or her disorder. These different factors are summarized in Table 1.2. Relatives who have an ill family member living at home or who have high levels of contact with him or her report higher levels of burden than other families (Anderson & Lynch, 1984; Jacob et al., 1987). Relatives heading single-parent households experience more burden than those in two-parent households (Carpentier et al., 1992). In addition, the presence of children at home also is associated with increased burden and distress, and working women are prone to experience more burden than women who are not working (Gibbons et al., 1984). Noh and Avison (1988) have suggested, based on Pearlin's (1983) theory of social roles and distress, that relatives who occupy multiple roles (e.g., parent, worker) are more likely to experience stress when the additional role of caregiving for the mentally ill family member is required.

The social support available to family members and the recent experience of stressful life events also are important determinants of burden, distress, and well-being related to coping with an ill family member (Noh & Avison, 1988; Potasznik & Nelson, 1984; Solomon & Draine, 1995; Webb et al., 1998). Membership in a self-help advocacy group appears to contribute to improved social support and adjustment in relatives (Hatfield, 1987; D.L. Johnson, 1990). Despite the growing prominence of NAMI and similar organizations, most relatives of persons with psychiatric disorders are not members of such groups, and because of the stigma associated with mental disorder, they lack confidants with whom they can discuss their problems and concerns. For example, Fadden et al. (1987) reported that half of all spouses with a mentally ill partner did not know any other people with an ill partner, and 25 percent felt they had no one to whom they could turn for help and support. It now is widely accepted that social support plays an important role in buffering the negative effects of stressful life events and other types of stressors for *all* individuals (Lazarus, 1966, 1991; Lazarus & Folkman, 1984; Franks et al., 1992), including clients with a psychiatric disorder and their relatives.

The severity of the client's actual symptoms and impairments in social functioning associated with the psychiatric disorder also are related to the amount of burden and distress experienced by his or her relatives (Mors et al., 1992; Reinhard, 1994). There is evidence that the specific type of symptom displayed by the client contributes to the burden of the disorder on the family. The *negative symptoms* of psychiatric disorder refer to symptoms that reflect a loss or diminished capacity in functions ordinarily present in individuals, such as social withdrawal, difficulty experiencing pleasure (*anhedonia*), low motivation, blunted affect, and problems with attention and concentration. *Positive symptoms*, on the other hand, reflect the presence of perceptions, thoughts, or behaviors in the client that are *not* usually present, such as hallucinations, delusions, bizarre behavior, or speech that is odd or difficult to follow. Families tend to find negative symptoms more burdensome than positive symptoms (Fadden et al., 1987; Hooley et al., 1987; Oldridge & Hughes, 1992; Raj et al., 1991; Runions & Prudo, 1983). For example, in a survey of fifty-two relatives with a mentally ill family member, McElroy (1987) found that the five most problematic behaviors were:

1. inability to achieve his or her potential;
2. lack of motivation;
3. inability to prepare for a vocation;
4. inability to work;
5. inability to adhere to or develop a predictable schedule.

Each of these problem behaviors clearly falls in the domain of negative symptoms.

There are several reasons why the negative symptoms of psychiatric disorders are a greater problem for relatives than the positive symptoms. First, negative symptoms tend to be more stable over time than positive symptoms (Mueser et al., 1991), and thus are more likely to be present and to have an impact on relationships with relatives. Positive symptoms usually occur during symptom exacerbations and then subside or go into remission following pharmacological intervention. In contrast, negative symptoms are more likely to be present during residual phases of the disorder and improve less from pharmacological treatments (Kane, 1990). Second, positive symptoms are more readily recognized as manifestations of the psychiatric disorder, because of their conspicuous presence, and hence are assumed by relatives not to be under the client's control. Negative symptoms, on the other hand, are frequently misinterpreted by relatives as "laziness" or a sign of character weakness rather than as symptoms of the psychiatric disorder and are a common source of criticism from relatives (Left & Vaughn, 1985). Third, by their very nature, negative symptoms tend to reflect deficits in social functioning that are more likely to impinge on the social lives of relatives than positive symptoms, which are more personal and experiential (Glynn, 1998). Thus, the severity of the client's negative symptoms and the associated problems in social functioning contribute to the burden of the disorder on other family members.

A final factor contributing to the burden and distress of relatives with a mentally ill family member is the gender of the client. Male psychiatric clients tend to engender greater amounts of burden in their relatives than female clients (Fadden et al., 1987; Mors et al., 1992). Differences in social role expectations between men and women may be one reason underlying the higher burden engendered by male clients. Some have suggested that societally defined roles may be more easily met by women than men (Farina et al., 1963; Busfield, 1982; Goldstein & Kreisman, 1988) and that socially deviant behavior is more readily tolerated in women than men (Clausen, 1975; Farina, 1981). Contrary to this interpretation is the argument that changes in sex-role expectations have increased in recent years primarily for women and may be one factor underlying the increased rate of affective disorders in women (Hafner, 1986). An additional consideration relevant to schizophrenia-spectrum disorders is that gender may be related to the severity and course of the disorder itself. Males tend to have an earlier onset of schizophrenia characterized by more frequent hospitalizations and worse social competence and social adjustment (Angermeyer & Kuhn, 1988; Goldstein, 1988; Haas & Garrett, 1998; Mueser et al., 1990).

It is apparent from the foregoing review that maintaining a close relationship with a psychiatric client is stressful. This problem can be compounded when the involved family member is the client's spouse. Some of the difficulties experienced by the spouses of psychiatric clients who become ill after their marriage are due to the shattering of their expectation that their partner will be socially competent and will assume a fair share of household, parenting, and economic responsibilities. Consequently, marital discord is common in marriages in which one spouse has a psychiatric disorder. Targum et al. (1981) found that 53 percent of spouses with a partner with bipolar disorder reported they would not have married that person if they had known about the disorder. Furthermore, high rates of divorce are common in married clients with affective disorder following their discharge from a psychiatric hospital (Merikangas, 1984; Beach et al., 1986).

The marital discord that is present when one spouse has a psychiatric disorder is usually reflected in disturbances in the couple's social interactions. These problems have been most extensively studied in couples in which one spouse has an affective disorder. Spouses with a depressed mate often report feelings of anger and hostility after an interaction, despite (or because?) of their attempts to suppress these feelings during the exchange (Kahn et al., 1985). Spouses tend to view their mate's depressive behavior as manipulative (Bullock et al., 1972). In support of this interpretation, Biglan et al. (1985) have analyzed sequential data from marital interactions suggesting that the depressive behavior of a spouse may function to ward off the partner's aggression. Beach et al. (1990) have summarized research on the interactions of couples in which one spouse has depression by pointing out that patterns of both negative reciprocity (i.e., extended exchanges of highly charged negative affect between partners) and passivity or avoidance are common problems in communication.

Not all families experience high levels of burden associated with caregiving, and some caregiving relatives report very positive aspects of their relationships, including companionship and receiving assistance from the client on tasks such as household chores (Bulger et al., 1993; Greenberg et al., 1994). Furthermore, client psychiatric status is often not predictive of relatives' caregiver gratification (Bulger et al., 1993; Pickett et al., 1997). However, whether the relative's relationship to the client is that of spouse, parent, child, sibling, or other, most relatives experience some degree of personal distress, even when their contact with the client is not high. Stress and family conflicts are common even for relatives who maintain contact with institutionalized clients. This distress is reflected by the range of negative emotions reported by relatives, as well as by the maladaptive strategies they adopt to cope with the client's frustrating behavior. The lack of accurate information many families have about the psychiatric disorder, combined with the burden of dealing with the client's unpredictable behavior, often leads to disagreements between relatives and the client. Poor skills for solving interpersonal problems among family members can lead to frequent disagreements, culminating in negatively charged conflicts and increased stress on everyone. High levels of stress in the family may in turn worsen the course of the psychiatric disorder. Next, we consider the evidence on the impact of negative familial affect on psychiatric disorders.

Negative Family Affect and the Course of Psychiatric Disorders

A large body of research has been conducted to examine the influence of negative affect and marital discord on the symptoms displayed by psychiatric clients. The most prominent line of investigation began in England more than forty years ago, consisting of a series of studies that looked at the relationship between negative family attitudes, referred to as *Expressed Emotion*, and the course of psychiatric disorders.

Expressed Emotion Research

The potential influence of negative family affect on mental disorder was discovered serendipitously in a study conducted by Brown and his colleagues (Brown et al., 1958). Brown et al. found that male clients with schizophrenia returning from a psychiatric hospital to live with siblings, distant relatives, or in hostels were less likely to have relapses than those returning to parental homes or their wives. A second study replicated the favorable effect of clients' living with siblings compared with parents or wives (Brown et al., 1962). The worse prognosis of the clients living with parents or spouses could not be attributed to differences in either the severity or the duration of their disorder, suggesting that some characteristic of the family environment predisposed clients to relapses. Brown and his colleagues hypothesized that clients living with close relatives might be exposed to higher levels of negative affect or intrusiveness, increasing their vulnerability to relapses.

To evaluate this possibility, Brown and Rutter (1966) developed the Camberwell Family Interview (CFI) to assess the affective climate of families with a psychiatric client. The CFI is a semistructured interview with individual relatives of clients recently admitted to a hospital for treatment. The client is not present during the interview. The relative's responses are tape-recorded and later rated for dimensions of Expressed Emotion (EE) by a trained rater. EE refers to the expression of critical, hostile, or emotionally overinvolved (e.g., dramatic, extreme self-sacrificing) attitudes toward the client. Ratings are made primarily on the basis of voice tone (e.g., pitch, emphasis, loudness), with verbal content of secondary importance. Relatives are rated as being "high EE" on the CFI if they frequently criticize the client, express a hostile or rejecting attitude, or display signs of pronounced emotional overinvolvement. Roughly half of the US households surveyed have at least one relative who is high EE.

The primary assumption of EE assessments obtained through the CFI is that negative or intrusive attitudes expressed by the relative during the interview are reflected in day-to-day interactions. Research on families engaged in problem-solving tasks supports this assumption. High EE relatives of both schizophrenia and affective disorder clients tend to be more critical, intrusive, and demanding during their interactions with their ill family member than low EE relatives (Hooley, 1986; Miklowitz et al., 1984; Mueser et al., 1993). There also is a tendency for clients to reciprocate these negatively charged statements, leading to extended exchanges of negative communication (Hahlweg et al., 1989). Thus, EE ratings appear to be a reflection of the affective climate in the families of psychiatric clients.

Prospective research has provided strong evidence that family EE is predictive of symptom relapses over the nine-month period following client's discharge from the hospital for treatment of an acute exacerbation. The relationship between EE and relapse has been most extensively studied for clients with schizophrenia; twenty-seven studies have been conducted (Butzlaff & Hooley, 1998). Other studies have shown that EE is also predictive of relapse in clients with affective disorders and eating disorders (Butzlaff & Hooley, 1998; Coiro & Gottesman, 1996). The results of EE research on schizophrenia and affective disorders are illustrated in Figure 1.1. It can be seen from this figure that clients living with (or in regular contact with) high EE relatives are about twice as likely to relapse during the nine to twelve months following hospital discharge as similar clients with low EE relatives. Furthermore, although some studies have found that family EE is related to specific client symptoms (e.g.,

Glynn et al., 1990), there is no consistent trend suggesting that EE is simply an artifact of client psychopathology. These findings suggest that the presence of strong negative affect in relatives toward the client may increase the level of ambient stress in the environment, resulting in a higher susceptibility to relapses and rehospitalizations.

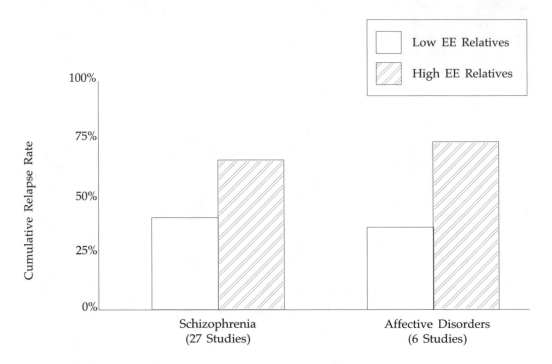

FIGURE 1.1   CUMULATIVE RELAPSE RATES OVER 9–12 MONTHS FOLLOWING HOSPITAL DISCHARGE FOR CLIENTS IN CONTACT WITH HIGH EXPRESSED EMOTION (EE) OR LOW EE RELATIVES

Although studies on EE have been influential in pointing to the need for family interventions for psychiatric disorders, this research also has generated much controversy. Justified concerns have been raised that the EE concept has been used by some professionals to blame and scapegoat families for the mental disorder (Hatfield et al., 1987; Kanter et al., 1987; Lamb, 1990). However, EE behaviors such as criticism or intrusiveness are best viewed as normal coping responses to the tremendous burden of maintaining a close relationship with a mentally ill family member (Greenley, 1986) rather than as psychopathology in the family. The presence of negatively charged interactions in families underscores the importance of establishing a collaborative relationship between professionals and families to improve their coping with the psychiatric disorder (Mintz et al., 1987; El-Islam, 1989).

Marital Adjustment and the Course of Psychiatric Disorder

Low satisfaction in a marriage in which one spouse has a mental disorder has been related to a poor course, particularly in affective disorders (Prince & Jacobson, 1995). Marital problems appear to be involved in the onset of at least some major depressions (Brown & Harris, 1978; Costello, 1982), and there is evidence that marital discord is predictive of a poor clinical outcome of depression (Goering et al., 1992). The absence of social support in unhappy marriages appears to be one crucial factor, as poor social support has been found to magnify the negative effects of stressful life events on depression (Lin et al., 1986).

Less research has examined the relationship between marriage, social support, and the course of anxiety disorders, and there is contradictory evidence as to whether marital factors or individual behavior therapy mediate their outcome (Emmelcamp & Gerlsma, 1994). Goldstein and Chambless (1978) suggested that marital problems often are associated with the onset and maintenance of complex agoraphobia. Barlow et al. (1984) found that agoraphobia in married persons was more effectively treated when therapy was provided to the couple rather than the individual (see also Barlow et al., 1981; Cerny et al., 1988), although some other studies have not reported this (e.g., Emmelcamp et al., 1992). In summary, there is evidence from research on both EE and marital adjustment that negative affect, lack of social support, and marital discord are associated with a poor prognosis of psychiatric clients. These findings, along with the burden of psychiatric disorder on other family members, can best be understood in the context of an interactive model of how the coping responses of relatives and clients determine the outcome of schizophrenia.

Stress-Vulnerability Model of Family Coping

To integrate research findings on the influence of client and relative factors on psychiatric disorders, we have developed a model that incorporates both biological and psychosocial parameters believed to mediate the outcome of the disorder (figure 1.2). We have adapted this model from the stress-vulnerability model developed for schizophrenia (Nuechterlein & Dawson, 1984; Rosenthal, 1970; Zubin & Spring, 1977) and Lazarus's model of stress and coping (Lazarus & Folkman, 1984; Lazarus, 1991). In our model, client *biological vulnerability* and *socioenvironmental stressors* are the major influences on the course of the disorder. These influences, however, can be mitigated by *protective factors*. Here, biological vulnerability refers to inherited or acquired negative alterations in brain structure or brain chemistry, socioenvironmental stressors describes the role demands, expectations, and life events impinging on the individual, and protective factors include the mechanisms or behaviors that decrease biological vulnerability or increase the capacity to deal effectively with socioenvironmental stressors. For example, consistent use of prescribed psychotropic medications and avoidance of other psychoactive substances will reduce biological vulnerability, while successful coping efforts on the part of the client protect against the noxious effects of environmental stressors. Client coping efforts are assumed to be impaired by both the disorder itself and other factors unrelated to the disease (e.g., poor role models, limited educational opportunities). Nevertheless, client coping skills are understood to be modifiable, although biological vulnerability may be a limiting factor.

In contrast to previous expositions of the stress-vulnerability model, our framework also explicitly incorporates family factors as critical influences on outcome. Like clients, relatives are exposed to socioenvironmental stressors, such as financial concerns, child-rearing challenges, and vocational problems. In addition, relatives experience stress due to the burden of the disorder, which may be chronic and severe when the client is highly symptomatic or unable to perform even very basic social role expectations. Thus, clients and their families are involved in an interdependent system in which the stress and coping of each member directly influences all others. The extent to which families can cope effectively with their stressors (whether related to the client or not) determines whether they will be able to help reduce the effects of stress on the client. When families are successful at coping, a favorable prognosis for the client is likely. On the other hand, when stress overwhelms the coping capacity of relatives, family stress will contribute to client stress (e.g., via the expression of negative affect), requiring increased coping. In the best case, the client is able to meet this demand with greater coping and the outcome of the disorder is not affected. In the worse case, the increased stress on the client can overwhelm his or her ability to cope effectively, leading to worse symptoms and decreased social functioning. These further impairments in client functioning can lead to an even greater burden on family members, resulting in a vicious cycle of negativity and impaired family functioning.

The ability of relatives to cope effectively with a mentally ill family member is influenced not only by the disruption that the disorder creates but also by their cognitive appraisal of the client's behavior and their access to social supports, as illustrated in Figure 1.3. Cognitive appraisal comprises relatives' knowledge about the client's disorder and their beliefs regarding the origins of the disordered behavior. Relatives who lack accurate information regarding their ill family member's psychiatric disorder or who believe the client's behavior is under the client's voluntary control are more likely to use coercive or negatively charged coping strategies to change the client's behavior. For example, several studies have found that relatives who view clients' symptoms as being under their control are more likely to be high in EE, to report more personal distress, and to have poorer family functioning (Barrowclough & Parle, 1997; Brewin et al., 1991; Robinson, 1996). In addition, relatives who have a greater fund of information about a client's mental illness use more coping strategies, report higher coping efficacy, and are less rejecting of the client than relatives with less understanding of the psychiatric disorder (Mueser et al., 1997). Finally, social support can affect relatives' cognitive appraisal by providing new information and different perspectives about the client's behavior or by directly influencing how the relative chooses to cope with the client (e.g., Solomon & Draine, 1995; Webb et al., 1998).

Our stress-vulnerability model of family coping has multiple implications for how BFT can lessen the burden on relatives and improve the long-term outcome of the client's disorder. In terms of client biological vulnerability factors, the therapist bolsters the protective effects of medication by promoting compliance. The negative effects of alcohol and drug abuse are minimized by the therapist actively intervening to combat these problems. For more minor problems, this might be limited to education and the use of communication skills by family members to express to the client their concerns and negative feelings about the abuse. For more serious abuse, the family might use the problem solving techniques to decide which limits to set and enforce, while the client might use problem solving to develop strategies to cope with persisting urges or select a treatment program.

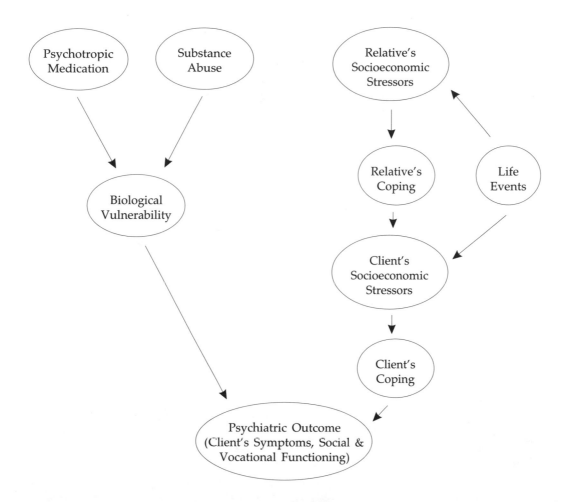

FIGURE 1.2 THE STRESS-VULNERABILITY FAMILY COPING SKILLS MODEL OF ADAPTATION TO PSYCHIATRIC DISORDER*

Efforts in BFT also are aimed at improving client coping efforts through teaching social skills and problem-solving skills for dealing with interpersonal stressors, as well as developing additional behavior management strategies for dealing with other types of stress. With respect to improving the coping of relatives, the therapist fosters a more adaptive appraisal of their ill family member's behavior by providing basic information about the nature of the disorder, factors that influence its course, and the limited personal control most clients have over their symptoms. In parallel, families

* *Adapted from Lazarus and Folkman, 1984; Lazarus, 1991; Nuechterlein and Dawson, 1984; Rosenthal, 1970; and Zubin and Spring, 1977.*

are encouraged to utilize the problem-solving and communication skills to manage other stressors in their lives, including vocational conflicts, financial constraints, and the like. By improving the ability of family members to interact more effectively and solve problems, the therapist helps to reduce the stress from family conflict impinging on both the relative and the client. Lastly, the therapist helps all family members improve their base of social support, both within and outside of the family, thereby increasing their resilience in the face of stress. Many families with a mentally ill member have constricted social support networks and are isolated due to embarrassment and feelings of helplessness (Lefley, 1996). Improving the quality of family members' relationships with people outside the family often has a beneficial effect on the quality of their lives.

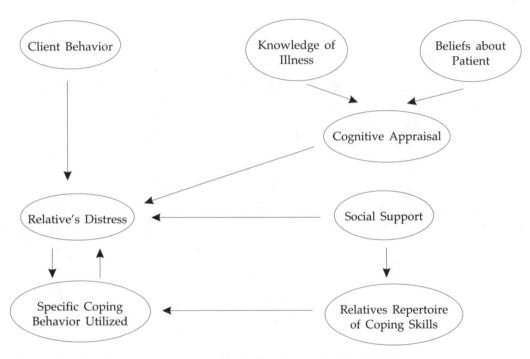

FIGURE 1.3 THE INFLUENCES OF DIFFERENT FACTORS
ON COPING BEHAVIOR AND DISTRESS OF RELATIVES IN FAMILIES
WITH A PSYCHIATRIC CLIENT

The Goals of BFT

Consistent with the stress-vulnerability family coping skills model previously described and the need to incorporate the family as members of the client's treatment team, the goals of BFT are multifaceted and tailored for each individual family. As summarized in Table 1.3, BFT is guided by three overall goals:

1. to improve the quality of life for the client;

2. to improve the quality of life for the client's relatives;

3. to improve problem-solving and communication skills to reduce ambient stress.

Smaller goals are included within each of these overall goals, such as improving the course of the client's psychiatric disorder, decreasing the burden on family members, and teaching the family how to work collaboratively to solve interpersonal conflicts and to achieve family goals.

TABLE 1.3
GOALS OF BFT FOR PSYCHIATRIC DISORDERS

I. To improve the client's quality of life
   A. Improve the course of the psychiatric disorder by:
      1. reducing symptom severity
      2. reducing vulnerability to symptom relapses
      3. lowering rate of rehospitalizations
   B. Enhance the client's capacity for independence and role functioning
   C. Strengthen the client's relationship with relatives and friends
   D. Help the client make progress toward or achieve personal goals

II. To improve the quality of life of the client's relatives
   A. Decrease the burden of the disorder on relatives by:
      1. developing realistic expectations for the client's behavior
      2. teaching relatives how to monitor the client's symptoms and compliance with prescribed treatments
      3. helping relatives learn to work with professionals to optimize outcomes
   B. Strengthen the relatives' relationships with the client, other family members, and close friends
   C. Help the relative make progress toward or achieve personal goals

III. To improve the functioning of the family as a unit and reduce ambient stress
   A. Help the family work together and with professional to monitor the client's disorder
   B. Replace negative communication patterns between family members with constructive, supportive communication skills
   C. Teach the family how to resolve conflicts between the members and achieve goals by using cooperative problem-solving tasks as a family

The goals of BFT are achieved by systematically using therapeutic techniques developed to improve family members' understanding of the psychiatric disorder and their ability to interact effectively, with a major focus on psychoeducational and social learning (e.g., social skills training) methods. The components of BFT can be organized into five sequential stages. During the *assessment stage*, an evaluation is conducted to identify the strengths, weaknesses, and needs of each individual in the family and of the family as a whole. Follow-up assessments are conducted on a regular basis to monitor progress toward treatment goals and to establish new goals. When the initial assessment has been completed, the therapist moves to the *educational stage*, providing information about the psychiatric disorder to family members, using a variety of psychoeducational techniques, such as didactic presentations, handouts, and eliciting the personal experiences of family members. Although several sessions are devoted exclusively to educating family members about the disorder early in BFT, the therapist helps the family integrate the information throughout the course of therapy by returning to this material on an "as needed" basis.

Following the educational sessions, the *communication-skills training stage* becomes the central focus of BFT. Using clinical methods based on social-skills training, a core set of communication skills is strengthened in all family members, with intensity of instruction on core and supplementary skills tailored to address problems or deficits unique to that family. Throughout BFT, the therapist is alert to opportunities to improve the quality of communication between family members using skills-training methods. After the family has achieved some proficiency at effective communication, the therapist proceeds to the *problem-solving training stage*, in which the family is taught a structured method for solving problems and achieving personal or family goals. These methods are designed to minimize tension between family members and to maximize their ability to reach effective solutions. For most families, the majority of BFT sessions are spent on problem solving, with families tackling increasingly more difficult problems or goals as they become more competent in the skill. In the last stage of BFT, the therapist helps family members develop *strategies for special problems*. Not all problems can be resolved by effective communication and problem-solving skills. The therapist's expertise in other behavior-change methods can be invaluable in helping families deal with these difficulties. Examples of strategies some families may benefit from learning include anxiety reduction methods (e.g., exposure therapy, systematic desensitization, cognitive restructuring), contingency contracting, and self-monitoring and self-control techniques.

In most cases, BFT unfolds over at least six months, and more often over one to two years. Even longer treatment periods may be helpful for some families. The majority of BFT sessions are spent helping family members improve their communication and problem-solving skills so that they can use these skills to resolve problems and achieve goals. Despite the strong focus on skill development and the relatively structured organization of therapy sessions that we recommend, BFT is not a "cookbook" approach that is applied in a uniform manner across all families. Rather, the BFT model provides a blueprint and foundation enabling the therapist to conceptualize problems faced by families who must cope with a psychiatric disorder by assessing the specific needs of each family, teaching relevant information and skills to address those areas of deficit, and evaluating progress during family therapy. As with all approaches to psychotherapy, BFT requires the art and clinical skill of the therapist to lay the mortar and bricks, using the blueprint to guide the process.

A Brief History of BFT

No single individual or group of people can be given full credit for inventing BFT. Rather, the BFT model has evolved over the past thirty years as practitioners developed strategies for working with families presenting a variety of clinical problems. Although any review of the history of BFT is necessarily selective, the work of several innovators is particularly pertinent to the BFT model we present here.

The first application of learning theories to the family involved using family members as surrogate therapists to implement behavior-change programs for the client (Falloon & Lillie, 1988). For example, Wolpe (1958) incorporated spouses into his treatment of anxiety disorders and Williams (1959) described teaching parents how to use extinction (i.e., the nonreinforcement of undesirable behavior) to eliminate temper tantrums in a young child. These practitioners recognized that the high degree of contact between family members and the potential reinforcement value of relatives to the client represented an opportunity to extend behavior-change programs beyond the office and therapy session into the natural home environment.

The next major innovation in BFT was the move toward conducting a functional analysis of the family unit. The core of a functional analysis is the recognition that at any point in time the behavior patterns between family members are maintained by the dynamic interplay of naturally occurring reinforcements and punishments. Hence, the behavior of all family members, including behaviors that may be maladaptive or have destructive effects, is viewed as "functional" within the family system, because it represents each individual's best coping effort at maximizing reinforcement and minimizing punishment. The implications of conducting a functional analysis are that successful modification of one person's behavior also requires changes in other family members. Early family interventions based on a functional analysis focused mainly on operant strategies for changing behavior in the home, such as the use of contingency contracting, clearly specifying the rewards and costs of specific behaviors, and token economy procedures. These approaches are best exemplified by the work of Patterson and colleagues with child problems (Patterson et al., 1967; Patterson, 1971), Stuart's (1969) approach with maritally discordant couples, and some of Liberman's (1970) work with couples and families.

As behavior therapists began to conduct functional assessments of problem behaviors in the family, new strategies were developed for changing entrenched and destructive patterns of communication. Based on the work of Bandura and Walters (1963; Bandura, 1969), who demonstrated that social behavior could be vicariously learned through the observation of role models, therapists began to use modeling and role-playing procedures to teach communication skills to family members. From the 1950s to the 1970s, a range of individuals contributed to the development, refinement, and "packaging" of a set of therapeutic techniques that systematically employed modeling, role-playing, and reinforcement to alter social behavior. The combination of these techniques, now known as *social-skills training* (Bellack et al., 1997; Liberman et al., 1989), had a profound impact on the practice of behavioral therapy with both individuals and families and has become one of the most widely used psychosocial interventions for psychiatric disorders. Following the lead of Liberman (1970), who described the use of skills training to solve communication problems in families, social-skills training methods gradually assumed an increasingly important role in family therapy for improving the quality of interactions. The programmatic use of social-skills training to teach communication and problem-solving skills became particularly prominent in the treatment of marital distress, as exemplified by Jacobson and Margolin's (1979) classic text on behavioral marital therapy, as well as other guides to behavioral marital therapy (e.g., Liberman et al., 1980; Bornstein & Bornstein, 1986; Baucom & Epstein, 1990).

A final innovation that contributed to the BFT model for families containing a psychiatric client was the development of methods for educating family members about specific mental disorders. As we discussed earlier in this chapter, there has been a growing awareness among professionals that family members and clients have a basic right to psychoeducation regarding psychiatric disorder, including its causes, diagnosis, course, and treatment. The earliest efforts to provide education to family members about psychiatric disorder in the context of the BFT model date back to the early 1970s, when Robert P. Liberman held classes to educate families, including clients, about psychiatric disorders and their management. Over the following decade, the BFT model for psychiatric clients was developed and refined to systematically integrate the functional assessment of the family unit and individual family members, psychoeducation, and training in communication and problem-solving skills.

Ian R. H. Falloon, who collaborated with Liberman, played a crucial role in the development of the BFT model for psychiatric clients by specifically defining the essential components of BFT and writing the first treatment manual for the application of BFT to families with a member with schizophrenia (Falloon et al., 1984; Falloon et al., 1988, 1993). The treatment manual of Falloon et al. (1984) served as a guide for the first controlled outcome study of BFT for schizophrenia (Falloon et al., 1985), with the favorable effects of BFT on reducing relapse rates replicated in a follow-up study (Randolph et al., 1994). Falloon's contribution to the operationalizing of the BFT model for psychiatric clients is reflected by the range of different psychiatric disorders to which BFT has been applied in recent years (Falloon, 1988; Miklowitz & Goldstein, 1997; Glynn et al., 1999).

The BFT model we present here bears a close resemblance to the model developed by Falloon, Boyd, and McGill (1984) for schizophrenia, which was strongly influenced by Liberman's seminal work with families in the preceding decade. Our thinking has also been informed by the NIMH Treatment Strategies in Schizophrenia study (Schooler et al., 1997), which is the largest controlled study of BFT conducted to date. This book was written because there has been a growing popularity in the application of the BFT model for many psychiatric disorders, including bipolar disorder, major depression, and anxiety disorders. In addition to describing how to apply the BFT model to a variety of different psychiatric disorders, we also address modifications in the model to families with relatives who differ from those families described by Falloon et al. (1984), such as married clients, clients who live with their adult children, and clients who live in long-term inpatient settings.

The Role of BFT in Treatment Planning for Persons with Serious Psychiatric Illnesses

BFT is designed to improve the relationships between psychiatric clients and their relatives. Based on the stress-vulnerability family coping skills model, improved relationships and coping skills also are expected to have a favorable impact on the functioning of each individual in the family and may improve the course of the psychiatric disorder. Nevertheless, as with any psychotherapeutic participation, the benefits of the work must be weighed against the costs in terms of time and energy. As has been noted above, families of persons with serious psychiatric illnesses face a variety of challenges, and a range of services with graduated intensity are likely to be most effective in meeting these needs (see Figure 1.4). Family members should be encouraged to participate in the lowest intensity level of service that yields both a stable and/or improving course for the client and a significant reduction in distress for the relative.

In particular, at a most basic level, we recommend that all family members have access to brief education about their relative's disorder within the context of a family-friendly agency. A family-friendly agency has many critical attributes. Families are treated respectfully and with interest and caring. Issues of confidentiality are dealt with in a forthright and sensitive manner, and the benefits of an open sharing of pertinent treatment-related information among the client, family member, and professional staff are recognized. Professionals accommodate the fact that many family members work during the day by ensuring some availability to service and staff during "off" times. Participation in family advocacy is endorsed through the provision of information and logistical support (rooms and refreshments for Alliance for the Mentally Ill meetings are often provided). As embedded in a family-friendly agency, brief education might encompass providing time-limited individual educational sessions on coping with serious psychiatric illness accompanied by suggestions for further reading. For many families, especially those low in expressed emotion or related to very stable clients exhibiting good social adjustment, this low level of service may meet their needs.

Even when provided with education and a family-friendly agency, however, some family members and/or clients will still exhibit high levels of dysfunction and distress. In these cases, we recommend participation in multiple-family groups, facilitated either by professionals (McFarlane, 1990; McFarlane et al., 1993; Schooler et al., 1997) or other family members (Burland, 1993; Burland & Mayeaux, 1995). Typically, these groups provide both social support and education to family members, using a semistructured format in weekly or monthly meetings. Results of participation can be very positive (McFarlane, 1990; McFarlane et al., 1993). However, a substantial proportion of individuals may not have their needs met by these groups. Logistical constraints may impede some family members from attending; others may feel alienated from the group because either they or their ill relative appear to be very different from most participants; still others may participate and yet remain highly distressed, particularly if their ill relative is very symptomatic. In such cases, we would recommend a course of individually based BFT until the client is stable and relatives' distress is lessened, followed by referral to a multiple-family group for maintenance of gains.

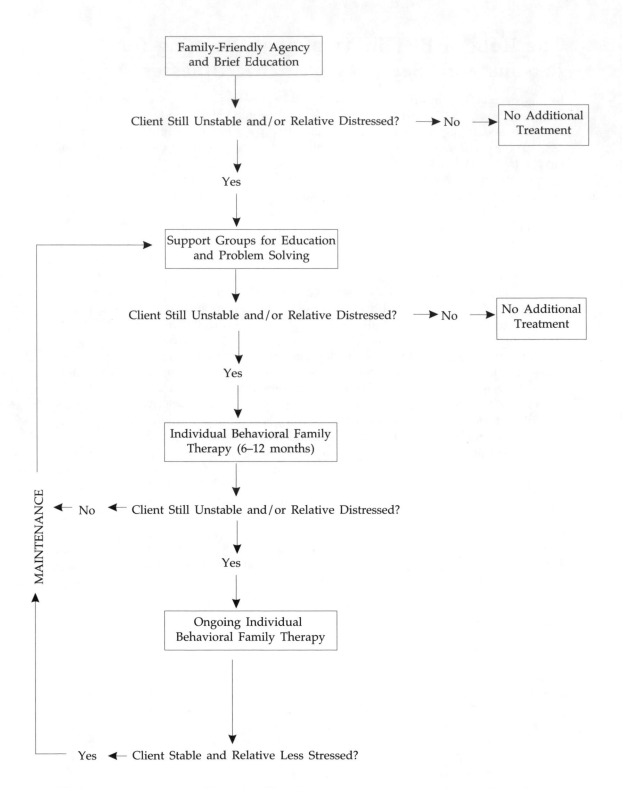

FIGURE 1.4 FAMILY TREATMENT PLANNING
FOR SERIOUS PSYCHIATRIC ILLNESS

Families with a relative who has severe, chronic psychiatric symptoms and a prolonged low level of functioning are good candidates for BFT, as well as families with a relative who has recently developed a disorder. Our collective experience working with several hundred families with a psychiatric client has primarily been with the disorders of schizophrenia (including schizoaffective disorder and schizophreniform disorder), bipolar disorder, major depression, and anxiety disorders (mainly posttraumatic stress disorder and obsessive-compulsive disorder). We also have experienced positive results with the BFT model working with other psychiatric disorders, such as dysthymia, cyclothymic disorder, atypical psychosis, substance abuse, and personality disorders (e.g., borderline personality disorder, schizotypal personality disorder). Clients with panic disorder, generalized anxiety disorder, other personality disorders, and refractory social phobia might also benefit. To illustrate the range of psychiatric disorders and family constellations who are appropriate for treatment, we provide brief clinical vignettes of some different clients and relatives who have benefited from BFT.

Case Examples

- A thirty-seven-year-old man with schizophrenia who was living with his parents and brother was engaged in treatment following a recent discharge from the hospital for treatment of a symptom exacerbation. The client had eight prior hospitalizations, beginning at age sixteen, many of them precipitated by medication noncompliance.

- A couple in their late 30s with a young child was referred for treatment because of familial stress. Marital discord was high, because of the husband's predominantly angry mood, difficulty with trust, and severe anxiety due to posttraumatic stress disorder. BFT was conducted with the couple to improve communication and to address differences in opinion regarding child rearing. Several sessions also included the child to evaluate and address his concerns about his father.

- A forty-year-old man with treatment-refractory obsessive-compulsive disorder was engaged in BFT with his parents, with whom he lived and upon whom he was extremely dependent. Therapy focused on teaching the family how to develop strategies to encourage and reinforce small steps toward greater independence for the client and on helping the parents identify personal goals to work on that were separate from the client.

- A twenty-year-old woman with a schizophreniform disorder who had recently experienced her first psychotic episode participated in BFT with her sister and brother-in-law, with whom she was living. The client continued to have residual symptoms and to function marginally. Treatment was aimed at educating the family on how to monitor the client's symptoms and facilitate her compliance with day treatment and medication.

- A forty-two-year-old married woman with a major depressive disorder and a history of hospitalizations was engaged in BFT with her husband. The woman felt overwhelmed by having to care for their five children and maintain the household. She was frequently criticized by her husband, who had little understanding of her depression. Therapeutic goals included decreasing the husband's negative behavior toward his wife and identifying ways of providing her help in accomplishing the household responsibilities.

- The parents and two adult siblings of a twenty-six-year-old man with a bipolar disorder were engaged in BFT. The client had four prior hospitalizations and lived at home with the parents and one brother. Therapy focused on decreasing the parents' intrusive behavior toward their son and using family problem solving to help the son achieve his goal of returning to college and completing his bachelor's degree

- A fifty-five-year-old man with a dysthymic disorder who was living independently was engaged in BFT with his sister, who lived close by. The client was socially isolated. Therapy focused on increasing social supports for the client and decreasing household stress in the sister's home, which she shared with another sister and her children.

- A man in his mid thirties with chronic schizophrenia who resided in a state hospital was engaged in therapy with his parents who were in their seventies. The parents visited with the client on a weekly basis. Therapy focused mainly on helping the parents develop more realistic expectations for their son's behavior based on a better understanding of his disorder and on improving the quality of communication between the parents and son.

- A young woman in her twenties with a dependent personality disorder and generalized anxiety disorder participated in BFT with her father, with whom she lived, and her brother, who lived independently. The woman had several prior psychiatric hospitalizations for the treatment of acute anxiety states, which she had responded to by trying to climb into her father's bed at night.

- A woman with a borderline personality disorder was engaged in BFT with her husband. Their relationship had been characterized by a rocky course with frequent separations and reconciliations, and the husband was bewildered by his wife's erratic shifts from "overvaluation" to "devaluation" in her behavior toward him. Therapy focused on providing information about the disorder, mainly to the husband, altering negative communication patterns, and using the problem-solving approach to resolve differences between them.

- A family that included a grandmother, a mother, her son with bipolar disorder, her daughter with a schizoaffective disorder, and another healthy son was treated with BFT. The son with bipolar disorder also had a substance use disorder. The family had few economic resources, and tension in the home was compounded by the son's stealing household items in order to purchase drugs. Much of the therapy was aimed at monitoring the symptoms of both clients and dealing with frequent crises using family problem solving.

BFT and Medical Conditions

Although our major focus in this book is on the application of BFT to families with a psychiatric client, the model is also appropriate to address problems in families with a relative who has a medical condition. A brief case description is provided below of the application of BFT to such a family.

Case Example

The family with a fifteen-year-old girl with juvenile diabetes was referred for family therapy because her poor compliance with diet and her failure to monitor her blood-sugar levels had resulted in two recent hospitalizations to stabilize her condition. Assessments and early work with the family indicated that the parents frequently displayed intrusive, critical behaviors toward their daughter in an attempt to coerce her to conform to her medical regimen as well as to meet other social and academic expectations. The daughter rebelled against her parents' tactics by becoming noncompliant with management of her medical condition, thereby exercising her own independence. The daughter's noncompliance was unwittingly reinforced by her parents as they responded to the imminent medical crisis by becoming less critical and expressing more concern about her disorder. BFT was aimed at teaching the parents how to express their concern about their daughter in a less coercive, more direct manner, and how to reinforce her for taking responsibility for managing her diabetes. The daughter's feelings about her parents' intrusiveness were validated in therapy, and she was taught how to constructively express negative feelings toward her parents when she found their behavior intrusive. When family members had learned the basics of problem solving, they developed a joint plan for monitoring the daughter's diabetic condition with a consequent improvement in compliance and no further hospitalizations.

Who Should Conduct BFT?

BFT is an intervention that should be provided by a mental health professional who has experience conducting psychotherapy and basic knowledge of psychopathology. The professionals who are the best candidates to learn and apply BFT for psychiatric disorders are psychologists, psychiatrists, social workers, and nurses with a clinical specialty degree (e.g., master's level). Therapists with a background in cognitive-behavioral assessment and therapy will be able to acquire the skills for conducting BFT more rapidly than other therapists, but many nonbehavioral therapists have been able to learn the BFT model and use it with success. A background in family systems approaches can be useful in learning BFT. However, family problems are conceptualized differently in BFT, and the overlap in clinical techniques between BFT and systems models is not extensive.

Some of the most important qualities of a therapist conducting BFT include good communication skills, warmth, sensitivity to the problems of each family member, and the ability to convey enthusiasm to the family about the treatment and to set positive but realistic expectations for change. Patience and a willingness to face obstacles and accept slow progress also help. The therapist must adopt a shaping attitude toward behavior change in the family, providing family members with ample reinforcement for small but significant steps toward improved functioning. Ability to provide structure in family sessions is another essential ingredient for an effective BFT therapist. Providing family members with a clear, organized structure for therapy sessions facilitates the teaching of new skills and decreases the anxiety associated with the unpredictability of some approaches to therapy. Finally, therapists need to be able to focus on the development of specific communication and problem-solving skills in the family, rather than play the more traditional role of the therapist as the family's problem solver. This last attribute is perhaps the most difficult one to acquire, because it can appear to run counter to the therapist's self-identity as a "helper." However, the long-term benefits of teaching families the skills to help themselves outweigh the short-term benefits of the therapist providing quick solutions to the family for their problems. Although the gains made by families in BFT often accrue over a long period of time, the rewards of this collaborative relationship between families and the professional are often substantial and enduring.

TABLE 1.4
QUALIFICATIONS FOR THE BFT THERAPIST

Psychotherapy experience
Basic knowledge of psychopathology
Good communication skills
Warmth
Sensitivity to the problems of each family member
Enthusiasm about the BFT approach
Ability to set positive and realistic goals for change
Patience in the face of slow progress
Ability to reward small steps toward improvement (shaping)
Skill at structuring treatment sessions

Summary

This chapter provided the therapist with background and rationale for using BFT to treat psychiatric disorders. We reviewed the development of a new paradigm in the mental health profession that views the family as collaborators rather than culprits in the treatment of psychiatric disorders. The factors leading to this paradigm shift were discussed, including the widespread acceptance of the biological basis of major psychiatric disorders (and the rejection of psychogenic theories of the etiology of psychiatric disorders), the deinstitutionalization movement, and the high burden placed on relatives in caring for an ill family member. We described the stress-vulnerability coping skills model of psychiatric disorders, which serves as a heuristic in guiding BFT treatment aimed at reducing stress in the family, in enhancing the coping of *all* family members, and in reducing clients' biological vulnerability (e.g., through use of appropriate medications). We provided a brief description of the BFT model and its history and discussed who may benefit from this intervention. In the next chapter, we provide a detailed overview of the BFT model and give information about the logistics of conducting the therapy, the structuring of treatment sessions, and core principles of clinical practice.

CHAPTER 2	# AN OVERVIEW OF BEHAVIORAL FAMILY THERAPY

In the preceding chapter we established a rationale for providing BFT to families with a psychiatric client. In this chapter we focus on practical considerations regarding the implementation of family therapy and describe in greater detail the BFT model. In the first section we address the *logistical details* of conducting BFT, such as who should participate, the setting, and the length, frequency, and duration of sessions. Next, we discuss the *organization of the BFT model,* providing the therapist with an overview of how the essential components of the model unfold throughout therapy. In this section we emphasize the importance of conducting routine assessments of family functioning and progress over the course of therapy and of planning each treatment session based on a formulation of the family's specific needs. In the third section we describe the *internal structure of BFT sessions.* In order to create a therapeutic environment that minimizes stress and maximizes the family's capacity to learn, a clear and predictable structure of treatment sessions needs to be established and maintained over the course of treatment. Last, we address *overarching clinical practices* that serve to guide the therapist conducting BFT. These practices include promoting an open sharing of information in the family, adopting a problem-solving orientation, blocking negative affect, and shaping homework compliance and family meetings.

Logistical Details

BFT is usually provided in a single-family format, which is more suitable to the engagement of families and training in communication and problem-solving skills than the multiple-family group format. However, multiple-family groups can be useful as a strategy for maintaining gains made in BFT and for providing ongoing social support and psychoeducational opportunities. We discuss further the role of multiple family groups in Chapter 9, "Termination and Strategies for Maintenance."

Who Should Participate in BFT?

Every effort should be made to engage the client in BFT, although we have conducted BFT successfully with relatives of clients who refuse to participate. This is far from ideal, however, and the therapist should be alert to opportunities to engage the client at any time during the course of family work. Those relatives who have the greatest involvement with the client, regardless of their specific relationship, will benefit most from participating in sessions. We have successfully conducted BFT for psychiatric clients whose concerned relatives included parents, stepparents, siblings, spouses, boy/girlfriends, offspring, as well as more distant relatives such as grandparents, aunts or uncles, and friends. The critical factor is that a caring relationship between the relatives and client exists, or that there is a desire to reestablish and strengthen the strained relationship between the family members.

Sometimes many of the relatives in a family can be engaged in BFT, including those with only minimal contact with the client, and the therapy serves as a rallying point to heal old wounds and reinforce family members' mutual concerns for each other. In other families, only one relative can be involved in therapy with the client, despite different relatives having regular contact with him or her. With such cases, the therapist works with the family members who are willing to participate and is alert to opportunities later in therapy to engage the other relatives.

The therapist attempts to involve all of the relatives in BFT who are living with the client. When the client does not live with relatives, those family members with whom the client has the most contact should be engaged in therapy. A general guideline is that family members who are in contact with the client at least weekly or biweekly are the best candidates for BFT.

In some families it is best to provide more therapy to relatives who have more contact with the client. This is particularly desirable when some of the relatives live with the client and others do not.

Case Example

A nineteen-year-old man with schizophreniform disorder and his family were engaged in BFT after his first psychiatric hospitalization. The client lived at home with his parents and had three older siblings who lived away from home, two of whom were married, all of whom showed concern about the client's well-being. After an initial meeting with the entire family, the therapist conducted functional assessments on the client and his parents and then engaged the entire family (including the spouses of the two married brothers) in the educational sessions. Following this, BFT sessions on communication and problem-solving training were conducted with the client and his parents, with the brothers attending occasional sessions. This allowed the therapist to devote the majority of therapy sessions to improving how the parents and client managed conflicts at home, while maintaining a lower level of involvement with the siblings.

The decision to provide some family members with less therapy should not be determined solely by the amount of contact with the client. A less involved relative can often be an important source of social support to more involved relatives or the client. In cases where a single relative is living with the client, it can be very helpful to engage a less involved relative in the full course of BFT, in order to bolster the social support available to the relative who must cope with the client's disorder at home. Engaging at least two healthy relatives in treatment can be especially useful when the client's disorder is severe, or when more than one relative has a psychiatric disorder. The burden of illness is greater in single-parent households (Carpentier et al., 1992). When two healthy relatives are unavailable, a friend, member of the clergy, or some other supportive person may be sought to fulfill this role in therapy.

The BFT model is most applicable to clients and relatives who are adolescents or older. BFT is not well suited for families in which the client is a child. Similarly, young children (e.g., under the age of twelve) in families containing an older psychiatric client should not be included regularly in BFT sessions. Children in these families may benefit from participating in special family therapy sessions designed to meet their needs (e.g., assessing the concerns of a child about a parent's disorder, providing basic information about the disorder).

Adolescents who are siblings of the client should be included in the family sessions whenever possible. Accumulating evidence indicates that siblings experience significant distress due to the disruptive effects of the disorder on the family. The needs of healthy siblings are often overshadowed by the crisis of a psychiatric disorder in the family. Siblings of clients frequently have concerns about their own vulnerability to the psychiatric disorders, and their relationship with the client may be affected by their feelings of guilt, anger, anxiety, and loss (Marsh & Dickens, 1997; Moorman, 1992; Swados, 1991).

Length, Frequency, and Duration of Sessions

The length of sessions is usually between forty-five and sixty minutes, depending on the number of participants and the progress the family has made on learning the information or skills targeted for a particular session. Briefer sessions lasting thirty to forty minutes can be conducted when the goals of the session have been accomplished and the therapist elects not to introduce additional material. Some families are capable of meeting for longer than an hour, especially when the client is not floridly symptomatic, and with these families occasional sessions as long as ninety minutes can be conducted. Longer sessions may be particularly helpful for some families during the educational phase of BFT, when a stimulating discussion may take place regarding the family's experience with the psychiatric disorder. Sometimes taking a brief break during the session can help family members keep focused and absorb new information and skills. Session length must be determined by the therapist's clinical judgment of the time required to teach material and of the constraints on his or her own time.

The frequency of BFT sessions gradually declines over the treatment period. During the early stages of BFT, usually the first ten to fifteen sessions, it is best to conduct sessions on a weekly basis until the family has achieved basic knowledge of the disorder as well as communication and problem-solving skills. Following a core of weekly sessions at the beginning of BFT, the frequency of sessions can be reduced to biweekly for several months, followed by every three weeks and then monthly sessions. An example of the declining frequency of BFT sessions would be: weekly for three months, biweekly for six months, every three weeks for two months, and monthly for three months. The decision to reduce the frequency of therapy sessions is based on a variety of factors, including: the progress the family has made in learning the requisite information and skills, the amount of negative affect present among family members, the severity of psychosocial stressors impinging on all members, and the ability of the family as a unit to manage these stressors. Reducing the frequency of family sessions before the family is ready can be stressful, leading to symptom relapses and rehospitalizations.

BFT was originally conceived as a time-limited intervention with the goal of teaching families the skills necessary to manage the problems of having a mentally ill family member without the help of a professional. To achieve a sustained benefit from BFT, a minimum of six to nine months of therapy is recommended, and most families require one to two years. Clinically, the duration of BFT is determined by the needs of each individual family. Time-limited treatment is an attainable goal for many families, but not others, particularly when a severely symptomatic client lives at home or when psychosocial stressors are high (e.g., poverty, domestic violence, substance abuse). In these cases, providing BFT on a long-term basis with less frequent contacts (e.g., every two to four weeks) may facilitate better family coping and prevent symptom exacerbations, leading to improved family functioning and decreasing the overall costs of treatment. This approach recognizes that many psychiatric disorders result in lifelong handicaps, which require long-term psychosocial interventions to produce favorable outcomes.

Setting

BFT can be conducted either in the clinic or at the home of the family (or client residence). There are advantages to conducting at least some sessions at home. Home-based sessions may enable the therapist to engage some relatives who would otherwise be difficult to involve in therapy. Sessions conducted at home also provide invaluable information about the environment in which the family resides and how family members interact in a familiar setting. An additional advantage to home-based sessions is that they often result in fewer cancellations, saving time and money in the long run. One compromise solution that works for many families is to offer several sessions at home at the beginning of treatment and then to shift the focus of sessions into the clinic.

The major criterion for the physical setting of family therapy sessions, either at home or in the clinic, is a quiet working environment that is conducive to learning. When young children are present in the home, it is best to make baby-sitting arrangements so that the children will not interfere with the session, or for family members to take turns caring for the children during the sessions. In addition, it is useful to contract with the family to limit use of the telephone during sessions. For home-based sessions, the living room, dining room, or around the kitchen table are good locations for family meetings. Clinic-based sessions should be conducted in a room large enough for family members to sit in a circle without feeling cramped. It is preferable for sessions to be conducted in a room with enough space for family members to get up and move around when performing role plays.

Organization of the BFT Model

BFT is a structured approach to working with families with a psychiatric client. We previously described BFT as consisting of five discrete components: assessment, education, communication-skills training, problem-solving training, and special problems. These components of treatment are ordinarily conducted in sequential order, although the specific areas may be reviewed or reintroduced at a later time on an "as needed" basis. A sixth component precedes the core components of BFT: engagement of the family. We briefly review the logic underlying the sequential ordering of these elements of treatment.

Components of Treatment

At the very beginning of treatment, the family must be engaged and motivated to participate in BFT, and expectations must be established regarding the nature of therapy. *The engagement* component of BFT sets the stage for the actual intervention that follows, and usually requires one to three individual or family meetings.

Before actual treatment can be initiated, an assessment of the family's strengths and weaknesses is required to guide the intervention. The purpose of the assessment phase of BFT is to identify the assets and deficits of each individual in the family that determine his or her ability to successfully pursue personal goals. Obstacles in the family to each relative's ability to achieve personal goals, such as the effects of the psychiatric disorder or lack of support from other family members, are then identified to aid in formulating a functional analysis of the family. A second purpose of the assessment phase is to evaluate the strengths and weaknesses of the family unit in managing the psychiatric disorder. Understanding how the family collectively deals with problems informs the therapist as to what changes in the family system need to be targeted to optimize outcome of the disorder and improve overall family functioning.

Individual interviews with each person in the family are conducted at the beginning of therapy to assess his or her personal needs and to begin the process of setting goals for therapy. The assessment of the family as a unit is conducted during meetings with the entire family, with a focus on evaluating family members' knowledge of the disorder, ability to communicate clearly and constructively, and problem-solving skills. Throughout the course of treatment the therapist assesses the family's progress toward acquiring targeted information and skills and toward the attainment of individual family members' personal goals. In addition, follow-up assessments devoted to individual family members and the overall family are conducted regularly throughout the therapy.

Immediately after the assessment of the family and individual members, sessions focus on *education*. The rationale for providing families with basic educational information about the psychiatric disorder before attempting to modify communication and problem-solving skills is that misunderstandings often are at the root of negatively charged family interactions involving the client. Relatives frequently blame the client for displaying characteristic symptoms of the disorder (e.g., referring to the client as "lazy") and have unrealistic expectations regarding the client's true capabilities. By educating family members about the symptoms and course of the psychiatric disorder, negative communications in relatives often can be reduced. Thus, parsimony dictates that families be educated about the psychiatric disorder before determining the need to modify their communication skills. Furthermore, education is vital early in treatment so that relatives can began to learn how to monitor the disorder, to reinforce the client's participation in treatment, and to respond to the possible signs of an impending relapse.

We recommend spending between two and four sessions educating the family about the disorder. Although this time is usually sufficient to cover the relevant material, families often require more time to fully integrate the information into their understanding of the disorder. Consequently, after the initial educational sessions have been conducted, the therapist must be alert in later sessions to opportunities for family members to apply their knowledge about the psychiatric disorder. From the experiential perspective, family members are continually being educated throughout BFT as they grow in their understanding of the disorder.

After an adequate educational basis has been established, *communication-skills training* commences. Basic competence in clear and constructive communication is an essential prerequisite to training in problem solving, because negatively charged communications or withdrawal often derail the problem-solving process. Not all families need extensive communication-skills training, although a brief review of effective communication can be quite helpful. For families that have significant problems with communication, more specific training is provided. A core set of communications skills are routinely taught to these families during this phase of BFT, including skills for active listening, expressing positive and negative feelings, and making requests. Supplementary communication skills are taught as necessary, such as how to compromise or request a time-out.

For families who are provided communication-skills training, between four and ten sessions are usually devoted to this. When the client and relatives have difficulty in communicating but share few daily experiences and thus encounter fewer problems (e.g., the client resides in a hospital or supervised residence), even more sessions may be spent improving communication skills. As with education about the disorder, the therapist must conduct additional training in communication skills later in therapy as the need arises. Since good communication is viewed as a necessary ingredient to effective family problem solving, the therapist monitors and prompts the family's use of communication skills throughout training in problem solving.

When family members are able to communicate clearly and effectively with each other, family treatment turns to training of *problem-solving skills*. The goal of problem-solving training is to teach skills that will enable family members to solve their own problems without the assistance of the therapist. A secondary goal of this component of BFT is to resolve conflicts and help family members achieve specific goals, which is accomplished mainly by guiding families through a sequence of problem-solving steps designed to optimize successful resolution. Four to twelve sessions are typically devoted to problem solving, although more sessions are appropriate when the duration of BFT exceeds one year.

Improved problem-solving skills, combined with effective communication and an understanding of the psychiatric disorder, address the major needs of most families. However, not all difficulties that families face can be overcome by problem solving, and in the final component of BFT, strategies for dealing with *special problems* are developed. For example, contingency contracting may be taught to help relatives and the client resolve disagreements about household chores. To develop these supplemental strategies, the therapist provides additional expertise based on his or her experience and clinical training. When necessary, the therapist takes additional steps to identify effective strategies for these problems, such as consulting with other mental health professionals and researching books and articles on the topic. Special problems are addressed last in the sequence of BFT components, so that an assessment can be made as to whether problems will improve as a function of education and skills training. Between one and five sessions are spent on special problems with most families. Table 2.1 provides an outline of the number of sessions devoted to each of the components of BFT.

TABLE 2.1
OUTLINE OF SESSIONS DEVOTED TO EACH COMPONENT OF BFT

BFT Component	Phase of Treatment	Number of Sessions
Engagement	Beginning	1–3 sessions
Assessment	Initially and throughout	1–3 sessions with each individual at the beginning of treatment; follow-up individual and family sessions every 3-4 months
Education	Early to Middle	2–4 sessions
Communication Skills Training (if needed)	Middle to Late	4–10 sessions
Problem-Solving Training	Middle to Late	4–12 sessions
Special Problems	Late	1–5 sessions

To summarize, BFT for psychiatric disorders follows a structured sequence in which the core components of education, communication-skills training, and problem-solving training are provided in a planned order. Once a component has been taught, the therapist may return to it at any time to provide additional training. However, in order to master each component, some degree of competence must be attained in the preceding component(s). Thus, it is ineffective to attempt to teach communication skills before family members understand the nature of the disorder. Similarly, families will not be able to learn problem solving before they can communicate effectively.

Negative communications and pressing problems cannot be ignored early in treatment, and they must be dealt with therapeutically in order to keep the family engaged in treatment. The therapist deals with these problems early in treatment by trying to minimize their distracting impact on the teaching of basic information and skills, rather than training new and more complex communication and problem-solving skills that family members are not yet prepared to learn.

The Internal Structure of BFT Sessions

The BFT therapist is proactive, rather than reactive. In contrast to focusing primarily on material brought in by the family, the therapist has a specific agenda of activities to be accomplished in each session. Prior to each meeting, the therapist identifies the skill to be taught and reviews information obtained in previous sessions to anticipate and prepare for obstacles to this skill training. A major advantage to maintaining a coherent organizational plan for BFT is that it specifies for the therapist the tasks that need to be accomplished in therapy. Just as the therapist systematically plans each treatment session and evaluates the family's progress toward goals, the therapeutic activities in each session also are structured in a consistent and predictable manner. By establishing a regular structure within treatment sessions that is maintained across the course of therapy, the therapist can allay the anxiety of family members (and the therapist!) who are unsure of what to expect. A clear internal structure for each BFT session also provides a framework to the therapist for conducting ongoing assessments of the family, addressing new problems as they arise, and teaching the requisite information and skills. The general structure of each BFT session conducted after the initial assessments is summarized in Table 2.2.

Each BFT session begins with a brief discussion of the past week. The goal of this review is to identify any significant problems or obstacles encountered by the family that may need to be addressed before the end of the session, and to evaluate whether skills taught in the session are being generalized to the home. Informal socializing is minimized, and the therapist maintains a concerned, friendly but businesslike manner.

Following this discussion, the therapist briefly reviews the progress each family member has made toward personal goals set after the educational sessions (see Chapter 4 on Family Assessment). Progress toward goals and problems are noted, and, when necessary, the therapist plans to set aside time at the end of the session to discuss obstacles toward achieving these personal goals. The review of personal goals is omitted during the educational sessions because these goals have not yet been elucidated.

Then the homework assignment and family meeting are reviewed. Compliance with homework is reinforced, and the family's understanding of information or competence in using skills is checked. When the family has not completed the assignment at home, members are usually requested to do part of it in the session. Time is then devoted to evaluating the family's understanding of the assignment, exploring obstacles to homework completion or conducting family meetings, and problem solving with the family to arrive at a plan for members to complete the homework assignment and meet together before the following session.

TABLE 2.2
INTERNAL STRUCTURE OF BFT TREATMENT SESSIONS

Time	Activity
2–5 minutes	Initial greetings-review of the week-identification of new problem areas
3–5 minutes	Review of individual family members' goals (conducted after educational sessions)
5–15 minutes	Review homework and family meeting
15–30 minutes	Continue work on previous educational or skills-training topic or begin work on new topic
5 minutes	Assign homework
5–15 minutes	(Optional) Problem solve on important, circumscribed issues identified at the beginning of session

Depending on the progress the family has made on the homework assignment and members' acquisition of the information or skills, most of the remaining session is spent either continuing work on the same area or introducing a new topic. For example, if the therapist taught the communication skill of "Making Positive Requests" in the previous session and family members have completed their homework assignment and demonstrate competence at this skill in the next session, the therapist would begin work on the next skill of "Expressing Negative Feelings." On the other hand, if family members have not followed through on homework or still need additional training in "Making Positive Requests," the therapist would continue to work on this skill.

Toward the end of the session a new homework assignment is given to the family and the plan for the next family meeting is reviewed. The therapist checks the family's understanding of the assignment and, when appropriate, helps them plan to remember to complete the assignment and when it will be done. After this assignment has been given, time that was scheduled earlier in the session can be devoted to solving pressing problems or helping family members make progress toward personal goals. Although informal chatting does not play a critical role in BFT, some families find it reinforcing, and to the extent that it occurs, it should be relegated to the end of the session, after the main work has been completed.

BFT resembles a classroom course that is taught to families, with the information and skills tailored to the individual needs of the members and their progress in therapy. Similar to how the teacher prepares for each class in advance, the therapist plans an agenda and sets goals for each BFT session. After the session has been completed, the therapist evaluates the family's progress toward achieving the goal and identifies obstacles to the acquisition of material planned in the agenda. A form for planning and evaluating the success of each BFT session is contained in the appendix.

It is preferable that this structure be maintained in all treatment sessions except those in which the family is in crisis. In these cases, immediate problem solving may necessitate postponing the review of homework and basic educational and skills-training work until later in the session or the next session. Over time, the therapist endeavors to hand over responsibility to the family for structuring its own therapy session. In this respect, the ability to structure family time toward resolving problems and achieving goals is modeled by the therapist in the early and middle stages of BFT and acquired by the family in the later stages of therapy.

Keeping to the planned agenda can be a daunting task, often requiring great therapeutic skill. Family members experienced in other less-structured psychotherapies may have an expectation that the objective of therapy is to divulge and explore personal issues and conflicts, with the therapist primarily listening and interpreting. Alternatively, socially isolated family members may see the therapy as an opportunity to talk informally and solicit the social support of the therapist, rather than learn new skills. The therapist can be distracted from the task of teaching information or skills to family members, and he or she must learn to recognize and minimize these digressions, without antagonizing the family. To help stay with the agenda, the therapist can:

1. use whatever topic the family has brought up to probe for BFT skill attainment or problem solving;

2. ask the family to postpone discussion of the topic until the end of the session;

3. begin the session by outlining the agenda to alert the family to the session goal and structure;

4. interrupt digressions by reminding the family of the topic at hand and its relevance to the management of the client's disorder and/or improved family relations.

Overriding Clinical Practices

From the beginning and throughout the course of treatment, the therapist consistently engages in several clinical practices. These overriding clinical practices are described below.

Promote an Open Sharing of Information in the Family

No family therapist can avoid dealing with the issue of confidentiality in the course of treatment. Clients often have concerns about what information will be shared with their relatives, and relatives may be equally concerned about being informed about the client's disorder. The best strategy for handling issues of confidentiality is to encourage all family members to share information pertinent to the treatment plan with one another in an open fashion. By stressing the importance of open communication to family members early in treatment, the therapist can avoid being placed in the uncomfortable position of being exposed to family secrets which can undermine good communication.

There are times, of course, when family members privately divulge information to the therapist with the expectation that the information will be kept in confidence. In these situations, the therapist must first make a judgment as to whether the information must be kept private in order to protect the family member from possible harm. For example, if a family member reveals that he or she is being physically or sexually abused, and fears possible recrimination from the perpetrator, the therapist may need to work privately with the person to take steps to rectify the situation without informing other family members. Such cases are rare. A more common occurrence is for a family member to tell the therapist something in private that the therapist believes would be useful to discuss with the entire family (e.g., a family member with a substance abuse problem has begun to use alcohol or drugs again). When this occurs, the therapist tells the person why it is important to discuss the issue with the entire family and either encourages the person to bring it up in the next family session or requests permission to bring it up. The person may need to be encouraged more than once before he or she is willing to bring up the problem in a family session.

The therapist strives to promote open communication between all family members, including the client. Furthermore, the therapist explains to the client that information about his or her psychiatric disorder (e.g., symptoms) and factors that can affect the disorder (e.g., medication compliance, substance abuse) are shared with the treatment team. This allows the therapist to work with the treatment team and to provide members with information about the client's functioning that they would otherwise not know.

Develop a Problem-Solving Orientation

From the earliest meetings with family members, the therapist assumes a problem-solving orientation. The problem-solving approach is reflected both in the therapist's own conceptualization of the specific needs and goals of the family and in the inculcation of this approach in the family members. Utilizing a problem-solving approach to develop and implement a comprehensive plan for the treatment of individuals and families has gained widespread acceptance in recent years, with multiple variations of the method applied to different clinical populations (D'Zurilla & Nezu, 1999; Mueser, 1998; Nezu, Nezu, and Perri 1990). Essentially, developing a problem-solving orientation requires the ability to conceptualize family conflicts or the unmet desires of family members as "problems" or "goals" that can be handled with the problem-solving approach.

The basic tenet of problem-solving is that specific issues can be resolved and goals attained by following a model that includes a fixed sequence of steps: (1) define the problem; (2) generate possible solutions to the problem; (3) evaluate the advantages and disadvantages of each possible solution; (4) select the "best" solution or combination of solutions; (5) plan how to implement the solution(s); and (6) follow up on the plan at a later time. In order to initiate the problem-solving process, the therapist and family members must be able first to recognize problems and goals, and then to initiate constructive dialogue based on the sequence of problem-solving steps. This sequence may need to be repeated to make progress on a problem or goal. A major premise of the approach is that even the most difficult problems *can at least be improved* through systematic problem-solving efforts, once efforts are undertaken.

Even before problem-solving skills are formally taught to the family, the therapist adopts a problem-solving orientation when dealing with difficulties raised by family members. By modeling problem-solving behavior before these skills are formally taught, the therapist demonstrates that even very difficult problems can be managed by taking a calm, systematic approach. Furthermore, family members become familiar with the steps of problem solving before it is the focus of therapy so that learning proceeds at a more rapid pace.

At the beginning of a session families often present a new problem that they believe needs immediate attention, and they may vigorously try to get the therapist to address these problems in the session. Some families present new problems every week, and no amount of problem solving seems capable of ending the perpetual string of crises. If the therapist attempts to solve every one of these problems, he or she is often able to provide temporary relief, but the family learns little, and their long-term outcome is usually poor.

The therapist adopts a pragmatic approach to problems that are raised in family sessions during the assessment, educational, and communication-skills training phases of therapy. When problems come to the attention of the therapist at the beginning of treatment session, the therapist makes an evaluation based on the following questions:

1. *Is the problem so urgent that unless it is addressed immediately the family will be unable to concentrate and learn new material in the session?* E.g., the client has experienced a clear symptom exacerbation or has become actively suicidal or threatening, someone has just gotten into trouble with the law, an accident has occurred or a family member has become seriously ill, someone is verbally threatening or has been assaultive, a robbery has taken place, financial problems have dramatically worsened, a family member faces certain eviction.

2. *Can the problem be addressed at the end of the session, rather than at the beginning?* E.g., a slight increase in the client's symptoms has been noted by relatives, the client is bothered by medication side effects, a significant transportation problem has suddenly arisen, a family member ceases attending sessions, a previously abstinent family member has resumed using drugs or alcohol.

3. *Is the problem so chronic and long-standing that it cannot be solved in a single session?* E.g., the client does not help around the house, someone has a chronic substance abuse problem, there are disagreements about how to manage money, a couple fights over disagreements in child rearing, a family member will not pursue a job, the client is frustrated about having no friends.

In the case of a true crisis that is so overwhelmingly distressful that family members will not be able to concentrate on learning other material (Case number 1), the therapist has no choice but to problem solve with the family at the beginning of the session. The therapist's goal here is to develop a plan with the family for dealing with the problem, while still leaving enough time later in the session to work on education or communication-skills training. Sometimes the entire session is needed to address the problem, but often an effective plan can be developed in the first fifteen or twenty minutes and the remaining time can be spent working on the core BFT components. The therapist helps the family arrive at the plan by chairing a problem-solving session, keeping the discussion highly focused, solution oriented, and as brief as possible. Although the therapist is modeling for the family how to conduct a problem-solving meeting, the goal at this stage of therapy is not to teach problem-solving skills to the family, but rather to resolve the problem at hand. The plan is then reviewed the following week, with modifications undertaken as necessary. The specific strategies used in leading a problem-solving discussion are described in Chapter 7, "Problem-Solving Training," with one section devoted to Crisis Problem Solving.

When the problem is both circumscribed and important but not immediately urgent (Case number 2), time can be allocated at the end of the session to arrive at a plan. After the therapist has evaluated the seriousness of the problem, the family's concerns are validated, and they are informed that time will be reserved at the end of the session to identify some solutions to the problem. As with Case number 1, the therapist leads the family through a focused problem-solving discussion and arrives at a plan that is followed up the next week.

The main distinction between Case number 2 and Case number 3 is that the problems in Case number 3 are long-standing conflicts or problems that require extensive time to address successfully, whereas the problems in Case number 2 are more limited and manageable within a single session. When a significant, chronic problem is raised, the therapist acknowledges the importance of the problem, but reminds the family that it has been experiencing this problem for a long time and that it will not be able to resolve it in a single session. The importance of developing skills that will enable the family to solve the problem is emphasized. The therapist makes a special note of the problem and then explains to the family that this problem will be addressed soon after they have learned the essentials of problem solving. For Case number 3, it is vital that family members know that the therapist recognizes the importance of the problem and understand when in the course of therapy the problem will be addressed.

Problems encountered by the therapist in conducting the therapy can be addressed using a similar strategy. It is often vital that the therapist address obstacles to teaching information or skills to family members in order for them to develop basic competence in these areas. Problems such as incomplete homework, a disruptive working environment for therapy (if it is conducted at home), lateness to sessions, the intoxication of a family member at the session, or medication noncompliance can be identified by the therapist and handled by taking a systematic problem-solving approach. These problems are raised by the therapist in a matter-of-fact style; he or she explains to the family that it is his or her job to make sure the family members learn certain information and skills that will help them cope more effectively in the future, and that a particular problem must be resolved if such learning is to take place. The family is then engaged in a problem-solving effort to resolve the issue the therapist has raised (see Chapter 7 for more on this).

The problem-solving orientation permeates the therapist's approach to both specific problems raised by the family and problems encountered during delivery of the treatment. By repeatedly using the basic steps of problem solving, the therapist models a constructive approach to the management of real day-to-day difficulties. This structured method helps bring order to the chaos within many families, decreasing tension both within the family and in the therapist.

Reduce Negative Affect in the Family

It is clear that negative affect in the family is painful and to be avoided, and much of BFT is aimed at reducing high levels of negative affect. We highlight the importance of negative affect here because of its potentially pernicious effects early in family treatment. By getting the family together for BFT sessions, the therapist may inadvertently increase contact between certain family members who would otherwise avoid each other in order to avoid conflict. The therapist must not allow conflict in the therapy session to undermine this coping strategy. It is incumbent upon the therapist to stem or interrupt negatively charged interactions between family members early in treatment. If conflict in the session is not minimized, the therapist may unwittingly contribute to increasing the amount of stress on the client, thus raising vulnerability to relapses and worse functioning.

The specific strategies used by the therapist to manage negative affect in the family vary throughout the different stages of BFT. For example, early in treatment the therapist deals with negative family affect primarily by interrupting critical relatives, reinforcing the client's participation in the sessions, acknowledging concerns, and redirecting the family to the goals of the session. As BFT progresses through education and communication-skills training, negative affect is addressed by reviewing relevant information about the illness and prompting more constructive communications. Later in therapy, negative affect may be handled by any combination of re-education, communication-skills training, or problem solving. Because of the importance of reducing negative affect in the family for a successful outcome of BFT, we will discuss strategies for accomplishing this goal in each of the chapters on the components of BFT.

Shape Adherence with Homework and Family Meetings

The strong emphasis on learning in BFT is underscored by the importance attached to homework throughout the entire course of therapy. Unless homework assignments are completed by the family, it is very difficult for the therapist to evaluate the extent to which the family has acquired the targeted information and skills, as well as to identify the problems encountered by family members when they try to use particular skills. From the beginning of BFT, families are informed about the rationale for homework, and problems completing assignments are addressed as they arise. With some families it may also be helpful to explain that only part of family therapy takes place in the session with the therapist and that the remainder of therapy occurs at home as family members try to apply their newly learned knowledge and skills on their own.

In addition to giving regular homework assignments, the therapist encourages the family to conduct weekly family meetings on a set day and at a set time agreed to by all family members. In the early stages of BFT, during the educational and communication sessions, these meetings can be quite brief (about fifteen minutes) and are focused on the discussion of specific homework assignments (e.g., review of educational materials or homework to practice specific communication skills). Later in therapy, as the family learns problem-solving skills, the length of the family meeting may increase as family members begin to address problems and goals. A major goal of BFT is for the family to continue to conduct family meetings after therapy has ended. Thus, the family meeting assumes an increasingly important role as therapy progresses, with the expectation that these meetings will serve as the major vehicle for reducing family stress, monitoring the psychiatric disorder, and helping family members achieve personal and shared goals.

Summary

In this chapter we acquainted the reader with the logistical issues involved in conducting BFT and provided a conceptual overview of the BFT model. Unique to this model is the high degree of specification of educational material, the succession of skills building that occurs across treatment sessions, and the level of planning that precedes each session. We discussed the internal structure of BFT sessions. Maintaining a consistent structure for BFT sessions reduces anxiety by providing clear expectations and increases the therapist's ability to follow an assessment-based agenda of education and skills training. We concluded the chapter with a review of clinical practices that are continued throughout the course of BFT, including promoting the open sharing of information in the family, modeling a problem-solving orientation, decreasing negative affect, and shaping compliance with homework and family meetings.

The following chapter will address the critical first step toward providing BFT, engaging the family in treatment.

CHAPTER 3	# ENGAGING THE FAMILY

To work with a family, you must first engage it in treatment. The time and effort needed to engage the family can be quite minimal, including as little as one or two meetings, or may require more intensive efforts, including multiple meetings with family members, support and education, and case management. Regardless of the amount of time required to engage the family, the therapist's skill at managing the initial contacts and motivating family members is one of the most important determinants of whether the family actually receives any treatment. Furthermore, the engagement process sets clear expectations for families that prepare them to participate in the active, learning-based approach that characterizes collaborative family work.

In this chapter we provide a guide for the therapist on how to engage the family in BFT. We consider the issues of when in the course of the disorder the family can be engaged, the steps of engaging and orienting the family to BFT, how to motivate family members and respond to common questions or misgivings, and how to deal with particular obstacles to successful engagement, such as the uncooperative or severely impaired client. Engagement represents the true beginning of therapy, and as such it sets the tone for the remainder of the therapeutic relationship.

When to Engage the Family

BFT can help families cope more effectively with a psychiatric disorder regardless of when in the course of the disorder treatment is provided. Families with a member who has recently become ill may benefit from learning basic information about the illness, including the fact that they are not to blame, and communication and problem-solving skills can prevent the development of a maladaptive pattern of criticism and social withdrawal. Families with a member who has been ill for a number of years often need help learning how to monitor the disorder, dealing with disruptive outbursts, and setting limits on the client's behavior.

Helping families negotiate emergent needs associated with the client's care, such as arranging for a psychiatric evaluation, making social service referrals for housing instability, or coaching the family on how to hospitalize the member, may be necessary before a therapeutic contract is established. With these families the therapist often must help relatives identify persons in their current social network who can assist them in meeting their most immediate needs. All of these contacts with the relatives should be seen as part of the engagement process. Thus, the therapist must be willing to invest considerable time and effort in working with some families before they are willing or able to commit to family therapy.

Steps of Engagement

The process of engagement involves three general stages: initiating contact with the family, motivating the family to participate, and orientation to BFT. A summary of the stages of engaging the family and the goals for each stage is contained in Table 3.1. We describe the specific activities of the therapist in each of these stages below.

We first address the engagement of clients currently working with a treatment team. Usually these are clients receiving treatment in the public sector or in a hospital setting. While many of the issues presented will be of interest to clinicians working with all families, we will also address topics of special concern when the client is not being treated by a treatment team. Most often, this occurs when clients are seen by a private psychiatrist and are participating in little, if any, additional treatment.

Initiating Contact with the Family

The primary goals of this stage is to introduce the family members to the therapist, to begin establishing a therapeutic relationship, and to provide a brief description of BFT. Sometimes this first meeting also serves to motivate the client or relatives to participate in family sessions, while other times more than one meeting is necessary.

It is generally preferable to initiate contact with the client first and with the relatives later, because the client is critical to the success of therapy and the treatment team usually has the strongest therapeutic alliance with him or her. Exceptions to this can be made when the client is making a slow recovery in the hospital from a symptom exacerbation and the treatment team has had contact with concerned family members. When the client is an outpatient who is being referred to BFT by his or her treatment team, the initial contact can be made in a meeting with all interested family members.

Unless the therapist is a member of the client's current treatment team, it is preferable if a team member introduces the therapist to the client and relatives. Alternatively, a member of the treatment team can explain to the family that the team believes family sessions will be beneficial, and that the therapist will contact them to discuss this possibility further. By initiating contact with the family through the treatment team, the therapist builds on the existing therapeutic relationship to add family therapy as another component of treatment. With some families, the initial groundwork laid by the treatment team is crucial to motivating the family to participate, rendering the therapist's task of engaging the family an easy one. With other families, the team helps make the contact, but the therapist must still motivate them to participate in therapy. Although it is best if a member of the treatment team can facilitate contact with the client and relatives, when the team has a poor relationship with the family or when there has been little or no contact with relatives, it may be better for the therapist to initiate contact without the help of the team. In such cases, the therapist can simply state, after introducing himself or herself, that the treatment team has recommended family sessions as a strategy for improving client functioning.

TABLE 3.1
STAGES OF ENGAGEMENT IN BFT

Stage	Goals
1. Initial contact with the family	• Convey concern about client and relatives • Begin to establish a therapeutic relationship • Briefly describe goals of BFT • Interest family members in learning more about BFT
2. Motivating the family to participate	• Discuss goals of BFT • Describe the format of BFT • Instill hope for change • Elicit willingness to participate in family sessions
3. Orientation of BFT	• Set positive expectations for change • Review goals and format of BFT • Discuss what is expected of family members • Discuss what family members can expect of the therapist • Determine logistics of family sessions (e.g., set appointment times for individual assessments and weekly family sessions) • Problem solve (e.g., scheduling, child care, transportation)

Initial Contact with the Client

During the initial contact, the therapist must strive above all to make a personal connection with the client that will form the beginning of their working relationship. To accomplish this, the therapist needs to demonstrate an interest and concern for the client and direct at least some of the conversation toward how the client is feeling and some of the problems he or she may be experiencing. We provide a vignette below that illustrates the utility of personally engaging the client before discussing the nature of family treatment.

Case Example

The therapist approached Bob, a young man with schizoaffective disorder, to discuss participating in BFT. The initial conversation quickly turned to a discussion of Bob's chronic auditory hallucinations, which he found extremely distressing. These hallucinations were particularly disturbing because the voice he heard always manifested itself as a sinister green knight. Bob explained that one of the ways he was able to cope with these hallucinations was by writing poetry. When the therapist expressed an interest in seeing his poetry, Bob was pleased to share his creative out-pouring. The therapist and Bob talked for about half an hour before the conversation shifted to BFT. By this time, a connection had been made between Bob and the therapist, who now knew something about each other. Soon after the conversation turned to family therapy, Bob agreed to participate in the program.

After the introductions, the therapist spends a few minutes getting to know the client before beginning discussion about family sessions. The therapist refers to the recommendation of the treatment team for family counseling sessions, describes the purpose of the family intervention, and provides a brief description of the nature of BFT. We provide an example below of how the therapist introduces the topic of family sessions:

> I would like to talk with you for a couple of minutes about a family counseling program that your treatment team thought might be helpful to you. The idea of this program is to try to help people who have experienced the kind of difficulties you have to work with their families and help them achieve their personal goals. Sometimes there can be a little tension between someone like yourself and their relatives, and one of the goals of family counseling is to lower stress on everyone in the family. Even when there isn't a problem with tension in the family, these sessions can help everyone learn more about these types of problems and communicate better, which can help you stay out of the hospital and be more independent in the community. The sessions are very positively focused toward the future and are mostly aimed at improving how family members communicate and solve problems together.

Note that the therapist avoids use of a specific diagnostic term unless he or she knows the client accepts this label. In presenting the purpose of BFT, the therapist does not assume there is significant stress in the family or problems in communication, although it is made clear that if such difficulties do exist, family sessions will help alleviate these stressors. The major objectives of BFT that are presented to clients are helping them improve their independence, achieve goals, and stay out of the hospital. The treatment is described as "positively focused" and aimed at "improving the ability of the family to communicate more effectively and solve problems together." This informs the client that therapy sessions are future oriented (as opposed to past oriented), minimally stressful, and concerned with enhancing family functioning. Concrete examples of what the client might get out of BFT are given, such as returning home and helping his or her family, who always seem upset. If the client acknowledges having a psychiatric disorder, the therapist can also add that the goal of BFT is to help the client and family learn more about this type of disorder so that they can become active members of the client's own treatment team.

This introductory description of BFT is sufficient to motivate many clients, who may then want to know more about the format of therapy, such as frequency and duration of treatment sessions. When clients express interest in family sessions but are unsure or pessimistic about how their relatives will respond, they are reassured that the therapist will raise the prospect of BFT with relatives, unless the client would prefer to do so first. Some clients want to talk more before they are ready to commit to participating in BFT. Key points on motivating these clients are discussed in the section below on Motivating the Family to Participate.

Initial Contact with Relatives

The initial contact between the therapist and relatives often takes place over the telephone but sometimes occurs in person at the clinic or hospital. The therapist's goal during this contact, especially if it is over the telephone, is to briefly highlight the goals of BFT and to elicit a willingness on the part of the relative to talk more in person about family sessions. We first describe how to interest the relatives in BFT when the initial contact occurs on the telephone.

The therapist begins the conversation with a personal introduction, mentions the mental health center or hospital from which he or she is calling, and explains which members of the client's treatment team have recommended family sessions. The therapist then explains how family treatment could be beneficial to the client and relatives, and then briefly describes the nature of BFT sessions. The therapist answers questions raised by a relative and at the conclusion of the discussion, if the relative is interested, arranges a time to meet in person to discuss the family program in more detail. Any other involved relatives are invited to participate in this meeting with the therapist.

The initial description of the advantages of BFT provided to the relative is similar to that provided to the client, with a few minor modifications. Although it is still preferable not to refer to a specific diagnostic term at this time, unless the therapist knows that the family accepts the diagnosis, the therapist can more freely use the term "illness" or "disorder" when talking with relatives, who almost always understand that the client has a psychiatric disability. In connection with this, relatives often resonate to the idea that family sessions will help them become members of the client's treatment team. The attraction of this goal is that it recognizes the importance of the family and holds the promise of teaching relatives more about the disorder and how to manage it. As when discussing BFT with the client, the therapist does not imply to the relatives that their family has poor communication or problem-solving skills, although it can be assumed that relatives who live with a mentally ill person do experience some stress associated with this. An example of how the therapist discusses BFT during an initial telephone contact with a relative is provided below.

Therapist:	Hello, Mrs. Smith? This is Dr. Jones calling from Riverview Mental Health Center. I believe that Ms. Handly, John's case manager, mentioned to you that I'd be calling?
Relative:	Yes, she did.
Therapist:	Good. I was calling to talk to you about a family counseling program we have that is designed to help clients achieve goals and stay out of the hospital. Ms. Handly and John's psychiatrist both thought this program might be helpful to John and your family.
Relative:	Does this mean you think that we *caused* John's problems?
Therapist:	No, not at all. We believe that as concerned family members you can do a lot to help John.
Relative:	I see. So what's this program about?
Therapist:	The goal of the program is to teach family members, including you and your son, more about his psychiatric disorder so that your family can become extended members of his treatment team. In addition to helping family members understand more about this kind of disorder, the program teaches families how to communicate better with each other, and how to solve problems using strategies that other families with similar problems have found helpful. An important goal for the program is reducing the stress on all family members by working with the whole family.
Relative:	Sounds interesting. Does the whole family have to participate? How long does this program last?
Therapist:	We have found that it is best when everyone who is involved with the client participates in family sessions, but it is not a strict requirement. Most families benefit when they participate in sessions for at least several months, and sometimes even more, although the sessions are held less frequently over time. Sessions start out weekly, and then after a while sessions are held every other week, and then monthly. It sounds like you might be interested in this program.
Relative:	Yes, I think I am.
Therapist:	Maybe we could set up a time when you could come over and we could talk about it a little more. How would that be?
Relative:	That sounds fine. Should I come alone, or with other family members?
Therapist:	It would be helpful if you could bring anyone else in your home who would be able to come. Who else do you think might come?

Family members may ask additional questions during this initial contact, such as about the nature of the psychiatric disorder, further details about the format of sessions, billing, or how to handle specific problems. The therapist addresses those questions which are most easily handled and explains that the more difficult concerns and problems are the types of issues that can be addressed in family sessions. It is important that the therapist not be perceived by family members as withholding information in order to entice their participation in family therapy. Rather, the more that family members understand about the goals of BFT and the nature of the psychiatric disorder, the more likely it is that they will be interested in participating in sessions. Thus, the therapist is willing to provide some educational information about the disorder over the telephone if the relative is interested, such as information about the client's diagnosis, medication, or causes of the disorder.

Motivating the Family to Participate

For many family members, a ten- to fifteen-minute conversation over the telephone is sufficient to interest them in family therapy and to get them to agree to set up a meeting time to talk with the therapist in person. The purpose of this meeting is to review the goals of family therapy, to answer more questions the relatives might have about the program, and to arrive at a firm commitment on the relatives' part to participate. After relatives and clients have agreed to participate in the family program, an orientation meeting is set up for the entire family to set clear expectations, which is the third step of engagement. Some families need more time after the initial contact to think about family treatment, to talk among themselves, and to talk again with the therapist. Most families who meet with the therapist after an initial telephone contact eventually agree to try family therapy.

Many of the skills for motivating clients and relatives to participate in BFT were alluded to in the previous section Initiating Contact with the Family. Some of these skills are basic interpersonal skills that are useful in any clinical situation. The therapist demonstrates clear interest and concern for the well-being of the client and relatives. The therapist focuses the discussion on the potential benefits of the treatment program. Families tend to endorse all of the main goals of BFT, including reducing rehospitalizations, increasing client independence and adjustment, minimizing stress on all family members, and making the family an extended part of the client's treatment team. By informing family members that BFT will improve their understanding of the psychiatric disorder, their communication skills, and their ability to deal with common problems, the therapist connotes the positive, learning-based approach of the treatment model. Furthermore, by providing basic information in response to questions about the psychiatric disorder and its treatment, the therapist shows a willingness to share his or her knowledge and to work collaboratively with the family.

In addition to these methods for motivating the family, we have found several other strategies to be useful when motivating and engaging families in BFT. These strategies are described below.

Letting Family Members Know They Are Not Alone

One of the greatest burdens experienced by clients with a psychiatric disorder and by their relatives is the feeling that they must cope with the disorder alone. The social stigma of mental illness, as well as the tendency of many people to deal with personal problems alone, results in constricting the social networks of many families and increasing their experience of stress. In order to overcome this sense of isolation, the therapist validates the experiences described by clients and relatives by empathizing and by helping them understand they are not alone, that many others share similar problems. The therapist explains that the family program was developed in order to address these types of common problems. The realization that others have similar experiences coping with mental illness helps families to understand that they are a part of a larger community. Whether or not the relatives become more involved with this community, such as through self-help or advocacy groups, the message that "you are not alone" is comforting to family members.

Allowing Relatives to Vent

Some family members have built up negative feelings over many years of trying to cope with their relative's disorder. Usually these feelings center on the client, but they can also be directed at the mental health system, insensitive treatment providers, or an inability to get consistent and accurate information about the psychiatric disorder. Relatives may need to vent some of these feelings to the therapist before they can be engaged and work constructively in family therapy.

The best role the therapist can play when dealing with a relative who expresses a great deal of anger is to be a good listener. Active listening skills by the therapist, such as paraphrasing what the relative has just said, are crucial because they let the relative know that his or her frustration is understood. The therapist can look for opportunities to point out that the family program can be helpful in addressing some of the problems, although he or she may have to hear the relative out in order to gain the relative's attention.

Relatives often feel relieved after several minutes of venting to the therapist and are then ready to discuss family treatment. Sometimes the relatives want to tell their whole story and more venting is needed. The therapist should allow time for this, while gently steering them toward discussion of family therapy and positive changes for the future. The therapist should not be discouraged by the presence of high levels of negative affect (i.e., "Expressed Emotion") in relatives, because such strong feelings are usually an indication of the relative's intense degree of involvement and commitment to the client.

Case Example

The sixty-four-year-old father of a thirty-six-year-old man with bipolar disorder was contacted during one of the client's hospitalizations about participating in family sessions. After an initial telephone conversation with the therapist, the father agreed to meet with the therapist to discuss the program further. Soon after the father arrived for the meeting, he launched into a lengthy, angry account of the many years of difficulty he and his wife had had managing their son and the poor treatment he had received from many professionals who were involved in their son's psychiatric treatment. After about twenty minutes the therapist was sure that engagement in therapy was a lost cause but allowed the father to continue. When the father had completed the main thrust of his story after forty-five minutes he appeared quite relieved and redirected the conversation himself to the family program. Comparatively little time was needed to discuss the family therapy before the father agreed to give it a try.

The place for relatives to vent their frustrated feelings is in a meeting with the therapist in which the client is *not* present. Venting by relatives in the presence of the client can be stressful to him or her and jeopardize engaging the entire family. If the initial engagement of the family occurs with the client present and relatives begin to vent negative feelings, the therapist must acknowledge and interrupt criticisms and then reinforce the client's participation in the meeting. Relatives who agree to participate in family therapy will have the opportunity to vent during the individual meetings that are held with the therapist during the first assessment phase of BFT. If venting appears to be critical to the engagement of certain relatives, an individual meeting can be arranged between the relative and the therapist, with the goal of this meeting being to allow the relative to vent *and* to engage their willingness to try family treatment.

Although providing a forum for relatives to vent their negative feelings can be vital to engaging them in family treatment, venting during family sessions is not constructive and can interfere with resolving important problems. Therefore, the therapist interrupts venting during family sessions by either prompting the relative to express a negative feeling about a specific behavior of the client or redirecting the conversation. One goal of BFT is to teach family members how to express negative feelings in a constructive manner so that these feelings do not build up over long periods of time and lead to angry outbursts. Until the family is engaged, however, allowing relatives to vent (when the client is absent) can be a useful rapport-building strategy.

Instilling Hope for Change

Some families with a mentally ill member have suffered for years with chronic problems, and a major impediment to successful engagement is their belief that change is no longer possible. These families are often "burned out" by the stress and demands of coping with a psychiatric disorder with little or no assistance, and their level of commitment to the client may be severely attenuated. Engagement of these families requires the therapist to instill some hope that change is possible, even when dealing with severe problems that have persisted for many years. At the same time, the therapist does not want to create false expectations by suggesting that the family program will cure the disorder. The best way to instill hope in families is for the therapist to let them know that he or she understands the nature of the difficulties they have experienced, and to explain that the family program was developed with the purpose of helping families learn how to deal with such problems. The therapist can give examples of families with similar circumstances who have benefited from participating in BFT.

An additional strategy with many of these families is to highlight the potential for using BFT to help plan for the client's future when the parents are no longer able to be actively involved in his or her care. We have found that many parents and siblings struggle with who will assume future responsibility to help ensure that the client's needs are met. Many families have not discussed this issue, and family members frequently have very different implicit assumptions about one another's roles. Often, they welcome the opportunity to begin to develop their skills so they can resolve this difficult but important issue.

The therapist may need to convince some relatives that short-term change is possible when the family presents with pressing problems that require immediate attention, and the therapy must make good on at least some of these changes if the family is to remain in treatment. This may require addressing problems before the family has been taught problem-solving skills. While the therapist must be the leader in solving problems at the early stage of therapy, successful resolution of pressing problems decreases the stress impinging on the family, thereby enhancing members' capacity to learn information about the disorder and communication skills.

Responses to Common Questions Raised by Families

Some common questions and obstacles are raised by family members about BFT. We have identified some of these problems below and suggest responses for the therapist that we have found helpful in engaging these families.

1. Relative: We've tried family therapy before, but it didn't work and everyone felt frustrated afterward. How do we know it won't just happen again?

Therapist: What was that experience like? *(Pause for answer.)* I understand that your previous experience with family therapy was not a very positive one. However, not all approaches to working with families are the same. This program is positively oriented toward helping families cope more effectively with the disorder and reducing stress. In some other approaches to working with families, a lot of time is spent exploring "family dynamics" and trying to understand "why" everyone behaves the way they do. Our program is aimed at teaching families more about the psychiatric disorder and how to communicate and solve problems more effectively. Many families who have participated in this program have benefited from it, and if you give it a try you may find that it is better than your previous experience.

2. Relative: Our ill family member doesn't even believe that something is wrong with him (or her). What's the point of having family counseling if the client won't even take the first step toward helping himself (or herself) by recognizing that he (or she) has an illness?

Therapist: We have found that families can benefit from this program even when the client does not think he (or she) has a psychiatric disorder. Your relative actually *has* taken a very important step by expressing a willingness to participate in family sessions. Sometimes clients deny they have a psychiatric disorder in order to preserve their self-esteem; they don't want to think of themselves as having a "mental illness." This doesn't mean they aren't willing to work to improve their lives or learn how to get along with their family better. We have found that the client doesn't have to admit to having a disorder for the family to work productively together in this program.

3. Relative: Our family member has been given so many different diagnoses, how do we know which one is correct?

Therapist: It can be difficult to establish some psychiatric diagnoses, because some symptoms are common across different disorders. Sometimes diagnoses change over time because the symptoms also change. This is particularly true during the early stages of the client's disorder. In order to arrive at the correct diagnosis, a careful clinical interview must be conducted. In our program, we will educate you about your family member's diagnosis using the best information available to us.

4. Relative: We've tried *everything* and nothing seems to help at all! How is this program going to make a difference when nothing else has?

Therapist: It can be frustrating to work so hard to cope with the disorder in a family member and to feel that nothing has worked. I think the most important quality in your family is that despite the problems that you have experienced, you still care a great deal about each other and you haven't given up yet. It can be hard to try something new when your previous attempts have not seemed to help, but I think you will find that these family sessions are different from other things you have tried. The goal of these sessions is to help families understand more about the disorder and to learn how to deal with common problems. If you *try* family counseling sessions you may find them helpful. The kind of problems you described to me probably won't go away on their own. If you find that family sessions are not very helpful, we can always agree to stop them after we have discussed your concerns. Thus, you might consider trying this family program because as the old saying goes, "nothing ventured, nothing gained."

5. Relative: Our ill family member can be very demanding and unpredictable, and we're concerned that counseling will upset the balance we have reached in our family. How can we be sure that these sessions will not upset him (or her) and make our lives worse?

Therapist: That's a good question. We have found that by making the client an integral part of the family sessions, and by attending to the needs of all family members, both clients and relatives can profit without upsetting the balance that has been achieved in the family too much. The goal of family work is to lower stress and improve the functioning of everyone in the family, and this can usually be accomplished by a therapist who is sensitive to the concerns of each family member.

6. Relative: Can you make my family member better? The only thing that would help me is if he gets better.

Therapist:	Helping your family member is exactly what this program is about. Although we do not yet have a *cure* for your family member's disorder, we know quite a bit about how to reduce common symptoms, prevent people from having to go back to the hospital, and improve their independence. By working with professionals, relatives can play an important role in improving their family member's disorder.
7. Relative:	We are interested in family sessions, but one (nonclient) relative doesn't want to participate and wouldn't come in today. Is that okay?
Therapist:	It often happens that some family members are interested in participating in these sessions and others are not. Not everyone *has* to participate for the family to benefit, but it is preferable if the key relatives can participate in at least some of the sessions. I think it is best if I can talk to your relative directly about this program over the telephone. I may be able to answer some of the questions or concerns he (or she) has and let him (or her) know that he (or she) is important to the family and the success of the program.

This last issue, in which family members inform the therapist that other key relatives do not want to be involved in family counseling, is a common one. It is imperative that the therapist attempt to speak directly with each family member about participating in counseling sessions and not accept the word of another relative that the member does not want to participate. Sometimes one family member will "protect" another from having to participate in family counseling, even though the other member is willing to try if presented with the opportunity. At other times, the therapist may be able to persuade a reluctant relative to participate or to attend at least a few sessions. In either case, the therapist needs to have personal contact with each relative to assess his or her willingness to participate in family counseling. The key points for motivating families to participate in BFT are summarized in Table 3.2.

When There Is No Formal Treatment Team

The preceding discussion has been predicated on the assumption that the client is currently being seen by a comprehensive treatment team that makes a referral for BFT. However, especially in the private sector, the client may have no defined treatment team. In such a case, a relative may approach a therapist about initiating BFT. When approached, the therapist has the initial objective of assessing whether BFT is in fact a reasonable treatment option for the family given its current circumstances.

When evaluating whether BFT is an appropriate intervention for the family at this time, the therapist might consider the following questions:

1. Do family members have time each week to commit to the therapy?

2. Does the family have the financial resources to cover the cost of treatment, or can it be made available at a more affordable fee?

3. Is the client willing to participate in the treatment? If not, how will the treatment objectives be modified?

4. Would family members derive more benefit from individual treatment to meet their unique needs?

TABLE 3.2
KEY POINTS FOR MOTIVATING FAMILIES
TO PARTICIPATE IN BFT

- Goals of treatment:
    Make the family a part of the treatment team
    Reduce relapses and rehospitalizations
    Enhance client functioning and independence
    Reduce stress on all family members
    Improve family's ability to work constructively together
    Help all family members achieve goals
- Sessions are positively focused and involve minimal stress
- BFT is different from other treatments family may have had
- Other families with similar problems have benefited from BFT
- Change *is* possible, even after many years of problems
- BFT is not a *cure* for psychiatric disorders, but it can help improve relationships between relatives and the client
- Family members decide what problems they want to work on
- The family is free to try BFT and quit if they do not find it beneficial

---

To ascertain the answers to each of these questions, the therapist can often benefit from scheduling a general introductory session with as many family members as are willing to attend. The objective of this session is to begin to develop a treatment strategy to meet the family's unique needs and to determine whether BFT can be helpful in meeting those needs.

Responses to each of the above questions can help inform an appropriate treatment strategy. For example, the mother of a man with treatment-refractory obsessive-compulsive disorder with whom we met very much desired to initiate BFT. Her son, however, had been estranged from her for years and had no interest in resuming contact. In this case, the mother was seen for individual sessions, which focused on both grief work concerning her son's situation and on developing suitable behavioral strategies to manage the limited contacts the two did have. In another family, the parents of a twenty-three-year-old daughter with schizophrenia who was living at home felt they were no longer able to establish and enforce any rules around the house without severely agitating their daughter. The daughter had no established routine and was not receiving any kind of rehabilitation. The family approached the therapist to see whether they could work together to make things better at home. As their funds were limited, the therapist contracted with the family for a total of fifteen sessions; the daughter attended intermittently. The parents worked toward the goal of establishing some household standards and finding and implementing a reinforcement program to help the daughter meet them. As an additional objective, the therapist linked the daughter up with services available to persons with serious psychiatric disorders in her community to reduce the financial burden on the family.

In short, when the family approaches the therapist, he or she must be prepared to make a preliminary evaluation about whether BFT is appropriate. If BFT is to be pursued, the therapist should anticipate needing to do more of the "legwork" to get the therapy up and running, as well as extending more effort into linking the family to other services that might assist in the management of a member with a psychiatric disorder.

Orientation to BFT

After the client and relatives have agreed to participate in BFT, an orientation meeting is set up with the entire family. This meeting does not need to be very long; twenty to forty minutes is sufficient for most families. If the client was recently hospitalized, the meeting is usually held either just before or immediately following discharge from the hospital. For families in which the therapist has met separately with the client and relatives to enlist their participation in BFT, this is the first meeting between the therapist and the entire family.

The primary purpose of the orientation meeting with the family is to set clear and positive expectations for its participation in BFT. We have found that setting clear expectations reduces the anxiety experienced by family members in the early stages of therapy and prepares them to participate actively in the sessions. In addition, by letting family members know in advance that activities such as role-playing and homework are part of the therapy, resistance to these aspects of BFT can be stemmed.

The therapist begins the orientation meeting with a positive comment about the family's agreement to participate in the program. As therapists, we prefer to go on a first-name basis with families we treat. We suggest to the family that we use first names at this point of the orientation, and we have found that families appear to be comfortable with this, even when some family members are significantly older than the therapist. Other therapists may prefer to remain more formal and continue to use Dr./Mr./Mrs./Ms. titles. The therapist explains that the purpose of the meeting is to review the goals of the family program and to discuss what will be expected of the family and what the family members can expect of the therapist. At this stage, the therapist hands out a sheet to each family member that summarizes the main points of the orientation. A copy of this orientation sheet is included in appendix 1 ("Orientation to Behavioral Family Therapy"); it can be copied or modified according to the specific needs of the therapist.

The orientation is divided into five main sections: *role of the therapist, goals, format, expectations of family members,* and *expectations of the therapist.* Most of the information presented here will have already been discussed with the family before, but it is useful to review it again in order to ensure that the family understands the program. The therapist uses the orientation sheet to guide the review of the program, briefly elaborating on each of the points included in the sheet, checking the understanding of family members, and eliciting and answering questions about specific points. At the end of the meeting the therapist schedules an individual assessment meeting with each family member and arranges a regular weekly time for the family to meet for therapy sessions. The individual meetings are conducted as soon after the orientation as possible, with the first family session following after that, preferably within two to three weeks of orientation.

We next describe the points highlighted by the therapist during the orientation meeting.

Role of the Therapist

The therapist explains that his or her role is to guide the family in learning new information about the nature of the client's disorder and its treatment, and to develop more effective skills for coping with the disorder. This point serves as a brief introduction to the orientation sheet and requires little additional elaboration.

Goals

The review of the goals of BFT flows naturally from the discussion of the therapist's role. The family already will be familiar with most of these goals from previous contacts with the therapist, and a brief paraphrase of each goal is sufficient before moving on to the next section.

Format

In this section the therapist describes the different components of BFT, including assessment, education, communication-skills training, problem solving, and special problems. When discussing the assessment of the family, it can be helpful for the therapist to say, "I will be conducting individual assessments with each member of the family, because it is important for me to get each person's point of view and to understand the changes that are most important to them." This explanation can assuage the concern of some relatives that the therapist views them as a "client" or having significant psychopathology.

The therapist can elaborate the discussion of the educational, communication, and problem-solving components of BFT by giving examples of the types of topics that are covered in each component (e.g., symptoms and medication are addressed in the *educational* sessions, skills such as expressing positive and negative feelings are sharpened during *communication-skills training*, and family members learn how to define a problem and "brainstorm" solutions in *problem-solving training*). These examples flesh out the components of BFT for family members, helping them understand better what they will be learning in therapy.

When discussing the format of family sessions, the therapist also addresses how often and for how long the sessions will be provided. The amount of detail given to families may vary depending upon the setting and agency in which the therapist works. In some settings BFT may be offered as a relatively structured program of fixed duration (e.g., twenty to thirty sessions provided on a declining contract basis over eighteen months). In other settings BFT may be provided more flexibly for either shorter or longer periods of time, depending on the needs of the individual family. In any case, the therapist needs to set expectations concerning the frequency and duration of sessions. If the overall time frame is open, the family is informed that sessions will be conducted on a weekly basis for the first several months and that then the frequency of the sessions will gradually decline. The therapist tells family members that progress in treatment and achievement of goals will be reviewed on a regular basis (e.g., every three months) and that the decision to end sessions will be made jointly by the therapist and family. This lets family members know that they have input into the length of family treatment.

Expectations of Family Members

BFT requires a high level of participation on the part of both the therapist and family. The therapist defines for family members what is expected of them as participants in BFT. The general theme of the expectations listed in the orientation sheet is that BFT is a learning-based approach that requires regular attendance at family sessions, practice during the sessions of specific interpersonal skills ("active role-playing"), and systematic rehearsal of these skills in their natural environment ("completion of all homework assignments"). Rather than presenting these expectations as necessary evils, the therapist takes the opportunity at this point to "drum up" enthusiasm in the family members by explaining that active participation in therapy will lead to learning new skills and a positive outcome. This message empowers family members by conveying to them that the means for learning how to improve their situations and achieve their goals lies within their own family.

During the discussion of the importance of regular attendance, the therapist also provides guidelines to the family for canceling a session (e.g., calling ahead of time to cancel a session, preferably at least one day in advance). When sessions are to be conducted in the family's home, the therapist explains that a quiet working environment is needed in order for family members to be able to learn the material. If contacts with the family have all been office- or hospital-based up to this point and some sessions will subsequently be conducted in the home, inquiries are made of the family to evaluate how they can secure a quiet working environment in their home.

We now provide an example below of how the therapist introduces and discusses the expectation that family members will do role plays and complete homework as participants in BFT.

Therapist:	You can see on your orientation sheet that "active role-playing" is the next expectation that is listed. Do any of you know what a "role play" is?
Client:	It's kind of like talking to someone, but it's not real.
Relative:	Isn't it playacting?
Therapist:	Yes, it's a little like both of these. "Role-playing" is a technique that we use in family sessions to help people practice certain communication skills. A role play is a simulated or pretend social interaction in which one person talks to another as though the situation were actually taking place. I like to use role plays to give people a chance to see

what it's like communicating in particular ways. In our family sessions everyone will be doing some role-playing, including myself. Some family members feel a little bit funny at first when they try role-playing, but usually they become comfortable with it after a short time, and sometimes they find that role-playing can even be fun and interesting. Any questions?

Relative:	I guess not.
Client:	You mean we *have* to do it?
Therapist:	Well, I have found it best when everyone tries some role-playing. I like to give people a lot of positive feedback for role-playing and to avoid criticism. This usually makes the experience a pretty positive one.
Client:	Okay.
Therapist:	Good. I wanted to say a couple of words about homework next. As we have talked about, the goal of this program is to learn new information and skills that will help your family deal more effectively with the disorder and help family members achieve personal goals. However, in order for this learning to take place, family members need to practice the skills outside of the counseling session to see how they work in their natural home environment. Homework assignments will be given to review information and practice skills, and completing these assignment is crucial to how much this program will benefit your family. By doing homework, you will be helping me understand which skills are working for you and which ones are not, and that helps me do my job better.

Expectations of the Therapist

The nature of BFT as a genuine collaboration between the family and the therapist is illustrated by discussing therapist expectations immediately after family expectations. Family therapy involves a contract between the family and therapist and these expectations let family members understand what they can expect from the therapist. The expectations identified on the orientation sheet are straightforward and do not require extensive discussion.

The therapist discusses the arrangements for crisis counseling at this time in the orientation. It is best if the therapist is available to the family for emergencies, at least some of the time, because this availability connotes a level of commitment on the part of the therapist that goes beyond the weekly scheduled therapy session. The family members should know when and how they can call the therapist for an emergency or between session consultation (e.g., directly at the office or at home, through the hospital switchboard or a beeper system), and whom they can call when the therapist is not available. In our experience, crisis calls from family members between therapy sessions are rare and therefore add little time to the therapist's workload.

As will be discussed more fully in the next chapter, the second half of the orientation meeting may provide an excellent opportunity to conduct a formal problem-solving assessment with the family, and to obtain a relationship history from couples. If time does not permit this evaluation at the end of the orientation session, it can be rescheduled for a subsequent meeting. After the therapist has arranged to meet individually with family members and a first family session has been scheduled, the orientation meeting is concluded.

Special Problems with Engaging Families

Several problems can emerge during the engagement phase of BFT that require special comment. Some families present for treatment with an ill family member who is minimally involved in treatment, very uncooperative, or severely impaired. With other families, a range of factors may interfere with their adherence to BFT, ultimately compromising the effectiveness of the intervention. We discuss these points in this last section.

The Uncooperative Client

Severe negativism and poor cooperation with treatment are not uncommon problems in psychiatric clients. The relatives of an uncooperative client sometimes contact the therapist, particularly when that client is living at home. Despite the best efforts of the therapist, some of these clients refuse to be engaged in BFT, and the therapist must determine what is in the best interest of the relatives.

There are two general options available to the therapist when the client will not consent to family therapy: (1) provide BFT without the client or (2) provide individual psychotherapy. Of course, a combination of these two options is a third possibility.

BFT without the Client

If at least two relatives have regular contact with the client and are interested in family sessions, they can be engaged in BFT without the client ever participating. Educational material can be covered, and relatives can take turns playing the part of the client when learning communication and problem-solving skills. This option is most viable when two (or more) relatives are highly involved with each other and the client, such as the parents of a psychiatric client living at home. In cases like these, BFT is most productive when it focuses on helping relatives jointly decide how they want to manage the psychiatric disorder at home, such as what limits to place on the client's behavior and cooperation with treatment.

Case Example

The seventy-five- and seventy-three-year-old parents of a forty-one-year-old woman with major depression who was living at home contacted the therapist for family treatment. The client at first refused to talk with the therapist on the telephone or participate in sessions, although she eventually did attend two sessions for about 15 minutes each. After two meetings between the therapist and parents, they agreed to try BFT, and twenty-four sessions were conducted over the following year and a half. The focus of these sessions was on education and problem solving, with little attention paid to communication, which was already good between the partners. The sessions focused on helping the couple develop more realistic expectations about their daughter's capacity for independence, establish and enforce clear household rules (e.g., not smoking in certain rooms of the house), and consistently use rewards (e.g., rides to destinations, spending money) to reinforce desirable behaviors. The couple reported benefiting from the BFT sessions and remained in telephone contact for over three years following the sessions.

Individual Psychotherapy

In some families in which the client is uncooperative, only one relative has a high level of involvement with that person or is willing to commit to working with the therapist. Relatives who bear the burden of caring for an ill family member alone or who have minimal social support often experience high levels of stress and are good candidates for individual therapy. Therapy with these relatives needs to include education about the illness, but usually it is less concerned with management of the disorder and more focused on helping the relative resolve issues regarding his or her relationship with the client. Responding to the pronounced withdrawal or negativism of uncooperative clients often requires individual therapy to address issues of loss that are less pertinent to families with more engaged clients.

The Severely Impaired Client

When the client is severely impaired, such as living in a long-term inpatient setting or chronically psychotic and disorganized, the therapist must consider the question of whether this is the right time for family intervention. If the family seeks treatment, then some therapy may be in order to address the issues that propelled it to the therapist. If the family has not sought treatment, on the other hand, the decision to offer BFT needs to be based on clear evidence of family strife or maladaptive coping strategies that can be rectified by intervention. Some of the methods for tailoring BFT for families with a severely impaired client are described in Chapter 8, "Special Problems."

Similar to the problem of the uncooperative client, relatives with a severely ill family member sometimes need help "mourning" the loss of a relative (Atkinson, 1994; Miller et al., 1990). Although family sessions that include the client can be productive in teaching relatives how to manage the disorder more effectively, issues of loss are best addressed by conducting some individual or family sessions without the client. When a very ill client is willing and able to participate in BFT, a combination of sessions with and without the client can be fruitful for meeting the needs of the family.

CASE EXAMPLE OF DWAYNE AND TANIA

Dwayne, a forty-four-year-old married African American Vietnam combat veteran with chronic, combat-related PTSD, contacted the family treatment staff after completing a residential treatment program. He was planning to return to live with his wife of twelve years, Tania. He was concerned because he and Tania had had a contentious marriage and they had been separated for the previous fifteen months. They still were "in love," however, and both wanted to give the relationship another try. Dwayne attributed much of their difficulty to conflicts regarding how much involvement they should have and how much support they should give adult children from previous relationships. These children were experiencing many legal and financial difficulties, and Dwayne wanted to concentrate his efforts on his relationship with Tania.

After meeting with Dwayne, the BFT therapist called Tania and told her briefly about BFT. Tania was very enthusiastic about participating. She was apprehensive that the reconciliation with Dwayne might be difficult. To further complicate matters, Tania had recently developed stress reactions at work and was on disability herself. She agreed to come to learn more about the program and then consented to participate. The therapist raised the issue with Dwayne and Tania about whether any other family members should be invited. While Dwayne and Tania agreed the children needed help, scheduling constraints and Dwayne's desire to work on the marital relationship resulted in a decision to just work with the couple.

At the end of each subsequent chapter of this book we will provide updates describing the progress made by Dwayne and Tania over the course of BFT.

Summary

In this chapter, we discussed the process of engaging the family in BFT. Successful engagement is crucial in developing a collaborative working relationship with the family that will improve the prognosis of the client's psychiatric disorder. The primary goals are to enlist the willingness of the family to participate in BFT, to set clear expectations for the type of changes that may be achieved, and to inform the family about the nature of the therapy itself. The engagement process unfolds over three stages: *initial contact, motivating the family to participate,* and *orientation to BFT.* We recommended strategies for dealing with obstacles to engaging families, such as the uncooperative or severely ill client, to enable therapists to "get their foot in the door" and to initiate proper treatment.

In the next chapter we describe methods for assessment of the family.

CHAPTER 4	# ASSESSMENT OF THE FAMILY

After successfully engaging the family, BFT begins with a comprehensive assessment of all participants. The primary objective of this assessment is to identify knowledge, communication, and problem-solving deficits that interfere with successful management of the client's disorder and achievement of a more satisfactory life for everyone in the family. The assessment format presented below assumes that the client is receiving appropriate psychiatric treatment including a correct diagnosis, ongoing symptom assessment to monitor clinical status and medication, and case management, as required. Since these assessments are independent of BFT, they will not be highlighted here.

As with all behavior therapy, BFT is an ongoing process of therapy informed by continuing assessment. Most of this chapter will be devoted to evaluations conducted at the beginning of the therapy. However, the therapist remains alert in every session to application (and omission) of relevant BFT skills. When this ongoing assessment reveals critical deficiencies, then supplemental instruction is undertaken.

Consistent with its conceptual foundation, the objective of the assessment process is to obtain information about the family's actual behavior so that specific problem areas can be identified and remediated. When describing situations that occurred, participants are prompted to provide specific details (e.g., "What exactly did you say then?"; "Specifically, what improvements would you like to see when you say you would like to get along better with your wife?"). Furthermore, when possible the therapist re-creates interpersonal situations through role plays in order to directly observe the behavior of family members.

Finally, a word about the multimodal nature of the BFT assessment process is necessary. The accuracy and utility of assessments are strengthened when reliable and valid data are collected from a variety of sources. Thus, a comprehensive assessment must be conducted. This involves interviewing family members individually and conjointly, as well as conducting a behavioral observation of their current problem-solving behavior. In addition, self-report instruments can be used to help in the evaluation of specific problem areas. For example, the mother of a mentally ill man who states she feels very discouraged can be asked to complete the Beck

Depression Inventory (Beck et al., 1961) in order to gain a better understanding of her level of depression. Table 4.1 contains a list of self-report instruments that may be useful for assessing specific areas of concern. Additional assessment instruments can be found by consulting books by Corcoran and Fisher (1987), Hersen and Bellack (1988), and Sederer and Dickey (1996).

TABLE 4.1
SELF-REPORT INSTRUMENTS FOR ASSESSING
SPECIFIC PROBLEM AREAS

Problem Area	Scale	Authors
Agoraphobia	Agoraphobic Cognitions Questionnaire CAGE	Chambless et al. (1984) Mayfield et al. (1974)
Alcohol Abuse	Michigan Alcoholism Screening Test	Selzer (1971)
	Dartmouth Assessment of Lifestyle Instrument	Rosenberg et al. (1998)
Anxiety	Beck Anxiety Inventory	Beck et al. (1988)
	State-Trait Anxiety Inventory	Spielberger et al. (1983)
Depression	Beck Depression Inventory	Beck, et al. (1988)
	Center for Epidemologic Studies Depression Scale	Radloff & Locke (1986)
Drug Abuse	The Drug Abuse Screening Test	Skinner (1982)
	Dartmouth Assessment of Lifestyle Instrument	Rosenberg et al. (1998)
Family Burden	Family Distress Scale	Passamanick et al. (1967)
	Social Behavior Assessment Schedule	Platt et al. (1980)

Problem Area	Scale	Authors
General Distress	The Brief Symptom Inventory	Derogatis (1993)
Marital Conflict	Areas of Change Questionnaire	Weiss et al. (1973)
	Dyadic Adjustment Scale	Spanier (1976)
Obsessive-Compulsive Behavior	Compulsive Activity Checklist	Riggs & Foa (1993)
	Maudsley Obsessive-Compulsive Inventory	Hodgson & Rachman (1977)
Phobias	Fear Questionnaire	Marks & Matthews (1979)
Social Anxiety/ Avoidance	Social Avoidance and Distress Scale	Watson & Friend (1969)
Spouse Abuse	The Conflict Tactics Scale-2	Straus et al. (1995)
Trauma and PTSD	Trauma History Questionnaire	Green (1996)
	Stressful Life Events Screening Questionnaire	Goodman et al. (1998)
	Impact of Events Scale	Horowitz et al. (1979)
	PTSD Checklist	Blanchard et al. (1996)
	Posttraumatic Diagnostic Scale	Foa et al. (1993)

Initial Assessment

Prior to beginning education and skills training, a behavioral analysis is conducted on each individual family member and on the family as a unit. Individual assessment is a vital component of BFT. First, it permits the therapist to obtain specific information about each family member's understanding of the psychiatric disorder at hand, as well as its impact on that person's life. Second, it provides a forum for each family member to share his or her perceptions and concerns in confidence, without comment or censure by other members. Third, it provides an opportunity for the therapist to strengthen the alliance with each of the participants by identifying his or her unique concerns. Fourth, it helps the therapist shape a problem-solving focus by beginning to reframe concerns and stressors as potentially solvable "problems" that family members are currently facing. Finally, the therapist begins to direct the selection of each participant's individual goal(s) for subsequent problem solving, which is the cornerstone of BFT.

Confronted with the urgency of many clients' and families difficulties, as well as the exigencies of a typical clinical practice, it may be tempting to omit or minimize assessment in order to begin education and skills training as soon as possible. Although the individual interviews may need to be postponed when a family presents during a crisis, we caution therapists against proceeding with the core BFT work before the individual assessments have been completed. Of fundamental importance, the strength of the rapport and regard that the therapist develops during the assessment sessions can be most beneficial in motivating participants. Families and individuals dealing with a serious psychiatric disorder often confront feelings of loss, lack of control, helplessness, grief, isolation, and despair. Frequently, they have not had the opportunity to talk about these issues with an empathic, nonjudgmental mental health professional; the behavioral assessment provides an invaluable forum in which to begin to do so.

Equally important, the behavioral assessment helps the therapist understand the issues with which each family member is coping. It is critical to note that these issues may be independent of the family member's concerns about the client. Family members are also subject to all the travails that humans face, ranging from alcohol and drug abuse to financial pressures, marital problems, child abuse, depression and anxiety, and vocational setbacks. By spending the time necessary to acquire information about these experiences from each participant, the therapist greatly enhances his or her ability to anticipate and plan for problems to be dealt with in the BFT. Furthermore, this assessment is necessary to identify the skills that each family member will most benefit from strengthening.

Initial Assessment Structure

The assessment process has four components:

1. a joint interview with all family members, including an in vivo assessment of problem solving;

2. an individual history interview with each family member;

3. a functional assessment with each family member;

4. development of an initial case formulation

These core components can be supplemented with additional evaluation instruments, as the therapist deems appropriate. In a typical two- or three-person family, the objective is to complete these initial assessments in the two-week period between the orientation session and the first BFT session.

BFT was originally designed to be a home-based treatment. Distance, scheduling difficulties, and the other logistics of home-based work often preclude its implementation in this manner. However, we encourage BFT therapists to schedule at least one meeting at the home of the relative or client during the assessment period. Even one or two home visits can provide valuable information about the participants' lives, and about how to promote skill generalization to the observed environment.

Joint Interview

During the same session as the orientation to BFT, the therapist may elect to conduct a joint interview with the participants. Several factors must be taken into account when deciding whether to conduct a joint interview at this time or to first conduct the individual interviews. Prominent anxiety in one or more family members may indicate that a joint interview at this time could increase stress to even greater, more uncomfortable levels. Poor attentional capacity or other cognitive impairments (e.g., participant asks many irrelevant questions) in the client may be frustrating to relatives during a joint interview and result in very slow gathering of information. Finally, the presence of high levels of negative affect in the family, especially relatives who are harsh and critical toward the client, is a good reason for postponing the joint interview until a more solid relationship has been established between family members and the therapist in the individual interviews.

Typically, the joint interview requires forty-five to sixty minutes and provides an opportunity for the therapist to begin to assess communication and problem-solving skills. The initial assessment of communication skills relies primarily on informal behavioral observation of family communication during meetings with the therapist, as well as reports of behavior at home. In general, the therapist is evaluating the presence of the positive and negative communication patterns outlined in Table 4.2. A more formal task has been designed to assess problem-solving efforts.

TABLE 4.2
POSITIVE COMMUNICATION SKILLS

Eye contact
Body facing speaker
Asking clarifying questions
Not interrupting
Paraphrasing the speakers' comments
Use of "I" statements, rather than "you" statements
Not overgeneralizing
Brevity
Immediacy of feedback
Low levels of criticism and hostility

After reviewing the "Orientation to Behavioral Family Therapy" sheet (Appendix 1) with the family (discussed more fully in Chapter 3), the formal assessment is initiated. Typically, the therapist begins by informing the family that, since this treatment is focused on strengthening problem-solving skills, a discussion of the way the family currently solves problems can be a way for the therapist to determine how he or she can be most helpful to the family. The therapist then asks family members how they recently dealt with one or two problem situations. Since some families may not have conceptualized difficulties they have encountered as "problems," the therapist can be prepared with examples of common problems that families may face, such as how the client came to be hospitalized this time (if relevant), coping with recent financial pressures, or resolving child-rearing disagreements.

As family members describe how they attempted to deal with a problem, the therapist examines the correspondence between their report and the steps of problem solving that are taught in the BFT. In particular, the therapist listens for indications that family members talked about the problem together, agreed on a definition of the problem, generated and then evaluated solutions, agreed upon at least one solution, tried to implement that solution, and evaluated at a later time whether the solution had resolved the difficulty. Obviously, most families will not describe their problem-solving efforts using these specific steps. The therapist may probe to determine whether each of these steps occurred. For example, he or she can ask if family members sat down to talk about the problem, or if anyone felt "left out" of the discussion.

After talking about how the family dealt with a recent problem at home, the therapist then asks the family to work on a problem during the session, in order to obtain a more precise understanding of how family members interact together. This in vivo problem-solving assessment usually requires about fifteen minutes. First, the therapist asks the family to identify a problem it currently needs to resolve or a goal it wants to achieve. Some families have difficulty identifying problems, so the therapist can be prepared with a list of problems that are suitable to the task. It is important that these problems are not highly negatively charged, to minimize the possibility that the family session will degenerate into a hostile, angry confrontation. Examples of problems that are suitable for this assessment are provided in Table 4.3.

TABLE 4.3
EXAMPLES OF TOPICS FOR PROBLEM-SOLVING
ASSESSMENTS

Some family members are dissatisfied with the division of household chores

Family members can't decide which TV program to watch or which movie to see

Need to schedule or make car repairs

Family members want to make home improvements

Family members want to plan an activity together

Getting kids to activities/school on time

Planning a vacation

Once the family has agreed on a specific problem, the therapist asks it to work independently to try to reach a solution. We use these instructions to set up the problem-solving task: *"I would like you to work on solving the problem of _____ for the next few minutes. Since this is a family effort, I will be letting you work on it all by yourself, without interrupting you. Everyone's opinion is important, so I would like all of you to participate. Tell one another how you feel about the issue, and then try to come up with a solution. When you are done, I'll give you some feedback on what I observed."*

The therapist then lets the family work on the topic for ten minutes, interrupting only to stop physical aggression or extreme verbal hostility, should it occur. In our experience, family problem-solving assessments rarely need to be interrupted for these reasons (i.e., less than one in fifty assessments). To facilitate the family working independently, the therapist can pull his or her chair slightly back, avoid eye contact with family members, and take careful notes of the procedure during this period. The therapist can use the checklist contained in appendix 2 ("Problem-Solving Assessment Checklist") to record which problem-solving steps the family completed during the interaction. If family members direct questions to the therapist during the problem-solving assessment, the therapist redirects them to the task, requesting them to *"do the best job that you can"* or *"try and work on this problem for a few more minutes and see what solutions you can come up with."*

After the task is completed, the therapist provides family members with feedback about what he or she observed. We have found that the family can benefit most from feedback that models BFT communication skills, emphasizes strengths as well as identifies weaknesses, and links behaviors observed in the problem-solving activity with subsequent BFT work. For example, after observing a ten-minute interaction, the therapist might state: *"I really liked the way you all had input into discussing how you could handle the conflict with your landlord. I think you might sometimes be able to arrive at an even better answer if you could consider more than one solution to the problem. One of the areas I think I can help you with is learning how to brainstorm lots of solutions before you pick the one you want to try."* In this statement, the therapist simultaneously models the BFT communication skill of expressing positive feelings, provides specific, behaviorally based feedback on relative strengths and weaknesses, and sets the stages for later BFT problem-solving training.

When working with families in nonconjugal relationships (i.e., parent-child or sibling relations), the joint interview can be concluded at this point and appointments set for subsequent individual assessments. With conjugal couples where one has the disorder, it is useful to extend the interview for another thirty minutes or so to obtain a brief history of the relationship as well as current areas of conflict (see "Couples Relationship Interview" form in Appendix 2). While the overall BFT approach is relatively nonhistorical and focuses on the "here and now," we have found it can be important to understand the current difficulties the couple may be facing in the context of its history together. For example, the stresses apparent in a relationship in which the development of a psychiatric disorder is a recent occurrence may be very different from those observed in which the disorder is long-standing. When the disorder has recently developed, a psychiatric hospitalization may be negatively evaluated, because it reduces income to the family from a job or the availability of a family member for housekeeping and child-care activities. In contrast, in couples where the disorder has been present for a long time and is more debilitating, the healthy spouse may experience a sense of relief during the hospitalization because he or she does not have to supervise the ill partner and there is a reduction in the amount of chaos in the home.

During this joint interview, the therapist also attends to the couple's level of commitment to the relationship. Marriage to a person with a serious psychiatric disorder can be extraordinarily burdensome (Hooley et al., 1987; Judge, 1994; Noh & Avison, 1988), and members of some couples may be actively contemplating separation, even as they commit to participation in BFT. While these issues can be fully addressed during the individual assessments discussed next, it can be useful for the therapist to begin to broach the subject during the joint interview by asking the members if they have ever separated or discussed separation in the past. These issues can then be the focus of communication and/or problem-solving training in therapy.

If the couple is seriously considering separation, the therapist must come to agreement with each person about how best to proceed. For example, the therapist can ask the two to delay all decisions until they have completed the course of BFT and can better decide whether the relationship is viable. In our clinical work, we have found that most couples who are struggling with serious psychiatric disorders and come to the orientation session to learn more about BFT are willing to make this commitment. The therapist may need to compromise on the length of the commitment (e.g., the couple will commit to staying together for at least three months of weekly BFT sessions, at which point a reevaluation will be made). If the couple is unable to agree to work together for at least a few months, or if one person clearly wants to end the relationship, we recommend not starting BFT, because it is unlikely that the couple will devote the necessary energy to make changes that will improve its relationship. If the members agrees to commit to BFT, then the therapist asks each to identify conflict areas, as well as positive aspects of the relationship and activities they enjoy doing together.

Individual Life History

After the joint interview is completed, two individual one-hour meetings with each family member can be consolidated into a longer, single meeting with each person, but there are several advantages to holding two, rather than one meeting. Meeting with each person twice enables the therapist to develop more trust with each family member, as the person is able to reflect back on the first meeting with the therapist before the second one. The time between two interviews also helps the therapist identify additional questions to ask based on information gathered during the first interview, as well as to formulate questions raised by information provided by other family members.

The emphasis of the first of these meetings is on obtaining a brief life history of the family member, while the second focuses on conducting an assessment of the individual's current life circumstances, goals and problem-solving efforts, and understanding of and adjustment to the psychiatric disorder. In the first session, the objective is to obtain a brief overview of the individual's social and familial development. The therapist begins the session by informing the family member that, while the focus in the BFT will be on working on the "here and now" problems, individuals often have previous life experiences that have a great impact on their current circumstances, and that the first component of the individual assessment involves identifying some of these issues. The therapist then addresses each of the topics included in the "Individual Life History Interview" (contained in Appendix 2). The therapist is also alert to any signs of psychopathology (e.g., clinical depression, alcohol dependence) in the relative, as this can have an important influence on appropriate goal-setting and treatment planning. As a probe to determine level of motivation and capacity for follow-through, the therapist can conclude the session by assigning a brief homework assignment to be brought back to the subsequent individual meeting. This can be an inventory or questionnaire that the therapist believes may illuminate an issue, or even just asking the person to write down three questions they have about the ill family member's disorder.

During the first individual meeting with each family member, the therapist can ask probe questions to evaluate whether there is a problem with aggression between family members. Domestic violence and sexual abuse are pressing problems in many families where there is no established psychiatric disorder (Straus et al., 1980), as well as in families with a mentally ill individual (Goodman et al., 1997). Problems of domestic violence and sexual abuse in families with a psychiatric client include aggression by relatives directed at the client (Jacobson, 1989) and vice versa (Straznickas et al., 1993). Detection of domestic violence in psychiatric clients is more difficult because they frequently fail to report such problems unless specifically asked (Cascardi et al., 1996; Jacobson & Richardson, 1987). Useful probe questions include: *How do you and your family members handle disagreements? Do you or your family members ever get angry enough to threaten or hit one another? Have you had any experiences of being physically hurt or forced into sexual activity?* Any positive responses to these questions are then followed up by gathering more specific details, such as the duration and frequency of assaults, whether injuries have been sustained, the person's perception of whether the violence is a problem, and efforts to cope with it.

Individual Functional Assessment

The second interview focuses more narrowly on current life circumstances and issues relating specifically to the ill family member. The therapist begins by collecting homework (if applicable). Then, the therapist asks the family member about his or her knowledge of the psychiatric disorder, including the name, etiology, perceived factors that influence course, and beliefs about pharmacologic interventions, following the interview format contained in the "Individual Family Member Interview: Summary Sheet" (see Appendix 2). In order to avoid putting the family member on the defensive or creating the appearance of challenging the person, the therapist can begin this part of the interview with a statement such as: *"I would like to spend a few minutes finding out about your understanding of your relative's (your) problems. It is important for me to find out how each member of the family perceives these problems in order to know how to best help your family."*

As might be expected, families display a wide range of knowledge about these issues. Some relatives are very well informed, even to the point of knowing recent trends in research, while others know little about the disorder. Other individuals are misinformed about the disorder, such as thinking antipsychotic medications are addictive, the client is simply "lazy" or "manipulative," or that substance abuse is the cause of the psychiatric disorder—all of which are beliefs that can contribute to a stressful atmosphere in the family and inhibit the client from gradually improving in a supportive, reinforcing family environment. Finally, some individuals may articulate beliefs, such as "It does not bother me that he smokes pot—he's too agitated otherwise" or "Say what you want about medication, I believe God will cure him with prayer," which conflict with tenets of BFT and warrant being carefully considered by the therapist prior to initiating the educational sessions.

The second part of the interview involves an assessment of the family member's burden and coping capacity. After inquiring into the primary difficulties created by the client's disorder, the therapist asks the family member more general questions about his or her daily routine, availability of social support, positive and negative reinforcers, and concerns about other family members. The family member is then asked to identify one or two of the most significant problems he or she is currently facing, and the therapist conducts a brief functional analysis of each one, using the format contained at the end of the "Individual Family Member Interview" form, with the actual wording of questions and probes tailored appropriately for the family member.

The final part of the interview involves helping the person begin to define one or two areas in which he or she hopes to achieve positive change over the course of BFT. These areas can be defined either as problems the person wants to resolve or as goals he or she hopes to achieve. Some people are reluctant to commit to personal goals, because they define their participation in BFT primarily as a way to help their family member recover. The therapist acknowledges this as the most important motivation for most family members who participate in BFT. However, he or she also points out that the personal well-being of *every* family member, not just the client, is important and has an impact on the overall level of stress in the family. By working toward individual goals over the course of BFT, all family members can benefit from the sessions. Furthermore, when all family members work toward achieving personal goals, there are many more opportunities for the family to practice the communication and problem-solving skills they will be developing. The family member need not immediately identify a personal goal on which to work, but by raising the issue at this point in the individual interview, the therapist sets the expectation that all family members will work on personal goals over the course of BFT.

Therapists will note that working on the personal goals of all family members has the benefit of "leveling the therapeutic playing field" for all participants. In concert with their relatives, many persons with serious mental illness are acutely aware of the burden their disorder places on their loved ones and the emotional and financial sacrifices that family members may have made for them. Asking every family member to set and work toward a personal goal in BFT helps minimize the role of the client's inadequacies as the organizing principle of the therapeutic work.

We first raise the issues of specifying personal goals at the conclusion of the individual assessment sessions, and we have developed a handout for orienting family members to the types of goals we ask them to select (the "Orientation to Goal Setting" sheet), which is contained in Appendix 1. After briefly discussing the task with family members, the therapist asks them to think about possible goals during the first few BFT sessions and informs them that when the education sessions have concluded the therapist will again meet briefly with them individually to help define the actual goals or problem on which they wish to work.

We have found the attainment of these individual BFT goals is dependent on a variety of factors. In general, the best goals are ones that are supported (or at least not actively opposed) by other family members, highly desired by the participant, would result in an improved quality of life, and are attainable within the anticipated length of BFT. Personal goals that involve other people are acceptable, as long as the goal is for the sake of that individual and others do not oppose it (e.g., the husband would like to go out with his wife one night per week, a daughter would like to regularly attend Weight Watchers with her mother). If the goal is very ambitious (e.g., obtaining a GED, losing fifty pounds), then the therapist can help the family member shape it into a series of attainable smaller goals that can be achieved during the length of the BFT (e.g., sitting for the GED exam; losing fifteen pounds).

One good area to explore during goal setting is leisure activities and increased socialization. Family members often stop engaging in enjoyable activities during times of stress, leading to dissatisfaction and vulnerability to depression. Helping family members identify goals of resuming leisure pursuits or seeing friends has the positive effect of both setting an attainable goal and increasing desired experiences.

The goals established by each family member should relate to *personal* problems and not be contingent upon change by another person. Thus, it is best if the problems and goals targeted for the relatives of the client are independent of their interactions or concerns for that person. Many relatives at first want to set a goal such as "the client will start taking his medication regularly." While the therapist notes that medication noncompliance is an issue to be addressed and empathizes with the relative's concern, he or she reorients the relative to the importance of selecting a personal goal. Typical goals that participants have successfully set and achieved include enrolling in an evening course, planning and taking a long-delayed vacation, quitting smoking, beginning an exercise program, going to the movies once a week, gaining better control over one's temper, obtaining a new job, reading a favorite novel thirty minutes a day, and reducing the burden of doing all the housework.

Case Example

A husband and wife in their thirties (with a three-year-old daughter) participated in BFT to learn how to better manage the husband's (Juan) schizoaffective (depressed) disorder and to improve their marriage. Marital strain was partly due to the relatively high frequency of Juan's relapses (at least once per year for the past several years) and the negative symptoms of inactivity and social avoidance. The wife, Colette, worked part-time as an accountant. Juan had not worked over the past five years. During the assessment Colette identified two long-term goals: (1) finishing her education and obtaining a Certification in Public Accounting and (2) having another baby. Colette indicated that she had been taking night classes but had recently dropped out because Juan could look after their child only a little. She said that Juan supported both of these goals. She identified four shorter-term goals that were functionally related to her long-term goals: (1) talk more often with Juan; (2) have Juan take care of their child more; (3) go on more family outings; and (4) get more help with cooking and cleaning around the house.

Juan stated two long-term goals: (1) getting a car and a driver's license and (2) finishing school and getting a job in the helping profession. Juan had completed 86 credits out of 140 toward a college degree and had been enrolled as a student before his last hospitalization. Juan said he felt that Colette approved of these goals. Juan identified three shorter-term goals that he wanted to work on during BFT: (1) being more socially active with friends (the couple had company over about once every two weeks); (2) talking more with Colette (Juan indicated that he tends to be a loner and has trouble thinking of good conversation topics, but felt that if he and Colette were able to communicate better their relationship would improve); and (3) improve his skills for coping with depression, including feelings of hopelessness and helplessness, low mood, and thoughts about hurting himself, which both impede his relationship with Colette and his daughter and interfere with his ability to further his education.

Initial Case Formulation

After completing all the assessments, the therapist then develops a case formulation (see the "Case Formulation" form in Appendix 2). The overall objective of this exercise is for the therapist to integrate the information obtained in the assessments in a way that guides the BFT work. This formulation has three parts. In the first section, the therapist notes assets and deficits in each family member's BFT communication and problem-solving skills. Information for this summary is compiled from informal observations of family interactions with the therapist, the in vivo problem-solving assessment, and reports of relevant behavior at home. Once this information is obtained, the therapist identifies which specific skills are most important to improve in BFT and which skills need to be monitored for further evaluation.

The second section of the formulation involves the identification of two or three core issues that appear to contribute most to client and / or family difficulties and whose improvement is likely to lead to a better prognosis for the client. Whenever possible the therapist focuses on issues that are known to influence the course of the psychiatric disorder. The most common of these topics is a tense emotional climate in the family between the client and relatives. Negative affect, such as reflected by high "Expressed Emotion" in relatives, has repeatedly been demonstrated to predict relapse in schizophrenia and affective disorders (Butzlaff & Hooley, 1998). Thus, if the therapist is to facilitate the client's recovery, it is incumbent upon him or her to reduce levels of this negative affect. Similarly, excessive self-sacrificing and intrusive behavior on the part of relatives can sometimes be detrimental to the client's recovery (Leff & Vaughn, 1985) and are related to the experience of greater burden on the relative (Jackson et al., 1990). If the behavior is identified, then the therapist can work toward developing autonomy in family members and helping each to support the independent efforts of others. Alternatively, the therapist may become aware of other circumstances that increase stress for the client and are thus likely to increase probability of relapse (e.g., the family's social isolation, conflict between other family members, substance abuse in a relative).

Medication noncompliance is associated with increased rate of relapse for clients with schizophrenia-spectrum disorders and bipolar disorder, and for some clients with major depression and obsessive-compulsive disorder. If it becomes apparent that either the client and/or relatives exhibit attitudes or behaviors consistent with medication noncompliance, modifying these behaviors becomes a critical goal for BFT. Finally, inadequate monitoring of the psychiatric disorder or the failure to respond to clear signs of a symptom exacerbation is another core issue for many families. Some families do not recognize the actual symptoms of the disorder and have difficulty responding to changes, while others seem paralyzed in the face of worsening symptoms, refusing to talk about them and delaying taking steps toward getting the necessary help.

We provide here only examples of common core issues that many families face, and many other issues are possible. The identification of which issues should be addressed in BFT is an inexact art that relies heavily on clinical judgment. Therapists need to be open to the possibility that the core issues they identify during the assessment are in fact not the central issues plaguing the family, and that lack of progress in therapy may necessitate a reevaluation and reformulation of which issues to address in the BFT work.

Case Example

A nineteen-year-old man with bipolar disorder participated in BFT with his parents and his fifteen-year-old sister. The client had developed his psychiatric illness two years ago and had been hospitalized four times since then, three times associated with a suicide attempt or suicidal ideation. The client's psychiatric illness was exacerbated by his polysubstance abuse, including alcohol, marijuana, and cocaine. Furthermore, this substance abuse resulted in strong family conflict, both between the parents and client, and between the parents themselves. The father tended to be highly critical of his son, because of both his substance abuse and his failure to pursue personal life goals, including completing his high school degree. His mother, on the other hand, tended to be emotionally overinvolved in her son's life. She had difficulty attending to her own needs, was often intrusive with her son, but also gave into him (e.g., giving him money, which he would spend on alcohol and drugs), and was overprotective. Her relationship with her son contributed to conflict with her husband, who accused her of indulging their son and making his problems worse. The sister was caught in the middle; she avoided taking sides while trying to take the role of the peacemaker, but she also felt left out and that she got little of her parents' attention.

The functional analysis pointed to three core issues to be addressed in BFT, which, if successfully resolved, would be hypothesized to improve the course of the client's bipolar disorder and improve the quality of life of all the family members. First, the client's alcohol and drug use interfered with the stabilization of his bipolar disorder, and both he and his mother had little understanding of the effect of psychoactive substances on the course of psychiatric illness. As a first step toward addressing this problem, family members would need basic education about the interactions between even moderate amounts of substance use and severity of bipolar disorder. Such education could help the client understand how to avoid depressions and reduce the mother's inadvertent reinforcement of her son's substance abuse. However, there was also evidence suggesting that the son's substance abuse was partly motivated by efforts to escape from the tense home environment, and that improving the family atmosphere would lower this motive for using substances. Therefore, a second goal of BFT was to improve the communication skills of the parents, decreasing both the father's level of criticism and the mother's intrusiveness, while increasing the rate of positive communication. A third goal was to enhance the ability of the family to work together, especially the parents. The parents tended to disagree frequently and were unable to present a "unified front" when addressing family problems. This contributed to their marital discord and inability to manage effectively their son's dual disorder of bipolar disorder and substance abuse. Improved family problem-solving skills were targeted in BFT in order to help the members work together more collaboratively and, when necessary, to enable the parents to more effectively set limits on their son's behavior.

Once BFT objectives are identified, the therapist can subsequently assign tasks that both help in the acquisition of specific skills and yield progress toward meeting the objective. For example, if the therapist notes a high initial level of negative affect by relatives directed toward the client, he or she can prepare to implement a variety of strategies in BFT to address this problem. For a typical family, these strategies might include:

1. being prepared to interrupt hostile exchanges in sessions quickly;

2. evaluating whether criticisms of the client are the result of poor information about the disorder and provide additional education as needed;

3. spending extra time on the "expressing negative feelings" skill during communication skills training;

4. doing problem solving to address anger management issues;

5. monitoring the level of hostility toward the client outside of sessions.

The third part of the case formulation involves recording, in behavioral terms, the actual problem or goal on which each family member has selected to work. These definitions then serve as the baseline measure for all subsequent assessments of progress on the problem.

Ongoing Assessment

Continuing assessment is the foundation of effective behavioral intervention. The ongoing assessment of the family is integrated into BFT in five ways. First, every session begins with a brief (five-to-ten-minute) assessment of homework completion, progress on individual goals, and family-meeting activities. Incomplete assignments or failure to make progress toward personal goals become a focus of work later in the session. For example, if a family member fails to return a completed communication-skills homework sheet, he or she can be asked to complete it in the session. Or, if progress toward a personal goal has not been made for several weeks, the therapist may help the person identify a small step that can be taken prior to the next session toward a goal. Obviously, identifying and alleviating obstacles that contributed to the failure to complete the assignment (e.g., lack of time, misunderstanding of the instructions, failure to see the relevance of the task) or make progress toward a personal goal is also an important part of this assessment process.

Second, brief formal assessments of progress toward personal goals are routinely scheduled (we recommend a three-month interval between assessments). During these assessment meetings, the therapist meets individually with each family member for fifteen to twenty minutes to evaluate formally and discuss the progress that has been made toward goals and what impediments must still be overcome. Alternatively, individual goals may be reviewed in the family meeting, involving all members in evaluating progress and identifying obstacles. This review usually replaces the regular BFT session that week and is scheduled at the same time.

Third, formal assessments of improvements in family communication and problem-solving skills are performed on a routine basis (e.g., every three to six months), similar to the assessments of progress toward personal goals. In these meetings, the therapist conducts an in vivo assessment of family problem solving, using the same procedures employed in the initial assessment. Following the problem-solving task, the therapist initiates a discussion with the family members about recent problems they have experienced, their success with using BFT skills to address these problems, and possible areas that they would benefit from improving in subsequent sessions. The in vivo assessment and family discussion provide valuable feedback about gains that have been made in previous sessions and bring into focus specific skills to be targeted in the forthcoming sessions.

Fourth, the therapist spends a brief period of time at the end of each month of BFT to review family members' behavior during sessions and their reports of activity outside the sessions, using additional copies of the "Case Formulation" sheet developed as part of the initial case formulation. On this sheet, the therapist can note the acquisition of specific BFT skills by each family member, as well as the therapist's progress toward achieving the one or two overriding objectives of the treatment selected in the initial case formulation (e.g., reducing negative affect in the family, increasing medication compliance).

Most important, the therapist is continually alert for evidence that family members use BFT skills when opportunities arise, both in the therapy session and outside of BFT sessions. For example, if a client mentions during a problem-solving session that earlier in the week "her mother really ticked her off and (she) told her so," the therapist may allot ten minutes at the end of the session to set up a role play to determine whether the client used the "expressing negative feelings" skill to convey her displeasure to her mother. If not, he or she can use this as an opportunity to reinforce the skills previously taught in the BFT to promote generalization and maintenance.

CASE EXAMPLE OF DWAYNE AND TANIA

We resume the case of Dwayne and his wife, Tania, whose engagement in BFT was described in the previous chapter. After Dwayne and Tania had agreed to participate in BFT, individual and joint interviews were scheduled. Additional information about Dwayne garnered from the initial meeting with him and discussion with his psychiatrist indicated that he had recently completed an imaginal exposure-based inpatient treatment program for combat-related PTSD (Foy, 1992). At discharge, Dwayne had achieved some reduction in his frequent flashbacks and intense intrusive memories, but he was still highly symptomatic. He continued to meet the diagnostic criteria for PTSD; he also suffered from panic disorder (without agoraphobia) and major depression. His panic attacks occurred while he was alone in a car, and thus he either rode a bike or asked a family member to accompany him when he drove. His depression was moderately well controlled pharmacologically with dispramine (250 mg/day).

During the joint marital interview, Dwayne and Tania reported they had been separated for approximately eighteen months, but that they still felt a strong emotional attachment to each other and had decided to resume living together as the BFT was initiated. The couple hoped to use the therapy to "iron out" some of the difficulties they expected to encounter over the next few months, including: (1) readjusting to daily life together; (2) coping with their substance-dependent adult sons; and (3) deciding how best to assure parenting for their sons' children. In the formal ten-minute problem-solving assessment, the following behavioral excesses and deficits were noted: poor eye contact, speakers frequently interrupting each other, Dwayne criticizing Tania, frequent "you" (compared to "I") statements, and little progress toward active problem resolution.

During Dwayne's life history interview, a history of severe childhood physical abuse and neglect, in addition to alcohol dependence in remission for two years, was identified. Subsequent to the individual functional assessment, Dwayne was asked to complete the Mississippi Scale for Combat-related PTSD (Keane et al., 1984). He achieved a score of 114 out of a possible 175, supporting a diagnosis of current PTSD (a cutpoint of 100 or higher is considered indicative of PTSD). During the individual functional assessment, Dwayne evidenced high levels of knowledge about the etiology, course, and treatment of PTSD. He identified his three most pressing current problems as: (1) setting appropriate limits on the extended visits of his sons; (2) structuring his time more effectively to include school or paid employment; and (3) developing more intimacy with his wife. He decided to work on the BFT goal of structuring his time more positively, by either obtaining a part-time job or enrolling in an auto technician certification program.

During Tania's assessment, it became clear that she was also extremely distressed. In her life history interview, she revealed that she and her sons had been severely physically abused in her previous marriage. The guilt she had over not escaping that situation earlier made it very difficult for her to set limits with her sons, and contributed to her conflict with her husband. In her functional assessment she demonstrated a good understanding of PTSD. She was, however, overwhelmed by her current circumstances and had recently been placed on short-term work disability for depression, nervousness, and losing her temper with a customer at her workplace. She established her BFT goal as becoming affiliated with the local Al-Anon program (Alcoholics Anonymous support group for relatives) to learn better ways to cope with her sons' addiction problems.

In addition to detailing the information outlined above, the therapist's case formulation defined three major objectives for the BFT with this couple: (1) to encourage more positive communication between Dwayne and Tania, primarily through the implementation of weekly family meetings and encouraging the expression of positive feelings; (2) to help the couple use the problem-solving approach and negotiation skills to arrive at an agreement about how much contact they would have and what responsibility they would assume for their sons; and (3) to help Tania obtain both ongoing informal social support and professional counseling to augment her BFT work.

Questions and Answers to Common Problems

1. *Question:* What if the therapist can't get a relative to identify personal goals to work on because his or her concern for the client is so great?

   Answer: Some relatives, usually parents, devote extraordinary amounts of time and energy to helping their ill family member and find it very difficult to focus on their own needs. This dedication often is beneficial for the client, but it can put undue pressure on him or her to improve more rapidly than is possible.

   We recommend a two-stage approach to encouraging relatives to set personal goals, or helping them actively pursue goals that have already been set. First, emphasize that the needs of every person in the family are important, including both the client and all relatives, and that meeting these needs will reduce overall stress in the family. Point out that the time and energy involved in coping with the disorder in the family has made it hard for relatives to take the time to care for themselves and pursue personal goals that will improve their quality of life.

   Second, if the relative still has difficulty setting goals or following through on them, explain that by pursuing personal goals, the relative demonstrates (models) for his or her ill family member important skills that are necessary for achieving a satisfactory quality of life. By reframing the pursuit of personal goals as directly benefiting the client through teaching a life skill, the relative is free to work on personal goals without changing the fundamental belief that he or she is participating in BFT only for the sake of the client.

2. *Question:* How does the therapist handle the individual assessment of relatives who are only peripherally involved with their family or who are likely to attend only some BFT sessions?

   Answer: The amount of time devoted to individual assessments should be tailored to their current role in the family. If a relative does not live at home but is closely involved with the client and relatives, a full assessment should be conducted. If the family member has relatively little contact with the client and other caregiving relatives (e.g., less than one contact per week), an abbreviated individual assessment can be conducted by condensing the two assessment interviews into a single interview. Some family members are difficult to engage in BFT, although they may be willing to come to a few sessions on an uncommitted "drop-in basis." For these persons, the individual assessment should be postponed until the relative has attended several sessions and appears more willing to commit to BFT sessions.

3. *Question:* How is the assessment conducted when the family presents for treatment during a period of crisis?

Answer: In some cases, a crisis involving the client serves as a major factor impelling the family to seek treatment (e.g., violence, a marked worsening in the client's symptoms, medication noncompliance, housing instability). With such families, the resolution of the crisis (or significant improvement) is often necessary in order to successfully engage the family. By their very nature crises require immediate intervention.

For families who present in a state of crisis, we recommend that the therapist interweave the family and individual assessments into taking steps necessary to resolve the crisis. Most crises require several sessions to resolve. Attending to the crisis demonstrates to the family that the therapist is responsive to its pressing needs. By simultaneously collecting assessment information through individual interviews and family meetings, the therapist is able to develop a case formulation that will guide the intervention when the crisis has be resolved.

Summary

In BFT, a comprehensive initial assessment combined with both planned and spontaneous ongoing evaluations are the foundations on which interventions are implemented. The therapist is vigilant in every interaction with the family to discern which BFT skills might be helpful in managing a particular situation and to determine whether the family is actually using those skills. By continually evaluating whether the skills are being used in the sessions and in the family's day-to-day life, the therapist obtains the information needed to direct subsequent interventions. The first of these interventions, helping the family learn about the client's psychiatric disorder, is discussed in the next chapter.

CHAPTER 5

EDUCATION ABOUT PSYCHIATRIC DISORDERS

Providing basic educational information about psychiatric disorders to the relatives of clients is the most common ingredient shared across the broad range of family treatment programs developed in the 1970s and 1980s (Falloon et al., 1984; Anderson et al., 1986; Jacobson et al., 1989; Beach et al., 1990; Hatfield, 1990; Miklowitz & Goldstein, 1990; Barrowclough & Tarrier, 1992). Prior to these more enlightened times, it was common for mental health professionals to ignore the educational needs of concerned relatives, viewing them instead as either culprits in causing the disorder or peripheral to the client's treatment. Answering family members' inquiries about even the most elementary facts regarding the disorder such as "what is its name?" and "what is the likely course of the disorder?" was considered by many professionals to be a violation of client confidentiality. As a result, relatives were often left in the dark about the psychiatric disorder as they struggled to cope with the bewildering behavior of a symptomatic client at home.

Until recently, professionals also provided minimal information to clients about the nature of their psychiatric disorder, assuming they were either incapable of or not interested in making informed decisions about the treatment of their own condition. Instead, most clients with serious mental illness were viewed as possessing limited insight and were relegated to the role of passive recipients of treatment. These assumptions have been challenged, and it is now widely recognized that clients are capable of learning more about their mental illness (Eckman et al, 1992; Wallace et al., 1992). Furthermore, educating clients about their disorder shows respect for the importance of allowing them to participate actively in making decisions about their own treatment, and this may avert noncompliance problems that arise out of resentment of an authoritarian, monolithic medical approach. This trend toward educating clients about their psychiatric disorder is reflected by the growth of educational programs for clients designed to meet these needs (e.g., Ascher-Svanum & Krause, 1991).

Educating the family plays a critical role in BFT because it lays the foundation for collaboration between the family and the mental health professional. Clients and relatives cannot become effective members of the client's extended treatment team until they have a good understanding of the symptoms of the disorder, its course, and the principles of treatment. Without such basic information, families remain heavily dependent upon professionals for monitoring the disorder and are unable to reinforce consistently the client's adherence to treatments and encourage small steps toward greater self-sufficiency. Thus, educating the family about the client's disorder is a cornerstone upon which the success of the overall treatment depends.

A word about tailoring education to the ill relative's recovery course is in order. Psychiatric illnesses have a wide range of outcomes, and it is incumbent on the therapist to try to meet the family's particular needs while reviewing the educational material. For example, approximately 10 percent of the individuals diagnosed with schizophrenia seem to have a very benign course, with only one or two exacerbations. These clients may be on antipsychotic medication, but appear to have very little residual symptomatology. On the other hand, approximately 25% of the individuals with the disorder have symptoms that appear resistant to even the best pharmacological intervention, and must live in a supervised setting for most of their lives (Harding & Keller, 1998). A therapist working with a family from the first group—where the client is asymptotic and functioning independently—might emphasize ensuring that the family has a good understanding of the benefits of medication compliance and a strong relapse prevention plan, while a therapist working with a family from the latter group might spend more time talking about new research on novel medications, which might give the family more hope.

Goals of Family Education

Four major goals can be identified for the educational component of BFT: (1) legitimizing the psychiatric disorder; (2) reducing negative feelings in family members; (3) enlisting the client's and the family's cooperation with the rehabilitation plan; and (4) facilitating the family's ability to monitor the disorder (see table 5.1). The rational for each of these goals is discussed below.

Legitimizing the Psychiatric Disorder

The symptoms of most nonpsychiatric disorders (e.g., coughing, angina, fever) are easily recognized as due to physiological problems that are beyond the client's control. In contrast, psychiatric symptoms (e.g., depression, anxiety, social withdrawal) are less readily viewed as reflecting a "disorder" and are more likely assumed to be under the client's voluntary control. One reason why people often believe clients have control over their psychiatric symptoms is that many symptoms are defined by the *absence* of particular behaviors or emotions (e.g., negative symptoms of schizophrenia, avoidance in anxiety disorders), rather than the conspicuous *presence* of other behaviors (e.g., bizarre behavior, frequent checking or ritualizing behaviors). It is easier to understand that auditory hallucinations may be due to a chemical imbalance (i.e., disorder) than severe social withdrawal, apathy, or avoidance. A second reason why some psychiatric symptoms may be thought to be under the client's control is that almost everyone has experienced at least mild levels of depression or anxiety with which they have successfully coped and that they have not allowed to interfere much with day-to-day functioning. These experiences can lead to a false impression that psychiatric clients could recover from the same problems if only they tried hard enough.

TABLE 5.1
GOALS OF FAMILY EDUCATION

Legitimizing the psychiatric disorder

- Promote family acceptance of the disorder
- Recognize the limits the disorder imposes on the client
- Develop realistic expectations for the client
- Reduce blaming of the client

Reducing negative emotions in family members

- Lower guilt, anxiety, rage, depression, and isolation
- Let relatives and clients know they are not alone
- Foster a collaborative spirit in coping with the disorder

Enlisting family members' cooperation with the treatment plan

- Explain pharmacological and psychological interventions
- Review components of client's comprehensive treatment
- Help relatives reinforce client's participation in treatment

Facilitating the family's ability to monitor the disorder

- Recognize early warning signs of relapse and changes in persisting symptoms
- Know how to respond to impending relapses by contacting the treatment team
- Monitor compliance with treatments and medication side effects

---

The goal of legitimizing the client's psychiatric disorder is achieved chiefly through providing information about symptoms and how the diagnosis is established. By helping family members understand that the client's problems are subsumed under a specific psychiatric diagnosis (with a likely biological basis) shared by other clients, the therapist promotes family members' acceptance of the disorder and the limits it may impose on the client. This enables all members to develop more realistic expectations of the client, while reducing blame placed on the client for displaying symptomatic behavior. At the same time that the psychiatric disorder is legitimated, the client is encouraged to take responsibility in areas where this seems possible, to avoid reinforcing the "sick role."

Reducing Negative Feelings in Family Members

As discussed in Chapter 1 and illustrated in Table 1.1, relatives of psychiatric clients experience a wide range of negative emotions, including guilt, depression, anxiety, and anger. Although some unpleasant feelings are inevitable in any relative who must cope with an ill family member, educating family members about the psychiatric disorder may alleviate negative feelings that are related to an incomplete or inaccurate understanding of the disorder. Parents with an offspring who has developed a psychiatric disorder often feel guilty, thinking that they may have caused the disorder or contributed to it, and are relieved to learn that problematic family interactions or child-rearing practices are not at the root of the disorder.

The siblings of clients frequently feel guilty for different reasons. They may experience a form of "survivor guilt," wondering why they were spared from a disorder that struck another family member so randomly. In some families, poor social functioning and problematic behaviors precede the onset of the psychiatric disorder by many years. In these families, siblings often cope with the stress by eschewing contact with the client and withdrawing from their family, which may later lead to feelings of guilt when the client's psychiatric disorder becomes more fully apparent. In addition to guilt feelings, many siblings have concerns about their own vulnerability to the psychiatric disorder or the chances that their children will develop the same illness. Educating siblings about the disorder, including the genetic risks associated with it, and providing a safe forum in which their concerns can be discussed with the client and other relatives, can help reduce their guilt and anxiety about shared vulnerability to the disorder.

Relatives often harbor angry feelings toward clients based either on their disruptive or nonresponsive behavior or on their failure to meet role expectations. In some families these angry feelings are freely communicated to the client (e.g., high Expressed Emotion interactions, as discussed in Chapter 1), while in others the relative may suppress expression of these feelings. Education that helps relatives recognize symptoms of the disorder, set more realistic expectations, and diffuses angry and hostile feelings toward the client can foster a more collaborative family spirit toward coping with the disorder.

Negative feelings such as anxiety, depression, and anger are common in both relatives and clients who try to cope with the frustrations of a psychiatric disorder. Families often feel alone with their experience because of social prohibitions against openly discussing mental illness in society. By informing the family that other people suffer from the same disorder, relatives and clients learn they are not alone, which can lower their sense of isolation. Some families may capitalize on this information and seek out other relatives or clients with similar experiences for additional social support through self-help and advocacy organizations (see section on Additional Resources at the end of this chapter).

Enlisting Family Members' Cooperation with the Rehabilitation Plan

Recovery from most serious psychiatric disorders requires both pharmacologic and psychosocial intervention; BFT is only one component of a comprehensive treatment program. The provision of most treatment requires the collaboration of the client, who must come to the mental health facility for appointments when scheduled and follow through on activities such as taking medication as prescribed, getting prescriptions filled when necessary, and completing assignments from skills training classes. Family support is vital to continued participation in the rehabilitation program, especially for disorganized, acutely ill, or unmotivated clients. Thus, the primary objectives of BFT are to review with the family both the pharmacologic and psychosocial treatments that the client is receiving, to answer questions, and to provide the rationale for the various rehabilitation components. At a minimum, the client is asked to identify the benefits and the side effects of his or her medications, and feedback from other family members concerning medication is also elicited (this topic is discussed more fully below). Similarly, the role of independent-living skills classes, socialization, supportive counseling, and vocational rehabilitation or placement in the client's treatment can be outlined, the client's progress in concurrent activities (e.g., day treatment, GED classes) can be monitored, and impediments to active participation identified for later communication and problem-solving skills efforts.

Facilitating the Family's Ability to Monitor the Disorder

Considering the episodic nature of most major psychiatric disorders, careful monitoring and a rapid response to early signs of a symptom exacerbation are crucial steps for preventing relapses and rehospitalizations. Family members often have greater contact with the client than mental health professionals, and they can be more sensitive to subtle changes in the client's behavior. For this reason, one goal of family education is to enable family members, including the client when feasible, to monitor the course of the disorder so that they can alert the therapist or treatment team in the event of an impending relapse. The purpose is not to replace treatment providers in monitoring the disorder, but rather to improve monitoring by incorporating the family into this role.

Knowing how to monitor the disorder requires family members to be able to recognize early warning signs and symptoms, as well as to evaluate the client's adherence to treatments (e.g., medication compliance, attendance at partial hospitalization or vocational programs). Through the family's understanding of the elements of treatment, they become more able to reinforce the client's adherence, and to troubleshoot when problems emerge. An additional factor is that educating relatives and clients about the side effects of psychotropic medications can facilitate the recognition of side effects that, if untreated, can undermine medication compliance. Facilitating the family's ability to systematically monitor the disorder and take decisive action when changes are detected has tremendous implications for improving the long-term course of the client's disorder.

Principles of Family Education

There are several fundamental principles of family education that serve to guide the therapist in BFT. As long as the therapist keeps these core principles in mind throughout the course of therapy, he or she will be able to make progress toward the goals of family education.

TABLE 5.2
CORE PRINCIPLES OF FAMILY EDUCATION

The therapist must be knowledgeable about the psychiatric disorder
Information is presented to the family in an honest, direct manner

- The therapist never withholds information to "protect" the family
- The therapist provides the best information available to the family, acknowledging the limits of professionals' knowledge when appropriate

Family education is an interactive process between the therapist and all family members

- The therapist does not rely solely on didactic teaching methods
- The therapist helps family members understand how information applies to their own experiences with the disorder

Family education is long term and continues throughout the entire course of therapy

---

The Therapist Must Be Knowledgeable about the Psychiatric Disorder

Clearly, if therapists are to succeed in educating family members about the psychiatric disorder, they must be sufficiently knowledgeable about it. Basic knowledge about the psychiatric disorder includes an understanding of the diagnostic criteria and symptoms of the disorder, its prevalence and longitudinal course, effective pharmacological and psychological treatments, and theories regarding its etiology. While therapists need not be accomplished researchers, the more they know about the disorder, the more comfortable they will be in the educational discussions. At a minimum, they should know more about the disorder than the family members and be at ease fielding questions about it.

Considering the range of psychiatric disorders that may be treated using the BFT model, therapists cannot be expected to have expertise in every possible area. Rather, they must be open to educating themselves when necessary about specific disorders so they will be able to teach the relevant information to the family. Similarly, therapists need not be able to answer every conceivable question raised by family members, but they should know how to find the answers to these questions through resources such as other professionals, books, or journals. In sum, the therapist must possess an adequate body of knowledge about the disorder and understand how to use other resources when necessary in order to educate the family. At the end of this chapter we provide a list of organizations, books, and journals that can be used by therapists and families to obtain additional information about specific psychiatric disorders.

Information Is Presented in an Honest, Direct Manner

Mental health professionals sometimes feel uncomfortable when talking to families about the client's disorder. All too often, professionals are keenly aware of their own limits in treating serious mental illness, and they recognize the difficult and long struggle many clients and families face. Nobody likes to be the bearer of bad news. An understandable response of some professionals is to "protect" families from what they perceive to be potentially upsetting information about the client's condition. This occurs particularly often early in the course of the client's disorder, when there may still be some doubt about the accuracy of the client's diagnosis.

The common, but erroneous, assumption is that relatives will be shocked and dismayed to learn that a family member has a specific psychiatric disorder. In our experience, the opposite is often true. Relatives frequently express gratitude to professionals who are direct in educating them about their family member's disorder, even when it is a serious and debilitating one, such as bipolar disorder, schizophrenia, or obsessive-compulsive disorder. In many cases, relatives have been acutely aware for years that something is wrong with a family member but have been frustrated by their inability to get straight answers from professionals about the disorder. These relatives sometimes express relief upon learning about the diagnosis. Information about diagnosis, symptoms, and prevalence of the disorder confirms their belief that something is wrong with their family member and opens doors for them to learn about how they can help the client and work together with the treatment team. Therefore, a vital principle of family education is that the therapist always strives to provide family members directly and honestly with the most accurate facts available about the disorder, never deliberately withholding information. Through direct communication with the family about the client's disorder, the therapist creates a supportive and collaborative working relationship with family members that can endure throughout the course of therapy.

Family Education Is Interactive

To help family members understand the psychiatric disorder, the therapist cannot rely solely on didactic teaching methods, but must make the educational sessions as interactive as possible. This means the process of educating the family requires that the therapist continually elicit the experiences of the client with the disorder and his or her relatives, probe the family members regarding their knowledge about educational topics to be covered, and ask questions that reveal their understanding of the material that has been presented. By adopting an interactive approach to education, the therapist is able to evaluate the family's acquisition of basic information about the disorder and to pace the presentation of new material accordingly. Furthermore, by continually seeking feedback and input from the family, the therapist avoids the pitfalls of overloading family members with information, resulting in boredom and disengagement.

Family Education Is a Long-term Endeavor

Usually only three or four sessions in BFT are devoted solely to formal family education, but education continues throughout the course of therapy. Information about psychiatric disorders is not easily absorbed by most families, and the therapist must always be on the alert for opportunities to help family members understand crucial facts about the disorder, including during sessions that occur later in the course of therapy. Most short-term educational interventions for families with a psychiatric client have met with only limited success (e.g., Sidley et al., 1991; Birchwood et al., 1992; Vaughn et al., 1992). A critical limitation of these interventions is that they do not allow enough time for the family to integrate the educational material and gauge its relevance to their own experience.

Relatives are often able to comprehend intellectually information about their family member's disorder, but require much more time to make the connection between this information and the client's symptomatic behavior. In most families, after the educational sessions have been completed, there will be occasions when relatives act toward the client as though they have "forgotten" basic information about the disorder. The therapist can point out to the relatives that the client's behavior is a symptom of the disorder or is related to medication, as illustrated in the case example provided below.

Case Example

The sister of a twenty-three-year-old man with major depression complained about his laziness in the fourteenth BFT session, which was focused on problem-solving training.

Sister: You can ask George to do something, even the simplest things, and he can't seem to get around to doing it. He's gotten to the point where he's so lazy that he's got to rest before he does anything he's asked to do. I don't see why he's so tired and sleeps so much.

Therapist: I'm not sure that it's laziness, Paula. Low energy and an increased need for sleep are symptoms of George's disorder, major depression, that can interfere with his day-to-day functioning. Also, when you don't have a lot of structured time in your day, you really lose a lot of energy. So, I don't think that he's lazy, but I can understand how it would be frustrating if you ask George to do things and he doesn't do them.

An alternative strategy is for the therapist to help family members actively process information they have about the disorder by asking them whether the client's behavior reminds them of any of the symptoms of the disorder. Sometimes after many months or even years, relatives experience a breakthrough in their understanding of the client's illness, leading them to a new level of awareness and ability to cope with their ill family member. The therapist's continued efforts toward educating the family are vital to helping families achieve a better understanding of the psychiatric disorder.

Format of Educational Sessions

Between two and five sessions devoted to education are recommended for most families. The educational sessions follow an agenda based on curriculum that has been prepared in advance, with the pace of teaching tailored to individual needs of the family. The information is summarized using a variety of visual aids, such as blackboards, flip charts, posters, and handouts. The teaching format resembles a cross between a classroom, with the therapist assuming the role of the teacher, and a group discussion, with the therapist acting as a facilitator. The conversation is guided by the therapist so as to cover the curriculum as planned, and he or she solicits the experiences and understanding of family members, their comments and questions, throughout the session.

In each family educational session, the therapist provides a brief overview of the material to be covered that day. An interactive discussion centered on that topic follows, with an emphasis on helping the family members comprehend how the information applies to the client. At the end of each session, the therapist gives the family a homework assignment. After the first educational session, the therapist begins each session with a review of the homework assignment and inquires whether family members have any questions about the information that was discussed in the previous session.

Educational Curriculum

The core curriculum taught to families in BFT can be divided into five broad topic areas, taught in sequential order: basic facts about the psychiatric disorder, the stress-vulnerability model, medication, preventing relapse through monitoring early warning signs, and a caregiver's guide to helping a relative with a serious psychiatric illness. The key points of these topic areas are provided in educational handouts (contained in Appendix 3), and are summarized in Table 5.3. Additional handouts on alcohol and drug use in clients with a psychiatric disorder, improving communication, and problem solving are also included in Appendix 3. These handouts do not provide an exhaustive review of the information that the therapist covers in the educational sessions. The therapist supplements the information in the handouts to meet the specific educational needs of the family (Mueser et al., 1992), using additional resources as necessary. Additional handouts designed for clients with a psychiatric disorder and their relatives can be found in Atkinson and Coia (1995), Bisbee (1991), Miklowitz and Goldstein (1997), and Wyatt (1994). The therapist may also choose to develop a special handout for a family following the format used in the handouts contained in Appendix 3.

TABLE 5.3
OUTLINE OF CURRICULUM FOR EDUCATIONAL
SESSIONS

Basic facts about psychiatric disorder
- Diagnosis
- Common myths
- Prevalence
- Course of disorder
  - Age of onset
  - Episodic nature
  - Long-term course
- How diagnosis is established
  - Clinical interview
  - No available medical tests
  - Review of history

Stress-vulnerability model of psychiatric disorders
- Psychobiological vulnerability to disorders
  - Genetic factors
  - Other biological factors
- Effects of alcohol and drug abuse and medication on symptoms
- Effects of stress of symptoms
  - Life events
  - Exposure to negative family affect
  - Lack of meaningful structure
- Family and client coping skills as mediators of stress
- How family members can help
  - Encourage adherence to treatment regimen
    - Medication compliance
    - Participation in psychosocial treatment/rehabilitation
  - Monitor symptoms of disorder
  - Create a supportive, noncritical family environment
  - Reinforce small steps by the client toward better role functioning and greater independence

Medication
- Effects of medication on disorder
  - Treatment of acute symptoms
  - Prevention of relapses
- Names of medications
- Side effects

- Strategies for managing side effects
  - Side-effect medications
  - Coping strategies
- Talking with physicians about medication
- Importance of taking medication on regular basis

Early warning signs of relapse
- Definition
- Common early warning signs
- Identification of early warning signs for the client
- Monitoring symptoms and early warning signs
- Formulating a plan if an impending relapse is suspected

A caregiver's guide to helping a relative who has a serious psychiatric illness
- High levels of tension are common in many families with a psychiatric client
- Critical communication patterns are a problem
- Extremely self-sacrificing behavior may create difficulties

Basic Facts about the Disorder

The first educational session focuses on providing the family with information about the client's diagnosis, the characteristic symptoms of the disorder, its prevalence, course, and outcome. For interested readers, an entire transcript from a first educational session with a family containing a client with schizophrenia is contained in Mueser and Glynn (1988).

After a brief overview of the topics to be discussed in the session, the therapist begins by explaining to the family the client's diagnosis. Although most families at this point in therapy already know the diagnosis, their knowledge about what the diagnosis actually means can vary greatly. To assess what the family members know about the diagnosis, the therapist asks each person in turn, including the client, to explain what he or she understands about the diagnosis. Accurate information is then acknowledged and false impressions are corrected by the therapist. As many family members may initially feel awkward using medical terminology, the therapist may begin by asking, *"What have you been told about (X)'s problems? Were you given a name or diagnosis?"*

There are many commonly held "myths" about serious psychiatric disorders, particularly those disorders in which psychotic symptoms may occur, such as schizophrenia and major affective disorders. For these disorders, it is important to review and dispel myths and misconceptions that have arisen from movies, news coverage, and conventional wisdom. For example, violent or bizarre crimes committed by psychiatric clients tend to be "sensationalized" by the media, leading to the impression that people with psychiatric disorders are often violent. Although it is true that psychiatric clients are slightly more prone to violent behavior than the general population (Hodgins et al., 1996; Mullen, 1992; Wallace et al., 1998), such violence is rare in the vast majority of clients. Some of the most widespread myths about psychiatric disorders are summarized in Table 5.4.

TABLE 5.4
COMMON MYTHS ABOUT PSYCHIATRIC DISORDERS

People with schizophrenia have a "split personality" or "multiple personality disorder."	People with schizophrenia have only *one* personality. A split personality or multiple personality disorder is a very different psychiatric disorder (a "dissociative disorder") that is quite rare.
Families cause psychiatric disorders.	Child-rearing practices, conflict, and poor communication in the family do *not* cause psychiatric disorders. Some disorders tend to "run in families" because of genetic factors, not because of problems between family members.
People with a psychiatric disorder are often violent.	People with a psychiatric disorder are usually not violent. Although some clients are prone to violence when their symptoms worsen, most withdraw from others when their symptoms are severe.
Alcohol or drug abuse can cause long-term psychiatric disorders.	Available research suggests that substance abuse can trigger a psychiatric disorder in vulnerable people, but does not *cause* the disorder.
Psychiatric clients can control their symptoms if they really want to.	Psychiatric clients have no more direct control over their symptoms than people with medical conditions such as hypertension or diabetes.
Psychiatric disorders are a sign of moral weakness.	Psychiatric clients are not morally weaker than other people. The symptoms of their disorder are due to biological factors that are beyond their control, not to moral inferiority.

This introduction to family education is illustrated in the transcript of a session with a client with schizophrenia (Sandra), her brother (Edward), and her mother (Molly).

Therapist:	The first thing I would like to do is to find out what the word *schizophrenia* means to each of you. Molly, what does schizophrenia mean to you?
Molly:	I think it's an inability to cope with reality.
Therapist:	People with schizophrenia have difficulty finding out what reality is and is not?
Molly:	Yes.
Therapist:	How about you, Edward?
Edward:	I have thought in the past that it's like a split personality, where you have your rational side and then on the other hand, you can change to the irrational side, which doesn't handle information properly or believes delusional things. Like someone having two separate sides to them.
Therapist:	Okay.
Edward:	And there is also paranoia.
Therapist:	Yes. Sandra, what do you understand by the word *schizophrenia*?
Sandra:	I think schizophrenia is a supersensitive state of the mind that does not screen out conscious material.
Therapist:	So, schizophrenia makes you very sensitive and attentive to your environment?
Sandra:	Yes, and when there is all this chaos around you, there are constant environmental intrusions into a normal, well-functioning life. That's why I sleep so much. It's my only respite.
Therapist:	It is a way of coping with the chaos, which I think you are describing very accurately. I want to begin our discussion of what schizophrenia is by first saying what schizophrenia is *not*. It is not like the traditional notion of a "split personality," although what you were describing, Edward, is similar to what we mean. Usually, when people talk about a "split personality," they refer to two personalities in the same individual; one personality doesn't know what the other is doing at all times. Schizophrenia is not that. That is called a "multiple personality disorder" or a "dissociative disorder."
Edward:	Like in the movies?
Therapist:	Right! Schizophrenia is a biologically based disorder that results in difficulty controlling impulses and difficulty discerning what is real and what is not. This is like what you were saying, Edward, that there is a part that is aware of reality, but there is also a part that is not in touch with it. However, we know that for people with schizophrenia, what they do makes sense to them based on their understanding of the environment. This means that if a person with schizophrenia does something that seems strange, like locking themselves in their room for days on end, if you talk with them they may tell you, "I'm afraid someone is out to get me, so I have to protect myself." So if you understand their perception of the world, then often their behavior becomes understandable, and it seems like a normal reaction. Like Sandra was saying about sleeping all the time—if you were always surrounded by chaos, then it would be normal to try to escape from it by sleeping.

At this point, it is useful to talk about how the psychiatric disorder has affected each family member, including the client. This can be accomplished by asking questions such as: *"I'd like to spend a few minutes finding out about how Julia's bipolar disorder has affected each person in your family. Julia, what influence has bipolar disorder had on your life?"* and *"Sally, what kind of an effect has Julia's disorder had on you?"* Almost invariably, the disorder has had a profound effect on each family member. This round-robin discussion helps to underscore the fact that everyone in the family is affected by an ill member's psychiatric disorder, which can contribute to creating a cooperative spirit of working together to overcome problems that have resulted from the disorder.

After the diagnosis has been briefly explained, the therapist provides information about the prevalence of the specific disorder. Family members also benefit from learning that the psychiatric disorder is present throughout all parts of the world and affects people regardless of their religion, income, race, etc. Data on the prevalence of the psychiatric disorder alleviates some of the burden on the family of feeling alone by demonstrating that many other families experience similar problems. The fact that the disorder is present cross-culturally helps give it legitimacy, reducing blame on the family for its cause.

A brief discussion of the onset and course of the specific psychiatric disorder is warranted next. Some individuals experience a relatively early onset of their psychiatric disorder (e.g., between the ages of sixteen and thirty), whereas others have a later onset. Most psychiatric disorders tend to have an episodic course, marked by variations in symptom severity, sometimes requiring hospitalizations for the treatment of acute symptom exacerbations, especially for schizophrenia and bipolar disorder but also for obsessive-compulsive disorder, post-traumatic stress disorder, and major depression. In addition, many clients are vulnerable to exacerbations throughout their life. However, the extent of the impact can vary greatly across disorders and individuals, and clients and families can learn how to minimize the impact as much as possible. This information helps families understand that serious psychiatric disorders are often lifelong disabilities, but that clients and relatives can take steps to cope effectively with the limitations imposed by the disorder.

The notion of matching the focus of the educational sessions to the needs of the family is critical with recent-onset clients with disorders such as schizophrenia and bipolar illness. With the current emphasis on community care and reducing hospitalizations, younger ill relatives of many families seeking BFT may never even have been hospitalized. These clients are often well-maintained on medication and may not have, as yet, suffered many negative consequences of their illness. Because optimal psychiatric and psychological treatment plans have changed so dramatically in recent years, research is lacking on whether, in the end, these clients will have the improved prognoses that their families so desperately desire. At this point, the therapist must walk the tightrope of sharing what we know currently about prognosis and predictors of best outcomes, while acknowledging that we are limited in what we know about the long-term outcomes of our newest treatment strategies.

Up to this point, the diagnosis, prevalence, and course of the disorder have been reviewed, but the specific symptoms have not yet been covered. Families need to understand how a diagnosis is established and know the characteristic symptoms of the disorder if they are to learn how to monitor these symptoms. The therapist explains that a psychiatric diagnosis is made based on a careful clinical interview designed to assess whether the client has experienced specific symptoms. A psychiatric diagnosis is based on the presence of specific symptoms, *in the absence* of medical conditions (e.g., a tumor, an endocrine disease) or the use of substances (e.g., alcohol, stimulants) that are known to produce such symptoms. Many families are surprised to learn that the psychiatric disorder cannot be diagnosed from common medical tests, such as an X ray, CAT scan or PET scan, or blood test.

Prior to the review of the specific psychiatric symptoms that are used to diagnose the disorder, the therapist can connote the client as having the role of "the expert" and solicit his or her aid in explaining the symptoms to the other family members (Falloon et al., 1984). This strategy gives the client a respected role in the discussion of symptoms and validates his or her experience with the disorder. For example, the therapist can say: *"I would like to spend a few minutes talking about specific symptoms of depression. It is easy for me to give you a definition of each of these symptoms, but when it comes down to explaining what these symptoms are actually like, Tina is the real expert. I would appreciate your help, Tina, in helping your family understand more about some of these symptoms. Is that okay with you?"*

Most clients agree to the role of "the expert." Even when clients do not believe they have the disorder in question, they are still often willing to take the role of "expert." In such cases, rather than continually repeating the specific diagnosis throughout the educational sessions, the therapist may opt to refer to the disorder and person with it using a less disputed phrase, such as "people with these kinds of difficulties" and "these types of problems." If the client does not accept the role of the expert, the therapist nevertheless reviews the different symptoms, but does not try to elicit the client's experience directly.

The review of the symptoms can be conducted using the following format. First, the therapist provides a definition of the symptom and provides one or two brief examples (e.g., *"A compulsion is the strong need to engage in a behavior or thought in order to reduce anxiety, even if it must be repeated many times. For example, washing one's hands many times throughout the day is a compulsion"; "A hallucination is a false perception; that is, the hearing, seeing, feeling, or smelling something when nothing is there. For example, hearing voices when no one is speaking"; "A delusion is a false belief; that is, a belief that is not shared by others and appears clearly to be wrong. For example, believing that other people want to hurt you, when nobody really wants to"*). Second, the client is asked whether he or she has experienced that symptom and, if so, is asked to describe what it was like. Third, the therapist asks family members whether they were aware that the client had a particular symptom. The therapist makes it clear to the family that not all symptoms must be present for a client to have the psychiatric disorder.

This three-step process is intended to help relatives recognize the characteristic symptoms of the disorder in their own family member. Often, the client reports that he or she has not experienced a particular symptom, contrary to the observations of either the therapist or family members. When this happens, the therapist refrains from trying to convince the client that the symptom is truly present and intercedes to prevent family members from trying to force the client to "own up" to having the symptom. Instead, the client's account is not challenged, although the nature of the symptom is still discussed with the relatives. Above all, the therapist seeks to create a civil, supportive environment in the family when discussing the symptoms of the disorder, allowing differences between family members to exist without erupting into arguments. In many families, this is the first experience they have had of talking about the symptoms of the psychiatric disorder with the client, and relatives are surprised to find that it is possible to have a peaceful discussion about the disorder, and to benefit from hearing each others' perspective. The information described above is summarized for schizophrenia, schizoaffective disorder, bipolar disorder, major depression, post-traumatic stress disorder, and obsessive-compulsive disorder in the series of handouts in Appendix 3 beginning with "Facts about . . ."

The Stress-Vulnerability Model

The introduction to the psychiatric disorder, ending with a review of the symptoms, leads naturally into a discussion of the causes the disorder. At this point, the stress-vulnerability model of psychiatric disorders is described, concluding with an overview of how the family can help improve the course of the disorder (recall figure 1.2).

After an overview of this topic, the therapist begins the discussion by explaining that everyone has his or her own biological vulnerabilities to experience the negative effects of stress in a particular way. Some people are prone to secrete excessive gastric juices, leading to ulcers. Others may be vulnerable to hypertension, cardiovascular disease, or eczema. Still others may have biological vulnerabilities in the balance of chemicals in the brain (neurotransmitters), resulting in psychiatric disorders. Although it has not yet been *proven* that imbalances in brain chemicals cause psychiatric disorders, many researchers believe that this is the case, and there is a great deal of evidence indicating that biological factors are involved in psychiatric disorders.

The therapist explains that the origin of the biological vulnerability is not fully understood, but that evidence suggests that both genetic (inherited) and nongenetic factors can play a role in determining vulnerability. The increased risk of developing the psychiatric disorder if a relative also has the disorder is described (see Table 5.5). In addition, it is explained that other risk factors may contribute to an individual's biological vulnerability to a psychiatric disorder (e.g., obstetric complications, maternal exposure to influenza during pregnancy). Depending upon whether other family members are known to have had the psychiatric disorder, the therapist can emphasize or de-emphasize the possible role of nongenetic factors in determining biological vulnerability to the disorder.

Biological vulnerability can be changed (for better or worse) by either drugs or stress. Certain medications can reduce biological vulnerability, presumably by correcting the imbalance in brain chemicals. These medications can lessen symptoms and minimize the chances of relapse. Other drugs can worsen biological vulnerability or eliminate the protective effects of prescribed medications. For example, cocaine abuse can precipitate symptom relapses, whereas alcohol abuse lessens the efficacy of many psychotropic medications prescribed for psychiatric disorders.

Stress on the client also can have a direct impact on vulnerability, thus worsening symptoms. Examples of stressors are provided, such as life events, negative family affect, or lack of meaningful structure, and their role in triggering the onset of the disorder is considered. The therapist can probe family members to evaluate whether the onset of the disorder or symptom exacerbations coincided with particular life stressors.

Although stress influences vulnerability to symptoms, family and client coping skills can mediate the effects of stress. In other words, as the client and relatives learn new and more effective strategies for handling stress, such as improved communication and problem-solving skills, the negative effects of stress on vulnerability are reduced, resulting in a less severe course and outcome of the disorder. An understanding of how biological vulnerability is influenced by stress, which, in turn, is influenced by family coping skills, helps family members see that they *can* have an impact on the course of a biologically based disorder. The therapist can further support this point by explaining that teaching stress-management techniques have been found to improve the course of medical illnesses such as breast cancer (Fawzy et al., 1990), hypertension (Blanchard et al, 1988), and diabetes (Surwit & Feinglos, 1983), as well as psychiatric disorders.

TABLE 5.5
PREVALENCE OF MAJOR PSYCHIATRIC DISORDERS IN THE GENERAL POPULATION AND FIRST-DEGREE RELATIVES OF CLIENTS WITH THE SAME DISORDER

Disorder	Prevalence of Disorder (%)	
	General Population	First-Degree Relatives
Schizophrenia	1	10
Bipolar Disorder	0.5-1	5-10
Major Depression	5	15
Chronic Anxiety Disorder	2-5	15-20

Data extracted from Cloninger (1987), Goodwin & Jamison (1990), Gottesman (1991), Kessler et al. (1994), and Robins & Regier (1991).

The discussion of the stress-vulnerability model ends with a brief review of how the family can improve the course of the psychiatric disorder. The basic roles that family members can play include encouraging adherence to treatment, monitoring symptoms of the disorder, creating a supportive family environment, and reinforcing small steps by the client toward better role functioning and greater independence. These points are summarized in a handout for families in Appendix 3 ("Stress-Vulnerability Model").

Medication

Medication is a mainstay of treatment for most clients with a psychiatric disorder. In order to maximize compliance with medication, families need to understand the clinical effects, types, and dosages of medication used, common side effects, how to talk with physicians about medication, and what to do about missed dosages.

Most of the medications used to treat major psychiatric disorders have two main clinical effects. First, they reduce acute symptoms of the disorder, such as hallucinations, delusions, pressured speech, depressed mood, or obsessions and compulsions. Second, when the medications are taken prophylactically, they substantially lower the chances of subsequent symptom relapses. Thus, medications are often prescribed on a long-term basis, and many clients need to take medication throughout their lives in order to minimize their risk of relapses and rehospitalizations. Even when relapses occur, clients who take medication regularly usually experience milder relapses that can be treated more quickly and with less medication than clients who discontinue their medication. The therapist explores the client's past compliance with medication and identifies factors that may have interfered with compliance (e.g., side effects, forgetting, lack of family support, financial constraints). Positive effects of medication are elicited from the family to reinforce its importance in treating the psychiatric disorder.

Next, the specific names of different medications used to treat the client's disorder are reviewed (e.g., antipsychotics for schizophrenia, antidepressants for major depression, mood stabilizers for bipolar disorder). The therapist finds out from the family which medications the client has been treated with in the past. The therapist explains that the *potency* of different medications (within the same class) differ, which is why some medications require higher doses than others. Once the correct dosage is given, the clinical effects of different medications are often similar, although each individual is unique in terms of which medication works best for him or her. There are some differences, however, in the profile of side effects across the medications.

The therapist needs to know the specific side effects of the medication that the client is taking, which are reviewed with the family. The client's past and current experience with medication side effects is evaluated, and strategies for dealing with side effects are discussed. Two of these strategies include talking to the physician about the side effect(s) and using specific coping strategies (e.g., isomorphic exercises for muscle stiffness caused by antipsychotics). Physicians may address medication side effects by altering the dosage, prescribing another medication for side effects, or switching the client to a different medication. It is vital that clients realize that they have a number of options for handling medication side effects other than ceasing to take their medication. Further, sometimes side effects are more easily recognized by relatives who may then alert the physician.

Often families have inaccurate information about the addictive properties of psychotropic medications. The therapist probes for these beliefs and explains, when appropriate, that the medication is not addictive (i.e., the client does not require higher amounts of medication to achieve the same clinical effect over time). Of course, this is not true for some psychotropic medications. Regular use of anxiolytics *can* lead to dependency.

Finally, the therapist discusses with the family how to handle missed doses of medication and anticipates possible problems with medication compliance. At the end of this educational topic, the family members should know the clinical effects of the medication, which specific medications and dosage levels the client is taking, why each medication has been prescribed (e.g., that the Ripserdal is an antipsychotic medication for the symptoms of schizophrenia, the Cogentin is for the side effects of the Risperdal, and the Restoril is to help with sleep), some of the side effects of the medication, and how to get more information from the physician about the medication. Information for families about medication is summarized in four hand-outs in Appendix 3: "Antipsychotic Medications," "Antidepressant Medications," "Mood Stabilizers," and "Antianxiety and Sedative Medications."

Early Warning Signs of Relapse

The episodic course of most psychiatric disorders provides important opportunities for the prevention of full-scale relapses through careful monitoring of early warning signs of relapse. The therapist explains that symptom exacerbations often develop gradually over a period of several weeks, with small changes preceding the more dramatic worsening of symptoms. If slight increases in symptoms are detected at a sufficiently early stage, relapses often can be prevented (or their severity mini-mized) through early intervention. The family can play a critical role in monitoring these increases in symptoms by alerting the treatment team when changes are suspected.

Each client has his or her own unique set of early warning signs that occur before a relapse. Some early warning signs of relapse are reflected by subtle changes in the client's mood or behavior (e.g., increased anxiety, irritability, depressed mood, social withdrawal). Other early warning signs may be slight increases in preexisting symptoms (e.g., reemergence or worsening of obsessions and checking behaviors, increased intensity of hallucinations, acting on delusions, more intrusive memories of a traumatic event). Still other early warning signs are idiosyncratic to the client (e.g., wearing black clothing, preoccupation with martial arts). Common signs of relapse are reviewed with the family with the aim of identifying several *observable* signs for the client that have preceded relapses in the past. If the client has only had one or two symptom exacerbations, it may be difficult to identify accurate warning signs for him or her. Here, discussion of typical early indicators of relapse is especially useful.

Once the key signs of an impending relapse for the client have been identified, they are written down. Then the therapist leads the family in formulating a plan for responding to early warning signs and preventing relapses. Each family's plan may differ slightly, but should include the following elements: checking early warning signs on a regular basis (e.g., weekly), calling a family meeting to discuss whether the changes have occurred, and contacting the treatment team if most of the family mem-bers agree that early warning signs have developed. A form that can be used for developing a family plan for responding to early warning signs of relapse is con-tained in Appendix 2 ("Relapse Prevention Worksheet").

A Caregiver's Guide to Helping a Relative Who Has a Serious Psychiatric Illness

The final educational topic serves as both a review of earlier material and a bridge to the communication work, which is the next component of the BFT. The key elements to improving prognosis—medication compliance, avoiding street drugs and alcohol use, finding something useful to do, and limiting family stress—are again detailed. Then, the role of family tension, including patterns of communication reflec-tive of high Expressed Emotion—criticism and extremely self-sacrificing behavior—

are described in lay terms. Families are encouraged to begin to attend to the presence of these patterns in their own lives, and to reduce them as much as possible. Families are also reminded that many of the strategies they learn in the communication- and problem-solving skills training will help reduce family stress. Oftentimes, both the relapse prevention worksheet and the caregiver's guide can be covered in the same session.

TABLE 5.6
EXAMPLES OF REVIEW QUESTIONS FOR EDUCATIONAL TOPICS

Basic Facts

What is the diagnosis?
What are some of the symptoms of this diagnosis?
How was this diagnosis made?
How common is the disorder?

Stress-Vulnerability Model

What is the cause of the disorder?
How does stress affect the symptoms of the disorder?
What is the effect of alcohol and drugs on the symptoms and relapses?
How can family members help the ill person?

Medication

What medications is the client taking for the disorder?
How do medications help the disorder?
What are the side effects of the medications?
What should you do if you have problems with side effects from the medications?

Early Warning Signs

Why is it important to monitor early warning signs and symptoms of the disorder?
What are the client's early warning signs of relapse?
What is your family plan, if you notice an increase in early warning signs in the client?

A Caregiver's Guide to Helping a Relative Who Has a Serious Psychiatric Illness

What are the four key elements of a recovery plan?
What are the benefits for the client in reducing high levels of stress and tension in the family?
Which relative communication and behavioral patterns tend to be related to client relapse?

Review Questions

One strategy for helping family members actively process educational information they have learned is for the therapist to ask open-ended review questions after each topic area has been covered. These questions also provide valuable information to the therapist about what the family has learned and in which areas the family needs further education. A convenient time to ask these questions is at the beginning of a session in which a new educational topic will be taught. Examples of review questions for each of the main topic areas are contained in Table 5.6.

Use of Educational Handouts

There are two basic approaches to the use of educational handouts in sessions devoted to teaching the family about the psychiatric disorder. One strategy is for the therapist to give an educational handout to each family member at the beginning of the session and have the family read the handout as the therapist reviews and elaborates on the material. This method is best when the therapist does not use other visual aids to summarize the material during the session (e.g., posters, flip charts), and when at least one or two family members have good reading skills. A second method is for the therapist to give family members the handout at the end of the session and request them to review it on their own as a homework assignment. This approach is preferable when the therapist uses posters or flip charts during the session, as the handouts can be distracting. We have had success in working with families with a member who cannot read by having other family members read the handouts to the illiterate relative. When none of the family members has adequate reading skills, handouts are skipped, and usually the total amount of time spent on education is abbreviated. A brief review of the critical educational information can be audiotaped and given to the family for review.

Family Meetings and Homework Assignments

We have explained in Chapter 2 ("An Overview of BFT") that at the beginning of BFT, families are taught to establish a regular time to meet together on a weekly basis throughout the course of therapy, ideally even after therapy has ended. The rationale for having weekly meetings without the therapist is that it provides families with a chance to review material that has been covered in the session and to practice skills on their own. After families have learned problem-solving skills, they will use this family meeting time to address problems and goals, using the therapist as a consultant on difficulties encountered in these meetings. Time is set aside at the end of the first session to discuss the importance of family meetings and to schedule a standard time and place for all family members to convene. The steps involved in arranging a weekly family meeting are summarized in Table 5.7. A key element to initiating and maintaining family meetings is to have one member assume responsibility for preparing for the meeting and calling it to order (e.g. "chair" the meeting). Some families prefer to rotate chair duties, while others prefer to have one member (often a responsible parent) assume the role on a more consistent basis. As part of the initial discussion on family meetings, the therapist guides the family in selecting a "chair" strategy most suitable for its needs.

During the educational and communication-skills training sessions, the therapist provides the family with specific homework assignments that can be completed during the family meeting time. When strong levels of negative affect are present, it is especially important that the family understand the purpose of the assignment, which should be clear, concise, and easy to accomplish. This structure will minimize the chances of conflict developing in the family meeting when the therapist is not present to interrupt it.

One type of homework assignment for the educational sessions is for family members to review handouts in the family meeting, writing down any questions that arise. Another type of assignment is for family members to obtain more specific information about the client's disorder or his or her treatment. For example, the client may be given the assignment to find out exactly what dosages of which medications he or she is currently taking. Assignments of this sort help family members learn practical information about the client's disorder. Still another type of homework assignment is for the therapist to write down several questions about information taught during the session and to request the family to answer those questions during their next family meeting. This strategy allows the family to actively process its understanding of the disorder and informs the therapist as to the need for additional education.

TABLE 5.7
STEPS TO ORGANIZING ONGOING FAMILY MEETINGS

1. Select a regular thirty-minute time block in which all family members are available for weekly meetings.

   Day   Time

2. During the week, have a sheet readily available upon which family members can list topics to discuss during meeting.

3. Chair assures that paper and pencils are available for recording notes and completing assignments during meeting.

4. Make sure there are no distractions during meeting (TV is off, meeting not scheduled during mealtime).

5. Chair assures that list of problem topics and BFT assignment brought to meeting are discussed. He/she makes sure meetings begin and end on time, that everyone contributes viewpoint, and that everyone acts respectfully and responsibly.

When assigning homework, the therapist provides a clear rationale for the assignment (e.g., "The purpose of this assignment is for you to review the information we discussed today about major depression and to see whether you have any questions about it"). The assignment is given in a direct, assertive manner, using phrases such as "I would like you to . . ." and "for the next week, your homework assignment will be . . ." After the assignment has been explained, the therapist checks to make sure the family has understood it correctly. The therapist communicates to the family that homework is an integral part of the BFT, just as important as attendance at the session itself.

Homework and family meetings are reviewed at the beginning of each session, with the therapist troubleshooting problems that prevented completion of the assignment. Typical problems with homework include: some or all family members forget the meeting time, the assignment is forgotten (or lost), the assignment is misunderstood, and unforeseen events disrupt the meeting plan. It is vital that the therapist immediately address obstacles to homework and formulate a plan to ensure completion of the assignment in the following week. If the therapist is consistently responsive to problems with family meetings and homework assignments from the beginning of BFT, he or she will be able to shape the family's compliance with these assignments, which become even more important later in therapy.

Blocking Negative Affect in the Family

High levels of tension, conflict, excessive criticisms, and put-downs are all common problems for some families early in BFT. Because education is the first component of therapy, families have the fewest resources for diffusing negative affect in these sessions. The therapist needs to be prepared to block strong expression of negative affect in the educational sessions in order to protect the client from stress, enable the families to acquire basic information about the psychiatric disorder, and maintain a good therapeutic relationship with the family. At this point in therapy, the therapist's goal is to stop the negative affect without attempting to teach communication or problem-solving skills, which will be the focus of later sessions. There are several options available to the therapist for stemming negative affect that erupts early in the course of treatment.

Reinforcing the Client's Participation

Relatives who are just beginning to learn about their family member's psychiatric disorder are especially prone to blaming the client, criticizing behavior, or questioning the client's true commitment to change. The therapist's first response to these challenges is to defend the client by reinforcing his or her participation in the family sessions, while at the same time acknowledging the relative's concern. By coming to the aid of the client, the therapist demonstrates that he or she will not allow the client to be scapegoated by the family, thereby avoiding the risk of alienating the client from subsequent family sessions. By simultaneously validating the relative's concern, the therapist maintains an alliance with the entire family and avoids taking sides.

One easy way to apply this strategy is to follow three simple steps:

1. acknowledge the relative's complaint;
2. connote the client's participation in the sessions as an indication that he or she is willing to work with the family;
3. explain that family sessions will address these types of concerns later in the course of therapy.

For example, if a relative (Louise) complains that the client (Jim) never helps out and is not really interested in change, the therapist can respond:

"I can understand why you might find it hard to live with Jim when he doesn't help out at home. However, I also think that it's really important to recognize that Jim has expressed a willingness to participate in these family sessions and to work on these types of problems with you. Jim deserves a lot of credit for agreeing to come to these sessions, and Jim, I'm glad you're here. Louise, I appreciate the fact that you raised this problem. These are the types of problems that we will be addressing in these family sessions, after we have spent some more time reviewing information about the disorder."

Stopping Arguments

In some families, tensions may quickly lead to arguments that, if unchecked, can disrupt the collaborative family atmosphere and prevent learning. Probably the most important thing for the therapist not to do when an argument erupts is to sit back and wait for it to end! Any dedicated effort on the part of the therapist to stop the argument is preferable to allowing it to continue.

The therapist attempts to stop strong, nonconstructive expressions of negative affect that lead to arguments at the earliest possible time. The communication of negative affect is not constructive when a person raises his or her voice, speaks in a hostile or sarcastic tone, is insulting or calls others names, overgeneralizes or uses accusing "you" statements (e.g., "you never care about anyone else"), or voices frequent criticisms or put-downs. When such negative interactions occur, the therapist interrupts, briefly acknowledges the complaint or conflict, and then explains that this type of communication is not helpful. The therapist explains what particular aspect of the communication was problematic (e.g., speaking too loudly, putting the other person down, making "blaming" statements), so that family members can try to avoid that behavior in the future. Then the therapist refocuses the discussion on the educational topic.

The therapist may need to interrupt the family several times in order to stop an argument successfully. When arguments develop quickly, usually because the family has had that same argument many times before, the therapist must first get the attention of family members. This can be accomplished by speaking even louder than the family (e.g., saying "STOP!" or "HOLD IT EVERYONE!"), whistling, raising a hand to signal "stop," or leaning forward or standing between two arguing family members to prevent them from seeing each other and continuing the argument. Once the therapist has the attention of family members, the problem with the negative communication can be addressed. Although the goal is to get the family back to work on the focus of the educational session, the therapist assures family members that this conflict (and others like it) will be addressed in later sessions, when their skills have developed further.

Taking a Break

Family arguments can be so disturbing to some members that it becomes difficult to continue immediately with the session. This is particularly true when a family member begins to cry during an argument. We strongly discourage therapists from ending a session early when one person becomes upset. By ending the session early, the therapist gives the family the message that there are certain family situations that cannot be handled, which immediately lowers the therapist's credibility as someone who can really help them.

Rather than ending the session early, the therapist can call for a brief break (e.g., five minutes), allowing family members to get up, stretch, leave the room, get a drink of water, and walk around for a few minutes. If someone was crying, the therapist can sympathetically suggest that they take a moment to wash their face. If someone was especially upset, the therapist can talk with them for a few minutes during the break to help calm them down. When the family reconvenes, the therapist says a few words about what occurred, explains that BFT is designed to help them deal with such conflicts, and continues with the agenda. If some family members continue to show visible signs of being upset, the therapist can abbreviate the remainder of the session plan, and spend some extra time at the end of the session talking with them and providing reassurance.

Allowing Family Members to Vent

Despite the therapist's best efforts, there are some family members who continue to show high levels of negative affect during sessions, which can jeopardize the outcome of therapy. In most cases, these individuals are relatives who have experienced years of frustration living with difficult clients, and who have received minimal help in coping from other relatives or mental health professionals. Although these relatives can be very difficult to work with, they also tend to have a strong commitment to the client and appear to benefit in the long run from BFT. Furthermore, they often enjoy a good, if tumultuous, relationship with the client and are important persons in the client's social support network.

When repeated attempts to block or contain negative affect from one person during family sessions are unsuccessful, the therapist should consider scheduling individual sessions with that person in addition to the ongoing family sessions. During individual sessions, the therapist can let the person vent feelings of anger or loss, and help them develop realistic expectations for the client. These individual sessions can strengthen the person's relationship with the therapist, validate that person's negative feelings without disrupting the family sessions, and give the therapist extra leverage for stopping strong displays of negative affect during the session (i.e., the therapist can tell the person that they will discuss the issue in their individual session). In most cases, when individual sessions are offered to a family member, it is on a temporary basis (e.g., two to five sessions) and not for the entire length of BFT.

Cultural Diversity

Two issues are critical in adapting BFT to a particular ethnic or cultural group—ascertaining information about the culture's ideas about psychiatric illness and its beliefs about family relationships. First, the therapist must be sensitive to different cultural interpretations of "mental illness," normalcy," and "deviant behavior" when educating the family about a psychiatric disorder. Perhaps the most important step is for the therapist to develop an awareness about his or her beliefs regarding members of different cultural groups, to correct stereotypes and misperceptions, and to develop a respect for alternative cultures and worldviews. As a part of this developing awareness, it is helpful if the therapist can initiate dialogue with family members as to how these issues affect them, including cultural perspectives on symptoms and psychiatric disorders.

It is imperative to note that different cultures, and individuals within a culture, vary in their perception of the nature and causes of psychiatric disorders (Vargas & Koss-Chioino, 1992). The therapist's primary role is to provide useful information about the disorder that can be integrated or accommodated into culture-bound beliefs, because the therapist is unlikely to change the core beliefs themselves. Thus, the therapist needs to be acquainted with the beliefs of the persons with whom he or she is working, and to be respectful of any alternative interpretations of behaviors that might be seen by the therapist to reflect a psychiatric disorder. The therapist should also be alert to the influence that the acculturation level of the family has on its beliefs. For example, individuals whose families immigrated to a host country four or five generations ago may hold beliefs very similar to those of the host country's general population, while those that are first generation may not. A close alliance between the therapist and the family that emphasizes points of agreement and possibilities for collaboration is critical to the long-term goal of teaching families about a psychiatric disorder and its management over time.

Second, the therapist will benefit from becoming acquainted with different cultural groups' notions about family ties and respect for authority. Eurocentric norms (i.e., adult offspring live independently from their parents and make their own decisions) often differ significantly from other cultural groups, and the more familiar the therapist is with cultural groups that differ from his or her own reference point, the less likely he or she is to inadvertently contribute to a therapeutic breach. Oftentimes, issues can be very subtle. For example, in BFT, open discussions with prescribing physicians about side effects are encouraged. However, some cultures would see such a conversation as confrontational and disrespectful of the doctor's authority. Unless the BFT therapist can help navigate this breach (for example, by eliciting the help of the most respected member of the family to talk with the doctor), the education will be of little value. McGoldrick et al. (1996; McGoldrick, 1998) offer an invaluable resource in thinking about the role of cultural differences in family therapy.

CASE EXAMPLE OF DWAYNE AND TANIA

During the discussion of the symptoms of PTSD concerning Dwayne, it became clear to the therapist that Tania also suffered from untreated PTSD as a result of a life-threatening robbery that had occurred two years previously. In the educational sessions, the therapist provided important information to the couple about PTSD, describing etiology (including the necessary exposure to a traumatic event), prevalence, course, and possible treatment options. These sessions also provided Dwayne with the opportunity to talk about some of his most troubling combat experiences, while the therapist shaped empathic listening skills in Tania (and to a lesser extent, for Tania to talk about the robbery while Dwayne listened). Both Dwayne and Tania indicated feeling relieved at finally being able to talk about some of their traumatic experiences.

The therapist also asked the couple to have weekly family meetings lasting at least fifteen minutes. Dwayne and Tania gave a variety of reasons for not meeting for the first two weeks, including not feeling comfortable talking together, being too "busy," and the assignment interfering with Dwayne watching television. The therapist conducted a mini-problem-solving session after this, and the couple decided to meet once a week for ten minutes prior to Dwayne's favorite show. They successfully sustained this meeting time through most of the therapy, and by the end of treatment the duration of these meetings had extended to twenty minutes.

Questions and Answers to Common Problems

1. *Question:* How does the therapist handle a client who objects to or challenges the diagnosis? What should the therapist do if a relative tries to force the issue with the client?

   Answer: Psychiatric clients often deny that they have a specific disorder and may forcefully object to the use of the diagnostic label in family sessions. In our experience, this happens more often among persons with schizophrenia, although it also happens with other disorders. Psychiatric clients may use denial as a strategy for preserving their self-esteem. Both clients and nonclients are aware of the stigma attached to mental illness. By denying that they have a disorder, clients avoid having to think of themselves as undesirable social outcasts. However, clients who deny having a specific disorder rarely claim to have no problems. Thus, in most cases, a client's denial of the disorder does not mean that the person will not work on specific problems or goals.

   The goal of working with such clients is to get past the diagnosis without allowing it to become an issue of contention. The therapist has no stake in convincing clients they have a particular diagnosis. The therapist strives to create a climate of mutual tolerance among participants in the family sessions, which includes tolerance of differences in opinion about the client's diagnosis (i.e., the therapist thinks the client has a specific disorder, but the client disagrees). If the client feels strongly about not having the diagnosis, the therapist can downplay use of the specific label.

   A similar strategy is adopted for dealing with relatives who try to convince the client that he or she has a disorder. Relatives are discouraged from attempts at such persuasion, and it is pointed out that clients can actively work with the family to deal with problems without acknowledging their diagnosis. A clinical example is provided below of such an interaction between a schizophrenic man, his brother, and the therapist that took place toward the end of their first educational session (the father was also present at the session).

Case Example

Brother: I have a question. You know we were talking and Bob said how he doesn't feel that he has got schizophrenia. Don't

	you think that instead of trying to overcome the symptoms and the effects they have on him, it would be better if Bob admitted he has schizophrenia?
Client:	I admit I'm gravely disabled, that's what the court said. I am. I cannot function in almost any controlled situation. I cannot function. My concentration is off. My brain, from taking all the drugs over the years, is deteriorating a little bit. I do receive spiritual aid and comfort, but that's something I'd prefer not to talk about.
Therapist:	Sure, I understand. I think Bob has shared a lot with us. He has admitted that he feels he has serious difficulties, and he has described some of the symptoms associated with schizophrenia.
Brother:	I think there has to be a realization. Even though we know it's real for Bob, he also has to grasp the fact that it's something he doesn't have to let take him over.
Therapist:	I hope the sessions will help Bob and your whole family learn to deal with some of the symptoms and experiences of this disorder. I don't know of any good way of convincing somebody that they have schizophrenia. But I do know that there are some useful ways of learning to cope and how to solve problems that can reduce stress on the family and can help Bob cope with the stress that he experiences in his everyday life. That's what's really important, because "schizophrenia" is just a term—
Brother:	—just a word—
Therapist:	Yes, a word to describe a set of symptoms. Bob has said he is willing to talk about some of his experiences and share them, and you are willing to work together as a family. That means the positive force of this family can improve the course of Bob's symptoms.

2. *Question:* What does the therapist do when family members continue to hold antiquated or incorrect beliefs about the psychiatric disorder, even after they have been provided with accurate information?

   Answer: Work toward educating the family over the long term and accept the fact that old beliefs die hard. Often, the therapist meets the family for the first time many years after the onset of the disorder. Family members may have developed their own ideas about the origins of the disorder and what helps it before they ever came into contact with professionals, who often give different explanations (as well as different diagnoses) for the disorder. Thus, unless the therapist tells family members something about the disorder that makes more sense than their current way of understanding it, they may continue to hold onto their old beliefs. Despite this, progress is possible if the therapist is aware of the family members' beliefs and repeatedly exposes them to an alternative point of view.

3. *Question:* How does the therapist educate the family about the disorder when it is unclear what diagnosis the client has?

Answer: When there is a lack of clarity about the diagnosis or another aspect of the client's disorder, despite reasonable efforts to gain the most accurate information possible, the therapist explains the uncertainty to the family, and educates them based on what is understood about the disorder. A clinical example of such a situation is provided below.

Case Example

A thirty-seven-year-old woman with a seriously debilitating psychiatric disorder and her parents were engaged in BFT. The client's symptoms presented a diagnostic dilemma. She engaged in frequent checking and ritualistic ("neutralizing") behavior, consistent with an obsessive-compulsive disorder (OCD). However, she had many bizarre delusions that suggested a possible diagnosis of schizophrenia. To complicate matters further, she had responded minimally to pharmacological interventions usually effective for either OCD (clomipramine) or schizophrenia (antipsychotics). The therapist dealt with the diagnostic uncertainty by explaining the difficulty of firmly establishing whether the client had either or both disorders. Then, the family was educated about the symptoms of both disorders.

Educational Resources for Therapists and Families

Therapists conducting BFT often need to obtain additional information about a psychiatric disorder. Sometimes family members raise questions to which the therapist does not know the answer. At other times, the client may have a psychiatric disorder with which the therapist is less familiar. While colleagues may be able to answer many questions, it is also useful for therapists to have other resources at their disposal. In addition, family members may benefit from joining advocacy and consumer mental health organizations, and from reading books on psychiatric disorders and how to cope with them.

We provide here a list of organizations, books, and journals to aid therapists in finding pertinent educational resources for themselves and the family with whom they work. Our list is not exhaustive, of course, but it provides relatively up-to-date information. Except for books or organizations that are not specific to one disorder, we have categorized the resources according to the psychiatric disorder. We chose to limit our list to three major categories of adult disorders: schizophrenia (including schizoaffective disorder, schizophreniform disorder, and schizotypal personality disorder), affective disorders (including bipolar disorder, cyclothymia, major depression, and dysthymia), and anxiety disorders (with a focus on post-traumatic stress and obsessive-compulsive disorders).

Several considerations led us to focus on these disorders. All of these disorders are relatively common. These disorders also tend to have a major impact on the individual's life and, consequently, often result in adult clients returning home to live with their parents or cause significant disruption to married life. In addition, there exists a considerable knowledge base for each of these disorders, including established pharmacological and/or psychological treatments. Finally, we have personally experienced at least some success conducting BFT with families containing a client with these diagnoses. Note, however, that these disorders are not the only ones that may benefit from BFT.

Within each diagnostic category, we have separated the resources into those for families and those for professionals. The books for families are aimed at the lay audience, written in an easily readable fashion. Therapists will also benefit from reading these books. The books and journals for professionals are more technical, although some more educated family members with an interest in more detailed information and recent advances in research may benefit from reading them. Significant numbers of relatives express an interest in learning more about current research on psychiatric disorders (Mueser et al., 1992), so therapists may choose to synthesize recent findings or recommend critical articles.

Summary

We began this chapter with a review of the rationale for educating family members about psychiatric disorders. Providing accurate information to the family about the psychiatric disorder is intended to legitimize and promote its acceptance, reduce negative emotions that are related to a poor understanding of the disorder, and facilitate the ability of the family as a unit to monitor the symptoms and take steps to prevent relapses through early intervention. The therapist's efforts in educating the family are guided by several core principles: the therapist is knowledgeable about the disorder; information is provided in an honest, straightforward fashion; the educational process is interactive, not strictly didactic; and education takes place throughout the entire course of BFT. Curriculum for the educational sessions was described, including basic facts about the disorder, the stress-vulnerability model, medication, and early warning signs of relapse. The chapter concluded with a section on additional educational resources for information about psychiatric disorders for therapists and family members. In the next chapter, we describe how to train communication skills in family members.

Resources

General

Organizations

The National Alliance for the Mentally Ill (NAMI), the largest consumer/advocacy organization in the United States; 200 North Glebe Road, Suite 1015, Arlington, VA 22203. Toll-free hotline 1-800-950-NAMI; local affiliates can be identified by looking up Alliance for the Mentally Ill (AMI) in the telephone book; www.nami.org.

National Alliance for the Mentally Ill Consumer Council; 200 North Glebe Road, Suite 1015, Arlington, VA 22203.

National Mental Health Association; 1021 Prince Street, Alexandria, VA 22314.; 1-703- 684-7722; www.nmha.org.

Books for Families

Andreasen, N.C. (1984). *The Broken Brain: The Biological Revolution in Psychiatry*. New York: Harper & Row.

Brown, E.M. (1989). *My Parent's Keeper: Adult Children of the Emotionally Disturbed*. Oakland, CA: New Harbinger.

Carter, R. E., Galant, S. K. (1998) *Helping Someone with Mental Illness: Compassionate Guide for Family, Friends, and Caregivers*. New York: Times Books.

Esser, A.H., & Lacey, S.D. (1989). *Mental Illness: A Homecare Guide*. New York: Wiley.

Garson, S. (1986). *Out of Our Minds: How to Cope with the Everyday Problems of the Mentally Ill—A Guide for Patients and Their Families*. Buffalo, NY: Prometheus Books.

Hatfield, A.B., & Lefley, H.P. (1993). *Surviving Mental Illness: Stress, Coping, and Adaptation*. New York: Guilford.

Johnson, J.T. (1988). *Hidden Victims: An Eight-Stage Healing Process for Families and Friends of the Mentally Ill*. New York: Doubleday.

Kaplan, B. (1964). *The Inner World of Mental Illness*. New York: Harper & Row.

Marsh, D.T., & Dickens, R. (1997). *How to Cope with Mental Illness in Your Family: A Self-Care Guide for Siblings, Offspring, and Parents*. New York: Jeremy P. Tarcher/Putnam.

Secunda, V. (1997). *When Madness Comes Home: Help and Hope for the Children, Siblings, and Partners of the Mentally Ill*. New York: Hyperion.

Vine, P. (1982). *Families in Pain*. New York: Pantheon.

Woolis, R. (1992). *When Someone You Love Has a Mental Illness*. New York: Putnam.

Schizophrenia

Organizations

Schizophrenia Association of America; 900 North Federal Highway, Suite 330, Boca Raton, FL 33432.

Books for Families

Backlar, P. (1994). *The Family Face of Schizophrenia: Practical Counsel from America's Leading Experts*. New York: Jeremy P. Tarcher/Putnam.

Burke, R.D. (1995). *When the Music's Over: My Journey into Schizophrenia*. New York: Basic Books.

Dearth, N., Labenski, B.J., Mott, M.E., & Pellegrini, L.M. (1986). *Families Helping Families: Living with Schizophrenia*. New York: Norton.

Deveson, A. (1991). *Tell Me I'm Here: One Family's Experience of Schizophrenia*. New York: Penguin.

Gottesman, I.I. (1991). *Schizophrenia Genesis: The Origins of Madness*. New York: W.H. Freeman.

Hemley, R. (1998). *Nola: A Memoir of Faith, Art & Madness*. New York: Graywolf.

Holley, T.E., & Holley, J. (1997). *My Mother's Keeper: A Daughter's Memoir of Growing Up in the Shadow of Schizophrenia*. New York: William Morrow & Co.

Johnson, A. (1995). *Humming Whispers*. New York: Orchard Books.

Keefe, R.S.E., & Harvey, P.D. (1994). *Understanding Schizophrenia*. New York: Free Press.

Kroll, V.L. (1992). *My Sister, Then and Now (Contemporary Concerns)*. New York: First Avenue Editions.

Kytle, E. (1987). *The Voices of Robbie Wilde*. Washington, DC: Seven Locks Press.

Moorman, M. (1992). *My Sister's Keeper*. New York: Norton. First-person account of a woman learning to cope with her sister's schizophrenia.

Mueser, K.T., & Gingerich, S.L. (1994). *Coping with Schizophrenia: A Guide for Families*. Oakland, CA: New Harbinger.

O'Brien, B.O. (1958). *Operators and Things: The Inner Life of a Schizophrenic*. New York: A.S. Barns and Company.

Schiller, L., & Bennett, A. (1994). *The Quiet Room: A Journey out of the Torment of Madness*. New York: Warner.

Sechehaye, M. (1970). *Autobiography of a Schizophrenic Girl*. New York: New American Library.

Sheehan, S. (1982). *Is There No Place on Earth for Me?* New York: Vintage Books.

Swados, E. (1991). *The Four of Us*. New York: Farrar, Straus, & Giroux. First-person account of the impact of schizophrenia on the family, told from each person's perspective.

Torrey, E.F. (1995). *Surviving Schizophrenia: A Manual for Families, Consumers and Providers*. New York: Harperperennial Library.

Walsh, M. (1985). *Schizophrenia: Straight Talk for Families and Friends*. New York: Morrow.

Wyden, P. (1998). *Conquering Schizophrenia: A Father, His Son and a Medical Breakthrough*. New York: Knopf.

Books and Journals for Professionals

Anderson, C.M., Reiss, D.J., & Hoggarty, G.E. (1986). *Schizophrenia and the Family*. New York: Guilford.

Atkinson, M.A., & Coia, D.A. (1995). *Families Coping with Schizophrenia: A Practitioner's Guide to Family Groups*. New York: John Wiley & Son.

Birchwood, M., & Tarrier, N. (Eds.) (1992). *Innovations in the Psychological Management of Schizophrenia: Assessment, Treatment and Services*. Chichester, England: Wiley.

Falloon, I.R.H., Boyd, J.L., & McGill, C.W. (1984). *Family Care of Schizophrenia*. New York: Guilford.

Hirsch, S.R., & Weinberger, D. (Eds.) (1995). *Schizophrenia*. Oxford, England: Blackwell Scientific Publications.

Kanavagh, D. (Ed.) (1992). *Schizophrenia: A Practical Overview*. London: Chapman and Hall.

Mueser, K.T., & Tarrier, N. (Eds.) (1998) *Handbook of Social Functioning in Schizophrenia*. Boston: Allyn & Bacon.

Nasrallah, H.A. (general editor) (1988-1992). *Handbook of Schizophrenia, Volumes I-IV*. Amsterdam: Elsevier Press.

Schizophrenia Bulletin. Published quarterly by the National Institute of Mental Health.

Schizophrenia Research. Published bimonthly by Elsevier Press.

Tsuang, M.T., Farraone, S.V., & Faraone, S.V. (1997). *Schizophrenia: The Facts (Facts Series)*. London: Oxford University Press.

Affective Disorders

Organizations

National Depressive and Manic-Depressive Association; 730 N. Franklin Street, Suite 501, Chicago, IL 60610-3526. Toll-free hotline 1-800-826-3632; www.ndmda.org.

National Foundation for Depressive Illness, Inc.; 20 Charles Street; New York, NY 10014.

Books for Families

Berger, D., & Berger, L. (1991). *We Heard the Angels of Madness. A Family Guide to Coping with Manic Depression*. New York: Quill.

Burns, D. (1980). *Feeling Good: The New Mood Therapy*. New York: William Morrow & Co.

Burns, D. (1989). *The Feeling Good Handbook*. New York: William Morrow & Co.

Copeland, M.E. (1992). *The Depression Workbook*. Oakland, CA: New Harbinger.

Copeland, M.E. (1994). *Living without Depression and Manic-Depression: A Workbook for Maintaining Mood Stability*. Oakland, CA: New Harbinger.

Court, B.L., & Nelson, G.E. (1996). *Bipolar Puzzle Solution: A Mental Health Client's Perspective*. Washington, DC: Taylor & Francis.

Duke, P., & Hochman, G. (1992). *A Brilliant Madness: Living with Manic-Depressive Illness*. New York: Bantam Books.

Halebsky, M.A. (1997). *Surviving the Crisis of Depression & Bipolar (Manic-Depression) Illness: Layperson's Guide to Coping with Mental Illness beyond the Time of Crisis*. New York: Personal and Professional Growth.

Jamison, K.R. (1993). *Touched with Fire: Manic-Depressive Illness and the Artistic Temperament*. New York: Knopf.

Jamison, K.R. (1995). *An Unquiet Mind*. New York: Knopf

Klein, D.F., & Wender, P.H. (1993). *Understanding Depression: A Complete Guide to Its Diagnosis & Treatment*. New York: Oxford University Press.

Manning, M. (1996) *Undercurrents: A Life beneath the Surface*. San Francisco: Harper San Francisco.

Mondimore, F.M. (1999). *Bipolar Disorder: A Guide for Patients and Families*. New York: Johns Hopkins University Press.

Papolos, D., & Papolos, J. (1992). *Overcoming Depression (Revised Edition)*. New York: Harper Perennial.

Plath, S. (1971). *The Bell Jar*. New York: Harper & Row. An autobiographical account of depression by the well-known poet who later committed suicide.

Rosen, L.E., & Amador, X.F. (1996). *When Someone You Love Is Depressed: How to Help Your Loved One without Losing Yourself*. New York: Simon & Schuster.

Steel, D. (1998). *His Bright Light: The Story of Nick Traina*. New York: Delacorte Press.

Styron, W. (1990). *Darkness Visible*. New York: Vintage. First-person account of the author's experience with depression.

Thompson, T. (1996). *The Beast: A Journey through Depression*. New York: Plume.

Vonnegut, M. (1975). *The Eden Express*. New York: Bantam. First-person account of the author's experience with schizophrenia (which is now recognized today as bipolar disorder).

Whybrow, P.C. (1997). *A Mood Apart: Depression, Mania, and Other Afflictions of the Self*. New York: Basic Books.

Wurtzel, E. (1994). *Prozac Nation: Young and Depressed in America*. Boston: Houghton Mifflin.

Yapko, M.D. (1997). *Breaking the Patterns of Depression*. New York: Doubleday.

Books and Journals for Professionals

Akiskal, H.S., & Cassano, G.B. (Eds.) (1997). *Dysthymia and the Spectrum of Chronic Depressions*. New York: Guilford.

Basco, M.R., & Rush, J. (1996). *Cognitive-Behavioral Therapy for Bipolar Disorder*. New York: Guilford Press.

Beck, A.T., Rush, A.J., Shaw, B.F., & Emery, G. (1979). *Cognitive Therapy of Depression*. New York: Guilford.

Beckham, E.E., & Leber, W.R. (Eds.) (1995). *Handbook of Depression (Second Edition)*. New York: Guilford.

Goodwin, F.K., & Jamison, K.R. (1990). *Manic-Depressive Illness*. New York: Oxford University Press.

Journal of Affective Disorders. Published monthly by Elsevier Press.

Klerman, G.L., Weissman, M.M., Rounsaville, B.J., & Chevron, E.S. (1984). *Interpersonal Psychotherapy of Depression*. New York: Basic Books.

Ludwig, A.M. (1995). *The Price of Greatness: Resolving the Creativity and Madness Controversy*. New York: Guilford.

Papolos, D.F. (1997). *Overcoming Depression*. New York: Harper Collins.

Paykel, E.S. (Ed.) (1992). *Handbook of Affective Disorders (Second Edition)*. New York: Guilford.

Whybrow, P.C. (1998). *A Mood Apart: The Thinker's Guide to Emotion and Its Disorders*. New York: Harper Collins.

Anxiety Disorders (Obsessive-Compulsive Disorder and Post-traumatic Stress Disorder)

Organizations

The Anxiety Disorders Association of America; 11900 Parklawn Drive, Suite 100, Rockville, MD 20852. (301) 231-9350; www.adaa.org.

The Obsessive Compulsive Disorder Foundation, Inc.; P.O. Box 70, Milford, CT 06460. (203) 878-5669; www.ocfoundation.org.

Books for Families

Allen, J.G. (1995). *Coping with Trauma: A Guide to Self-Understanding*. Washington, DC: American Psychiatric Press.

Foa, E.B., & Wilson, R. (1991). *Stop Obsessing! How to Overcome Your Obsessions and Compulsions*. New York: Bantam Books.

Gentry, M. (1997). *After the Accident: Triumph over Trauma*. New York: Tinker Press.

Granoff, M.D., & Lee, A. (1996). *Help! I Think I'm Dying!: Panic Attacks & Phobias: A Consumers Guide to Getting Treatment That Works*. New York: Mind Matters.

Greist, J.H., Jefferson, J.W., & Marks, I.M. (1986). *Anxiety and Its Treatment*. New York: Warner.

Mason, P. (1990). *Recovering from the War*. New York: Viking.

Matsakis, A. (1996). *I Can't Get Over It: A Handbook for Trauma Survivors (Second Edition)*. Oakland, CA: New Harbinger.

Raine, N.V. (1998). *After Silence: Rape and My Journey Back*. New York: Crown.

Rapoport, J.L. (1989). *The Boy Who Couldn't Stop Washing*. New York: Dutton. About recent advances in understanding obsessive-compulsive disorder.

Steketee, G., & White, K. (1990). *When Once Is Not Enough: Help for Obsessive Compulsives*. Oakland, CA: New Harbinger.

Sterns, A.K. (1984). *Living through Personal Crisis*. New York: Ballantine.

Sterns, A.K. (1988). *Coming Back: Rebuilding Lives after Crisis and Loss*. New York: Ballantine.

Veninga, R.L. (1985). *A Gift of Hope: How We Survive Our Tragedies.* New York: Ballantine.

Books and Journals for Professionals

Barlow, D. (1988). *Anxiety and Its Disorders: The Nature and Treatment of Anxiety and Panic.* New York: Guilford.

Blanchard, E.B., & Hickling, E.J. (1997). *After the Crash: Assessment and Treatment of Motor Vehicle Accident Survivors.* Washington, DC: American Psychological Associaton.

Davidson, J.R., & Foa, E.B. (Eds.) (1993). *Posttraumatic Stress Disorder: DSM-IV and Beyond.* Washington, DC: American Psychiatric Press.

Foa, E., Olasov, B., & Rothbaum, B.O. (1998). *Treating the Trauma of Rape: Cognitive-Behavioral Therapy for PTSD.* New York: Guilford.

Foy, D.L. (Ed.) (1992). *Treating PTSD.* New York: Guilford.

Fullerton, C.S., & Ursano, R.J. (1997). *Posttraumatic Stress Disorder: Acute and Long-Term Responses to Trauma and Disaster.* Washington, DC: American Psychiatric Press.

Horowitz, M. (1986). *Stress Response Syndromes (Second Edition).* New York: Jason Aronson.

Journal of Anxiety Disorders. Published bimonthly by Plenum.

Journal of Traumatic Stress. Published quarterly by Plenum.

Resnick, P.A., & Schnicke, M.K. (1993). *Cognitive Processing Therapy for Rape Victims.* Thousand Oaks, CA: Sage.

Steketee, G.S. (1993). *Treatment of Obsessive Compulsive Disorder.* New York: Guilford.

Swinson, R.P., Antony, M.M., Rachman, S., & Richter, M.A. (Eds.) (1998). *Obsessive-Compulsive Disorder.* New York: Guilford.

Turner, S.R., & Beidel, D.C. (1988). *Treating Obsessive-Compulsive Disorder.* New York: Pergamon.

Wilson, J.P., & Keane, T.M. (1997). *Assessing Psychological Trauma and PTSD.* New York: Guilford.

CHAPTER 6	# COMMUNICATION SKILLS TRAINING

Mental health professionals who are familiar with the relationships between psychiatric clients and their relatives have long observed problems in communication in many families. Early clinicians and theoreticians, mostly with a psychoanalytic orientation, interpreted disturbances in family communication as a reflection of pathological family processes that played a role in the etiology of the psychiatric disorder. More recently, there has been a growing recognition that stressful family interactions are a natural byproduct of living with and trying to cope with a psychiatric disorder in the family. When people are under duress, both clients and relatives alike, communication often breaks down, resulting in higher levels of stress on all family members. A major goal of BFT is to reduce stress in the family by improving the communication skills of clients and their relatives.

There are three major reasons for teaching communication skills, as discussed below.

1. **Reducing negative emotion in the family.** According to the stress-vulnerability coping skills model of psychiatric disorders, as discussed in Chapters 1 and 4, environmental stressors impinge on the client's biological vulnerability, leading to an increased risk of relapse. One important source of stress that has been repeatedly linked to higher relapse rates is the presence of negatively charged family interactions (e.g., relatives who are high in Expressed Emotion; Leff & Vaughn, 1985). High levels of criticism, intrusiveness, and extreme attempts at controlling the client's behavior are common sources of stress on clients, and often reflect frustration on the part of relatives. Furthermore, negative, emotionally charged interactions often fail to resolve conflicts and can intensify problems, worsening the stress on everyone in the family.

   Strengthening effective communication skills in families can prevent some conflicts from developing and resolve others with a minimum of stress. Good communication between family members can help to create a supportive, positive atmosphere in the family in which the efforts of every person are recognized and gradual gains by the client are systematically reinforced. Such an affective climate can enhance the quality of life of all family members and lower the chances that the client will experience a relapse or rehospitalization.

2. **Helping family members compensate for client's deficits in information-processing ability.** Clients with psychiatric disorders often have deficits in their ability to process social information accurately (i.e., "social cognition"; Penn et al., 1997). Some clients have difficulty recognizing other peoples' emotions through their facial expressions and fluctuations in voice tone. Many clients have problems concentrating for even moderate periods of time, so that their ability to follow conversations and respond appropriately to others is impaired. Another common problem for psychiatric clients is their inability to make inferences in situations that would seem obvious to others. Thus, clients may find it hard to "take a hint" from another person because they are unable to pick up on subtle cues (e.g., a bored facial expression, frequent looking at his or her watch).

   Communication-skills training helps family members learn how to compensate for clients' deficits in social cognition. Communications that are brief, behaviorally specific, and (when appropriate) refer to specific feelings are more easily understood by clients. Teaching family members how to check whether the client has understood them (e.g., by asking the person to describe their understanding of what was said) can further improve communication, thereby avoiding conflicts that occur when the client misunderstands his or her relatives.

3. **Improving the interpersonal skills of clients (and relatives).** Poor, ineffective social behavior is one of the most prominent signs of psychiatric disorder that prevents clients from enjoying close interpersonal relationships. Some clients are unassertive; they speak in a meek, quiet voice tone and avoid eye contact. Others are loud and offensive, frequently interrupting, talking in an angry voice tone, and monopolizing conversations. There is a wide variation in problems in social skill that may be present in psychiatric clients. Relatives (as well as other people in the general population!) are not immune to these problems in skill. Similar to clients, although usually not as severe, relatives may also have deficits in social skills and these problems can interfere with their ability to be effective in social interactions. Improving these skills in family members will help them achieve instrumental and interpersonal goals that are necessary for improving their quality of life.

Before we describe how to improve communication in families via social skills training, we first provide a definition of "social skills" and an overview of the specific communication skills taught in BFT.

What are "Social Skills"?

A variety of different definitions of social skills have been proposed over the years. Liberman et al. (1989) provide a general definition of social skills as "all the behaviors that help us to communicate our emotions and needs accurately and allow us to achieve our interpersonal goals" (p. 3). Hersen and Bellack (1977) provide a more detailed definition of social skills as the "ability to express both positive and negative feelings in the interpersonal context without suffering consequent loss of reinforcement. Such skill is demonstrated in a large variety of interpersonal contexts and involves the coordinated delivery of appropriate verbal and nonverbal responses. In addition, the socially skilled individual is attuned to the realities of the situation and is aware when he is likely to be reinforced for his efforts." (p. 512)

Common to all definitions of social skill is the predominant focus on the behavior of individuals during social interactions. Social skills are the specific behaviors emitted during interactions that enable people to be effective in getting their point across. Starting a conversation, communicating a feeling to a loved one, returning an item to a store, responding to criticism, obtaining directions, or having a job interview are all examples of situations that require the smooth integration of a range of different behaviors if the desired outcomes are to be achieved.

The behavioral elements of social skill can be divided into three broad categories: nonverbal skills, paralinguistic features, and verbal content. *Nonverbal skills* refer to specific behaviors such as facial expression, eye contact, and use of gestures during an interpersonal exchange. Facial expression and eye contact are especially important nonverbal skills. Facial expressions help convey the feelings of the speaker, which should be consistent with the content of the message. Eye contact enables the speaker to better engage the listener's attention.

Paralinguistic features are the characteristics of vocal speech, including voice tone and loudness, fluency, duration of utterances, and appropriateness of turn taking (latency of response), that take place during the ebb and flow of a conversation. Similar to facial expression, voice tone communicates the feeling of the speaker, which should be consistent with the verbal content. A common problem in families with a psychiatric client is the duration of speech utterances. Relatives sometimes speak uninterrupted for long periods of time, with the result that the client loses track of what is said and fails to get the message. This can be frustrating to both relatives and clients. The problem is easily rectified by teaching family members to speak for briefer periods of time. Definitions of nonverbal and paralinguistic skills are included in Tables 6.1 and 6.2.

Verbal content refers to what is actually said in the communication, including the specific choice of words, regardless of the manner in which it was spoken. Problems in verbal content emerge when the speaker is vague or overgeneralizes (i.e., lacks behavioral specificity), or when irrelevant subject material enters the conversation. The combination of nonverbal skills, paralinguistic features, and verbal content determines the success of the person in getting his or her message across. In some circumstances, clear and expressive nonverbal and paralinguistic skills are more critical to making a point than the content of the message itself. For example, saying "I really feel frustrated when you don't take phone messages for me when I'm not home" in a meek voice tone while avoiding eye contact can be ineffective, because the negative verbal content is neutralized by the unassertive manner in which it is said.

On the other hand, exaggerated nonverbal and paralinguistic expressiveness, particularly in the absence of clear and specific verbal content, can also be a problem. For example, saying "You're the laziest person I know!" in an irritated voice tone and with an angry facial expression fails to provide the listener with information about which specific behaviors are a problem and how the problem can be prevented from happening again. Communication-skills training focuses on improving the nonverbal, paralinguistic, and verbal-content dimensions of social skill.

TABLE 6.1 DEFINITIONS OF NONVERBAL SOCIAL SKILLS

	Appropriate	Inappropriate
Eye Contact	• Looks at other person • Moves eyes while talking	• Looks away from other • Has fixed stare
Facial Expression	• Smiles, frowns, wrinkles forehead, serious when necessary	• Deadpan, no movement
Gestures	• Moves head and hands while talking	• Stiff, no movement • Exaggerated movements
Interpersonal Distance	• Stands a few feet away	• Too close, too far • Inappropriate touching
Body Posture	• Body is erect while talking • Appears relaxed	• Slumps • Very tense
Body Orientation	• Body positioned toward the other person(s) involved in interaction	• Body turned away from other person(s) involved in interaction

Curriculum for Communication-Skills Training

Most interventions for families with a psychiatric client share the common aim of improving interpersonal communication. BFT is distinguished from other approaches by its strong, explicit focus on assessing and improving communication skills using methods derived from social learning theory. Specific curriculum has been developed by Falloon et al. (1984) and Liberman et al. (1989) for teaching communication skills to families in BFT. The curriculum we describe here includes three core skills that are taught to all families and three supplementary skills that are taught on an "as needed" basis. The duration of formal skills training is titrated based on family need.

TABLE 6.2 DEFINITIONS OF PARALINGUISTIC FEATURES

	Appropriate	Inappropriate
Voice Tone and Pitch	• Tone goes up and down with expression of feeling	• Monotone, unusual inflection
Affect	• Emotional tone consistent with verbal content	• Emotional tone inconsistent with verbal content
Loudness	• Speaking at a volume that is audible and comfortable to the listener	• Speaking too softly or too loudly
Speech Fluency	• Speaking without repeating or skipping words	• Speech dysfluencies such as stammering
Amount of Speech	• Roughly equal amounts of talking between different parties	• One person does most or very little of talking compared to other
Latency of Response	• Responds without long pause • Speaks at a moderate pace	• Pauses for a long time • Speaks too quickly or too slowly

The three core skills include expressing positive feelings, making positive requests, and expressing negative feelings. *Expressing positive feelings* is a crucial communication skill for family members to use to reinforce specific desired behaviors in other members (e.g., cooking a meal, getting up on time, doing a favor). All family members need to request things of each other at times, and *making requests* in a positive, noncoercive manner is most likely to be successful. When family members live together or are close to each other, it is inevitable that people will sometimes annoy or upset each other. *Expressing negative feelings* constructively can prevent such situations from occurring again, and is an important skill to have to strengthen a supportive family environment.

The supplementary skills include active listening, compromise and negotiation, and requesting a time-out. *Active listening* refers to the behaviors someone uses to show another person that he or she is hearing to what is being said (e.g., looking at the person and nodding his or her head). Because family members know each other so well, they often think they know what the other person is going to say even before he or she says it. The skill of active listening ensures that the listener pays attention and demonstrates to the other person that he or she has understood the other's point.

In some families, members tend to dig their heels in when conflicts or problems arise, making a resolution impossible. Teaching families *compromise and negotiation* can prevent tension and resentment from occurring due to intractable problems. *Requesting a time-out* is a useful skill to teach families in which disagreements tend to quickly escalate into destructive, emotionally charged arguments. By stopping the argument and waiting until tempers have cooled down, everyone is given an opportunity to deal with the conflict in a calmer state of mind.

For the purposes of teaching, each of these six skills is broken down into three to five component steps, including both verbal and nonverbal elements. The steps of each skill are displayed in Table 6.3. There are several common ingredients to these communication skills:

1. communications are brief;

2. the focus is on the "here and now" (or recent past), rather than on the distant past;

3. reference is made to specific behaviors instead of personality or character traits;

4. specific verbal feeling statements are used to express the experience of positive and negative emotions; and

5. good eye contact and appropriate interpersonal distance are encouraged;

6. statements typically initiated with "I," rather than "you."

These characteristics have been found to promote good communication and to lead to the resolution of problems in both clinical and nonclinical populations.

Selecting the Intensity of Communication-Skills Intervention

In light of the limited time available to both family members and therapists, it is imperative to use BFT session time wisely. Some families exhibit obvious deficiencies in communication, and here an intensive period (four to eight sessions) of BFT formal skills training is warranted, prior to the initiation of problem-solving skills instruction. However, other families have strong communication skills at the outset of the BFT, and thus only a brief review of key points may be needed. It is recommended that therapists use the orientation, assessment, and education sessions to observe the communication skills used by the family in order to make a determination about whether formal skills training would be beneficial. Both in-session and reports of out-of-session interactions can provide important information. In determining whether additional skills training is necessary, the therapist is seeking to identify whether patterns of interaction reflecting the common ingredients of communication skills taught in BFT already predominate. These principles, which promote strong positive interactions among family members, include:

TABLE 6.3   CURRICULUM FOR COMMUNICATION SKILLS TRAINING

Core Skills

Expressing Positive Feelings
> Look at the person
> Tell what he/she did that please you
> Tell how it made you feel

Making Positive Requests
> Look at the person
> Tell what you would like that person to do
> Tell how it would make you feel

Expressing Negative Feelings
> Look at the person with a serious facial expression
> Tell what that person did that upset you
> Tell how it make you feel
> Suggest how it could be prevented in the future

Supplementary Skills

Active Listening
> Look at the speaker
> Nod your head
> Ask clarifying questions
> Paraphrase what you heard
> Wait until the speaker finishes before responding

Compromise and Negotiation
> Look at the person
> Explain your viewpoint
> Listen to the other person's viewpoint
> Repeat what you heard
> Suggest a compromise (more than one may be necessary)

Requesting a Time-Out
> Indicate that the situation is stressful
> Tell the person that it is interfering with constructive communication
> Say that you must leave temporarily

In addition to attending to the consistent presence of the ingrediants listed above, the therapist should also be alert for statements reflecting attitudes considered "high" in Expressed Emotion, as discussed in more detail in Chapter 1. These would include frequent statements made to or about the client in a critical tone of voice and/or a preponderance of negative observations or feedback. Frequent exposure to these types of statements is associated with higher rates of relapse in persons with serious psychiatric illness, and thus also raise the need for focused intervention.

If the therapist observes that most communication in the family is in accordance with the positive principles highlighted above and does not reflect high levels of criticism or hostility, then a one-session review of key communication points is recommended between the education and problem-solving components of BFT. If the therapist notes a consistent deficiency in using these principles and/or high levels of criticism (in content or tone of voice), then more formal communication-skills training is merited. These two levels of communication-skills intervention are discussed more fully below.

The Single-Session Review for Skilled Families

This session, which is scheduled between the end of the educational sessions and prior to the initiation of problem solving, has two goals: (1) to provide a rationale for family members to continue to use the strong skills they have been exhibiting, and (2) to conduct an overview of the six key principles of communication outlined above. In preparation for the communication review session, in the final educational session family members are given a copy of the handout "Keys to Good Communication" (see Appendix 4) and asked to read it prior to the next meeting. At the beginning of the communication session, the therapist informs the family that he or she has been carefully observing the communication style of the family members since meeting them and provides feedback on their strengths, especially as they pertain to the key points noted above (these key points should be listed on a flip chart or blackboard for easy reference; they are also included in the last page of the "Keys to Good Communication" handout). After providing this feedback, the therapist then develops the rationale for continuing to converse following these principles. He or she asks two sets of questions in supporting the rationale. The first alludes to the value of all persons being clear in their speech, and can be ascertained in response to questions such as *"Why do you think it is important to communicate clearly in families?"* or *"What problems can arise when people misunderstand each other in families?"* The second piece of the rationale challenges the family to use the information they acquired about the impediments associated with serious psychiatric illness to clarify why strong communication would be especially critical in a family in which a member has this illness. This might include *"What symptoms of XX's illness might get in the way of him (or her) understanding you all clearly?"* or *"How do you think you might compensate for that?"*

After the rationale for strong communication is elicited from the family, the therapist reminds the family that the next session initiates the most critical aspect of the BFT—formal problem solving on issues of concern to the family. In preparation for this work, the therapist wishes to assure that the family continues its effective communication, and so the remainder of the current session will be allocated to demonstrations of three core communication skills—expressing positive feelings, making positive requests, and expressing negative feelings—which are critical to successful problem solving. (These skills are discussed more specifically below.) The therapist notes that the format of all three skills is similar—it includes using an "I" statement with a feeling, and being brief and specific—and displays examples on a flip chart or blackboard.

Next, the therapist asks each participant to demonstrate at least one skill during the session and asks family members on the "receiving" end of the feedback to convey that they are listening, through the use of good eye contact, nodding, asking clarifying questions, and restating what is said to them to be sure they have understood the speaker accurately. Note that, in contrast to the more elaborate training outlined below, these exercises do not need to be connoted as behavioral rehearsals and can use "real time" expression of feelings, rather than role plays of interactions that have already occurred. After each demonstration, family members are encouraged to provide feedback on the use of the key principles. The session concludes with a final "round-robin" of expressing positive feelings, and then family members are given the "Structure-Problem Solving and Goal Attainment" handout to read in preparation for the next session.

Extended Communication-Skill Training in Less-skillful Families

Between four and eight sessions are usually devoted to training in communication skills in families requiring more intensive intervention; family members also often need to be prompted to use these skills in later sessions, and booster sessions to review skills are also helpful. Everyone in the family actively participates in communication training sessions, which are primarily interactive, rather than didactic, and involve experiential role-playing as a major vehicle for learning the skills.

We recommend that therapists begin by teaching three core skills in order—expressing positive feelings, followed by making positive requests, and then expressing negative feelings. By focusing first on the expression of positive feelings, family members learn how to reinforce each other for engaging in desirable behaviors, thereby leading to increases in these behaviors. In many families, the initial focus on communicating positive feelings has the effect of improving the overall affective tone of the family, and leads to more cooperative behavior. The second skill of making requests provides a formula for asking someone to do something in a positive, noncoercive manner. The ability to make such requests is an important prerequisite to expressing negative feelings, which also involves making a request for behavior change. After family members have shown improvements in these first two skills, expressing negative feelings is taught, with the major emphasis on how to communicate unpleasant feelings in a constructive manner. The handout "Keys to Communication" (see Appendix 4) contains material for communication-skills training and should be distributed to family members.

Communication skills are taught using the procedures of social-skills training, a set of behaviorally based teaching methods that have been "packaged" as a clinical technique. Since the 1960s, social-skills training has become one of the most widely used strategies for teaching more effective interpersonal skills to both clinical and non-clinical populations (Mueser, 1998).

Social Skills Training with Families

Principles of Social Learning

The clinical procedures involved in social-skills training are based on several principles of social learning, including social modeling, behavioral rehearsal, positive social reinforcement, shaping, and programmed generalization. These principles are briefly described below.

Social modeling refers to the use of role models to demonstrate desired communication behaviors. A great deal of social behavior, perhaps most, is learned through the observation of others rather than through direct experience. In social-skills training, the therapist models specific communication skills for the family by using simulated social interactions (role plays) to demonstrate these skills. Before the role play, family members are informed as to which skill will be modeled, and immediately after the demonstration the therapist's behavior is discussed. In addition to the use of modeling in role plays to demonstrate a specific skill, the therapist also models good communication skills in his or her other interactions with family members.

Behavioral rehearsal is the practice of a specific communication skill by a person in a role play. Behavioral rehearsal gives family members opportunities to practice a communication skill in a situation that resembles a true life interaction, while receiving feedback about how to improve their performance in that situation. In order to acquire and generalize communication skills in BFT, family members engage in multiple behavioral rehearsals and receive feedback designed to improve their skills.

After each behavioral rehearsal, the person receives *positive social reinforcement* in the form of praise about those aspects of the interaction that were performed well. Reinforcement is provided by both the therapist and family members in order to strengthen specific component skills, such as those listed in Tables 6.1 through 6.3. *Shaping* is the rewarding of successive approximations toward a desired goal. Over repeated behavioral rehearsals of communication skills in role plays, each followed by positive reinforcement about specific component skills, the person's performance gradually improves and becomes more effective. Shaping takes place both within the session and over the course of BFT.

In order for skills training to improve the family's spontaneous interactions, communication skills must transfer from the clinic session to the natural home environment. *Programmed generalization* is the systematic use of homework assignments to ensure that skills that are taught in the session are practiced at home. Through the use of homework assignments, obstacles to the generalization of communication skills can be identified (e.g., the person forgets to use the skill, other family members respond negatively to the person when the skill is used), and steps can be taken to overcome these obstacles.

Social Skills Training Procedures

In the extended training, one to two sessions are usually spent teaching each of the three core communication skills, with a similar number of sessions (as necessary) devoted to each supplementary skill. Teaching communication skills follows the same social-skills training format that has been employed in multiple settings. This format is summarized in Table 6.4 and described below. For additional information on social-skills training, see Liberman et al. (1989) and Bellack et al. (1997).

TABLE 6.4   STEPS OF SOCIAL-SKILLS TRAINING WITH FAMILIES

1. *Establish a rationale for learning the skill.* Elicit comments from each family member about why the skill is important. Provide additional reasons as necessary.
2. *Present the component steps of the skill.* Review each step of the skill using posters or handouts. Briefly discuss why each step is important.
3. *Model (demonstrate) the skill for the family.* Explain that you will give an example of how to use the skill. Choose an everyday situation to demonstrate. When the skill has been modeled, ask family members which steps of the skill they observed.
4. *Engage a family member in a role play to practice the skill.* Choose a situation that recently happened. Simulate the physical conditions of the original situation (e.g., have family members stand or sit facing each other), rearranging furniture if necessary. Instruct the family member to try the skill in a role play. Request other family members to monitor performance.
5. *Provide positive feedback about the role play.* Elicit positive feedback from family members about specific behaviors in the role play. Provide additional positive feedback as necessary. Cut off criticism from family members until positive feedback has been given.
6. *Provide corrective feedback.* Point out one specific behavior in which the family member could improve. Explain what the person could do differently to be more effective in using the skill.
7. *Engage the family member in another role play of the same situation.* Request the person to do the role play again, this time making one change in behavior based on the corrective feedback. Use additional modeling, coaching, and/or prompting to help the person further improve his or her ability to do the skill.
8. *Provide additional positive and corrective feedback about the role play.* Always provide (and elicit from family members) positive feedback first, then give corrective feedback. If improvements can still be made and the person is willing, do one or two more role plays of the same situation.
9. *Engage another family member in a different role play, followed by feedback and more practice (steps 4 to 8).* Have every person practice the skill in at least two role plays of a specific incident, eliciting feedback from family members. Provide ample encouragement and reinforcement for effort and improvement.
10. *Assign homework to practice the skill.* Explain the rationale for homework, give out homework sheets, and review how they should be completed. Elicit and answer questions about the assignment. Ask family members when they can complete their assignment each day and how they will remember to do it.

Establishing a Rationale

The first step of teaching a skill is to establish the rationale with family members for the importance of learning the skill. For example, expressing positive feelings about a specific behavior that someone has done can increase the chance that they will do that behavior again in the future. Two strategies can be employed to develop the rationale for a communication skill. First, the therapist can elicit the rationale from family members by using the Socratic method and asking the family probe questions that will prompt a discussion about situations where the skill can be used and the consequences of not using the skill. For example, when establishing the rationale for learning how to express negative feelings, the therapist can ask, *"What happens when you have a negative feeling and instead of expressing it, you just hold it in?"* and *"Why is it important to be able to express negative feelings constructively, rather than by yelling and shouting?"* Asking these types of questions gets the family involved in communication training from the beginning. Second, the therapist can provide additional reasons for a particular communication skill if the family has not identified those reasons in response to the questions asked. Examples of probe questions and the reasons for learning each of the communication skills are provided in Table 6.5.

Presenting the Components of the Skill

When the rationale has been established, the therapist reviews the components of the skill being taught, using the steps outlined in Table 6.3. We recommend that therapists use posters, flip charts, or blackboards to present the steps of the skill to the family. By creating a central focus of attention, the therapist can make sure that everyone is engaged and comprehends the material being covered. An alternative is for the therapist to give each family member a handout containing the steps of the skill (see Appendix 4 for copies of handouts for each skill and homework assignments).

The therapist briefly discusses each step of the skill, explaining (or eliciting from family members) the importance of each component. For example, it is important to look at the person when communicating in order to get that person's attention and make sure he or she is listening. When communicating negative feelings, it can be helpful to make a clear feeling statement (e.g., "I felt angry," "I was annoyed") so the other person knows exactly how the speaker was feeling, and does not have to infer it based on the person's voice tone and facial expression. Only a few minutes are required to review the components of the skill.

Modeling the Skill

At this point, the family is familiar with the importance of the skill and how it is broken down into basic steps. The therapist next models the skill so that family members can see how the steps of the skill fit together in a realistic interaction. The therapist can informally provide an example of how the skill can be used, or he or she can set up a role play to demonstrate the skill. In either case, before modeling, the therapist tells the family what skill will be demonstrated and instructs members to attend to the specific steps of the skill.

TABLE 6.5
PROBE QUESTIONS AND RATIONALE FOR TEACHING
COMMUNICATION SKILLS

Expressing Positive Feelings	• Why is it important to express positive feelings to each other? • What happens when you express positive feelings to someone about something that he or she has done? • How do you feel when someone says something positive about something you have done?	• Expressing positive feelings to each other makes you feel good. • Telling someone you appreciate what he or she has done increases the chances that he or she will do that again in the future. • When positive feelings are communicated to people about something they have done, it makes them feel appreciated and not taken for granted.
Making Positive Requests	• Why do you need to be able to make requests of other people? • What happens when you make demands of other people? How is it different when you constructively request someone to do something?	• Everyone needs to be able to make requests of each other in order to get needs met and to get things done that are important to them. It is a necessary part of living together. • People often feel resentful when someone demands that they do something, and often they refuse to comply with the request. Constructive requests that are positive, not coercive, are more likely to be granted.
Expressing Negative Feelings	• Why is it sometimes important to be able to express negative feelings?	• Expressing negative feelings can tell people how their behavior affects you.

CONTINUED ON THE NEXT PAGE

TABLE 6.5 (CONT.)

	• What happens if you don't express any negative feelings that you have?	• If you don't express negative feelings, they can build up inside of you, and you can eventually explode in anger over some trivial matter.
	• What happens if you express negative feelings in a hostile manner, such as by shouting or screaming?	• If you yell, sometimes the other person becomes defensive and yells back, and the problem only gets worse, not better.
	• Why is it helpful to constructively express negative feelings to someone by explaining what specific behaviors upset you?	• Constructively expressing negative feelings can lead to a change in the other person's behavior, averting similar situations in the future.
Active Listening	• When someone is talking to you, why is it important to let that person know you are listening?	• Active listening lets the person know he or she has your attention and that you care about what he or she is saying.
	• Why can paraphrasing what the other person has said be helpful?	• Paraphrasing (or repeating back what you heard) tells the person that you have understood his or her point.
Compromise and Negotiation	• When people are having a disagreement, how can compromising be helpful?	• Compromising enables people to resolve disagreements because each person gets at least part of what he or she wants.

TABLE 6.5 (CONT.)

	• Why is it sometimes necessary to negotiate in order to reach a compromise?	• The first compromise that someone suggests is not always acceptable to the other person. Negotiation often helps people reach a compromise that they agree is good.
Requesting a Time-out	• How can taking a break during a heated argument be useful?	• Taking a break when an argument becomes stressful can help everyone cool off. It is easier to solve disagreements when people are calm.
	• What happens sometimes when you feel tensions rising during a disagreement and you continue to argue?	• When tensions get worse, it becomes more and more difficult to solve problems.

The introduction to a communication skill, including establishing the rationale, discussing the steps, and modeling of the skill, are illustrated in a case example provided below. The transcript is from the ninth BFT session with a family that included a male client and his parents. In this session the therapist introduces the skill of expressing negative feelings. The transcript begins after the therapist has reviewed progress toward goals and the previous week's homework assignment.

Therapist: Today I will be introducing a new communication skill in our family session: expressing negative feelings. I'd like to know your ideas about why it's important to be able to express negative feelings.

Client: People can know how you really feel instead of holding it all in and letting things build up.

Therapist: Exactly. You can avoid that "straw that broke the camel's back." By expressing negative feelings when you have them you don't let things build up and build up until something relatively minor happens and all those feelings that have been built up come out at once. What other purposes can communicating negative feelings serve?

Father: I think in a way it can help to correct a situation.

Therapist: I agree, that's an important point. If you communicate a negative feeling and you are specific enough about what the person did that

| | caused that feeling, often you can prevent that from occurring again in the future. It gives the other person an opportunity to change their behavior. |

Mother: But that doesn't mean that they will change their behavior!

Therapist: That's true, you can never be guaranteed that expressing a negative feeling will cause the other person to change. However, I have found that if you express the feeling in a constructive way, there is a better chance that the person will listen and try to change.

Mother: I guess it's worth trying.

Therapist: Right. The skill of expressing negative feelings can be divided into four different steps, as shown on this poster *(points to poster)*. Why do you think it's important to look at the person?

Father: To get his attention, or hers! *(laughing, looks at his wife)*.

Therapist: Good. And what's so important about having a serious facial expression?

Client: It lets the person know you're not kidding, that you really mean it.

Therapist: Right. The second step is to tell the person what they did that upset you. Here the goal is to be as specific as possible, so the person knows exactly what they did . . .

[The remaining steps of the skill are discussed before the therapist models it as below.]

Therapist: I am going to give you some examples, based on my own experience, of how to express a negative feeling and how not to express it. I've been living with a roommate for the last year, and one source of conflict between us is she leaves clothes around the house. I know that for myself it is more useful to say, "Dawn, would you please pick up your clothes that are in the living room and hang them up? It bothers me when they are laying around—it just makes me feel a little tense," as opposed to saying, "You are very inconsiderate, you're lazy, you're a slob, you're the worst roommate I've ever had," which is tempting to say sometimes. What do you see as the difference between saying it those two ways?

Mother: The first way you said it, at least you told her what upset you.

Therapist: That's right, I was specific about which of her behaviors upset me, leaving her clothes around *(therapist points to second step of the skill on the poster)*. Which way did you think was a better way to communicate feelings?

Client: When you said it "bothered" you and made you "tense," I thought that was pretty clear, but not too hard on your roommate. I think she would be insulted if you started calling her names.

Therapist: I agree, calling someone names like "slob" or "lazy" isn't going to help solve the problem very much . . .

After the therapist has modeled the skill, the remainder of the session is spent providing family members with opportunities to practice the skill in role plays. The nature and uses of role plays have been described in the orientation meeting (Chapter 3), so that by this time in BFT the family is aware that role-playing is used to teach communication skills. The goal of each session in which a new communication skill is introduced is to engage each family member in at least two role plays of that skill.

Role-playing

The therapist explains to family members that he or she would now like to give them an opportunity to practice the communication skill in a role play. The therapist turns to one family member, preferably not the most dysfunctional individual in the family, and asks that person to think of a situation that recently occurred where he or she could have used the skill. It does not matter whether the person actually used the skill, or even said anything at all. Rather, it is only important that it would have been appropriate for the person to use the skill in that situation. It is best if the situation involved another family member who is present at the session, but this is not absolutely necessary. The role play should be conducted with only two active participants in order to assure that participants focus on the key points in the skills training.

When the family member has identified an example, he or she briefly explains it to the therapist. If the situation is suitable, the therapist requests the person to help set up the role play. Although role plays can be conducted with everyone remaining seated and not moving from their chairs, we prefer to recreate the situation more vividly by having participants in the role play get out of their seats, move into positions that resemble the situation, and rearrange furniture, as necessary. This active approach makes it easier for family members to "get into" the role play and for the therapist to clearly demarcate the beginning and end of each role play.

The family member, with the help of the other person who was involved in the situation, arranges the role play situation accordingly. If the situation involved someone who is not present at the session, the family member enlists the help of someone present to play that role. When the role play is set up, the therapist instructs the family member to act as if the situation is actually occurring and to show what happened. If the person did not say anything in the original situation, the therapist instructs him or her to try using the skill that has just been discussed. To make sure that the person has understood what he or she is supposed to do, the therapist can ask the person to explain the goal in the role play. The person playing the other role is told to respond as he or she did (or would do) in that situation. The remaining family members are requested to observe the person in the role play and prepare to provide constructive feedback.

Providing Positive Feedback

The actual role play then commences, continuing for several exchanges and usually lasting between thirty seconds and two minutes. The therapist ends the role play by saying "Stop" or "That's good" (this can be combined with a hand signal, such as holding up a hand to signify "stop" like a traffic cop, or forming a "T" with both hands like "time-out" in a game). Immediately after stopping the action the therapist elicits positive feedback from other family members about the person's performance in the role play by asking questions such as *"What did you like about the way _____ did that role play?"* and *"Which steps of the skill did you see _____ doing in that interaction?"* The family member should be provided with specific, positive feedback about his or her attempt to use the skill. Feedback focuses both on the basic components of the skill, repeatedly drawing the attention of family members back to the steps of the skill listed on the poster, and on other relevant dimensions of social skill, such as voice tone and facial expression (see Tables 6.1 and 6.2). The therapist gives limited general positive feedback to encourage effort (e.g., *"You did a good job"*), focusing primarily on specific attributes of the performance (e.g., *"I really like the way you were so clear about saying what you wanted. I thought your voice tone was nice and warm, too"*). Similarly, when family members provide general feedback, they are encouraged to be specific about what they liked. Negative comments are interrupted until the positive comments have been made. Feedback in all cases is given directly to the person practicing the skill, not to the therapist. The total amount of time spent giving positive feedback after a role play is usually one to three minutes.

When the role play performance has been poor, or when dealing with family members who tend to be overly critical, the therapist can elicit positive feedback by framing a specific question. The therapist identifies one component of the person's role play that was performed adequately and solicits feedback from family members about that aspect. For example, if "John's" eye contact was good during the role play, the therapist could ask family members, *"What did you think about John's eye contact just then?"*

Providing Corrective Feedback

After positive feedback, corrective feedback is given about how to improve performance of the skill. Rather than focusing on what the person did not do or what they did poorly, corrective feedback informs them about how to do the skill better next time. Corrective feedback can be given by anyone in the family or by the therapist. However, we recommend that in the early stages of communication-skills training, as the family is becoming more familiar with the social-skills training approach and the therapist is gauging their comfort with learning the skills, the therapist take responsibility for providing most of the corrective feedback. When the family appears at ease with social-skills training, the therapist can elicit these comments from family members. Corrective feedback is given in very limited doses, with usually one or two suggestions provided each time. As with positive feedback, the focus of corrective feedback is both on the components of the skill that are listed on the poster and on other nonverbal and paralinguistic elements.

The major reason for giving corrective feedback is to help the person improve his or her performance in the next role play, which is based on the same situation as the previous one. Therefore, immediately after the corrective feedback is given, the person is requested to engage in the same role play again and to make one or two minor changes in behavior. For example, the therapist might say, *"I noticed that when you made your request you didn't speak very loudly. I'd like you to do that role play one more time and this time to try to speak more loudly. Okay?"*

The choice of which behaviors to focus on improving from one role play to the next is determined by two factors:

1. the salience of the behavior; and

2. how easily the behavior can be changed.

For example, (1) speaking in a very low voice tone is a very salient social skill deficit, because it is difficult to hear, and even if the person is heard, he or she will often not be taken seriously; (2) most people find it easy to learn how to be more behaviorally specific in their communications, but facial expressiveness may be difficult to improve, especially in clients with blunted affect. This does not mean that the therapist ignores problem areas that are difficult to change. Instead, the therapist alternates between easier and more difficult skill components as the focus of change.

Additional Behavior Shaping

After the corrective feedback has been given and a second role play is conducted, the therapist once again elicits positive feedback from the family members. At first, attention is drawn to the specific skill component(s) that the person changed from the first role play to the second, with additional feedback given for other positive aspects of the performance. After providing the positive feedback, the therapist either continues working on that person's skills for one or two more role plays or goes on to the next family member. The decision about whether to continue working with the same person is determined by level of skill at the end of the second role play and his or her apparent willingness to continue working. If the decision is made to go on to the next person, corrective feedback for the second role play is skipped, because the person will not have the opportunity to immediately use this feedback in the following role play. If the therapist chooses to do some additional work with the same person, corrective feedback and suggestions for improvement are given. In addition, other skills training methods may be employed at this point (e.g., coaching, prompting), which are described in the section following this one titled Supplementary Skills Training Procedures.

The process of engaging family members in role plays and providing them with feedback is illustrated below. The excerpt is taken from the first session in which the skill of expressing positive feelings was introduced, the fourth BFT session. The participants in the session included June (the client) and her mother, Sheila. The session took place in the family's apartment. The transcript begins after the mother has done several role plays and feedback has been given.

Therapist:	June, I was wondering whether there was something that your mother did in the past few days that pleased you.
Client:	Her cooking.
Therapist:	Good. Is there something specific? Some specific dish that she made?
Client:	Yeah, London broil.
Therapist:	Okay, and when she made that, did you tell her that it pleased you?
Client:	I think so.
Therapist:	Good. I'd like to do a role play with this situation. Where were you when you said that?
Client:	I think I told her from the kitchen.
Therapist:	Okay, could you reenact that for me? Where were you standing?
Client:	By the door.

Therapist:	Would you go and stand over there?
Client:	Okay. *(She moves into position.)*
Therapist:	And Sheila, where were you?
Mother:	I was in the kitchen. *(She gets up and moves into position.)*
Therapist:	Please show us what you said.
Client:	Mom, you really outdid yourself this time.
Mother:	Great! What did I do that made you so happy? What did you like?
Client:	Everything. You see, there's nothing on my plate! *(turning to the therapist)* This kind of conversation goes on every day.
Therapist:	Good, let's stop the role play here. *(Speaking to Mother)* Sheila, what did you like about the way June said that?
Mother:	I appreciate that she let me know how she felt. *(Turning to June)* I like the fact that you don't take me for granted. I like to feel appreciated.
Therapist:	So you liked what she told you?
Mother:	Yes.
Therapist:	Good. Was June able to follow all of the steps of expressing positive feelings that we have listed here *(pointing to the poster)*?
Mother:	Pretty much. Sometimes she doesn't look at me when she's speaking, but I don't think it's because she's insincere.
Therapist:	That's a good point. June, you said you sometimes talk to your mom from the next room. It can be hard for people to hear you and to know what you mean to say when you yell from the next room. I'd like you to do this role play again, and this time come into the room, sit down next to your mom, and look at her when you tell her you were pleased by the dinner she cooked.
Client:	All right. *(She leaves the room, reenters, and pulls a chair up next to her mother.)* Mom, I really enjoyed that dinner. You've really done it again. That steak was really delicious.
Mother:	Thank you, June.
Therapist:	You did a very good job, June. I like the way you brought the chair over and how you sat down right next to your mother. You looked at her this time. Did you notice the difference this time, Sheila?
Mother:	Yes, I did.
Therapist:	Good. Keeping in mind the other points of this skill *(pointing to the poster)*, you said June was able to look at you this time. The second point of this skill is saying what the person did that pleased you. Was she specific about what you did that pleased her?
Mother:	Yes, June, you complimented me about my cooking.
Therapist:	Right. June, I also liked the fact that you were so clear about how you felt. You said you "really enjoyed" the dinner. That was a good example of how to combine all the steps of this skill together.

After one family member has had the chance to practice the skill in a few role plays, the therapist goes on to the next person, using the same approach of identifying a recent situation, setting up role plays, and giving positive and corrective feedback. If everyone in the family has had a chance to practice the skill and there is still time for additional practice, the therapist can set up more role plays based on other situations that recently happened.

Giving Homework

Toward the end of the session, when everyone has become familiar with the skill through their participation in role plays, the therapist gives a homework assignment to practice the skill on their own. Homework sheets are distributed to each family member, to be completed based on their efforts to use the skill out-of-session. The purpose of these sheets is for the family members to record situations where they tried to use the skill or where they could have used the skill but forgot to. The homework sheets (see Appendix 4) provide space to write down for each day of the week who was involved in the interaction, the nature of the situation, and what the person said. Family members are requested to identify at least one situation each day where they used the skill (or could have used it) and to record this situation on the homework sheet. The assignment should be completed at the end of each day. The therapist briefly reviews the rationale for giving homework (i.e., it gives family members an opportunity to practice the skill in their natural environment while providing critical information to the therapist on how skill development is proceeding). Finally, the therapist helps family members anticipate problems in completing the assignment. Family members are asked where they can put their homework sheets so they will not forget to complete them, and whether there are any obstacles they can identify that could interfere with doing the assignment. To facilitate compliance with homework on communication skills, family members are requested to bring their homework sheets to their own family meetings (held without the therapist) and to discuss some of the situations each person has identified where the skill was (or could have been) used. Obstacles to completing homework can be addressed at these family meetings.

An example of how to give the homework assignment is provided below from the same family session transcript as the previous example.

Therapist:	You came up with some really good examples today. Like I said before, it's very important for you to practice these skills so you can become skillful and comfortable with them. In order to help you remember to practice, I have a homework assignment for you *(hands out homework sheets)*. This assignment involves using the same skill of expressing positive feelings that we've been going over today. What I'd like you to do is to record each day, at the end of the day, a person who pleased you. I would also like you to write what the person did that pleased you, and what you said. Think about everyday sorts of things that you can comment on, such as looking good, helping, cooking meals, just being pleasant, and so on. Sheila, where could you put your homework sheet where you won't forget about it?
Mother:	I'm often in the kitchen, so I could put it on the refrigerator.
Therapist:	Good. And June, where could you put your sheet?
Client:	I think I'll put mine on my dresser.
Therapist:	All right. When we meet again next week, please bring your homework sheets so that we can go over them together. Also, I'd like you to bring your homework sheets to your own family meeting and discuss how your practice of this skill is going.

In the next session, after reviewing progress toward goals, the therapist asks for the homework assignments and reviews them with the family. The therapist gives positive feedback for completed or partially completed assignments. Then, the therapist uses one or two of the specific situations identified by each family member on the homework sheet to set up additional role plays. By conducting role plays based on situations recorded on the homework sheets, the therapist is able to judge each family member's ability to use the skill, and to provide further training via feedback and more role-playing. After role-playing a situation based on the homework assignment, the therapist can ask family members (including the person in the role play) whether the person's behavior was similar to what actually happened. This provides information to the therapist about whether the skill has successfully generalized to the home environment.

During the session after a new skill has been introduced, the therapist evaluates the extent to which family members have acquired that skill. One way of accomplishing this is to cover the poster with the steps of the skill for the first role play conducted with each family member during that session. The unprompted performance of family members is a good indication of their competence with the skill. After the role play, the poster is then shown to the person and the component steps of the skill reviewed, along with the provision of positive and corrective feedback. As in the session in which a new skill is introduced, repeated behavioral rehearsals in role plays and feedback gradually lead to improvements in the skill. If a family member records a situation on the homework assignment in which the skill could have been used, but was not, he or she is requested to practice the skill in the role play. If no homework was completed, the person is prompted to identify a recent situation where he or she could have used the skill, which is then role played, as in the first session (also, see later section in this chapter on Homework Noncompliance).

An example of the review of the homework assignment for the skill of making positive requests is provided in the excerpt from the session transcript below.

Therapist: The last time I was here we talked about making positive requests, and I asked you to fill out some papers to record times during the week when you made requests of other people. I'm glad to see that each of you wrote down something that happened.

                (Therapist inspects the homework sheets, and selects the client's sheet to begin the review.)

Therapist: James, I see that you had a few situations where you were able to make requests of other people.

Client: Yeah, I had one where I wanted my friend to come over so we could play music together.

Therapist: That sounds like a good one. Let's do a role play of it. Did you ask your friend over the telephone?

Client: Yes. I said it to him twice on the phone, and he didn't come, and then I said it to him once when he was over here.

Therapist: Let's see how you said it to him when he was over here. I'll play your friend.

Client: Alan.

Therapist: Okay, so I'll be Alan. Where were you?

Client:	We were in the living room. He dropped by to get some tickets. I got tickets for the Beck show.
Therapist:	Okay. What I'd like you to do is to show me how you made a request of Alan that night.
	(Therapist and client move into position for role play.)
Client:	I don't remember exactly what I said.
Therapist:	That's okay, just do it as if it were happening right now. Be your natural self.
Client:	Okay, I can do that. *(Begins role play)* Alan, I was wondering if you would give me a call Saturday afternoon and we could get together and jam. I'd like that—it's important to me.
Therapist:	I'd like that too. We haven't played in a while. If I don't call you, would you call me?
Client:	Sure, if I'm awake! *(End of role play.)*
Therapist:	Good! Was that kind of the way the conversation went?
Client:	Kind of, but I don't think I was that articulate.
Therapist:	*(Turning to other family members)* What did you like about the way James communicated that just now?
Brother:	James, I think that it was very sincere, the way you said it was important to you.
Therapist:	Yes, I agree. James, I also liked your eye contact. You were looking right at him.
Client:	Yes, it felt good to do that.
Therapist:	What did you think of James's feeling statement?
Mother:	He really said two feeling statements. *(Turning to James)* You said that you would like Alan to come over. You also told him that it was important to you to get together so you could jam.
Therapist:	Yes, you did a real nice job then, James.

This role play illustrates the client's competence at the skill of making positive requests. In this same session, other family members showed similar levels of competence in their role plays, so the therapist proceeded to introduce the next communication skill of expressing negative feelings.

Based on the skill performance of family members in the role plays of situations identified on the homework assignment, the therapist decides whether to continue working on the same skill for the remainder of the session or to begin work on the next communication skill. If compliance with homework has been good and family members have demonstrated basic competence at the skill, the therapist introduces the next skill following the same methods as with the first skill. The therapist should allow for at least a half hour to introduce, model, and engage family members in role plays of a new skill. If less than a half hour remains in the session, the therapist can conduct additional role plays or end the session early. However, if the performance of family members is still marginal or compliance with homework has been poor, the remainder of the session is spent practicing the skill in role plays.

Within each skills training session, the majority of time is spent actively practicing the skills in role plays and providing feedback designed to improve the person's performance. Table 6.6 provides a general framework for how time is spent during a communication-skills training session. The emphasis in skills training is on having the person show how they handled a particular situation, rather than tell about it. Feedback is tailored to produce small changes in the skill, which, over a succession of role plays, gradually approximates the targeted skill (i.e., shaping). Above all, the therapist strives to create a learning environment that consistently recognizes and reinforces the efforts of family members to learn new skills, and that minimizes criticism and negative feedback.

TABLE 6.6
ALLOCATION OF TIME IN COMMUNICATION-SKILLS
TRAINING SESSIONS

Time	Activity
5–10 minutes	Review goals and family meeting
10–15 minutes	Review homework, conduct skills training on homework situations
5–10 minutes	Establish rationale for new communication skill
10–25 minutes	Model new skill, engage family members in role plays, provide feedback
5–10 minutes	Assign homework

Supplementary Skills Training Procedures

In addition to modeling the skill at the beginning of the session and providing positive and corrective feedback, there are other strategies that the therapist can use to help family members acquire communication skills. In general, these strategies are best to use when simple instructions and feedback fail to produce the desired changes in behavior in the role play. Several of these methods are described here.

Modeling

There are several different ways that therapist modeling can help family members improve their communication skills. Three different uses of modeling are described below.

Supplementary Modeling

Just as modeling a new skill at the beginning of a session demonstrates to family members how that skill can be used, *supplementary modeling* throughout the session can facilitate further improvements. If simple instructions prove insufficient for improving a family member's social-skill performance from one role play to the next, the therapist can model the skill in that same role play situation, taking the place of the family member. When modeling the skill, it is best if the therapist exchanges places with the person for the role play and instructs the person to pay particular attention to the component of the skill that the therapist wishes to highlight. Immediately after the skill has been modeled, the family member and therapist exchange places again and the person tries the skill in a role play of the same situation. Positive reinforcement is then provided in the usual manner, with special attention given to the component of the skill that was the focus of the modeling.

For example, if the therapist instructs a husband to be more behaviorally specific when making a positive request to his wife in the next role play, but he is not able to do this, the therapist could use modeling as follows:

Therapist: *(Speaking to the husband)* I would like to model for you how to make a positive request. Let's change positions. I'm going to pretend to be you in this role play. What I would like you to do is to pay special attention to how I am very specific when I make the request. Any questions?

Then, after the therapist has modeled the skill in the role play, he or she could ask:

Therapist: What did you notice about the request I just made? Was I specific? *(The therapist points to the second step on the poster for making a positive request.)*

Husband: Yes, you were quite clear about what you wanted done.

Therapist: Right. Let's change places back again *(husband resumes former position in the role play)*. I'd like you to do that role play once more, just like you saw me do it, and this time be sure to be specific about what you would like done. Okay?

Supplementary modeling is an excellent strategy that can often be used to help family members improve their communication. The therapist need not be concerned about overusing this method. Many family members find it easier to learn communication skills through observing another person demonstrate the skill than through detailed verbal instructions. They often also feel that their feelings are legitimized or validated when the therapist role-plays expressing them.

Negative Modeling

Negative modeling refers to the use of modeling by the therapist to demonstrate how not to communicate, rather than to show appropriate communication skills. Negative modeling can be especially helpful when the therapist is unsuccessful using other methods to change negative communication styles in a family member. This strategy is initiated by the therapist explaining the nature of the communication problem to the relevant family member and then stating that he or she will do a role play to demonstrate that problem. The family member participates in the role play while the therapist negatively models the behavior. This approach gives the family member an opportunity to see what it is like to be on the "receiving end" of a negative communication. After the role play, the therapist discusses with the family member why the behavior was problematic.

For example, some family members tend to make positive statements to another person that are often followed by negative comments, which have the effect of canceling out the positive feeling. One therapist working with a wife who displayed this communication problem used negative modeling in the following manner:

Therapist: Susan, I noticed that sometimes when you have a positive comment to make, you say something a little negative right after it.

Wife: I guess I do that sometimes.

Therapist: I would like to do a brief role play with you to demonstrate how that can be a problem. Let's both get up and stand in the middle of the room here. I'm going to greet you and I'd like you just to act as you naturally would. Is that okay?

Wife: Sure.

Therapist: *(Begins role play)* Hello there, Susan, good to see you! You sure look nice in that dress, but how come you're wearing those shoes. They don't match?!

(Wife, looking puzzled, begins to examine her shoes and appear indignant.)

Therapist: All right, let's stop this role play here. Susan, how did it feel when I gave you that compliment?

Wife: It didn't seem like a compliment. I was wondering what was wrong with my shoes.

Therapist: That's right, when you say something positive and then say something negative right after, the negative comment sticks with the person. Of course, Susan, your shoes are just fine. I was just pretending as an example for this role play.

Special caution should be taken when using negative modeling to assure the family member that the therapist is not making fun of him or her. This strategy is used sparingly with families.

Discrimination Modeling

This strategy represents a combination of standard (positive) and negative modeling. *Discrimination modeling* is used to highlight a particular component of social skill, usually a nonverbal or paralinguistic element. The therapist first explains to the family that he or she will do two role plays in a row, and their task is to notice the difference between the two examples. Then, the therapist first models a very poor example of the skill, followed by a very good demonstration of the skill. After the second role play, the therapist elicits comments from family members about the difference between the role plays and which one was more effective. Discrimination modeling is useful in illustrating the importance of social skills such as voice tone (e.g., meek or hostile vs. appropriately firm and assertive), voice loudness, eye contact, and the use of verbal feeling statements.

Coaching

Coaching refers to the use of verbal prompts given during the role play to improve a specific social-skill component. Coaching is usually done by whispering the next step of the skill to the family member engaged in a role play, who follows this step accordingly. After the role play is completed, positive feedback is given as usual, especially regarding the component that was coached. Another role play of the same situation is conducted, but this time the therapist does not coach the family member.

For example, it is common for people to omit clear, verbal statements about their feelings when practicing communication skills, even after they have been reminded to make a feeling statement before the role play. When this happens, the therapist can stand next to the person during the role play and whisper into his or her ear at the appropriate time, "Tell how it made you feel" or "Tell how you would feel if he or she did that to you." The therapist can even coach the person to make a specific statement during the role play, such as "I felt angry when . . ."

Family members are often surprised and amused the first time the therapist uses coaching during a role play. However, people usually appreciate the help offered by the therapist, and succeed in improving their skills in subsequent role plays. Coaching can be used relatively often with some families. However, the therapist should be careful not to coach too much. Some family members are slow at integrating the different components of a skill in a role play, but are capable of doing so without coaching if given the time. Useful assessment information is also obtained by allowing the family member to complete the role play without interference.

Prompting

Prompting is just like coaching, except that instead of giving verbal reminders during the role play, nonverbal cues are given. To use prompting, the therapist explains before the role play that he or she will employ a specific prompt to remind the person to work on a particular skill, and that prompt is demonstrated. Then, the therapist positions him or herself so that the family member can clearly see the therapist during the role play, who then prompts the person to use the skill as needed throughout the behavior rehearsal. After reinforcement is given, the role play is repeated, with the therapist fading the prompting.

Prompting is especially effective for improving voice loudness and eye contact. For voice loudness, the therapist can use the prompt of motioning his or her thumb upward to indicate "speak louder." To improve eye contact, the therapist can prompt by pointing to his or her eye at the relevant times during the role play. See Liberman et al. (1989) for additional hand signals to use as prompts for training communication skills. In most cases, prompting needs to be used in multiple role plays and gradually faded in order to produce durable changes.

Therapist Modeling of Good Communication Skills

We have described how the therapist often uses modeling in role plays to teach families specific communication skills. In addition to this important use of modeling, the therapist strives to model good communication throughout all of his or her interactions with family members. Therapists need to develop an awareness of their own interpersonal styles and make special efforts to ensure that their behavior is consistent with the guidelines outlined in this chapter. For example, when requesting a family member to engage in a role play, the therapist says, "I would appreciate if . . ." or "I would like you to . . ." (making a positive request), rather than "I want you to" or "It's your turn to . . ." The therapist generously praises family members (using the skill of expressing positive feelings) for their efforts and the small improvements they make, always taking care to be as behaviorally specific as possible. The therapist uses "active listening" skills in every session to show family members he or she is listening and understanding what is said, and to acknowledge each person's feelings. The therapist even judiciously uses expressing negative feelings with the family, such as conveying concern about problems with homework completion, irregular attendance at sessions, or repeated disruptions or distractions during the session.

Likewise, the therapist avoids common pitfalls when communicating with families. For example, the therapist does not interrupt family members or raise his or her voice except to stop negative exchanges. He or she is prepared, however, to try to get conversations "on track" quickly if digressions occur. When conflicts develop, the therapist does not try to find "who is at fault" and assign blame, but instead gathers information pertinent to resolving the problem. Thus, the therapist's own behavior serves as an example throughout BFT of how good communication skills can help families cope with and overcome difficult, long-standing problems.

Hints for Training Specific Communication Skills

To inform therapists about some of the nuances involved in teaching communication skills to families, we briefly discuss each skill and provide hints about how to present it to the family and engage its cooperation.

Core Communication Skills

Expressing Positive Feelings

One of the major purposes of teaching this skill is to increase mutually desirable (reinforcing) behaviors among family members through the frequent, spontaneous expression of positive feelings. Clear behavioral specificity and positive feeling statements help people know that the small things they do for each other are appreciated, which results in a more supportive family atmosphere. Overall, this skill is one of the easiest and most rewarding skills to teach, and families tend to respond very positively to it.

When teaching this skill, the therapist will encounter some family members who seem to be unable to identify anything that another person has done recently, especially a relative, that pleased him or her. Sometimes family members assume an indignant or superior manner when reporting that nothing other people do pleases them, as if to say, "Nobody ever thinks of me." With these individuals, it is best if the therapist does not rush to provide numerous examples of possible things that other people have done that pleased them. Instead, the therapist patiently waits a little while and gives the person some time to think of a recent example. This places subtle pressure on the person to identify some instance, however minor, in which someone pleased him or her. Other family members can help the person remember an example by mentioning recent events.

We have found that expressing positive feelings is a useful skill to integrate into every session for families in which negative affect predominates. For example, at the end of each session, the therapist can lead a round-robin of expressing positive feelings. Each participant in the session, including the therapist, expresses a positive feeling about something that someone else did that pleased him or her. These communications are not role plays, but are actual interactions between the participants. By prompting these positive feelings, family members receive important reinforcement for their effort in participating in the BFT sessions.

Making Positive Requests

The ability to make positive requests is critical for people who live together and naturally have some interdependence. Positive requests are useful not only for asking people to do favors, but also for requesting changes in behavior, including annoying behavior. Thus, a family member can elect to make a positive request of a relative instead of expressing a negative feeling. For example, if someone is playing the stereo loudly at night, the person can state, "I would really appreciate it if you could turn down the music after 11:00 PM; it would make it easier for me to sleep" (a positive request), rather than saying, "It annoys me when you play the stereo late at night because I can't sleep (an expression of a negative feeling)." This is a convenient strategy for resolving minor problems in many families, especially when there is a reluctance to express negative feelings or some individuals are particularly sensitive about having negative feelings expressed to them.

Family members often have difficulty making clear feeling statements (e.g., "I would appreciate," "I would like," It would make me feel good") when they request something. Discrimination modeling can be useful for highlighting the importance of positive feeling statements when making a request. For example, saying, "I would appreciate it if you could pick up my cough medicine at the drug store" is more effective than "Could you pick up my cough medicine at the store?" Sometimes the feeling statement is tagged on at the end of the request, like an afterthought. We encourage family members to make feeling statements as soon as possible when they make the request, and we explain that this increases the chances that their request will be gratified.

Another point is that family members should be aware that a positive request is a *request*, not a *demand*, and that the other person is free to deny the request. Therefore, the therapist is alert to requests that are made in a threatening or coercive manner, with the implication that they cannot be refused. When demands are made, the therapist prompts the person to rephrase their demand as a positive request.

A final consideration is whether an explanation needs to be given when making a request. In most cases, the more someone explains why he or she would like something done, the greater the chances are that the other person will agree to do it. For many day-to-day interactions, however, such explanations are not necessary, because the reason for the request is obvious. We have found that if someone makes a substantial request that will require considerable effort on the part of the other person, providing an explanation as to why the request is important is very helpful.

Expressing Negative Feelings

This is one of the most difficult communication skills for family members to learn, because it involves unlearning other ways of dealing with negative feelings (e.g., suppression, making hostile and critical statements). When teaching this skill, it is important for the therapist to emphasize the constructive nature of appropriate expressions of negative feelings. That is, by communicating a negative feeling to someone about something he or she did and suggesting how it can be prevented in the future, the speaker attempts to rectify the situation. Thus, the goal of expressing negative feelings is not simply to achieve a catharsis.

Sometimes family members are quite clearly in conflict about a particular issue during the first session in which expressing negative feelings is taught. It might appear attractive to the therapist to train family members in this skill using the situation at hand. However, we recommend that family members first be involved in role plays of situations that are not currently pressing (e.g., something that happened over the past week) before attempting situations that are current. We have found that family members who are not familiar with the steps of expressing negative feelings are sometimes resistant to changing their behavior in role plays in which they deal with issues about which they have strong feelings. The artificial nature of role plays allows family members to distance themselves from their usual feelings and to try new and different ways of communicating. This "distance" is especially important for the first few role plays of this skill, because strong negative feelings can disrupt a person's ability to learn new interpersonal skills.

Recipients of expressions of negative feelings are informed that their primary responsibility is to convey that they are listening. Rather than responding by giving their own point of view, they are instead encouraged to demonstrate to the speaker, through verbal and nonverbal responses (e.g., looking the speaker in the eye, asking clarifying questions, paraphrasing what they have heard), that they have heard what has been said. During in-session role plays, they are explicitly given the role of "listener" and given feedback for their listening behavior at the end. In families where conflict is high and members are defensive, the therapist encourages recipients of expressions of negative feelings to first paraphrase what they have heard prior to making any other response. This restatement provides family members with a moment to collect their thoughts and consider their response.

An example of shaping this listening behavior is provided below. Kathy, a depressed 32-year-old woman, and Bill, her 35-year-old husband, are the clients.

Therapist:	Kathy, the last time we worked on expressing negative feelings I was disappointed that you forgot to do your homework. Did you have a chance to practice the skill this week?
Kathy:	Yes, it was mostly Bill who upset me. *(Bill, the husband, looks annoyed as therapist inspects homework sheets.)*
Therapist:	I see here that you expressed a negative feeling to Bill on Tuesday about the mortgage being late. I would like to see how that happened. Kathy, where were you when you talked about this with Bill?

Kathy:	Sitting at the table after dinner. Bill was across from me, like we are here.
Therapist:	Bill, do you remember this and what you said?
Bill:	Yeah.
Therapist:	Okay, Kathy you can begin.
Kathy:	Bill, I am really upset that the mortgage was late. Our credit rating will be ruined.
Bill:	Well, if you took more . . .
Therapist:	Wait, Bill, what is your job when someone is giving you negative feedback?
Bill:	Oh, yeah, but . . . well, to show I am listening.
Therapist:	Right. How do you do that?
Bill:	Look at her, nod my head, restate what she said to make sure I heard it right.
Therapist:	Great. How about giving it another try?
Bill:	I see, Kathy. You are upset because the mortgage got paid late and you are afraid about our credit rating. Me too. We just seem to be short each month. The money problems are terrible.
Therapist:	Bill, before we get into that topic, I would like you to give Kathy some feedback on her expression of negative feelings. Did she use all of the steps?
Bill:	Well, she told me she was upset and scared, and she was specific. She didn't make a request, though.
Therapist:	That's right. She was clear and specific, but did not suggest a change. And Kathy, what did Bill do that made you feel he was listening?
Kathy:	He sounds like he understands how concerned I am. He recognized I'm scared about our credit.
Therapist:	I thought so too. Now, it sounds like the money problems need to be the focus of some problem solving in the next couple of weeks. Let's put that up on the board as an area of concern.

Note that the therapist helped each family member to give feedback to the other for his or her effort in keeping the conversation calm and using the BFT skills. In addition, while the therapist acknowledged the financial issues, he or she avoided becoming embroiled in them during the communication skills training.

Family members often have difficulty labeling their own specific feelings, even when those feelings are quite evident in their nonverbal and paralinguistic skills. We have observed that when people are able to specify a negative feeling verbally, their voice tone and facial expressions become slightly less affectively charged, and it becomes easier for the listener to understand why the person is upset. When teaching how to express negative feelings, the therapist can generate examples of negative feelings from family members (e.g., anger, frustration, annoyance, anxiety, pain, fear, sadness), listing the different emotions on a poster. Then, when someone has difficulty labeling a specific feeling, the poster can be taken out and the person can choose from the list of feelings. Teaching people to express negative feelings may involve helping them to identify the subtle physiological cues that accompany feelings, such as increased heart rate, feeling "hot," and agitation. The sooner a person can be aware of a negative feeling and communicate it to another person, the easier it will be for the situation to be resolved and for the feeling to subside.

In addition to the steps of expressing negative feelings, there are three general rules for using this skill:

1. use "I" statements and avoid blaming "you" statements;

2. express one negative feeling about one behavior at a time and do not string together a series of negative comments; and

3. communicate the feeling as soon as possible after the incident occurrs, rather than after waiting a long time.

The examples we have provided here have focused chiefly on the expression of negative feelings such as anger, irritation, annoyance, etc. It is important to note that often angry feelings reflect a sense of being "hurt" or rejected by another, and therapists are encouraged to challenge participants to discriminate between angry and hurt feelings, and to articulate their feelings as accurately as possible. Listeners are sometimes more readily able to accept that their behavior has "hurt" another person then that it has "angered" them.

Expressing negative feelings can also be used to express other feelings that may not be related to another person's behavior, such as depression, anxiety, or boredom. Family members are encouraged to express such feelings to each other, when possible identifying events or behaviors related to those feelings or ways that another person can help them cope with them.

In this section, we have emphasized using the expression of negative feelings as a first step in rectifying problematic situations. As family members acquire stronger skills, they may also wish to discuss troubling past events that they have been unable and/or unwilling to discuss successfully in the past. While the objective of gaining this skill is not to focus on events that happened long ago, therapists may occasionally find that participants would like to discuss past affectively loaded events, using the skills they have recently developed. The therapist must weigh the benefits of spending time on these issues against the cost of delaying work on other skills. One strategy that the therapist can use is to defer these topics to final sessions, when the highest levels of all skills have been attained, and then allocate special time to the one or two most important issues.

Supplementary Communication Skills

Active Listening

Active listening is taught when family members do not appear to attend to what others say. They may interrupt others, misinterpret them or ignore what they have said, or simply appear inattentive when they are talking. The net effect is that the speaker does not feel heard, which can lead to frustration and conflicts. Active listening is an especially useful skill to teach families who are prone to rapidly escalating arguments. Active listening skills such as paraphrasing what the other person has said tend to facilitate peaceful conflict resolution, because family members are more likely to feel understood.

The therapist can choose to teach active listening at any point in BFT after the educational sessions have been completed, including before teaching expressing positive feelings. When the therapist decides to teach active listening, an entire session should be devoted to it (or more than one if necessary). The session is conducted in much the same manner as those for the other skills, following the format of establishing the rationale, discussing the steps, modeling the skill, etc.

One difference between teaching active listening and other communication skills is the way in which role plays are structured. In order to model and practice listening skills in role plays, someone needs to take the part of the "speaker." The therapist elicits the help of another family member, who can be the speaker and talk about something for a couple of minutes during the role play. Before the role play is initiated, a topic is chosen by the speaker that he or she can talk about. The topic should be something innocuous, such as a movie or TV program the person saw, a party the person recently attended, plans for cooking a meal, or upcoming holidays, rather than a conflict-laden topic. The role play lasts for several minutes (longer than role plays for the other skills), followed by feedback and additional practice in the usual sequence.

Homework assignments for active listening skills also differ from those for the other communication skills, because this skill is more difficult to monitor on a daily basis. Instead of daily monitoring, homework is given to family members to practice active listening in their weekly family meeting. At this meeting, each person spends five minutes with another person practicing his or her listening skills. Other family members observe which specific listening skills the person used (see "Active Listening Skills" in Appendix 4), and provide positive feedback at the end of the time period. The homework sheet for "active listening" contains spaces for family members to record which specific steps of the skill they observed during these practice periods at home.

Compromise and Negotiation

Deficits in this skill usually do not become apparent until problem-solving training has begun. During problem-solving, some families have great difficulty agreeing on a definition of the problem or on the best solution(s) for solving that problem. Teaching families how to compromise and negotiate can facilitate their ability to solve problems cooperatively. In some families, competence in this skill can obviate the need for most formal problem solving, because "problems" are resolved before they fully develop. Compromise and negotiation can be taught before training in problem solving begins, and should be grounded in good active listening and expressing negative feeling skills.

If the therapist chooses to teach compromise and negotiation, at least one full session should be devoted to it. The format for teaching this skill is the same as for the other communication skills (for more on how to teach this skill to psychiatric clients, see Douglas & Mueser, 1990). When learning the steps of compromise and negotiation, people tend to have the most difficulty with the fourth step, "repeat back what you heard" (see Table 6.3). People are used to listening to the other person's perspective and then giving their own, without ever clearly showing that they have understood what the other person said. The consequence is that each person continues to argue his or her own position, believing that he or she has not been fully understood, and never getting to the point of discussing compromises. Thus, familiarity with the skill of active listening facilitates learning compromise and negotiation.

Although we have broken down compromise and negotiation into five simple steps, this skill can require more time and patience than other skills, because the first or second compromises that are offered may not be suitable to one of the parties. The art of negotiation is to keep the dialogue going, with each person offering suggestions while maintaining a state of calm and mutual tolerance. The nature of a compromise is that it reflects a "middle ground" alternative in which each person gets at least part of what they want, and neither person "wins" or "loses" outright. When confronted with a major difference between family members, in order to encourage them not to give up and to continue to negotiate toward a suitable compromise, the therapist communicates optimism and confidence to the family that they will be able to reach a compromise if they continue to work on it. This does not mean that every issue is negotiable (e.g., the client wants to smoke in bed). However, there is room to settle most differences between family members through compromise and negotiation.

Requesting a Time-out

When angry or frustrated feelings become overwhelming, constructive communication is impossible and further attempts at conflict resolution can only worsen the situation. Teaching family members to request a time-out when they are feeling upset and tensions are rising can buy time that everyone can use to calm down. Then, when family members convene again at a later time, people are able to approach the problem in a better frame of mind that is more likely to lead to a successful resolution.

For many families, teaching expressing negative feelings is sufficient to prevent angry feelings from building up to the point where they interfere with constructive communication. Some individuals, however, have great difficulty recognizing their own angry feelings until they become severe and out of control. This skill is a useful strategy for these individuals (and their relatives), and it should be taught after teaching expressing negative feelings. A key aspect of teaching this skill involves ensuring that each family member can identify his or her earliest internal cues of provocation. Thus, the therapist can ask each participant in turn, *"How do you know you are getting angry? What cues do you feel in your body?"* Many individuals are able to identify somatic cues, such as tightness in chest, "band around my head," flush face, etc.; others may need prompting or directed questioning for this task. The goal is for each participant to learn to identify his or her internal cues of intense anger, so that they can be used to prompt a request for a time-out.

When one person becomes angry or upset during a disagreement, either that person or the other person can request a time-out. Some people find it very difficult to walk away from a situation when they become angry, and they may intensify the confrontation by demanding an immediate resolution to the problem. It may be very difficult to teach such individuals how to request a time-out, and attention may need to focus instead on teaching the skill to other family members who may become involved in such conflicts.

The need to teach requesting a time-out often appears in a session in which tempers flare and prompting family members to use expressing negative feelings meets with limited success. In these situations, the therapist can intervene to do in vivo training of this skill by first modeling it and then prompting it in the relevant family members. We have found that this approach is helpful in resolving these emotionally charged situations. It is also desirable to give the family a homework assignment to practice this skill (see Appendix 4) and to review the skill again in the following session. Most families do not need to be taught this skill. However, in families where disagreements often lead to angry, unproductive arguments, even after training in other communication skills, requesting a time-out may be an important skill to use to restore calm during a conflict.

Some family members use this skill to calm down and only need the therapist to validate this coping strategy and normalize its use. We illustrate one such case example below.

Case Example

A 26-year-old bipolar woman participated in BFT with her 23-year-old sister and their parents. Early in treatment, family conflicts would quickly deteriorate into accusations, shouting matches, and tears, and the therapist was kept busy maintaining control of the session and keeping the family focused on learning the pertinent information and skills. All family members had made slow but steady progress in their communication skills. Toward the beginning of the fourteenth BFT session, after the family had already started training in problem solving, the mother expressed some discouragement over her progress.

Mother:	I don't think I'm learning much. I still fly off the handle when I get mad.
Therapist:	Well, I think we talked about how hard it is to break certain habits of communicating. It's hard to stay calm when you're feeling upset, and I think that's just a normal reaction for people to have.
Mother:	How about when your temper gets the best of you and you start to shake—I mean actually shake?
Therapist:	Do you find that happening to you?
Mother:	Yes! Definitely!
Therapist:	What do you do when that happens?
Mother:	Well, I can tell the shaking is a cue that I need to take a break. I know I'm not thinking rationally, and I just have to stop and not think and clear my mind. And then I'm in control again. But it takes a while.
Therapist:	It takes some time.
Mother:	Yes, the better part of a half hour.
Therapist:	Does that happen to other people?
Sister:	Yes, at work. You just get so frustrated, just can't control it, and you walk away so you don't explode.
Therapist:	Does that work, is it effective?
Sister:	Yes, it helps a lot.
Therapist:	It's better than staying in the situation and losing control.
Sister:	Yes, and saying something you really didn't mean, only out of a fit of anger.

Therapist:	Right. It's more effective to walk away from the situation and take what we call a "time-out."
Mother:	Right, and then come back and face it when you can think about it.
Client:	I do that sometimes.
Sister:	I know, it used to be a lot worse around here a while ago. Everybody was just "on" everyone else. I can feel how different it's been in the family—people are calmer. We can actually relate to each other and get along, but before it was horrible, everyone was on each other's nerves, yelling at this, yelling at that.
Therapist:	So, do you think that your mom's learning some things? She was frustrated. Do you think she's doing better?
Sister:	Yes, sure. She just gets frustrated and gets upset sometimes, but I don't think she's worse. I think she's a little calmer.
Mother:	I am getting better, learning.
Therapist:	Good!

Communication-Skills Training in Later BFT Sessions

More often than not, family members require some ongoing attention to their communication skills as they begin to learn problem solving. The therapist can expect "relapses" of old, ineffective, aversive communication styles when tensions rise and family members become frustrated. When such problems reappear, the therapist stops the action and prompts family members to use the skills that they learned in communication-skills training. Once the therapist has taught a specific skill to a family, he or she can assume that each family member is capable of using that skill if prompted. For example:

Father:	(Speaking to his son in an angry voice tone) If I've told you once I've told you a thousand times, LOCK THE DOOR after you come in at night!!
Therapist:	It sounds like you feel upset about what your son did last night. Is that true? (Notice how the therapist checks out his or her observation that the father is upset.)
Father:	You bet it is. He only thinks of himself.
Therapist:	I'd like you to tell your son how you feel right now, using the steps of the skill "expressing negative feelings" that you have practiced before.
Father:	(Speaking to son) I'm really mad that you left the door unlocked last night again. Can't you remember next time?
Son:	I'm sorry, Dad. I forgot.
Therapist:	(To father) I think you really did a good job just then of telling your son exactly how you felt when he left the door unlocked. This might be an important problem to spend some time on today . . . either making a positive request or problem solving about it.

The first strategy the therapist takes when old communication habits reemerge is to prompt the family member to use the skill without reminding him or her of its component steps. If the person is able to employ the skill after this prompt or requires only minimal feedback to improve communication, then the therapist has confirmation that the person is capable of using the skill. On the other hand, if the person has forgotten the steps of the skill, the therapist can take out the poster (or handout) containing the steps and review the skill again. When this is necessary, it means that the family member no longer has the skill in his or her behavioral repertoire, and additional time is set aside for retraining that skill.

We have found that it can be helpful to take a break from problem-solving training to conduct an occasional review session on communication skills. Review sessions employ the usual combination of modeling, role playing, and feedback to enhance performance. If the family has had a special problem on one specific skill, the entire session can be spent reviewing that skill. In other cases, the booster session can be devoted to reviewing several communication skills.

Some families are consistently able to use the communication skills when they are prompted by the therapist, but do not use them spontaneously on their own. Two strategies can improve the generalization of communication skills to the natural interactions between family members. First, additional homework can be given to practice the skills at home, and these assignments are then reviewed in the following session. When family members have difficulty remembering to use the skills at home, a problem-solving discussion can be held to generate ideas for how they can remember to use the skills (e.g., handouts with the skills can be posted prominently at home, family members can prompt each other to use the skills).

Second, the therapist can interrupt a family member when he or she fails to use a specific communication skill, but not prompt the person as to which skill was not used. Instead, the therapist encourages the family member to consider which communication skill he or she could have used. This requires the person to select the appropriate skill from an array of possible skills, a process which can facilitate the person's ability to spontaneously use these skills. Ultimately, it is desirable for family members to be able to monitor and prompt good communication between each other in order to build in a positive feedback loop. Therefore, the therapist engages other family members in identifying problems in communication and rectifying these problems through prompting the relevant skills.

Homework Noncompliance

As in all stages of BFT, non-compliance with homework needs to be addressed at the earliest possible time. It is common after the first one or two sessions on communication-skills training for some family members to forget to complete their homework assignments. The therapist responds to this situation by first praising those family members who completed their assignment. Mild disappointment or concern can be expressed to those members who did not complete the assignment, although the therapist should not try to lay a "guilt trip" on them. Then, family members who did not complete the assignment are given the homework sheet and are asked to complete it as best they can. The difficulties that family members experience recalling specific events that occurred over the past week are acknowledged, and the rationale for recording something every day on the homework sheet is repeated. Then, role plays are conducted and feedback is given based on the situations identified by the participants. At the end of the session, the therapist takes some extra time to discuss with family members obstacles to completing their homework. If more than one family member did not do the homework, the therapist does not introduce a new communication skill, focusing instead on additional practice on the same skill.

If everyone in the family "forgets" to do the assignment after the first communication-skills training session, the same strategy described above is followed. However, if noncompliance persists, the therapist needs to confront the problem even more directly. The therapist takes a problem-solving approach to considering the factors underlying noncompliance. First, the therapist checks that family members understand the rationale for homework; that is, homework provides the therapist with crucial information about how the skills are working for family members in their own environment. This can be accomplished by restating the rationale and/or asking family members to describe their understanding of the reason for assignment. Second, the therapist evaluates whether the assignment is sufficiently clear to the family. For example, family members may believe they are supposed to complete the sheet only when they have successfully used the skill, rather than when an appropriate situation has occurred; or family members may believe that the skills are to be used only in rare situations, such as when one becomes very angry or has a big favor to ask, rather than in everyday situations, such as when someone does something mildly annoying or a small request is made. Third, the therapist explores obstacles that may have interfered with homework completion. If significant obstacles are identified, the therapist takes out a problem-solving sheet and leads a discussion to develop a plan for how to overcome those obstacles.

The therapist communicates honest and direct concern to the family about their homework noncompliance, rather than frustration or annoyance. Family members may have concerns that the communication skills feel awkward to use or are unrealistic. These (and other) concerns are acknowledged and addressed by the therapist. For example, the therapist can explain that many people feel a little awkward when first trying out these communication skills on their own, but that they usually become more comfortable over time and eventually feel quite natural. While not everyone uses these skills, many people do, and these skills have been found to improve communication in many families. The therapist should not discount his or her ability to help shape family members' homework compliance over time, as well. For example, he or she can schedule telephone check-ins between sessions to "see how the homework is going," or reduce expectations by asking family members to complete the assignment every other day, if they are unable or unwilling to do it daily. We have found that working earnestly and diligently with families to facilitate their follow-through on homework results in some degree of compliance in the vast majority of families.

Pitfalls to Good Communication

Throughout BFT the therapist is alert for the presence of negative communication styles that can undermine successful conflict resolution. Sometimes these styles change as family members become adept at using more effective communication skills. However, often the therapist must intervene to correct destructive communication styles that can otherwise disrupt cooperative family work. For example, family members may interrupt each other while talking, presume to speak for others, or give mixed verbal and nonverbal messages, all of which can interfere with effective communication. A list of the most common pitfalls to good communication, based on Lester et al. (1980) and Mueser and Gingerich (1994), is contained in Table 6.7.

TABLE 6.7
ALTERNATIVES TO COMMON PITFALLS TO EFFECTIVE COMMUNICATION

Communication Problem	Example	Alternative
Shouting, Yelling, or Screaming		Speak in a firm, calm tone of voice.
Interruptions		Allow person to finish before talking.
Coercive Statements ("shoulds" and "musts")	"You should know when to put out the trash."	"I would appreciate it if you would take out the trash every night before dinner."
Mixing Positive and Negative Statements	"You look nice today, but why did you wear those shoes?"	"I really like the dress you're wearing today."
Blaming "You" Statements and Fault-Finding	"You made me mad all day."	"I felt angry when you didn't give me a ride this morning."
Speaking for Other ("we" statements)	"We are concerned that you have been sleeping a lot lately."	"I am concerned that you have been sleeping a lot lately."
Mind Reading	"You're angry at me for forgetting your movie date."	"You look angry. Are you feeling that way?"
Name-Calling or Trait-related Put-downs	"You're so inconsiderate."	"I get upset when I see your clothes laying all around the living room. I would appreciate it if you would pick them up."

CONTINUED ON THE NEXT PAGE

TABLE 6.7 (CONT.)

Dealing with Multiple Problems	"You lay around all day, don't take your medication, and haven't taken a shower in weeks."	"I'm concerned that you have been laying around the house all day doing nothing."
Overgeneralizations	"You always skip lunch."	"I noticed that you skipped lunch yesterday and today."
Dwelling on the Past	"You didn't visit me in the hospital this time, just like the first time I was in the hospital two years ago."	"I was disappointed that you didn't visit me in the hospital this last time."
Making Threats or Giving Ultimatums	"If you don't take your medication, I'm going to put you back in the hospital."	"I'm concerned that if you don't take your medication, your symptoms will return and you may have to go back to the hospital."
Getting off the Topic	Husband: "You leave clothes lying around." Wife: "Well, your desk is pretty messy."	Husband: "You leave clothes lying around." Wife: "It's true that I do that sometimes."
Giving Inconsistent Verbal and Non-verbal Signals	"It's okay with me if you want to do that" *(sighs and rolls eyes).*	"I don't feel good about you doing that."

The therapist takes decisive action when any of these problematic communication styles appear during a family session. Of course, the therapist must first have already established a therapeutic relationship with the family before he or she can address these problems. As soon as this relationship is established, however, even before formal communication-skills training begins, the therapist responds to these negative styles by correcting the family member(s). This is accomplished by interrupting the family discussion, pointing out the communication problem, briefly explaining why it is a problem, and suggesting a better alternative. When discussing with the family how to correct an aversive communication style, it can be helpful to bear in mind specific strategies that promote effective communication. Many of these strategies have been alluded to throughout this chapter, and they are summarized in Table 6.8.

TABLE 6.8
GOOD COMMUNICATION SKILLS

Making eye contact
Using "I" statements
Being brief and to the point
Sticking to one topic at a time
Using reflective listening skills (paraphrasing, head nods)
Being specific about what you like and dislike
Being specific about what you want and don't want
Using "feeling" statements
Giving praise
Respecting the other person's opinion
Acknowledging the other person's feelings

Responding to Negative Affect

During the first several sessions of communication-skills training, the therapist responds to marked displays of negative emotion in the family in the same manner as in previous sessions. That is, the therapist intervenes immediately, acknowledges the basis for the conflict, corrects criticisms based on a misunderstanding of the client's illness, sets aside time at the end of the session for problem solving (for a pressing problem) or explains that the problem will be addressed in forthcoming BFT sessions (for a chronic problem), and calls for breaks when the affect becomes very intense. In the sessions leading up to communication-skills training, the therapist begins to establish "ground rules" for effective family interactions, addressing pitfalls to good communication and alternative skills for enhancing communication (Tables 6.7 and 6.8).

After the therapist has taught expressing a negative feeling to the family, he or she prompts members to use this skill when negative feelings become apparent. Negative feelings such as anger, annoyance, frustration, or anxiety are often evident in the voice tone (e.g., sarcasm) and nonverbal behavior (e.g., glaring, avoiding eye contact) of family members, but the specific feelings are not verbalized nor is it clear exactly what the person is upset about. In such cases, the therapist can begin by describing the behavior that he or she has observed to the family member. Without further prompting, just describing the behavior often enables the person to articulate his or her negative feeling and the source of his or her concern. If necessary, the therapist can follow up by exploring specific feelings that the person might be having, and then prompting him or her to use the skill of expressing negative feelings.

Occasionally, arguments will erupt in the family that lead to a tense, hostile environment, even after the family has received training in communication skills. The therapist's first line of attack is to address pitfalls to good communication, to prompt family members to express negative feelings appropriately, make positive requests, etc. As family members become more able to defuse major conflicts successfully in the session through the use of communication skills, they are encouraged to use these skills for handling disagreements that occur both in and out of the session. The bottom-line message that the therapist gives to the family after communication skills have been taught is that he or she must use these skills in the sessions to resolve conflicts. If family members refuse or are unable to alter their behavior accordingly, the therapist can teach requesting a time-out or simply call for a break until family members have calmed down and are prepared to communicate constructively and cooperatively. The therapist never permits the family to have a "free-for-all" during a conflict, which would not serve the BFT goal of teaching more effective communication skills.

CASE EXAMPLE OF DWAYNE AND TANIA

The therapist's primary objective of communication-skills training with Dwayne and his wife was to increase the amount of time that they spent in face-to-face contact. The initial in vivo and homework assignments revealed a deficit in the nonverbal and verbal skills required to keep a conversation going (e.g., good eye contact, asking clarifying questions, etc.), and remediating these problems was an important initial goal. Subsequently, the therapist worked to increase the time the couple spent actually discussing its daily activities and its current problems by gradually lengthening the time of its weekly assigned family meetings and encouraging short conversations on other days.

It was also very clear to the therapist that the couple rarely gave each other positive feedback. In order to increase positive exchanges between Dwayne and Tania, the therapist gave additional homework assignments to express positive feelings and often ended sessions with a round of positive feelings expressed by the couple and the therapist.

As is typical with many families of combat veterans with PTSD, Dwayne and Tania tended to withdraw and avoid conflict and disagreement. While they acknowledged that they had differences (e.g., how much support they should provide to their sons), they rarely discussed these topics and were reluctant to practice the expressing negative feelings exercise because they were afraid that it would lead to an overt conflict. To address these concerns, the therapist decided to emphasize repeated in-session (rather than at home) practice over a number of weeks to permit the couple to use the skill in a "safe" setting in which the other person used active listening skills. Because the couple was so inexperienced in conveying unpleasant feelings directly, the therapist used modeling extensively to teach the skill. Finally, to reduce potential tensions, the therapist routinely reframed topics involving negative feelings as problems to be addressed in subsequent problem-solving training.

Questions and Answers to Common Problems

1. *Question:* How does the therapist get reluctant family members to engage in role plays?

Answer: There are a number of different factors that can contribute to the reluctance of family members to participate in role plays. The most common reason is that many people feel awkward when role-playing at first. The therapist acknowledges these feelings and takes steps to help the family member feel as comfortable as possible in role plays. These steps include additional therapist modeling, ensuring that the person understands what he or she is supposed to do in the role play, giving plenty of positive reinforcement for any efforts, attempting to change behavior very gradually from one role play to the next, not pushing the person to do too many role plays in a row, and soliciting ongoing feedback from the person about his or her comfort with role plays.

Another factor that can facilitate the engagement of family members in role plays (or undermine it) is the therapist's own attitude and feelings about role-playing as a therapeutic tool. If the therapist is doubtful about the utility of role plays, or feels that requesting family members to role play is demeaning or an imposition, he or she will unwittingly communicate these beliefs to the family. For example, if the therapist attempts to engage family members in role plays by tentatively asking, "Would you mind participating in a role play?" or "Are you willing to do a role play?," family members are given the subtle message that the therapist believes role plays are unpleasant and nonessential. Therefore, overcoming resistance to role-playing is easiest if the therapist conveys a confident and upbeat attitude about the value of role plays to improving communication. In line with this, the therapist is not apologetic when requesting family members to participate in role plays, but instead directs the family in a good-natured but firm and matter-of-fact manner (e.g., "I would like you to do a role play on this . . ."). Using these skills, therapists can successfully engage the vast majority of family members in role plays.

2. *Question:* How does the therapist counter the complaints of family members that the communication skills seem "unnatural" or that people do not really talk that way in the "real world"?

Answer: As previously discussed in this chapter, family members are informed during communication-skills training that new skills often feel unnatural at first, but that most people become used to them after a while. There are two possible ways of responding to the added concern that nobody uses these skills in the "real world." The first strategy is to acknowledge that good communication skills are frequently not used in day-to-day living but that when people do use these skills, they are usually better able to solve their problems and achieve their goals.

The second strategy is to remind family members that people with psychiatric disorders often have difficulty processing social information accurately. By putting extra effort into communicating clearly—such as making sure that verbal feeling statements are congruent with nonverbal communications, being behaviorally specific, keeping brief and to the point, and frequently repeating back what the person has heard—family members can overcome these limitations on information processing and improve their communication with the relative who has the psychiatric illness. Thus, whether or not people use these skills in the "real world," the skills can help families with a psychiatric client communicate more effectively.

3. *Question:* When should the therapist continue working on communication skills and when should he or she move on to problem-solving training?

Answer: Because communication-skills training seeks to improve the skills of each family member, progress usually varies among the different participants. Some family members improve faster than others, whereas psychiatric clients with significant social-skill deficits lag behind. The decision about when to begin problem-solving training is based mainly on the aggregated progress family members have made in their communication skills. If some degree of progress is evident in most participants, the time is ripe to move on, even though significant deficits may remain. The therapist makes note of the most prominent communication problems and looks for opportunities to remediate these deficits in the course of problem-solving training.

In addition to work on communication that occurs during problem-solving training, the therapist may elect to renew the focus on communication skills later in therapy. For some families, good communication is more important than problem-solving skills. For example, families who spend relatively little time together often share few problems and may not need to get together regularly for the purpose of problem solving. The quality of the relationship between these family members hinges primarily on their ability to communicate with each other, not to solve problems or achieve goals.

For other families, good problem-solving skills are more crucial than communication skills. For example, family members may raise their voices, interrupt each other, and become heated in their discussions, but nevertheless remain focused on the problem and arrive at a workable solution. In these families, so-called problems in communication are not functionally related to problem-solving skill, and need not continue to be a major focus of attention after the communication skills training segment of BFT.

4. *Question*: What does the therapist do when family members say they use the communication skills (even though they don't!) before the skills have been taught?

Answer: It is not uncommon to encounter a family member who claims to be an expert at using the communication skills, but whose actual skills leave much to be desired. Rather than disagreeing with the person about his or her skills, the therapist responds positively by welcoming the relative's expertise and saying that he or she will be able to help the therapist teach the skills to the other family members. Communication-skills training is then conducted in the usual fashion, with the therapist selectively using this family member to model skills, while also engaging the person in role plays and providing feedback to modify his or her skills. When all of the family members claim to know the communication skills, the therapist can connote training as a "review" of these skills.

5. *Question*: How does the therapist deal with family members who insist on dwelling on the past, despite efforts to refocus them on the present?

Answer: Families with a long history of tumultuous and strained relationships may have difficulty putting their past behind them. If the therapist is forced to repeatedly refocus the family on the present, and its preoccupation with the past appears to interfere with its ability to plan for the future, more direct steps need to be taken to help it deal with the past. One strategy is for the therapist to schedule a family session that is devoted solely to discussing issues that occurred in the past. The purpose of this meeting is for family members to talk about their feelings and perceptions about what happened. No attempt is made to reach any kind of a resolution, to establish who is at fault, or to change anyone's interpretation about past events. During this meeting, the therapist makes sure that family members abide by the rules of good communication. The therapist reviews the purpose of the meeting with the family in advance. If the meeting seems productive and the family members wish to continue it, a follow-up meeting is held. At the conclusion of the meeting(s), the therapist restates that the focus of the remaining BFT sessions will be on learning skills that are relevant to issues they currently face or expect to face in the future.

Sometimes one family member dwells on the past, but others do not. Similarly, after one or two sessions devoted to discussing the past, one person may continue to want to talk about it. If the need appears to be great or the person's preoccupation disrupts the family sessions, the therapist may elect to conduct some individual sessions with that person or refer him or her for supplimental individual therapy, although clear limits should be set on the number of session conducted.

6. *Question*: How can family members be encouraged to express negative feelings to each other?

   Answer: The unwillingness to express negative feelings toward another family member usually stems from one of two concerns. Firstly, the person may be worried that expressing negative feelings to a relative will result in an angry backlash; instead, he or she prefers to keep quiet and "not rock the boat." This concern is often based on past experiences in which negative feelings have been communicated in a nonconstructive manner, leading to greater conflict and tension. Second, the person may be concerned that expressing negative feelings will lead to an increase in the client's symptoms. The relative may understand the relationship between stress and relapse, and choose not to express his or her negative feelings in order to minimize the other person's risk of a relapse.

   The same basic strategy is employed to address both of these concerns. The therapist helps family members understand that if they express negative feelings in a constructive, skillful manner, they will not provoke an angry backlash or symptom exacerbation. Rather, in most situations the appropriate expression of negative feelings will decrease stress on family members and facilitate cooperative living.

   One way that the therapist can convey this to the family is to lead a discussion about the differences between constructive and destructive expressions of negative feelings (e.g., the former are behaviorally specific and suggest changes for the future; the latter are often vague and criticize the person for who he or she is). A second strategy is to elicit feedback from family members after a negative feeling has been expressed appropriately in a role play or for a homework assignment. The therapist asks the person to whom the negative feeling was expressed specific questions to assess the accuracy of the other person's concerns about expressing those feelings. For example, we worked with a couple in which the husband had a history of multiple suicide attempts. His wife was afraid to express negative feelings to her husband for fear she would precipitate a relapse. To help her test out these concerns, on several occasions after she had appropriately expressed a negative feeling to her husband we asked him whether he found her communication stressful or whether any of his symptoms had worsened. In each instance he denied any negative effects. Over time and with more practice his wife began to feel more confident that she could communicate her negative feelings to her husband without any untoward consequences.

Summary

In this chapter we reviewed the rationale for improving communication skills in families with a psychiatric client. The primary reasons for communication-skills training include reducing tension in the family, teaching family members how to compensate for information-processing deficits in clients, and improving social skill in both clients and relatives. We summarized how to evaluate whether a family requires more formal communication-skills training or only a brief review of communication skills is necessary. We described different types of social skill that are the focus of training (nonverbal behaviors, paralinguistic features, verbal content), and reviewed the curriculum for communication skills that are taught in BFT.

Communication-skills training is conducted using the procedures of social-skills training, a "packaged" set of clinical methods for changing interpersonal behavior. The bulk of this chapter addressed how communication skills are trained in the family using social-skills training techniques. For each skill that is taught, the reason for learning that specific skill is first discussed with the family and then demonstrated (modeled) by the therapist. One at a time, family members repeatedly practice the skill in role plays, and after each role play they receive positive feedback and corrective feedback designed to improve their performance. At the end of each session, family members are given homework assignments to practice the skill outside of the session, and these assignments are reviewed in the following session.

Toward the end of this chapter we discussed the training of communication skills in later BFT sessions and strategies for handling common problems, including homework noncompliance, negative affect, and pitfalls to good communication. In the next chapter we describe how problem-solving training is conducted with families.

CHAPTER 7

PROBLEM-SOLVING TRAINING

Improving the ability of families to solve problems is a fundamental task of BFT. The primary therapeutic objective of BFT is to teach families a systematic way of resolving their own problems. Thus, while the therapist may be helpful to family members in solving specific problems and achieving desired goals, the major emphasis of BFT is on helping families learn to solve problems themselves and make progress toward their own goals.

This emphasis on developing problem-solving skills does not occur in a vacuum. A core assumption of BFT is that problem solving can be taught most effectively to families who have an understanding of the client's psychiatric disorder and who possess strong communication skills. Thus, structured problem-solving training typically *follows* the educational and communication-skills components of the therapy. As long as family members can keep the conversation flowing in a non-affectively charged manner, then even very difficult problems that have engendered a great deal of prior conflict can be resolved successfully using this method.

Although the *training* of problem-solving skills in family members takes place later in the course of BFT, the therapist uses this method from the beginning of treatment. For example, the therapist adopts a problem-solving approach both in developing and refining an initial treatment plan for the family *and* in dealing with family crises that arise early in treatment and cannot be deferred until formal problem-solving training. The use of a systematic approach to solving problems can be especially helpful in aiding a family to maintain structure and cope effectively when confronted with urgent situations that threaten to overwhelm it (e.g., violence in the home, imminent eviction). By demonstrating to the family how a step-by-step approach to solving problems can successfully resolve a crisis, the therapist acts as a powerful model to help motivate family members to develop proficiency at the technique.

Finally, as outlined in BFT, effective problem solving involves *all* family members working cooperatively to define the problem, to generate and evaluate solutions, to develop a plan, and to implement the plan and monitor its success. Because problem solving involves a combined family effort, its success is dependent upon the active participation of all members. If the therapist has been successful in the shaping of the scheduling of weekly family meetings prior to this point, then these ongoing meetings will lend themselves well to problem-solving activity. If the therapist has not yet succeeded in prompting the family to conduct weekly meetings on its own, then structuring these meetings becomes an even more important goal for the therapist. Regular family meetings held in the absence of the therapist provide the family with an opportunity to practice its problem-solving skills and to generalize these skills to more real-life family situations. The successes and obstacles encountered by families during these family meetings also provide valuable information to the therapist about which problem-solving skills the family has acquired and which skills are still in need of further development.

Overview of Problem-Solving Training

Briefly, problem-solving training involves teaching families a systematic way of solving problems that is designed to minimize negative communication and maximize successful resolution. The focus is on teaching a process, rather than on resolving particular issues. The basic tenet of problem-solving is that specific issues can be resolved and goals attained by following a procedure that includes a fixed sequence of steps: (1) define the problem; (2) generate possible solutions for the problem; (3) evaluate the advantages and disadvantages of each possible solution; (4) select the "best" solution or combination of solutions; (5) plan on how to implement the solution(s); and (6) follow up on the plan at a later time. Initially, the therapist models the use of these skills for the family; then, family members are coached until they demonstrate successful use of the technique independently.

Developing a Problem-Solving Orientation

Every day, family members may confront any of a series of life challenges, from the relatively minor (e.g., a broken washing machine, unexpected traffic making someone tardy to an appointment) to the profoundly life-changing (e.g., career transition, illness, birth or death in the family). The first requirement of effective problem solving involves defining or redefining a life challenge or desired goal as a problem to be solved. In D'Zurilla and Goldfried's (1971) terms, this involves "adopting a problem-solving orientation."

Throughout the earlier stages of BFT, the therapist helps highlight the importance of this overriding problem-solving orientation whenever he or she addresses urgent issues (e.g., family crises, nonattendance, or homework noncompliance) using the problem-solving method. Reviewing progress toward personal and family goals also affords the therapist the opportunity to model a problem-solving orientation. Impediments or lack of progress toward goals can be reframed as "problems" that will require solving once the family has developed its skills in this area.

Case Example

The wife of a client set a personal goal of quitting smoking during the BFT. As the therapy progressed through education and communication-skills training, weekly reviews of her smoking revealed that she had some success (e.g., not smoking while at work, attending a smoking cessation class), but she was still confronted with strong urges to smoke in the evening at home. As she raised these problems in the sessions prior to the teaching of problem solving, she was asked to put the problem "controlling urges to smoke while watching TV" on her problem list for work once the problem-solving training has been initiated.

Rationale for Problem-Solving Training

As with all the components of BFT, the initial presentation of problem-solving training involves motivating family members to master the skill by encouraging them to consider how it might be useful in their lives. The therapist can then augment their responses with a strong rationale for efforts to develop expertise in the skill. Consistent with the rationale developed for earlier skills training, the therapist will be most effective when he or she is able to personalize this initial presentation to highlight the family's strengths and weaknesses in previous attempts at solving difficult problems.

The therapist begins developing motivation by asking family members why they think it might be important to improve their ability to solve problems together. To avoid disparaging their current efforts, the therapist can inquire why family members think it might "be good to *sharpen up* problem-solving skills." The therapist then leads a discussion about how the family attempted to solve a recent problem it encountered (e.g., car trouble, getting help for a sick family member, dealing with financial stress). As the family discusses how the situation was managed, the therapist probes for behaviors relevant to the steps of problem solving (e.g., "Did you all sit down and have a meeting to discuss the problem?," "Did everyone share ideas?," "How was it decided who would take responsibility for implementing the solution?," "What goes well in your family as you attempt to solve problems?," "What would you like to improve in your family's problem solving?"). The therapist then summarizes the family's efforts, highlighting those problem-solving skills that were present (e.g., "So, you all sat down together after dinner Sunday and put your heads together to see how you could avoid being evicted") and identifying where it had difficulties solving the problem (e.g., "It sounds as if you generated many good solutions, but then had a really hard time agreeing which one was the best one to try").

Problem-Solving Training Format

At the beginning of problem-solving training, the family can be given a copy of the "Structured Problem-Solving and Goal Attainment" handout (see appendix 5) for review. To facilitate learning the steps of problem solving, the first training session involves working on a relatively easy problem that can be resolved within the session and that affords the therapist the opportunity to demonstrate the technique success-fully. As a rule of thumb, therapists should avoid selecting problems for their initial training efforts for which they cannot think of one to two workable solutions. Two examples of good problems for most families on which to begin working include planning a family outing and resolving apparent difficulties in implementing weekly family meetings. During this first training session, the therapist should be prepared to generate one or two suitable topics and to then lead the family in solving the problem by taking the roles of *chair* and *secretary* (described below). An important goal for the therapist in this session is to complete the sequence of problem-solving steps and arrive at a solution by the end of the session that family members can try to imple-ment before the next BFT session. By taking an active role in leading the problem-solving discussion, the therapist can model successful use of the technique.

To promote generalization of problem-solving skills from therapy sessions to meetings at home, specific family members assume the role of *chair* and *secretary* dur-ing successive sessions of BFT; the therapist prompts these family members to lead a productive problem-solving session. The roles of chair and secretary can be consoli-dated into a single role fulfilled by one family member, or maintained as separate roles fulfilled by two different members. The primary role of the therapist in training problem-solving skills is to teach the chair how to structure the discussion and to show the secretary how to record the family's problem-solving efforts. Therefore, most of the interaction by the therapist is directed toward the chair and the secretary during the training, rather than toward the family as a whole. During the first few problems, the therapist may need to take a more active role, prompting the chair by asking questions such as "Did you get feedback from everybody?" or "I'm not sure who has agreed to complete that part of the solution; did you decide?" and prompt-ing the secretary with questions such as "Could you please read the definition of the problem you wrote down?" and "Did you write down that last solution?" As family members gain more expertise in problem solving, the therapist gradually fades him-self or herself out. At the highest levels of mastery, the family can hold an entire problem-solving session during a BFT session with no input from the therapist at all!

The chair assumes the task of systematically guiding the family through com-pletion of the steps of problem-solving. The chair is responsible for outlining the task required in each step by reading the instructions, eliciting input from each family member during each step, and keeping the discussion task-oriented. He or she is also responsible for calling a time-out and rescheduling the meeting if strong emotions prohibit effective problem solving. The secretary's role is to maintain a written record of the family's problem-solving efforts using the form contained in appendix 5 (the "Problem-Solving/Goal Setting Record"), to halt the discussion if necessary to keep up with the record, and to review progress made towards solving a problem. Family members are encouraged to keep their records from problem-solving meetings in a notebook stored in a location to which all family members have access, such as the living room. While written records may seem tedious, they help keep the conversa-tion on task and contain "back-up" solutions if the initial plan does not solve the problem.

In the early problem-solving sessions, assignment to the role of chair and secre-tary can be rotated so all family members have the opportunity to share responsibilities and master the technique. Subsequently, family members are encouraged to elect a chair and secretary for each problem. In some families a high level of disorganization can interfere with the ability to learn the problem-solving format. One strategy for simplifying the training process is to combine the roles of chair and secretary during the initial training sessions and to separate the roles later, when family members have gained some familiarity with the method. By consolidating the roles of chair and secretary during the initial stages of problem-solving training, the therapist is able to focus most of his or her attention on one rather than two family members.

In some families, and in some cultures, there may be a natural or cultural ly defined "leader" of the family. In such families, encouraging someone other than the natural family leader to play the role of the chair may be both awkward and counterproductive. Family members may find it difficult to follow the lead of the chair if he or she is not also the natural family leader. In addition, families may be less likely to use the problem-solving approach on their own if it does not appear consistent with the power hierarchy that exists in the family. Thus, the therapist may elect to focus on that member as the chair of the problem-solving process.

Because the overall objective of the BFT sessions is *training* in the problem-solving technique, the therapist structures the sessions to promote progress toward this goal. In the early problem-solving sessions, it is important for families to gain a sense of mastery and success with the technique by working on everyday difficulties such as keeping the house clean or getting something repaired. By working initially on simple, less emotionally charged problems, families have the opportunity to learn the steps of problem solving and experience its benefits. If families raise more demanding problems in the early phases, it is recommended that the therapist explicitly defer them until the family has achieved mastery in problem solving.

Helping family members maintain an upbeat, constructive, optimistic attitude as they proceed in their problem solving is a valuable tool in promoting skill acquisition and generalization. Research on mood and problem solving has demonstrated that positive mood states result in the generation of more creative and effective solutions to problems, whereas negative moods can interfere with efforts to resolve difficult issues (Isen et al., 1987). Maintaining a cooperative, positive atmosphere in the family may facilitate the teaching of problem-solving skills as well as produce better solutions to the problems at hand. At the conclusion of the problem-solving task, the therapist gives the family ample positive feedback for strengths it evidenced (e.g., "I really liked the way you generated so many potentially workable solutions, and that everybody suggested something"), as well as constructive feedback when necessary (e.g., "I didn't hear you evaluate any of the other solutions after you decided that you liked the second one").

As with the other skills taught in BFT, the therapist notes and praises efforts to use the model. He or she also recognizes the importance of shaping small improvements in behavior over time. Most important, at the end of each session, the therapist prompts family members to recognize and acknowledge other members' positive problem-solving efforts. Generalization of skills outside the session can be promoted by increasing the availability of social reinforcement.

Occasionally, families have difficulty identifying problem areas on which to practice the technique. The therapist must be prepared to suggest topics for training when this occurs, based on either the results of the initial behavioral assessment or the ongoing assessment embedded in previous BFT sessions. After working on three or four problems, some families may exhibit consistent deficits in only one or two aspects of the problem-solving technique, such as the failure to arrive at specific definitions of problems, or being unable to evaluate solutions thoroughly. In such cases, the therapist may spend an entire session concentrating on just one or two steps of the problem-solving sequence to remediate deficits in these areas.

Therapists and family members need to recognize that problem solving is an ongoing process that often must be repeated several times before a successful resolution is achieved. Even under the best circumstances, families may arrive at a carefully considered solution that is successfully implemented, yet fails to resolve the problem due to unforeseen obstacles. Particularly when initial efforts lead to limited (or no) success, it is important that the therapist reframe any setbacks as "learning opportunities" and resume problem solving with a positive attitude. In such a situation, the family is encouraged to use the new information it has obtained to reevaluate the solutions generated, suggest new ones if needed, select or revise a potential solution, and implement it in a continued problem-solving effort (for more on this, see the later section in this chapter called Debugging Problem-Solving).

Clinical Examples of Problem-Solving Training

Each therapist needs to develop his or her own personal style for introducing the rationale and teaching the steps of problem-solving. To give an example of how one therapist initiated problem-solving training, we provide an excerpt from a transcript below.

Case Example

The family members participating in BFT included a thirty-one-year-old man with major depression and his mother. This example is taken from the eighth BFT session, the first session in which problem solving training was initiated.

Therapist:	Today I would like to begin working on how you solve problems together. Do you remember how in one of our first sessions I gave you a problem to talk about and I told you we would be working on ways of solving problems?
Mother & Client:	Yes.
Therapist:	We have found that problems come up in every family. Even if they are little problems, they do come up. And what's important isn't what solutions you come to, but the way you go about trying to solve the problem. What happens in many families is that they talk about problems but they never come up with any constructive solutions, and it's still a problem when they're done talking. What happens then?
Mother:	The problem can get worse and worse.
Client:	And everyone gets mad at each other and starts blaming each other.
Therapist:	Yes, that happens a great deal. We have found it useful to provide families with some structure for solving problems.

	We have come up with a six-step formula for helping families talk about and solve problems together. Being able to solve problems as a family can reduce stress. Do you remember from our discussion about depression how stress can worsen the symptoms, sometimes requiring clients to go back to the hospital?
Client:	Yes, I'm sensitive to stress.
Therapist:	That's right, so it's real important to keep stress at a minimum, and coming up with effective ways of solving problems can reduce stress in the family. I have some forms I'd like to give you that summarize the steps of problem solving. Let's review each of these steps *(the steps of problem solving are reviewed).*
Therapist:	I'd like you to try problem solving with this approach today. I need someone to help keep track of our problem-solving, to be the "secretary" and write down the solutions we think of. Sam, could you be the secretary?
Client:	Isn't being the secretary women's work?
Therapist:	Actually, anyone in the family can be the secretary for a problem-solving discussion. The person just has to write down how the problem is defined, what the solutions are, and so on. Do you think you can do that?
Client:	Sure. *(Sam and his mother get a pen, and a hard surface, and get problem-solving sheet out.)*
Therapist:	Good. One problem that has been going on that I would like you to talk about is your family meetings. I would like you to practice problem solving in your family meetings, but it seems like it has been difficult for you to come up with a specific time to meet.
Mother:	Yes, it has. We ran into a scheduling problem last week because we went to see my other son.
Therapist:	Okay, well, is finding a good meeting time a problem for you, or is there another problem that you would like to work on? Sam, is coming up with a consistent time for your family meeting a problem?

(The therapist is making sure that both the mother and client agree to work on this topic.)

Client:	I have a lot of free time on my hands, so I can meet anytime.
Therapist:	Is it a problem picking a time to meet on a regular weekly basis for both of you?
Client:	I guess so.
Therapist:	Well, this is just a suggestion from me. Is there another problem, that you would rather work on?
Mother:	No, I think this is a good problem. It's a pretty simple problem and you said it's better to start on an easy problem.

Therapist: That's true. Let's start at the first step of problem solving. The first step is defining the problem. Sam, how would you define this problem?

As described in the previous section, the therapist's principal role in problem-solving training is to teach the chair how to guide the family in an orderly fashion through the six steps of problem solving. After the therapist has modeled for the family how to chair a problem-solving meeting, his or her focus shifts toward shaping the skills of the family members in chairing similar meetings. To illustrate how the therapist works directly with the chair to improve structuring skills, we provide a clinical example from the session transcript of one family.

Case Example

The family included a twenty-eight-year-old man (Fred) with obsessive-compulsive disorder who was living at home with his mother (Darlene) and thirty-two-year-old sister (Ann). The client had a history of numerous psychiatric hospitalizations and was only partially responsive to psychotropic medications and behavior therapy. The transcript is taken from the twentieth BFT session, which was conducted following a brief rehospitalization of the client. The opinion of both the client and his relatives was that this rehospitalization was at least partially precipitated by the client's tumultuous relationship with a new girlfriend (Cathy), another psychiatric client. Although problem solving training was initiated on the ninth session with this family, their progress in acquiring the requisite skills was slow due to a number of family crises and the client's disruptive symptoms. The example begins in the middle of this session, when the family has just completed the second step of problem-solving on the client's goal of breaking up with his girlfriend. The mother is the chair of the session.

Therapist: What's the next step of problem solving?
Mother: We're supposed to discuss each solution. The first solution was Fred going back to the hospital.
Client: I want to go back to the hospital. I want to go back.

(After a long pause, it is evident that the mother is stymied, so the therapist prompts her.)

Therapist: Darlene, could you remind everyone what it is you are supposed to discuss about each solution?
Client: I want to run away to the hospital!
Mother: All right. What are the main advantages and disadvantages of each solution?
Client: I want to go back to the hospital. Can I go back to the hospital?

(The mother is distracted by the client's persevering about returning to the hospital. The therapist prompts the mother to refocus the client on evaluating each solution.)

Therapist:	Darlene, what are you supposed to do at this point with Fred asking if he can go back to the hospital?
Mother:	Fred, you're off track here. You need to concentrate on this one solution. Tell us, what do you think are the advantages and disadvantages of running away to the hospital as a solution for breaking up with Cathy?
Client:	I don't know.
Sister:	A disadvantage of that solution is that you don't like being locked up, and you'd be locked up if you went to the hospital. You haven't liked that in the past.
Client:	Yeah, I don't like being in the hospital.
Mother:	Okay, so that's one disadvantage of going to the hospital, being locked up. What are the advantages of this solution?
Client:	At least I would get away from her!
Mother:	That's right. The next solution is Ann assisting Fred in communicating with Cathy. What's the advantage of that?
Client:	Yeah, that's a pretty good solution.
Mother:	Why is that a good idea?
Sister:	It's great because Fred doesn't have to communicate with her at all, and he won't be feeling sorry for her or feeling bad for her or getting upset or feeling depressed about it. Fred could get on the phone and say it's over and hand the phone over to me, and if she has anything else to say I could explain it to her.
Mother:	Is that solution better than the first one?

(The therapist interrupts to remind the mother that each solution is discussed independently in this step of problem solving.)

Therapist:	Darlene, don't compare the different solutions at this step of problem-solving. Just go down the list and discuss the advantages and disadvantages of each solution.
Mother:	We still don't have a disadvantage to this solution. What's a disadvantage of Ann assisting Fred in communicating with Cathy?
Sister:	Well, the bad thing about it is that Cathy might not believe me as much as she would believe Fred himself.
Client:	That is a problem.
Mother:	Okay, let's go on to the next solution. Fred will tell Cathy that it's over. What's the advantage of that?
Sister:	She'll believe him and leave him alone.
Mother:	And what's a disadvantage?
Client:	None.
Sister:	None, except that it might be hard for Fred to do.
Mother:	All right then. The fourth possible solution is Fred telling Cathy that they should see other people.

(The remaining solutions are discussed, Darlene moves the discussion to the next step, and Fred with Darlene's and Ann's help, chooses the solution of telling

Cathy himself that their relationship is over. The therapist praises Darlene for her skill in chairing the discussion before she moves on to planning how to implement the solution.)

Therapist:	Darlene, I really liked the way you kept everyone on track when discussing each of the solutions and how you were able to come to an agreement about the best solution to Fred's goal of breaking up with Cathy.

Steps of Problem Solving

Once an overriding problem-solving orientation has been engendered during BFT, the family is also given specific training in each of the steps of the method. We identify below important nuances of each of these steps and strategies for enhancing the skills of family members. The key points for each step are summarized in Table 7.1 and are included in the educational handout "Structured Problem-Solving and Goal Attainment" contained in appendix 5.

1. *Problem Definition*

   The first skill involves defining challenges or stresses as problems to be solved or goals to be achieved. This usually involves helping the family move from a global statement of difficulty (e.g., "money is tight") to a more specific, clearly defined problem (e.g., "we are consistently short about $300 every month" or "we need $1500 to get the car engine overhauled"). Defining the problem in precise terms helps assure that every family member is trying to solve the same problem and minimizes ambiguity as to whether the problem has been solved or not.

   Vague problem definitions may lend themselves to wasted efforts. Consider the case of the "money is tight" problem described above. Without further specification, one family member may understand the problem as "money is tight because we don't know how to budget" while another may conceptualize the problem as "money is tight because I don't get enough overtime work anymore." Obviously, the resolution to the budgeting problem involves different potential solutions (e.g., read a book on budgeting, take a class in money management) than the problem of decreased overtime pay does (e.g., talk to the boss to see if more overtime is available, ask for a raise, consider changing jobs).

   Family members are encouraged to give themselves ample time to define problems clearly and specifically. Of all the steps in problem solving, defining the problem adequately often requires the most time. This is particularly true when family members have not discussed the problem before, or when previous discussions have resulted in hostile conflict or angry withdrawal of family members. Every person is considered to have valuable input, and each is encouraged to offer his or her perspective on the situation and to offer a potential definition or refinement of the problem. Family members are encouraged to use active listening skills such as good eye contact and asking clarifying questions when they are not offering their own ideas.

TABLE 7.1
KEY POINTS IN SUCCESSFUL PROBLEM SOLVING

1. *Problem Definition—problem is*
   - narrowly defined
   - behaviorally described
   - integrated from contrasting views

2. *Brainstorming Possible Solutions*
   - minimum of five suggestions is ideal
   - all suggestions are noted
   - no evaluation
   - every member encouraged to contribute at least one suggestion

3. *Evaluating Alternative Solutions*
   - every suggestion should be evaluated
   - evaluations can be brief

4. *Choosing Optimal Solution When Family Members Disagree*
   - modify or combine solutions to arrive at an acceptable one
   - agree to try one solution and then the other if the first is not completely successful

5. *Planning Implementation*
   - written records are helpful
   - anticipate and plan for possible obstacles
   - rehearse situations that may be difficult
   - each plan should have a monitor and a planned review time

6. *Review of Implementation*
   - anticipate that more than one attempt may be required to resolve any problem
   - implementation should always be reviewed
   - work from problem-solving sheets so other brainstorming alternatives are available if needed
   - praise all efforts

Family members are instructed to work toward a *consensual* definition of the problem, shared by all family members. Sometimes reaching consensus is quite simple, as in the case of a family deciding that a car transmission must be fixed or that a toilet seat must be repaired. At other times, reaching a shared definition can be difficult and necessitate an extended discussion. For example, a husband may be concerned that his wife "does not care for me because she always comes home from work late," while the wife may feel "I know he's upset, but he doesn't understand how hard my job is and how impossible it is for me to be home at the time he wants." During the problem-definition stage, each family member states his or her view in specific terms, highlighting precise behaviors of concern. Then, family members explore ways to combine the disparate views into a shared definition.

Family members can use the expressing negative feelings communication skill in initiating problem-solving discussions. In the example just described, the husband may begin by saying, "I feel lonely and unloved when you don't come home until 9 PM. In the future, I'd feel more relieved if you made it home by 7 PM." The wife can then clarify that she works late as a response to job requirements, rather than as a rejection of her husband, and might offer a problem definition such as "I come home later than you want and this makes you feel bad." If the husband accepts this reframing as an accurate definition of the problem, then the couple can generate solutions that might help the wife get home a little earlier (e.g., going to work earlier, skipping lunch once or twice a week, reducing availability for new work assignments) or reduce the husband's distress while he waits (e.g., going to the gym after work, working later himself, reading a novel, watching the news on television).

Sometimes, as family members struggle to define the problem, they voice contrasting views. One family member may object to the habits or behaviors of another, who denies there is any difficulty. In such a situation, the family can be encouraged to combine the contrasting views in the definition of the problem. For example, one family member may object to another member's smoking, while the smoker may believe it is his or her right to smoke and the nonsmoker is the one with the problem. When the family members bring this up as an area of conflict, they can be encouraged to join the two viewpoints, and use that combined definition as the basis of subsequent problem solving (e.g., "Sue's smoking in the house really irritates Beth, and Sue hates Beth nagging about her smoking").

2. *Generation of Alternative Solutions*

Once the family has agreed on a definition of the problem, the second stage of problem solving involves the generation of a variety of possible solutions. The chair (prompted by the therapist, if necessary) directs this brainstorming activity and encourages each family member to participate. Every solution is acknowledged and recorded by the secretary on the problem-solving sheet. No evaluation of solutions is permitted at this point, and the chair is directed to interrupt any evaluative statements made by family members during this second step (e.g., "that solution didn't work"). Family members are encouraged to be open-minded and creative as they attempt to generate possible resolutions to the difficulty. We suggest families try to identify a minimum of five possible solutions in order to maximize the chances that one successful solution will be found.

Some families find it difficult to generate solutions freely, and instead try to agree on a solution and formulate a plan after articulating only one or two possibilities. The therapist can help the chair broaden the discussion by prompting him or her to reread the direction to the second step aloud (see "Problem-Solving/Goal Setting Record" in appendix 5). In addition, in early problem-solving training, the therapist can suggest one or two more unconventional or outlandish solutions (sometimes referred to as "wild cards") to model a more free-flowing exchange of ideas and to inject some levity into the discussion.

3. *Evaluation of Solutions*
   Once the family has generated five or six solutions, the chair then directs a brief evaluation of the advantages or disadvantages of each one. The chair first reads the instructions to the family for the evaluation of solutions step, then states the first potential solution on the list and asks for input as to its major advantages and disadvantages. The secretary records one or more advantages and disadvantages of the solution, and then the chair moves onto the next solution, with the same process being repeated until all of the solutions have been evaluated. Evaluations can be brief; identifying the one or two advantages and disadvantages of each solution is usually sufficient.

4. *Selecting the Best Solution(s)*
   Once the family has considered the benefits and costs of each solution, it must select the best solution or combination of the solutions to implement. In the first few problem-solving sessions, the therapist clearly informs the family that it is *its* responsibility (rather than the therapist's) to choose the solution that might work best. However, the therapist can be helpful by outlining selection criteria that increase the chances that the solution selected will succeed. These criteria include choosing a solution that is easy to implement, requires only resources already available, and appears likely to result in at least some progress toward resolving the problem.
       When family members have defined the problem clearly and systematically evaluated all of its possible solutions, they frequently arrive at a quick consensus on which solution to attempt first. Nevertheless, family members sometimes have different opinions on the best solution, and a compromise must be negotiated. To this end, family members are first prompted to use their listening skills to ensure that they understand each member's point of view. If no consensus results and the various solutions cannot be combined, then the family is encouraged to select one of the options to implement *first*, with the agreement that the alternative will be implemented if the first is not fully successful.

5. *Implementing the Best Solution*
   Once a solution has been selected, a plan is needed to ensure that it is successfully implemented. In most cases, the successful resolution of a problem or attainment of a goal requires family members to do something outside of the therapy session. The successful implementation of the solution(s) is enhanced when:
   A. specific family members assume responsibility for completing the various components of the solution;
   B. there is a plan for how necessary resources will be obtained (e.g., money, expertise);
   C. a realistic time frame for each task has been developed;
   D. potential obstacles have been anticipated and overcome; and

E. one participant agrees to monitor implementation of the plan and report on it during BFT sessions and family meetings.

The different points that require consideration during the discussion of how to implement a particular solution are contained in the "Problem-Solving/Goal Setting Record," which also includes spaces for the secretary to record the agreed-upon plan. When solutions involve multiple efforts or activities by many family members, it can be helpful to develop an "assignment sheet" and post it at home. This sheet serves as a reminder to both the family member who has agreed to monitor progress toward solving the problem and the other members.

Families may benefit from rehearsing specific aspects of the plan for solving a problem or achieving a goal. For example, a family member may practice what to say to a phone company representative when he or she calls to inquire as to why a payment was not credited. When behavioral rehearsal would be beneficial, the therapist can help the family set up a role play and provide feedback to the participants in order to enhance its performance, as described in the previous chapter on communication-skills training. Sometimes role-playing the initial part of the implementation plan in the session increases the resolve of the family members to follow through on the plan outside of the session.

6. *Review of the Implementation and Solution*
An integral part of problem solving involves evaluating whether the problem has been successfully resolved by the selected solution(s). This process involves determining whether the solution has been implemented as planned and whether it has been effective. In the early stages of problem-solving training, the review of previous problem-solving efforts is scheduled after the discussion of progress on individual goals. During this review, impediments to successful problem solving may be identified, which can serve as the basis of activity in the current therapy sessions. Families are also encouraged to monitor problem-solving progress in their weekly meetings.

Solutions need to be implemented if they are to be successful in resolving problems or achieving desired goals. The chair prompts the family member who agreed to serve as the monitor to review the planned implementation of the solution and then lead a family discussion on the success of the solution. A failure in implementation is approached in a problem-solving manner in order to identify where impediments arose (e.g., resources were not obtained, a family member forgot to complete a task) and to develop a plan to resolve the implementation difficulties

Case Example

The mother of one client attempted to develop a plan to take a vacation, contingent upon saving a small amount of money each month toward her expenses. After two months, it became clear that her financial pressures were such that she would not be able to save money if she continued to give money to her adult children. However, she had not anticipated *their* financial stresses as an obstacle to *her* saving, and thus had not planned to deal with this situation. Once she had identified the impediment, however, during BFT sessions she was able to rehearse, effective responses to her children's request for money and then use these responses at home in subsequent weeks when they requested funds.

Sometimes, even a well-implemented solution fails to resolve the problem. In such a case, the chair (with the therapist prompting if necessary) again orients the family to the potential solutions previously generated to solve the problem, oversees a brief reevaluation of their benefits and costs in light of the failed first attempt, and prompts selection and planning for a new alternative.

Case Example

A client who wanted to lose weight decided to implement a long-dormant weight-training program to achieve this goal. After one month, the strength and tone of his muscles had improved, but he had not lost any weight. He reviewed with his mother the original list of solutions he had generated and decided he needed to combine calorie restriction with the weight-training program to achieve his goal. By using this combination of solutions, he was much more successful in losing weight.

Generalization of Problem-Solving Skills

Weekly meetings held by the family on its own are a potent strategy for generalizing the problem-solving skills acquired in BFT sessions to the home environment. The beneficial effects of participation in BFT are greatest when the family continues its scheduled weekly problem-solving meetings after formal therapy has ended, and the therapist needs to convey this fact to the family. However, despite the apparent advantages of conducting ongoing family meetings after the end of BFT, most families do not continue to meet on their own, nor do they continue to maintain written records of their problem solving. Impediments to these meetings include work or school schedule changes, pressures from other life circumstances and responsibilities (e.g., a new baby, a physically ill relative requiring care), or family members moving away. Therapists must be aware of this and prepare families by helping them practice their problem-solving skills in a less formal manner and without keeping problem-solving records.

After family members have had the opportunity to hone their skills in the steps of problem solving and maintaining a written record, the therapist can prompt the family to work on a problem in a BFT session without the assistance of the record sheet. To do this, the therapist introduces a brief rationale for the importance of knowing the steps of problem solving by pointing out that problems may spontaneously arise when a record sheet is not available or when it is inconvenient to conduct a more formal problem-solving meeting. In such situations, the steps of problem solving can still be followed to arrive at a tentative resolution. Then, the therapist instructs the family to try to solve the problem using the appropriate steps, intervening as needed to keep the family on track.

Similar to homework assignments to practice formal problem solving, families are requested to practice steps of problem solving without maintaining written records during their family meetings at home, and in spontaneous situations when conflicts arise. Also in line with training in formal problem solving, the therapist can observe the family's efforts at solving problems without the formal structure, and identify trouble spots that are the focus of more targeted training. As families develop their skills at less-structured problem solving, the therapist can explore with them the relative advantages and disadvantages of each approach to problem solving, and identify which method the family is most likely to employ on its own and when BFT sessions have ended. This discussion will help the therapist and family prepare for how problems will be resolved when they no longer have regular meetings with the therapist.

Debugging Problem Solving

We have emphasized that successful problem solving often requires multiple efforts before any progress is made. Many problems can be solved after a single family meeting is conducted, provided that the agreed-upon plan is followed through. However, some of the more thorny problems that families face defy easy resolution, and it is only through repeated, determined, and systematic efforts that solutions are found. Teaching families a method for reviewing their unsuccessful problem-solving efforts, pinpointing trouble spots, and modifying action plans can enable them to tackle some of the more challenging and divisive problems they face. We refer to this standardized approach to dealing with unresolved problems as "debugging problem solving."

The essence of debugging unsuccessful problem-solving efforts is to teach the family to systematically review the completed problem-solving sheet *in reverse* (i.e., beginning with the sixth step, proceeding to the fifth step, and so forth). As family members review their sheet and discuss each step in reverse order, they are taught to stop at the first step in which a clear obstacle was encountered, and to arrive at a tentative solution for resolving that particular difficulty. When family members have agreed how to alter the problematic step of the problem-solving sequence, they then proceed to review and modify (when necessary) those steps that *follow*, in the correct order. Thus, if the family is debugging a problem solving effort and finds that a difficulty was encountered in the fourth step of problem solving (Choose the Best Solution), this step would be altered, and then the fifth step (Plan How to Carry out the Best Solution) would be modified. The family would then complete the sixth step (Review Implementation) at a later time. This process is summarized in the flowchart contained in Figure 7.1, and is elaborated in the following two paragraphs.

When the family members review the implementation of a problem-solving plan (step six), they first evaluate whether the plan was actually carried out (step five). If the plan was *not* carried out as intended, the family determines how to ensure that the plan will be implemented next time, and this modified plan is put into effect.(e.g., in the original plan, mother was supposed to purchase transportation tokens, but she did not have enough money by the end of the week; in the modified plan, she will purchase the tokens at the beginning of the week after receiving her money). If the plan *was* put into effect, but it did not have its desired consequence

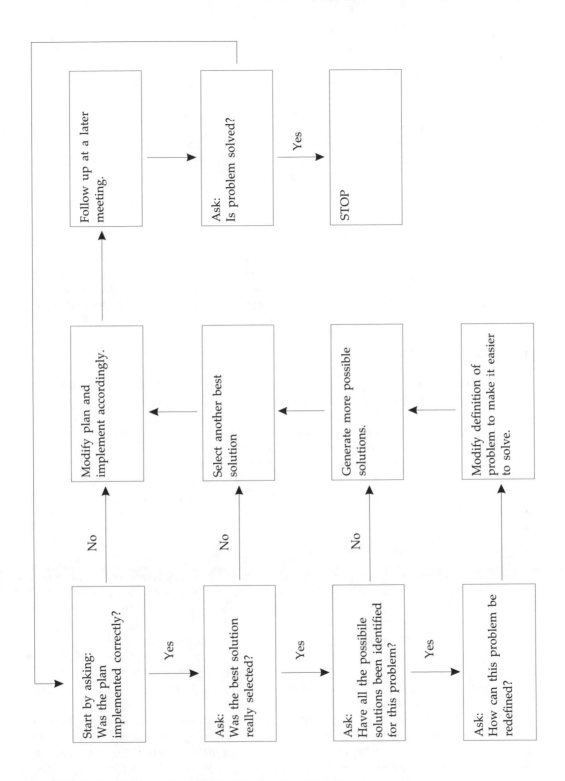

FIGURE 7.1   DEBUGGING PROBLEM SOLVING

(i.e., step five was implemented correctly), the family proceeds to evaluate whether or not the "best" solution was chosen among the solutions generated. This requires the family to reconsider the advantages and disadvantages of each solution to determine whether another solution should be tried (steps three and four). If the family agrees that another solution would be better, this solution is selected (step four), and a new plan is made for implementing the new solution (step five). On the other hand, if family members believe that the best solution was in fact implemented, despite its lack of success, they go to the previous step (two) of evaluating whether all the possible solutions to the problem have been identified. If not, additional solutions are identified (step two) and discussed (step three), a new best solution is selected (step four), and a new implementation plan is made (step five).

With the very most difficult problems, the family may determine that all the possible solutions have been identified and thoroughly discussed, the best solutions were selected, reasonable plans were made and successfully implemented, but that the problem has not yet been solved nor has significant progress been achieved. In these cases, the debugging process leads the family back to the first step of problem solving and requires it to evaluate how the problem or goal might be defined differently so as to make its resolving more manageable.

Case Example

A client who had been partially responsive to treatment of bipolar disorder attempted with the help of family members to achieve her goal of getting a job. Numerous family problem-solving meetings were held concerning this goal, but despite many efforts the client continued to be unsuccessful in obtaining employment. Finally, the client and relatives agreed to modify the definition of the goal to "engaging in constructive activity outside of the home." The family was more successful with this new goal, and problem-solving efforts resulted in the client securing a volunteer job.

Crisis Problem Solving

Just as the problem-solving approach is used to resolve family conflicts and help family members achieve personal and shared goals, the method is also employed to handle crises that occur over the course of family therapy. If family members have learned the basic problem-solving format and present with a crisis at the beginning of a session, the therapist prompts the family to use its problem-solving skills and steps in to help when necessary. When crises develop prior to the introduction of training in problem solving or before families have had the opportunity to hone their skills sufficiently, the therapist adopts a problem-solving orientation and leads the family in a discussion toward the resolution of the crisis, systematically following the steps of the method (including completing a "Problem-Solving/Goal Setting Record" sheet). In the absence of miracle solutions to the pressing problems families sometimes face, problem solving represents a pragmatic, reliable method for managing crises that threaten to overwhelm family coping and upset the therapeutic balance necessary to achieve long-term improvement in BFT. To illustrate the use of problem solving by a therapist in a crisis situation, we provide a case example below.

Case Example

The family in treatment was very poor and lived in a crime-infested and drug-ridden neighborhood in the inner city. Four family members participated in most BFT sessions: the mother, two of her children—Leroy, twenty- seven years old, who had a schizoaffective disorder, and Tamara, thirty-one, who had schizophrenia, and Tamara's daughter, Sally (fifteen). Two months prior to the first BFT session, Sally had given birth to her first child. The family had recently been under high stress following the grandmother's death from tuberculosis and the ongoing evaluation by the city health department as to whether any other family members also had been infected.

When the therapist arrived at the home for the seventeenth session, it was immediately apparent that Tamara was extremely agitated. When her daughter's boyfriend came into the apartment shortly after the therapist arrived, Tamara began to curse loudly at him. She picked up the globe from a hurricane lamp and made gestures threatening to throw the lamp at him. Other family members were frightened and unsure of what to do. The therapist took control by standing between Tamara and her daughter's boyfriend, politely requesting him to leave, and gently escorting him out of the apartment. Tamara appeared to be very paranoid and the therapist began to problem solve with the family, taking the role of the chair. The problem was defined to everyone's satisfaction as "Tamara feels she might hurt someone." The following solutions were generated:

1. Go to the community mental health center.

2. Go to the nearest hospital.

3. Go to the hospital where the therapist works.

4. Take additional medication.

5. Leave the apartment.

6. Other family members leave the apartment.

After discussing each solution, the family members agreed that going to the therapist's hospital was best, since they knew the treatment staff and Tamara needed immediate attention. To plan how to implement the solution, the following steps were determined:

1. Call the treatment team coordinator at the hospital.

2. Arrange for admission.

3. Arrange for transportation (a cab was called).

4. Have mother accompany Tamara.

5. Request case manager to meet Tamara when she arrived at the hospital.

The family followed through on the plan, and Tamara was voluntarily admitted to the psychiatric hospital two hours later.

186 BEHAVIORAL FAMILY THERAPY FOR PSYCHIATRIC DISORDERS

Putting Problem Solving in Context

Effective problem-solving training requires a substantial effort on the part of the therapist and the family. Given the breadth and severity of many of the devastating problems psychiatric clients must confront (e.g., poverty, limited social networks, few opportunities to achieve self-worth, distressing symptoms), the problem-solving method recommended here may seem almost trivial. As one of our colleagues described it, "With all the crap my clients face, offering them problem-solving training seems like spitting into the ocean." However, three important considerations mitigate against this demanding conclusion.

First, formal problem solving can be conducted on some of the more profound concerns in life, as well as the mundane.

Case Example

A client was given a homework assignment several weeks prior to termination to complete a problem-solving exercise on any topic to "sharpen up his skills." When he returned two weeks later, he reported he had decided to problem solve what he deemed to be the most important issue in his life—choosing a religion! He had systematically considered a variety of potential faiths, evaluated each, and decided (in step four) to attend a number of different services and speak with the clergy at each. After two months of this, he identified a religion in which he felt comfortable, and expressed great relief that he was "back on track."

Second, the problem-solving procedure can be used as a component of effective goal setting and for the attainment of larger objectives. We have found that clients and relatives can make great progress by breaking major goals into a series of smaller goals, which can each then become the focus of specific problem solving. Using this framework, we have helped clients obtain employment, live independently, establish intimate relationships with partners, and break out of the cycle of substance abuse and dependence. Attainment of these goals has had a major impact on the lives of these individuals and counters the concern that problem-solving efforts can offer only modest benefits.

Finally, many therapists are confronted every day with families living in horrible circumstances who appear to be in perpetual crisis. Often, these families must cope with extreme poverty, serious physical illness, crime, unemployment, trauma, and/or discrimination. For these families, the presence of serious mental illness is just one of many devastating realities. As mental health professionals interacting with these clients, we can become acutely and painfully aware of the limitations of our traditional interventions. While short-term improvements may be possible, long-term changes seem especially elusive. Because it is brief, structured, and focused on immediate topics, problem-solving training can help families at least organize their resources and try to address systematically their most urgent concerns. Utilizing this approach is rarely detrimental, and can help guide the therapist's effort when the circumstances appear overwhelming, as exemplified by the following case example.

Case Example

The mother of a thirty-five-year-old woman with chronic schizophrenia was engaged in BFT, and after several sessions her daughter agreed to join the sessions. The daughter lived in a rehabilitation residence, but was in contact with her mother several times a week. The mother described herself as "at the end of her rope" because her daughter's history of intermittent compliance with antipsychotic medication had resulted in her being evicted from several other residences in the past. Prior to therapy, a pattern had evolved in which the client would stop taking her medications, the mother would attempt legal action to prevent her daughter's eviction, eviction would nevertheless occur, and she would then call or come to her mother's house, where her mother would reluctantly take her in. The mother resented her daughter's poor cooperation with treatment and disliked spending time with her because of her poor grooming and hygiene, excessive smoking, and complaining.

The educational sessions were aimed at helping the mother understand that her daughter's behavior was related to the symptoms of her schizophrenia and that other families experience similar problems. Communication-skills training was focused primarily on increasing positive interactions between the mother and daughter. The early stages of problem-solving training were aimed at improving the quality of time that mother and daughter spent together. Over the course of a number of sessions, specific "rules" were agreed to and gradually implemented in which the daughter could earn outings with her mother through medication compliance, regular bathing, and not smoking when they were together. Later in therapy, history began to repeat itself as the daughter again became noncompliant with medication. As before, the mother started to engage a lawyer, contact the residence, and explore other housing options. However, through the process of problem solving with her daughter, the mother changed tactics and decided to let her daughter make her own decision about taking medication. The therapist, mother, and daughter agreed that should the daughter be evicted and become homeless, additional problem solving would be necessary to identify alternative housing arrangements. Despite the mother's belief that if left to her own devices the daughter would continue to be noncompliant with medication and face eviction, she did become compliant and was never evicted. This crisis was a turning point in therapy, which was terminated successfully after about nine months. Follow-ups indicated that the daughter's residence continued to be stable and the improvement in her relationship with her mother had been sustained. Problem solving was critical to this difficult case for two reasons. First, it provided the therapist with a clear structure for organizing therapy sessions to address specific problems, including crises. Second, it gave out hope and empowerment to the family that long-standing problems could improve through the use of systematic approach to resolving difficulties.

A sample of the wide variety of problems which have been successfully addressed by problem-solving in BFT is contained in Table 7-2.

TABLE 7.2
PROBLEMS CLIENTS HAVE SOLVED USING BFT
PROBLEM SOLVING
1. Getting up on time.
2. Managing money better.
3. Planning a vacation.
4. Keeping the toilet seat down.
5. Losing weight.
6. Managing urges to use cocaine.
7. Finding a part-time job.
8. Stopping physical violence in the home.
9. Implementing a successful feeding schedule for a new baby.
10. Limiting contact with intrusive in-laws.
11. Reducing depression.
12. Finding a girlfriend.
13. Keeping the house clean.
14. Helping an estranged father and nine-year-old daughter resume a relationship.
15. Avoiding pregnancy.
16. Deciding whether to continue in BFT.
17. Finding a residual treatment program.
18. Maintaining passing grades in college.
19. Handling suicidal thoughts.
20. Managing persistent auditory hallucinations.

Making Difficult Decisions

Problem solving is ideally suited for helping families work together to make changes in response to a pressing problem or desired goal. However, families are sometimes faced with complex situations that do not immediately lend themselves to the steps of problem solving and require that a preliminary decision or choice be made before the initiation of problem solving. Typically, such decisions involve major lifestyle changes, such as whether the client should continue to live at home, whether to enroll in school, to begin using alcohol again, or to stay in a troubled marriage. To help families make these difficult decisions in a systematic and thoughtful manner, the therapist can introduce the task of conducting a *decisional balance*.

A decisional balance involves teaching families to follow a sequence of steps similar to problem solving, including: (1) define the decision to be made; (2) generate a list of the advantages and disadvantages of one decision, and the advantages and disadvantages of another decision; (3) discuss the relative advantages and disadvantages; (4) select the best choice; (5) plan on how to implement the decision; and (6) follow up the plan at a later time. An example of a decision balance completed by a family to weigh the advantages and disadvantages of quitting cocaine is provided in Table 7.3.

TABLE 7-3

EXAMPLE OF A DECISION BALANCE LISTING THE
ADVANTAGES AND DISADVANTAGES OF USING
COCAINE AND ABSTAINING FROM COCAINE

	Advantages	*Disadvantages*
Alternative A: **Using Cocaine**	might have fun too much money will see friends	may get depressed feels like old times may end up in hospital will be a newcomer again at Cocaine Anonymous makes family upset counteracts medication
Alternative B: **Not Using** **Cocaine**	can buy clothes with cash feel proud	will be bored, lonely no friends to spend time with

Option which offers best combination of advantages and disadvantages: Alternative B, although staying off will be hard.

Once a course of action has been chosen, a variety of problems or goals can often be identified, to be worked on one at a time. For example, with the client who completed the decision balance on cocaine use (Table 7.3), his decision to avoid cocaine use resulted in a series of new problems, including:

1. dealing with cocaine urges;

2. establishing a social network of sober persons; and

3. securing transportation to Cocaine Anonymous meetings.

The client and family were then able to define each of these as a specific problem or goal to be addressed using the steps of problem-solving that they had previously learned.

Dealing with Negative Affect

Training in problem solving is predicated on the development of strong communication skills in the previous BFT sessions. However, especially intractable communication difficulties may impede successful problem-solving. For example, if one family member is very hostile or continually interrupts another, it may be difficult for the relatives to make progress solving a problem. In such a case, the therapist can "break-out" of the problem solving for five or ten minutes for some remedial communication-skills training. This training may involve helping the hostile individual express his or her observations in a more constructive way, using the techniques described in Chapter 6. In addition, the family member who is the focus of the negative input may be encouraged to give feedback to the speaker so that he or she can understand the detrimental impact of his or her poor communication style. Alternatively, a family member who monopolizes the discussion can be given some practice in active listening, while all family members can be reminded that everyone's input is valuable.

It may be difficult to determine initially if a particular comment or interaction is so harsh or controlling that it will prohibit continued problem solving. Frequently, the therapist can obtain valuable information by just observing the family without comment, for five to ten minutes, and then providing remedial training on critical communication or problem-solving deficits. For example, one therapist said, "What I'd like to see you do is work on this problem as if I weren't here. I'm going to sit here and join in where you need a little help. But for a while I'd like to sit back and see how you would handle this alone." However, the therapist should be prepared to act immediately to block character assassinations, threats of violence, or physical aggression.

Sometimes negative affect escalates among family members as a conflict becomes apparent, but the family does not initiate problem solving to address the issue. In these situations, the therapist can prompt family members to take a problem-solving approach to resolving the disagreement, which often results in a decrease in family tension. If this situation happens on repeated occasions, the therapist needs to consider additional strategies to teach families to initiate their own problem-solving discussions rather than relying on the therapist to prompt them. One such strategy is to identify a family member who is less likely to become embroiled in family arguments and teach that person how to recognize emotionally charged situations and prompt family problem-solving. Another strategy is to teach family members the communication skill of requesting a time-out, which is followed (after members have calmed down) by a problem-solving discussion.

CASE EXAMPLE OF DWAYNE AND TANIA

The couple selected three general topic areas for most of their problem-solving efforts:

1. Dwayne enrolling in an auto technician certification program;

2. improving its ability to manage money; and

3. working together to resolve some of the legal and child-care difficulties their sons were incurring.

Dwayne and Tania used the steps of problem solving to make progress on all three problems, although they clearly needed to continue to work on them after termination of treatment. Specifically, Dwayne located and enrolled in a specific auto technician certification program, but then discontinued it when his PTSD symptoms became exacerbated following a civil disturbance. The family's money problems became less severe after Dwayne decided to take a more active role in managing a disability pension he was awarded retroactively during the course of therapy. Although it continued to be a source of tension, the couple agreed not to allow any of its adult children with substance abuse problems to reside with it, but to try to continue to be actively involved in the grandchildren's lives.

In learning the problem-solving process, Dwayne and Tania quickly acquired a high level of skill in steps one through four (defining the problem through selecting the best solution). They consistently had difficulty implementing their chosen solutions, however. Typically, they would "forget" to review the implementation plan during their family meetings, or they would encounter an unanticipated obstacle and stop efforts at that point. It seemed clear to the therapist that the couple had not been sufficiently acquainted with problem solving as a process that requires repetition and persistence to achieve successful results. The therapist addressed this deficiency by allocating later problem-solving sessions solely to reviews of continued implementation efforts on earlier problems, and by prompting the couple members between BFT sessions (either by telephone contact with Tania or with Dwayne in person during brief clinic visits) to remind them about their planned next step and to discuss obstacles encountered. These strategies were helpful in improving Dwayne and Tania's ability to follow through on their problem-solving efforts outside of the BFT sessions.

Questions and Answers to Common Problems

1. *Question*: What do you do when family members have a problem with one person's behavior, but that person does not view his or her behavior as a problem?

   Answer: The first step in dealing with a problem that not all family members agree upon is to try to compromise on a definition that will allow all members to "own" the problem. Although this is often feasible, sometimes a compromise definition cannot be reached. In such cases the therapist can encourage the family to work on the problem, even though some members may have more limited investment than others. As the family problem solves, the therapist can keep an eye open for opportunities to involve the member who is less invested in solving a problem. A clinical example is included here to show how a therapist handled this type of situation.

Case Example

The family included three siblings who lived together, a pair of twenty-four-year-old twins, one with major depression and the other with bipolar disorder (Derrick and Daniel), and their twenty-eight-year-old sister, Gwen. The family was referred for BFT following a recent hospitalization of Derrick. Daniel experienced only mild residual symptoms and both he and Gwen worked. Following Derrick's discharge from the hospital, Gwen and Daniel expressed frustration about his dependency and inability to engage in constructive activity. The transcript is taken from the eleventh BFT session. Problem-solving training began on the ninth session.

Therapist:	Let's do some problem solving today on one of the things that you brought up. The one that I've heard the most is that Daniel, you say you take care of Derrick a lot, and Gwen, you've said that you don't think Derrick does enough to take care of himself. Derrick, has that been the gist of what you've heard from these guys so far?
Derrick:	Yes.
Therapist:	How can we define this as a problem that we could work on? Derrick, do you see this as a problem?
Gwen:	You know that it's a problem, but he's comfortable with it.
Daniel:	He's like a case, he just hangs out.
Therapist:	Hold it, let's let Derrick answer the question. Derrick, is it a problem for you?
Derrick:	No, but they say I make problems for everybody.

(The therapist sees that Derrick is open to discussion of the problem, although he does not view it as a problem. The therapist proceeds to explain that the problem can still be worked on.)

Therapist:	It's okay for us to work on a problem that Derrick, or anyone else, doesn't see as a problem. Derrick doesn't see it as a problem, but Daniel and Gwen do.
Daniel:	Because Derrick can't cope with it being a problem.
Therapist:	Okay, how can we word this? What's the problem for Daniel and Gwen?
Gwen:	That Derrick does nothing.
Daniel:	That Derrick takes all his money and spends it on dope and cookies.
Therapist:	Let's pick one of these things. Is it a problem that he spends all his money, or that he buys drugs, or is it a problem that he's not doing chores? Let's just pick one of these problems.
Daniel:	That's not the point. He has nothing to do. Even if he doesn't go to the program, he should have something to do. Even—
Gwen:	—I'm worried about the money, because I don't know—

(Both Daniel and Gwen are talking at the same time, and the therapist slows down the conversation by focusing on Daniel's perception of the problem.)

Therapist:	—Okay, hold it. I'm trying to listen to both of you at once. Daniel, you're saying that the problem is Derrick not having anything to do during the day.
Daniel:	Right. Is that a concern for you, Gwen?
Gwen:	Yes.

(The therapist tries to hone in on a definition to which both Daniel and Gwen agree.)

Therapist:	So, it sounds like the problem is that Daniel and Gwen have a problem with Derrick not having anything to do in the day. Is that true?

Gwen:	Yes.
Daniel:	Not quite. The problem is that Derrick doesn't do anything all day.
Therapist:	Okay, so Daniel and Gwen have a problem with the fact that Derrick doesn't do anything all day.
Daniel:	Yes.
Gwen:	Okay.
Therapist:	Let's write that down.

(After helping the family agree on a definition of the problem, the therapist requested Gwen to chair the discussion and Daniel to be the secretary. With the therapist's help, Gwen led her siblings through the remaining steps of problem solving.)

2. *Question*: Can the therapist put a problem on the problem-solving agenda?

Answer: Yes, just as any family member can identify a problem or a goal to address in problem solving, the therapist can also choose a problem for the family to work on. There are some problems that the therapist may encounter when working with a family that undermine his or her ability to work effectively with the family and achieve a successful outcome. It is the therapist's responsibility to recognize these obstacles and take steps to overcome them, often by using the problem-solving approach. Some of the most important problems for the therapist to place on the agenda are: symptom exacerbations of the client, medication noncompliance, alcohol or drug abuse, violence or threats of violence, frequent lateness to therapy sessions or cancellations, homework noncompliance, and the failure of the family to conduct family meetings outside the therapy session. Usually when one of these problems becomes apparent, the therapist seeks to address it at the soonest possible time.

3. *Question*: What does a therapist do when the family does not have meetings on its own?

Answer: There are several reasons why some families fail to meet on their own. As with other homework assignments, family members may not perceive the relevance of family meetings in reducing stress and achieving goals, or the nature of the assignment may be ill-defined. Many people have a traditional understanding of how psychotherapy works and assume that attendance at therapy sessions is sufficient for improvement to occur. Family members' understanding of the purpose of family meetings can be assessed through direct questioning by the therapist, and clarification can be provided when necessary.

   In some families the continued presence of strong levels of negative affect serves as a barrier to family meetings. Family members may have tried meeting together but ceased because of unpleasant experiences, or they may avoid meeting because of tense family atmosphere or the expectation that the meeting will be negatively charged. This problem can be especially prominent early during BFT (e.g., within the first ten sessions). The presence of negative affect can be evaluated by asking the family to conduct a problem-solving meeting at the beginning of the therapy session while the therapist observes the interaction. In addition, observation of other family members provides information about the presence of negative affect.

When negative affect interferes with family meetings, especially when conflict is clearly evident in sessions, additional communication-skills training may be necessary before family meetings are scheduled. If family members tend to heat up quickly during problem-solving discussions, giving the family very circumscribed homework assignments to practice specific steps of problem solving during its family meetings can minimize the chances of negative affect erupting. Then, the family gradually can be given additional steps of problem solving to practice on its own. For example, during a treatment session the therapist could guide family members through defining the problem and generating solutions (steps one and two) and then give them an assignment to evaluate the solutions (step three) during a family meeting held at home, with the remainder of the problem-solving steps completed in the next session. If the family is successful, the therapist could assign it to complete steps two and three on its own for the next problem, and so on.

Finally, there are some families who, despite the therapist's best efforts, never have family meetings on their own. These families may face severe stressors (e.g., poverty, ill health, domestic violence, substance abuse), be very disorganized, or have low educational levels that limit their follow-through on family meetings. At some point when working with these families, the therapists must accept the fact that family meetings are no longer a realistic expectation, and alternative strategies for training in problem solving can be employed, including focusing on helping family members follow the steps without a written record or formal meeting. Another strategy is to de-emphasize formal problem-solving training, focusing instead on improving communication within the family. Better communication skills may facilitate the ability of these families to resolve problems without following the step-by-step formula.

4. *Question*: How can problem-solving training be conducted with a severely impaired client and one relative?

Answer: The severity of some clients' symptoms may effectively preclude (or greatly limit) his or her active participation in family problem-solving. Symptoms such as persistent auditory hallucinations or delusions, impaired attention or concentration, or chronic apathy or depression can be especially problematic in some clients and may require frequent reorientation of the client to the problem topic. Family problem solving is a joint undertaking that requires at least two partially functional people to participate. When only one other relative participates in BFT sessions with a very ill client, the goal of teaching the dyad to problem-solve may need to be modified, or even discarded altogether.

Three suggestions may prove helpful when working with families containing one relative and a severely ill client:

A. *Teach the elements of problem solving and use them in the session to address problems and goals, but do not have the family use the method at home.* The therapist can assist the healthy relative by participating in problem-solving discussions during the session without the expectation that the skill will generalize to the home environment. Although this represents a deviation from the main goal in BFT of teaching problem solving as a skill that families can use independently, it provides a useful vehicle for dealing with many of the problems such families bring to therapy.

B. *Increase the focus on communication-skills training and decrease the focus on problem solving.* Severely impaired clients seem to have less difficulty improving their communication skills than their problem-solving skills. Problem-solving training involves teaching a more complex skill that relies more heavily on cognitive processing than training in communication skills. By spending more time enhancing family communication, the therapist may decrease the frustration that is inevitable when a relative tries to problem solve with a very ill client.

C. *Increase the focus on teaching the relative how to manage the client's symptomatic behavior and decrease the focus on problem solving.* Single relatives of very ill clients experience many problems coping with the dysfunctional behavior and can benefit from learning specific strategies for managing this behavior. Some of these strategies are described in the next chapter ("Special Problems").

5. *Question*: What if the problems appear too emotionally charged or complicated to solve successfully based on the family's current level of skill?

   Answer: Therapists are encouraged to avoid complicated or affectively loaded issues when initially helping families learn problem solving. Occasionally, therapists can find themselves "in over their heads" with a complex problem before they realize it. Dividing the problem into smaller, more manageable sub-problems and deferring ones that are not urgent or require a higher level of skill is a useful strategy in such an instance. A case example illustrates how a therapist handled this situation.

Case Example

Soon after beginning training in problem solving, a husband and wife agreed that one problem was that their ten-month-old son was still awakening during the night and disrupting them. At first pass, this seemed a suitable issue for early problem-solving training. The therapist began to shape a problem-definition discussion, only to have the topic quickly evolve into multiple problems, including:

1. the baby would need to be weaned to sleep through the night;

2. the mother had no intention of weaning the child for at least a couple of months;

3. the father was jealous of the intimacy between his wife and child, and he wanted the baby out of the bed that they shared; and

4. the father felt helpless because he could not comfort the baby when he fussed; only nursing soothed him.

The therapist realized early in the discussion that this problem had many facets and would require extended effort over the coming weeks.

She used it as an opportunity to help the family conceptualize large issues as being composed of many interwoven problems. She listed each concern on the blackboard labeled "for later problem-solving." When seven or eight of these topics had been listed, she asked the family to identify the one that seemed easiest to solve and likely to have some positive benefits. The husband and wife decided to work on preparing to wean the baby. The other problems were left on the board, and over the next few months, they conducted problem solving on them, as time permitted.

Summary

Teaching families how to solve problems using a systematic process is a core ingredient of BFT. Using both in-session and at-home assignments, families are encouraged to practice a six-step problem-solving process: (1) agree to a definition of the problem or goal; (2) brainstorm possible solutions; (3) evaluate solutions; (4) select the best solution(s); (5) plan and implement the best solution(s); and (6) review the implementation and revise as necessary. In teaching this skill, the therapist coaches successive family members in leading a successful problem-solving discussion. While in-session work emphasizes learning the process, families are encouraged to organize family meetings at home to practice use of the problem-solving strategy to resolve specific difficulties confronting them. The therapist's overall objective is to help all family members attain a high level of problem-solving skills. In addition to teaching the steps of problem solving, the therapist also instructs families in a technique for helping them make difficult decisions, the decisional balance. When conducting a decisional balance, family members construct a list of both the advantages and disadvantages of one choice, and then the advantages and disadvantages of the alternative choice. The systematic evaluation of the pros and cons of the choices can facilitate families in making calm and thoughtful choices about issues that may be the source of significant conflict among members.

CHAPTER 8

SPECIAL PROBLEMS

The focus of BFT is on teaching families basic information about psychiatric disorders and improving their communication and problem-solving skills in order to optimize the prognosis of the psychiatric illness. For families to achieve satisfactory outcomes, however, this information and these skills are often necessary but insufficient. A wide variety of different problems may accrue as either a primary or secondary result of the psychiatric disorder, ranging from substance abuse to aggression to severe social impairment. Client difficulties in these and other areas can be extremely burdensome to all family members. Occasionally, it may become clear that caregiving relatives are evidencing strong limitations in their own ability to cope. While effective problem solving may attenuate some of either the client's or the relatives' difficulties, augmenting this effort with other clinical strategies may permit a quicker and more sustained improvement. In this chapter, we describe interventions that address some of these supplemental needs. While not every issue can be addressed, the most common problems found in families are highlighted here.

In large part, the resolutions achieved through effective problem solving reflect the creativity and potential efficacy of the solutions generated by the family. However, family members usually lack access to the range of solutions known by professionals who have formally studied methods to achieve desired behavior change.

Consider the case of a recent assault victim with post-traumatic stress disorder who comes to a BFT session with her husband and indicates she wants to work on insomnia, nightmares, and the feeling that she always has to be "on guard." Both she and her husband are very disturbed by these difficulties, which creates great tension in their relationship. The couple may generate a variety of solutions for the insomnia (e.g., the wife could get more exercise during the day so she is tired at night, she could ask the doctor for sleep medication, she could try to avoid watching upsetting television before she goes to sleep, she could learn relaxation, she could cut down on the amount of alcohol she drinks). However, it is unlikely that the couple would be aware of specialized psychological treatments for post-traumatic stress disorder, such as cognitive restructuring, imaginal and *in vivo* exposure therapy, and stress inoculation training, which would be likely to improve her sleep disturbance (Keane et al.,

1985; Foa and Rothbaum, 1998; Foy, 1992; Marks et al., 1998). It would be incumbent upon the therapist to provide this information and help the couple evaluate whether such interventions might be helpful in this circumstance.

The BFT therapist has the responsibility to stay abreast of effective treatments of psychiatric disorders and to recognize opportunities to use them with specific families. To facilitate recovery, the therapist must be prepared to supplement the traditional components of the therapy with additional strategies and interventions to meet the special needs of the participants. The implementation of a special strategy typically requires the expenditure of time and effort on the part of both therapist and family. Thus, the therapist must conduct an informal cost-benefit analysis to evaluate whether additional work on a specific concern is merited based on whether:

1. the problem seriously compromises the life of the afflicted individual or his or her family;

2. there is an intervention that is likely to be effective;

3. the outcome of that intervention is likely to be superior to that achieved though the use of BFT communication- and problem-solving skills alone; and

4. the therapist and family have the time and resources to develop and implement these additional strategies.

In general, we recommend caution when implementing special strategies. As therapists, we are aware that the multitude of problems confronted by persons with a serious psychiatric disorder can seem overwhelming, and it may be tempting to try to address many of them concurrently. However, simply acquiring the core BFT skills can be time and labor intensive. It is usually best to see whether improved communication- and problem-solving skills enable families to successfully resolve difficulties before engaging either the client or relatives in other efforts that may inadvertently dilute their commitment to BFT. For most families, special strategies are developed to address problems that have not improved substantially with enhanced communication and problem solving. With some families, however, the use of additional strategies for other problems is merited before the completion of communication and problem solving.

In this chapter, approaches to many of the topics relevant to the seriously ill psychiatric client are discussed. In addition, we describe strategies for managing some of the most common problems presented by the relatives of persons with severe mental illness, as well as problems that can affect either the client or relatives. The list of topics is not exhaustive. Therapists with expertise in other interventions will find many opportunities to augment their BFT work with their additional skills. Similarly, therapists will no doubt encounter clients and family members who have problems in areas not discussed here. We encourage therapists to use this chapter as a springboard to designing the most effective family intervention programs for their clients and to utilize other available resources in developing strategies for helping families manage special problems (e.g., Bellack & Hersen, 1998; Bongar & Beutler, 1995; Dobson & Craig, 1998).

The Logistics of Special Interventions

In this book we have presented the formal components of BFT before discussing special problems. In general, delaying work on special strategies increases the likelihood that the family will have the time necessary to acquire the core skills. Despite this fact, special strategies can be provided early in BFT, if warranted, and interwoven at any point during the therapy sessions. Effective resolution of many of these problems can take months, and efforts may need to continue in concert with teaching the BFT components.

For example, if it becomes clear at the end of the functional assessment that there is a conflict in the family over how the client spends her money, the therapist may opt to spend ten to fifteen minutes at the end of several sessions monitoring the situation, setting up data-collection systems (if needed), encouraging practice of communication skills on this topic (e.g., prompting a family member to express positive feelings to the client when she budgets her money well and to express negative feelings when she manages money poorly), and helping the family and client establish a contingency contract regarding money management. Although part of each family session may be devoted to the special problem of money management, discussion of this problem takes place after completing the formal BFT agenda, such as in the last ten minutes of the session. By following this schedule, the therapist assures that sufficient time is spent teaching the basic BFT skills while still allowing time to address unique concerns. Furthermore, the therapist avoids getting embroiled in potentially emotionally charged topics at the beginning of a session, which may interfere with subsequent skills training during the meeting.

For the remainder of this chapter we discuss specific strategies for dealing with common problems in families over the course of BFT. We first discuss problems most likely to be presented by clients, followed by problems most common in relatives. Finally, we recommend strategies for dealing with difficulties that are shared among family members, or that are equally likely to be present in either relatives or clients.

Strategies for Client Problems

Clients often experience a variety of different problems that are responsive to special interventions provided in the context of BFT. The most common problems include: negative symptoms (i.e., low motivation, poor attention, reduced speech content or frequency, lack of pleasure, isolation) and/or secondary depression, suicidality, poor time management and disorganization, persistent psychotic symptoms, deficits in social functioning, and comorbid substance abuse. Each is discussed briefly below.

Negative Symptoms and/or Secondary Depression

While it is clear that negative symptoms of schizophrenia and the core symptoms of depression are two separate symptom domains, they share many of the same characteristics and may benefit from similar family interventions. In particular, both types of symptoms usually result in social withdrawal, loss of motivation, and isolation. Family members sometimes misinterpret negative symptoms or depression as more under the client's control than florid psychotic symptoms and express their frustration and exasperation over the client's lack of focus and inactivity. Further-more, both negative symptoms and depression are commonly observed in individu-als across a wide range of psychiatric disorders, although their etiology may be different. For example, numbing of responsiveness and social withdrawal are com-mon symptoms of post-traumatic stress disorder, and depression is very common in obsessive-compulsive disorder.

We use a three-step approach in addressing negative symptoms and secondary depression. First, if depression or negative symptoms are prominent, we recommend a thorough psychopharmacological evaluation to determine if a different medication regimen may improve the symptoms. Overmedication with antipsychotics can lead to side effects that are similar to negative symptoms (e.g., akinesia). Some clients with schizophrenia or schizoaffective disorder benefit from adjunctive antidepressant medication in addition to antipsychotic medication. There are numerous types of antidepressant medications that can be tried if one class produces only minimal benefits.

Second, we discuss the nature of depression and negative symptoms at greater length with family members during the education sessions, emphasizing that these symptoms are not voluntary while acknowledging the concern and frustration experi-enced by relatives. We then interweave this educational material into subsequent ses-sions as clients and family members continue to raise concerns. Helping the family understand the impairments that are characteristic of the client's disorder can enable family members to set more realistic expectations for recovery.

Third, we encourage the family to do problem solving on some of the issues related to depression and negative symptoms that most concern them. For example, we have worked with families who have addressed problems such as helping the cli-ent cope with severe depressive feelings, finding ways for the client to do something worthwhile with his or her time at least ten hours per week, helping the client make friends, and improving client sleep patterns. A core issue here involves identifying goals that are personally meaningful to the client and to which the person is willing to commit in spite of his or her relatively low motivation level. Often, this means beginning with very small objectives, which can then be broadened and expanded over time.

Suicidality

Suicidal ideation is quite common among clients with a serious psychiatric dis-order, and unfortunately the risk of suicide is high (Roy, 1986). Many of the core BFT skills are useful in helping families cope with a member who has suicidal thoughts. In the educational phase of BFT, family members can be informed that suicidal ideation is a common symptom of psychiatric disorders and that the reemergence of such thoughts may be an important early warning sign of relapse. During communication-skills training the therapist can encourage the client to express suici-dal thoughts and feelings to his or her relatives in order to enlist their aid in coping with the distress and/or seeking a professional evaluation. The problem solving approach can be use to help the client identify strategies for dealing with frequent suicidal thoughts.

In addition to these strategies, families in which the client has made a prior suicide attempt usually benefit from developing a specific written plan early in BFT for how to cope with a possible suicide crisis in the future. Such a plan is similar to the family plan for responding to early warning signs of relapse and includes:

- a description of the symptom as it pertains to the client (e.g., "John talks about life not being worth living and reports thoughts about hurting himself");

- the identification of a relative or relatives who can monitor the client and respond to emergent or increased suicidality;

- the names and telephone numbers of relevant members of the treatment team; and

- telephone numbers of crisis hotlines.

Some of the therapist's expectations and goals may need to be modified when working with clients who have chronic suicidal ideation or who have made many suicide attempts. Often, one major goal of BFT is to reduce rehospitalizations. However, an alternative goal for highly suicidal clients is to teach them how to use the psychiatric hospital to protect themselves during a suicide crisis (i.e., by signing in voluntarily). With such clients, a goal of BFT is to reduce suicide attempts, even at the cost of increasing hospitalizations. The therapist needs to explain to the family that an elective hospitalization to avoid a suicide attempt is a positive step forward and not a defeat.

Case Example

A couple was engaged in BFT and the husband had been hospitalized on seven prior occasions, each time precipitated by a suicide attempt. As a result of this history the wife was chronically anxious, afraid to leave her husband alone and afraid to express any negative feelings to him. Over the course of BFT the husband was helped to identify specific symptoms that were associated with previous suicide attempts (increased depression, social isolation, thoughts that he would be better off dead) and to communicate his feelings to his wife. A specific plan for dealing with a suicide crisis was agreed upon. No suicide attempts or hospitalizations occurred over the ten-month course of BFT. At follow-up it was learned that the client had signed himself into the hospital on one occasion in response to suicidal thoughts but had made no suicide attempts. Despite the hospitalization, the couple felt progress had been made in coping with his disorder.

Even the most diligent and concerted efforts by therapist and family are occasionally unsuccessful in preventing suicide. In the rare situations when a suicide actually takes place, it is vital for the therapist to continue to work with the family to help members process and deal with their loss. Most families benefit from participating in at least one to three sessions after a suicide. Such a discussion can include family members who did not participate in BFT sessions as well as regular attendees. When facilitating an open discussion with family members about the suicide of a loved one, the therapist may express his or her own feelings about the client and sadness at the family's loss. During this time, the therapist may be able to provide critical information about the disorder to help relatives understand that suicide is a common problem and that no one is at fault. The therapist should be aware that he or she may be held responsible for the suicide or partly blamed by family members. It is best if the therapist acknowledges relatives' feelings of loss, avoids becoming overly defensive, and points to the difficulties even professionals experience trying to prevent suicide in psychiatric clients. The therapist can consider whether some relatives will benefit from a referral to a self-help group of survivors of suicide or to individual grief counseling.

Poor Time Management and Disorganization

Clients with serious psychiatric disorders often have difficulty planning and managing their time effectively, resulting in missed appointments, failure to meet household and social responsibilities, and frustration in family members, friends, and professionals. Factors contributing to this poor time management may include demoralization, apathy, fewer external demands resulting in less of a daily routine, and high levels of distraction and poor concentration due to either persisting symptoms or cognitive impairments.

One useful strategy to address this problem is to encourage the client to carry a small daily organizer to write down his or her scheduled appointments, make lists, and keep reminder notes. This organizer can then be consulted routinely two to three times per day. To achieve this goal, the therapist can first make a positive request that the client obtain a daily organizer. The therapist then asks the client to bring the organizer to the next session and spends fifteen minutes modeling for the family how to help the client write down the appointments he or she has for the next week. The therapist then requests the client to review the next day's appointments each night before going to bed, checking off each appointment as it is attended and then bringing in the organizer to the next session. This assignment both encourages the client to carry the organizer and consult it frequently, and also collects data on attendance at scheduled activities. In reviewing the organizer the next week, the therapist expresses positive feelings for any achievements (e.g., client completed the assignment for three days) and then continues the assignment for the next week to shape progress toward the goal. With particularly impaired clients this brief review can be scheduled as part of the family meeting, with relatives assuming the role of shaping and reinforcing the client. With relatively few shaping efforts, less impaired clients are able to assume this task independently.

Persistent Psychotic Symptoms

Even optimal pharmacological treatment often fails to eliminate all of the psychotic symptoms in clients with severe mental illness. Some clients with persistent psychotic symptoms are able to manage these symptoms effectively and continue to meet their various social roles (e.g., work, getting along with family members, paying their bills). They may volunteer little information about their symptoms, which may cause little or no discomfort. Other clients may be distressed by unremitting hallucinations or delusions, especially those with a negative or threatening tone or that interfere with their ability to watch television, read, work, or interact with others.

We suggest four strategies for addressing persistent psychotic symptoms. The first two strategies require that the client have at least partial insight into the fact that his or her psychotic symptoms may be the result of a psychiatric disorder (or a "chemical imbalance in the brain"). This insight can develop gradually over several years or more rapidly during the educational sessions in BFT. Since the first two strategies involve helping the client develop coping strategies for the psychotic symptoms, without partial insight into those symptoms the client will lack the motivation to learn and use different methods of coping. The third and fourth strategies do not require client insight into the psychiatric nature of psychotic symptoms.

First, clients can use self-instructional talk to remind themselves that they are having psychotic symptoms.

Case Example

A client with schizoaffective disorder was troubled by severe paranoia while riding mass transit. He was certain that others on the subway were talking about him and could read his mind, although he could not understand how they were able to accomplish this feat. He was unable to attend his day treatment program or to visit his family because he avoided mass transit. After participating in the educational sessions of BFT he talked openly for the first time about having these suspicious beliefs. Gradually over several weeks he began to accept that these beliefs might be symptoms of his illness, since he could discover no logical explanation for them and he had begun to learn more about the biological nature of his psychiatric disorder. He began riding the subway on his own and reminded himself each day that any paranoid thoughts he had were symptoms of his illness and were not reflective of the behavior or attitudes of people on the subway. He was eventually able to ride the subway every day, although he still had days when he felt the need to be "on guard" as he did so. He also found that sitting near the front of the subway and limiting eye contact with others was helpful.

Second, clients often benefit from developing a repertoire of tasks for distracting themselves from distressing psychotic symptoms. For example, to cope with intrusive auditory hallucinations, clients may listen to music, hum, sing, or watch a favorite television show. To cope with delusions, such as the belief that the television is talking to them, clients can learn to engage in another activity, such as reading, sleeping, playing cards, going for a walk, or calling a friend. Once the problem area has been defined (e.g., "sometimes I feel like the people I am close to want to harm me"), the client and his or her family can use the formal problem-solving method to generate different options for dealing with the issue. Examples of distractor activities are provided in Table 8.1. Further information about self-control of psychotic symptoms can be found in Breier and Strauss (1983), Carter et al. (1996), and MacDonald et al. (1998); suggestions for teaching clients how to cope with chronic psychotic symptoms are available in Tarrier (1992; Tarrier et al., 1993).

TABLE 8.1
ADAPTIVE STRATEGIES FOR COPING WITH CHRONIC
PSYCHOTIC SYMPTOMS

Modality	Strategies	Examples
Behavior	1. Increasing nonsocial activity	a. Walking b. Engaging in nonsocial leisure activity (e.g., doing puzzles, reading, hobby)
	2. Increasing interpersonal contact	a. Initiating conversation b. Doing leisure activity with someone else
	3. Reality testing	a. Seeking opinions from others
Cognition	1. Shifting attention	a. Thinking about something different (e.g., something pleasant, plans) b. Passive diversion (e.g., watch TV) c. Blocking all thoughts
	2. Fighting back	a. Telling voices to "stop" (e.g., thought stopping)
	3. Self-instruction	a. Telling oneself "be responsible," "take it easy," "you can handle it" b. Problem solving (e.g., asking oneself "What is the problem?," "What can I do about it?," "What else can I do?," etc.)
	4. Ignoring symptom	a. Listening or thinking about symptom b. Reflecting back on content c. Accepting symptom
	5. Prayer	

Sensation/ Physiology	1. Decreasing arousal/ sensory input	a. Relaxation, deep breathing
		b. Blocking ears, closing eyes
	2. Increasing arousal/ sensory input	a. Physical exercise
		b. Listening to loud, stimulating music
	3. Aversive conditioning	a. Snapping a rubber band against the wrist (combining symptom with aversive stimulus)
		b. Conjuring up an unpleasant image

Third, it can be helpful to provide relatives with practical advice on how to interact with a family member who has persisting psychotic symptoms. Some relatives desperately try to dissuade the client from his or her beliefs through confrontation or logical argument. The unfortunate consequence of many of these interactions is an escalation of tension and estrangement between the client and his or her relatives. Furthermore, confrontation may actually increase rather than decrease the convictions psychiatric clients have about their delusional beliefs.

In BFT, therapists try to help relatives comprehend how real delusions seem to clients, even though these beliefs are clearly false to others. One method for illustrating this strength of belief is to compare it to the experience of people who have phobias. Most people know someone who has had a phobia and understand the strong fear experienced by the person. The belief underlying a phobia is no more rational than the delusional beliefs held by some clients, and in either case it is impossible to simply convince the person that the belief is irrational or that the person "shouldn't" experience the negative feelings associated with it. Instead, relatives are encouraged to respond to statements indicative of psychotic experiences by reflective listening, validating and empathizing with the underlying feelings, and avoiding arguments with the client.

Case Example

A daughter with schizophrenia felt unable to attend Thanksgiving family dinner because she believed her relatives could read her mind and that one of her cousins wanted to kill her. The family had been unable to convince her that these beliefs were inaccurate, trying in vain over a three-month period. Alluding to the stress-vulnerability model of psychiatric disorders, the therapist pointed out that family gatherings can be overstimulating to persons who are vulnerable to sensory overload and that it is good that the client recognized in advance that she might be overwhelmed at the dinner. The therapist focused on improving the parents' empathic listening skills and validating the client's feelings of being unsafe. Then, the parents were prompted to suggest a compromise activity for Thanksgiving Day. After a couple of behavioral rehearsals, the mother said, "I feel bad that you will not be able to come to the family dinner. I am very sad that you think your aunts and uncles would want to hurt you, but I understand that this is how you feel right now. I still want to see you on Thanksgiving, however, and I'd feel relieved if we could stop over at your apartment on the way home and bring you some leftovers. That way you won't be alone and you'll have some turkey." The daughter quickly agreed to this plan. The therapist then helped the parents determine how they wanted to field questions about the daughter's absence at the dinner.

A fourth strategy for the management of psychotic symptoms is to employ cognitive therapy principles designed to help clients evaluate the evidence supporting their delusional beliefs (Chadwick et al., 1996; Fowler et al., 1995; Kingdon & Turkington, 1994). Several controlled studies have demonstrated that cognitive therapy can be effective at reducing the severity of psychotic symptoms in schizophrenia (Drury et al., 1996a, 1996b; Kuipers et al., 1997; Tarrier et al., in press). In applying cognitive therapy to the treatment of psychotic symptoms the therapist establishes a collaborative relationship with a client aimed at exploring the basis for delusional beliefs and considering whether alternative interpretations might be better supported by the available evidence. Rather than adopting a confrontational approach to evaluating psychotic processes, the therapist teams up with the client and helps by posing questions that enable the client to evaluate his or her beliefs and possible alternatives. Individual cognitive therapy can be provided conjointly with BFT or can be incorporated into BFT sessions themselves.

Cognitive approaches to psychotic symptoms can be directed at the client's belief systems or the practical consequences of those beliefs. Sometimes it is easier to make headway by addressing problems related to delusional beliefs than attempting to change the beliefs themselves. In the case example provided below, we describe how some of the principles of cognitive therapy can be integrated into the BFT work to decrease the impact of delusional beliefs on client behavior.

Case Example

A mother and her forty-four-year-old son with schizophrenia were the participants in the BFT sessions. After many years of living with her son, the mother decided that she wanted to live alone in her own place. During the course of exploring different possible living situations for the son, he expressed the belief that he was married and that he should go and live with his wife. This belief was a delusion that the client had stated on previous occasions but that had previously had little impact on his behavior. The client was unwilling to consider other living arrangements since he felt his best option was to live with his wife. The mother reported that this delusion had been present for several years and that attempts to confront the delusion had been unsuccessful. Using the problem-solving method, it was determined that if the client wanted to live with his wife, she would need to be found, and a series of searches would be needed. On the first occasion, the mother spent several hours with her son driving to possible locations where he thought his wife might live, each attempt being unsuccessful. On the second occasion, the client and his mother met with a real-estate agent who is also a friend of the family so that the client could describe what he thought the house his wife lived in looked like. Possible neighborhoods were identified, but subsequent exploration was also unsuccessful in locating her. As they were driving home from the second attempt to find his wife, the mother asked her son what he thought they should do if they couldn't find his wife. The son suggested that finding an apartment might be a suitable alternative until his wife could be located. Two months later the son moved out into his own apartment. His transition into more independent living was successful. In the three years since he moved out of his mother's home, no further attempts were made to locate his wife.

Deficits in Social Functioning

Communication and problem-solving skills are taught in BFT using the principles of social-skills training (Bellack, et al., 1997; Liberman et al., 1989). These skills can be useful in both family and nonfamily interactions in the context of BFT. We have often helped clients and other family members practice communication skills to manage problematic work and social situations.

Case Example

The nineteen-year-old son of a patient believed he had been unfairly passed over for a promotion at work. He very much wanted to discuss the issue with his supervisor but said that he did not know what to say and felt too worried to even try. His father encouraged him to plan his conversation with his supervisor during a family session. Over a series of role-playing sessions, the son gradually improved his ability to express his concern over the promotion to his supervisor in a confident, skillful manner. He agreed to speak with his supervisor before the next family meeting and inform his parents about the outcome. He learned from his supervisor that he had not been at the company long enough to be considered for a promotion but was praised for his work performance.

Other participants in BFT have used communication skills to manage conflict with roommates, negotiate with the utility company regarding an unpaid bill, ask someone out on a date, request additional tutorial help from a professor, and work with a lawyer concerning a landlord dispute. In short, once participants have acquired the core BFT communication skills, they can generalize their use across a variety of settings and dilemmas. In addition, the same principles of social-skills training can be used in BFT to teach other basic communication skills to family members, such as initiating and maintaining conversations, self-assertion in responding to criticism, and discussing medication issues with the physician. For individuals with substantial impairments in social skill, relatives can be taught the rudiments of social-skills training so that the therapist can initiate training of specific skills in the session and relatives can facilitate the practice of each skill at home. This strategy allows the therapist to monitor gradual improvements in social skills while economizing on the time required to train new skills in the family sessions. A comprehensive curriculum of commonly taught social skills, including the individual steps to each skill and examples of the role play situations, can be found in Bellack et al. (1997).

Comorbid Alcohol and Drug Abuse

Comorbid substance abuse is a complicating factor in many clients. Clients with severe mental illness are significantly more likely to develop alcohol and drug-use disorders compared with the general population (Regier et al., 1990). Surveys of the prevalence of substance-use disorders, including substance abuse and dependence, indicate that 50 to 60 percent of clients with a severe mental illness experience problems related to substance use during their lives, and that 25 to 40 percent of clients meet criteria for a current substance-use disorder (Cuffel, 1996; Mueser et al., 1995). Therefore, most therapists providing BFT for psychiatric disorders can expect substance-use disorders in a significant proportion of their clients. As we discuss below, it is critical that the therapist address substance abuse over the course of BFT if positive outcomes are to be achieved.

Comorbid substance-use disorders in severe mental illness (i.e., "dual diagnosis") are associated with a wide range of negative outcomes (Drake & Brunette, 1998). For example, dually diagnosed clients are prone to more relapses and rehospitalizations, higher rates of aggression and suicidality, financial and legal problems, and increased health risk behaviors such as unprotected sex and trading sex for drugs. In addition to the effects on psychiatric illness, the multiple effects of substance abuse (e.g., stealing money, not fulfilling expected household tasks, threatening or aggressive behavior) can have a major impact on family functioning, including higher levels of conflict with family members, increased burden of managing the illness, and higher family expenditures (Clark, 1996; Dixon et al., 1995). A common consequence of this substance abuse is that the coping resources of the family can become overwhelmed, leading to an erosion of support for the client and ultimately to a breakdown in the family support system. The net result is that, if untreated, dual diagnosis can lead to a weakening or severing of family ties, contributing to housing instability and homelessness. An important goal of BFT is to prevent the loss of family support for dually diagnosed clients that can have catastrophic effects on the course of severe mental illness.

BFT can be used effectively to address the problem of dual diagnosis. BFT adapted for dual diagnosis is guided by two general goals. First, an important aim of the intervention is to reduce substance abuse and, when possible, to help the client achieve abstinence from alcohol or drugs. The second goal of the family intervention is to reduce the negative consequences of the client's substance abuse on other family members. A client's substance abuse can affect the functioning of everyone in the family, threatening supportive bonds. Even when the client's substance abuse continues to be a problem, BFT can enable family members to maintain a supportive relationship and to avoid some of the long-term consequences of substance abuse, including social isolation and homelessness.

Stages of Treatment

BFT with the dually diagnosed client is informed by the concept of stages of treatment (Osher & Kofoed, 1989). The stage concept is based on the observation that dually diagnosed clients who recover during treatment proceed through a series of distinct stages, including engagement, persuasion, active treatment, and relapse prevention. Each stage has a unique goal and interventions are tailored to the goal corresponding to the client's current stage. By attending to the client's current stage of treatment, the therapist can optimize outcomes by properly matching interventions to the client's current motivational state (Mueser, Drake, & Noordsy, 1998).

During the *engagement* stage, the client does not have a therapeutic relationship with the therapist. Without a working relationship, defined as regular contact between the client and the therapist, efforts to address substance abuse are invariably unsuccessful. Therefore, the goal of the engagement stage is to establish a therapeutic alliance with the client. In the *persuasion* stage, a therapeutic alliance has been established, but the client does not view substance abuse as problematic or is unwilling to work on it. The goal of this stage of treatment is to help the client understand that substance abuse is a problem and to motivate him or her to begin working on this problem. A client is considered motivated to work on substance abuse when he or she has begun to make efforts to cut down or stop using substances. When the client has demonstrated motivation to work on his or her substance abuse, he or she is in the *active* stage of treatment, wherein the goal becomes helping the client further reduce substance use and preferably attain abstinence. Finally, when the client has not experienced problematic substance use for at least six months, he or she is in the *relapse-prevention* stage, in which the goal is to prevent or minimize the possibility of a substance-abuse relapse and to expand recovery to other areas of functioning, such as social relationships and work.

Just as individual work with dually diagnosed clients is guided by the stages of treatment, so is family intervention, as described below. A key issue here is recognizing that families differ in their own beliefs about the benefits and costs of substance use, and the therapist is best advised not to make any a priori assumptions about these beliefs. Careful ongoing assessment is needed.

Engagement. Engagement of families with dually diagnosed clients follows the same basic principles as engagement for BFT, as outlined in Chapter 3. Clients with a dual diagnosis are intermittently compliant with treatment, and their families may also present special challenges for engagement. Successful engagement of both dually diagnosed clients and their families, therefore, often requires outreach into the community to connect with the families in their own natural settings. Reaching out to families, evaluating the concerns of relatives, and being flexible in terms of location and length of family sessions are important ingredients for successful engagement.

During the initial contact with family members, the therapist needs to be careful not to push substance abuse to the forefront of the discussion unless he or she knows that family members view it as a problem. Many family members are not aware of the interactions between substance abuse and mental illness, and most relatives and patients express little interest in learning more about substance abuse (Mueser et al., 1992). Thus, when engaging the family, the therapist does not state that reduction of substance abuse is an important treatment goal unless he or she knows the family will support this goal.

Persuasion. The primary goal of the persuasion stage is to convince the client and family members that substance abuse is an important problem that needs to be addressed. The primary therapeutic strategy in BFT for accomplishing the goal of persuasion is psychoeducation. Over the course of the educational sessions, families receive basic information about the nature of the psychiatric illness, medications and their effects, and the stress-vulnerability model. Discussion of the stress-vulnerability model provides a convenient opening for a more detailed discussion of the interactions between psychiatric illness and alcohol and drug abuse. At the end of the educational module on the stress-vulnerability model, families are introduced to the fact that commonly abused substances, such as alcohol, marijuana, and cocaine, can easily upset the client's biological vulnerability, worsening symptoms and functioning. Following discussion of this model, the clinician can introduce the educational handout provided in Appendix 3, that is specifically designed to address substance-use disorders in psychiatric illness. This educational handout provides a discussion of the motives clients often endorse for using substances, the common consequences of substance use, and definition of terms such as "substance abuse" and "substance dependence." This handout can be used to facilitate a discussion among family members about the client's substance use, its interactions with the psychiatric illness, and its effects on other family members. As with all education sessions in BFT, the therapist's goal is to facilitate an open, honest, and accepting discussion of the issues at hand. In discussing substance use and mental illness with families, it is especially useful to point out that persons with a psychiatric illness are more sensitive to lower amounts of alcohol and drugs due to their psychobiological vulnerability (Mueser, Drake, & Wallach, 1998). This helps family members understand that "normal" substance use in persons with a psychiatric illness often results in negative consequences that would not occur in people without a psychiatric disorder.

For many families these educational sessions are sufficient to persuade the participants that substance abuse is a problem, and for those families active treatment strategies are appropriate. However, some families remain unconvinced of the importance of substance abuse even after the educational sessions, or their commitment to working on substance abuse is limited. For these families it can be helpful to take a *motivational interviewing* approach to the problem of substance abuse. Motivational interviewing is a set of strategies designed to help individuals understand the effects of substance abuse on their lives and develop a commitment to working on this problem (Miller & Rolnick, 1991). Motivational interviewing involves helping the client identify goals that are personally important, determining how to achieve those goals, and then highlighting the discrepancy between the attainment of those goals and the client's continued substance use. When individuals see their substance use as interfering with their own goals, a dissonance is created, leading to a motivation to reduce or eliminate substance use. The term "motivation" in this approach refers to the fact that the client's own goals are used to harness motivation to change substance abuse.

The same principle of identifying goals and developing discrepancy between substance abuse and attainment of those goals can be applied in BFT using family problem solving. If families are not convinced that substance abuse is an important problem, the therapist uses problem solving to identify other important family and personal goals on which to focus. When goals have been identified, the therapist explores with family members the steps needed to achieve those goals, searching for opportunities to encourage family members to consider the possible obstacles posed by substance abuse. Significant progress may need to be made toward achieving a specified goal before the problem of substance abuse becomes apparent and the necessary discrepancy between achieving the goal and continued substance abuse develops.

Case Example

A woman with major depression and alcoholism participated in BFT with her husband with the purpose of decreasing her hospitalizations and suicide attempts and improving functional capacity. Despite reviewing information in the educational sessions about the negative effects of alcohol on mood, the couple remained skeptical that the client's alcohol abuse (which usually ranged from three to six drinks per day) contributed to her depression. In the problem-solving sessions, the therapist took a motivational interviewing approach to the client's alcohol abuse and shifted the focus to helping the client secure employment, a goal that was supported by the wife and her husband because of their tight financial circumstances. Over the course of several months of working toward this goal, the client was successful in obtaining competitive employment but experienced difficulties maintaining her expected work schedule. Family problem solving led to the observation that alcohol consumption appeared to be associated with problems on the job, especially getting up in the morning and arriving at work on time. The couple first agreed to try cutting down on the client's drinking in order to determine whether improvements in job performance occurred. Not only did reduced drinking improve her work performance but the client also reported decreases in her depression. Over the next few months, the couple concluded that moderate drinking was difficult to regulate, and the client became abstinent from alcohol. To support his wife, the husband stopped drinking at home.

The persuasion stage is also an appropriate time to facilitate discussion of what impact the client's substance abuse may have on other family members. As family members develop their communication skills, the therapist can encourage them to talk with one another about the impact of substance abuse on their lives. These discussions can be painful for both the client and relatives, but they can also help boost the family's commitment to working on substance abuse together. In facilitating these communications, the clinician tries to maintain an open, accepting family atmosphere that is free of blame and conducive of change on the part of the client.

Although the goal of the persuasion stage is to motivate the client and family to address substance-abuse related issues, attention must also be given to minimizing the effect of substance abuse on relatives. Problem solving is a useful strategy for addressing the effects of substance abuse on family members. Other special strategies may be identified, such as limiting family contact with the client when he or she is intoxicated.

Active Treatment. When families are in the active treatment stage the focus shifts to reducing substance abuse or attaining abstinence. Problem solving provides a useful format for achieving this goal. Problem solving can be used to identify "high-risk" substance-abuse situations and to develop alternative strategies for either managing or avoiding those situations. Clients with a dual diagnosis endorse a variety of different motives for using substances (Addington & Duchak, 1997; Carey & Carey, 1995; Fowler et al., 1998; Noordsy et al., 1991; Warner et al., 1994), but most motives fall into one of three categories: coping with distressing symptoms, socialization, and pleasure and recreation. Exploring with a client his or her motives for using substances can provide a useful focus for family problem solving in addressing how clients can get their needs fulfilled in ways other than using substances. For example, a client who uses marijuana mainly for recreational reasons can be engaged in family problem solving aimed at developing alternative leisure and recreational pursuits.

Clients in the active treatment or relapse-prevention stages may benefit from participating in self-help groups for addictive disorders, such as Alcoholics Anonymous (Noordsy et al., 1996). Clients with schizophrenia-spectrum disorders appear to be less likely to benefit from these groups due to their social deficits, although some clients have positive experiences. As self-help groups vary in their attitudes toward psychiatric illnesses and psychotropic medications, it is helpful if the therapist becomes knowledgeable about local groups that will be most receptive to dually diagnosed clients.

Sometimes relatives are persuaded that substance abuse is a problem, while the client remains unpersuaded. The clinician has several options when the client and relatives are in different stages of treatment. The therapist can use problem solving to take a motivational approach to client-centered goals, as described in the previous section on the persuasion stage. In order to accomplish this, the therapist works collaboratively with the relatives to identify goals with the client and then develops discrepancy between achieving those goals and the client's substance abuse. Alternatively, the therapist can encourage family members to use problem solving in order to address the substance-abuse problem despite the client's lack of commitment to working on this problem. In these situations, family problem solving can take the form of helping members negotiate and compromise about ways of reducing the harm associated with substance abuse. In addition, to the extent that family members control certain client resources (such as the client's finances), family problem solving (or "contingency contracting") can be used to decrease a client's substance use. Clients sometimes become motivated to work on their substance-use problems after they have experienced some of the benefits of reducing substance use.

Relapse Prevention. In the final stage of treatment, relapse prevention is aimed at helping family members maintain an awareness of the client's vulnerability to relapse and working to improve other areas of functioning, such as social relationships. Maintaining awareness of the potential for relapse can be facilitated by completing a relapse-prevention plan for substance abuse using the same worksheet as that completed for the psychiatric illness. Problem solving can be useful for addressing other areas of functioning.

Other Treatments for Dual Disorders

For some dually diagnosed individuals, substance abuse can be severe and persistent despite arduous treatment efforts. Family intervention is an important treatment strategy for clients with a dual diagnosis, but other interventions may be required as well. For example, individual-based motivational interviewing (Miller & Rollnick, 1991), cognitive-behavioral counseling (Graham, 1998), and assertive community treatment (Drake et al., 1998) can be important treatment approaches for dual diagnosis. In addition, group-based interventions designed either to help individuals understand the effects of substance abuse on their lives and develop motivation to work on substance abuse, or to improve social skills for handling substance-abuse related and other social situations can be useful group interventions for dual diagnosis (Mueser & Noordsy, 1996). Therapists need to consider the broader treatment needs of dually diagnosed clients in order to determine whether and how family interventions may be supplemented by other treatment strategies. Specific guidelines for the treatment of dual disorders, including individual, group, and family formats, as well as pharmacological and residential approaches, are provided in Mueser, Drake, Noordsy, and Fox (in preparation).

Strategies for Relatives' Problems

Two problems often present in the relatives of clients with severe mental illness, problems that pose special challenges for the BFT therapist: substance abuse and extreme levels of emotional distress. We discuss special strategies for managing each of these problems in this section.

Substance Abuse in Relatives

Considering the fact that about 13 percent of the general population has a lifetime history of alcohol-use disorder and 6 percent has a history of a drug-use disorder (Regier et al., 1990), chances are high that therapists conducting BFT will encounter relatives with a substance-use disorder. Although information concerning substance abuse in a relative may be revealed during the initial assessment, therapists also need to be aware of signs in therapy that suggest the possible presence of such disorder. Signs to look for include unexplained absences, frequent appointment cancellations, apparent intoxication during sessions, significant conflict with other relatives, problems working, and financial problems. If the therapist suspects substance abuse in a relative, an attempt is made to confirm (or reject) the suspicion through an individual meeting with the person.

When a relative acknowledges a substance-use problem and expresses some motivation to work on the problem, the role of the therapist is straightforward: he or she tries to facilitate the relative's efforts to address the problem. Such facilitation may include assisting the relative to set goals for reduced substance use or abstinence, helping the person identify triggers for substance use and strategies for managing high-risk situations and urges to use substances (e.g., Sobell & Sobell, 1993), referral to self-help groups (e.g., Alcoholics Anonymous, Narcotics Anonymous, Rational Recovery, Al-Anon for other family members), or referral for individual counseling and (if the problem is very severe) inpatient treatment. Relatives with chronic substance abuse usually require comprehensive treatment over a long period. The therapist can facilitate the relative's entry into the system of available treatments.

Relatives who deny substance abuse in the presence of overwhelming evidence suggesting it, or who minimize problems ensuing from their substance abuse, or who are unmotivated to work on it, pose a difficult problem to the therapist. These relatives have agreed to participate in BFT in order to learn how to manage the client's psychiatric disorder, not to receive treatment for their own problems. If the therapist pushes the relative too hard toward working on substance abuse, he or she risks alienating that person and losing his or her participation in BFT. In these cases, we advise the therapist to continue the main work of BFT, remaining alert to opportunities to address substance-abuse related problems (e.g., through clear communication of feelings, problem solving) and to develop motivation in the relative to address the problem.

Similar to our description of how to use problem solving to motivate clients to address their substance abuse in the previous section, this approach can also be used with relatives who do not view their substance use as a problem (or who are unwilling to work on it). Rather than directly confronting the substance abuse, the therapist works with the family to identify goals that are then the focus of problem solving. In working toward these goals, the therapist attempts to shape the family discussion so that the possible interactions between the relative's substance abuse and steps toward achieving desired goals are considered. When relatives see their own substance abuse as interfering with a desired goal, they may become motivated to reduce their use of substances. In order to use the problem solving to harness a relative's motivation to work on substance abuse, it is important that the therapist help the family identify a goal to work on that has high relevance and personal meaning for that relative.

Extreme Levels of Emotional Distress

Although clients make substantial contributions to their own families (Greenberg et al., 1994), caring for and maintaining a close relationship with a person with a serious psychiatric illness can nevertheless take a significant toll on the psychological well-being of relatives (Cooper, 1996; Lefley, 1996; Song et al., 1997). For example, Coyne et al. (1987) reported that 40 percent of adults living with a client with depression met a standardized criterion for referral to treatment for distress, and 36 to 75 percent of relatives caring for a client with schizophrenia have been found to meet similar criteria (Gibbons et al., 1984; Oldridge & Hughes, 1992). Although an explicit goal of BFT is to reduce caregiving burden through the components of psychoeducation, communication-skills training, and problem solving, extreme levels of depression or anxiety may occur in some relatives that require interventions more specifically tailored to address these problems.

The first approach to managing extreme levels of emotional distress in relatives is to maintain a "holding environment" (i.e., a calm, consistent, predictable, hopeful therapeutic setting) and deliver the core components of BFT in order to determine whether they are successful in reducing the distress. Severe depression and anxiety in relatives often motivates them to participate in family intervention, which provides a certain level of professional support, reassurance, and hope that in and of itself can be therapeutic. In addition, correcting misconceptions about psychiatric illness and its treatment, improved communication, and problem solving focused on helping relatives get their needs met can have a potent effect on distress. Finally, the severity of disruptive client behaviors can influence distress in caregivers (Provencher & Mueser, 1997); more effective psychiatric treatment of the client in the course of BFT, such as improved pharmacological management and illness monitoring, can reduce the severity of these behaviors and thus their effects on relatives.

When extreme distress in relatives persists throughout BFT, or is so severe as to disrupt the ability of the therapist to teach the core BFT components, there are several possible options that may be pursued. Many people benefit from reading self-help books for dealing with depression and anxiety disorders (see titles listed at the end of Chapter 5 and at the end of the "Facts About . . ." educational handouts on psychiatric disorders in Appendix 3). When the distress is quite debilitating, referral for individual psychotherapy can provide the relief necessary for the relative to continue to be an active participant in BFT. Some relatives experience severe depression when a close family member develops mental illness, and grief work with a therapist may help them process this loss (Miller, 1996). In addition, referral to a psychiatrist for a medication evaluation may be helpful for some relatives experiencing extreme levels of distress. In the course of making such referrals, it can be helpful if the therapist reviews with the relative, either individually or in a BFT session, information about the psychiatric disorder using an educational handout, such as one contained in Appendix 3 of this book or one specially tailored to the relative's disorder.

A common consequence of extreme distress is social withdrawal, both from family members and others. For individuals who experience persistent distress despite psychotherapeutic or pharmacological interventions, referral to a support group can be helpful. There are numerous different types of self-help support groups aimed at helping individuals cope with anxiety and depression and at promoting self-efficacy through informal shared problem solving. The therapist can help the relative explore possible groups by consulting the telephone book or local newspapers.

Strategies for Problems Often Found in Clients or Relatives

Some problems are encountered in both clients or relatives, such as intoxication during the BFT session, anger and violence, and anxiety problems. Other problems are shared across family members, such as difficulties with intimacy and conflict over child rearing. We describe strategies for handling these problems in this section.

Intoxication during the BFT Session

Occasionally, the therapist will encounter a situation in which the client and/or relatives appear intoxicated at the BFT session. Several strategies are available to the therapist to deal with this situation. First, during the orientation meeting, the therapist can make a request to family members to not imbibe before BFT sessions, explaining that alcohol or drug use will interfere with their ability to acquire critical skills. If substance abuse is a significant problem for a member, the therapist can contract with the person not to use substances on the same day of a family session, or, if substances have been used, the person will call the therapist to reschedule the appointment.

Second, the therapist can lead (or prompt) a problem-solving discussion to address his or her concern that substance use prior to sessions will compromise the efficacy of the treatment. Third, if the family member's intoxicated state is disruptive to the BFT session, the therapist can ask the person to leave the session. In dealing with this problem, the therapist must walk the thin line between addressing the problem so that the requisite BFT skills can be taught and trying to maintain an alliance with all family members.

Anger and Violence

Many families struggle with the issue of controlling anger and violence in the home, and these problems tend to be even greater in families in which one member has a psychiatric disorder (Goodman et al., 1997; Mueser et al., 1998; Jacobson & Richardson, 1987). The violence present in families with a psychiatric client can take many forms, ranging from verbal threats to moderate levels of physical aggression (e.g., pushing, shoving) to more severe aggression (e.g., hitting, punching, kicking). In a survey of recently hospitalized psychiatric clients, Cascardi et al. (1996) reported that 63 percent of clients living with a domestic partner had been exposed to physical violence and that 46 percent of clients living with family members had been exposed to violence. For many clients, the violence was reciprocal, with clients being both the aggressor and the victim. Although rates of victimization were similar for males and females, women were more likely to have sustained physical injuries. These findings underscore the importance of being alert to violence in the families of psychiatric clients.

The BFT therapist may first become alerted to a problem of anger or violence when discussing the client with other treatment providers and reviewing the clinical records, or when querying how the family handles disagreements as part of the joint or individual assessment interviews. Alternatively, the issue may become more prominent as family work continues and the therapist learns more of its day-to-day functioning. In any case, the therapist must recognize signs that anger management and violence are a problem for a family and be ready to intervene when necessary. A useful instrument for assessing violence in families is the Conflict Tactics Scale-2 (Strauss et al., 1995). However, because of its forthright nature, many of the items on the Conflict Tactics Scale-2 can be disturbing, and family members benefit from being oriented to the scale first.

We have found that several strategies can be helpful in addressing the problem of violence in families. At the most basic level, both communication and problem-solving efforts can be used to address the problem. In many families, anger and violence ensue when members lack the ability to give immediate, constructive feedback to one another about upsetting or frustrating events.

Case Example

A client with schizophrenia receiving BFT approached neighbor children yelling at them and swinging a golf club because they "were making too much noise," and he thought they were talking about him (a delusion of reference). In doing an analysis of the incident, it became clear that the client had been disturbed for days because the children were yelling right outside his window, but he had not been able to identify an appropriate way to convey his concerns and resolve the issue. When a problem-solving approach was taken, he defined the problem as "the children outside were loud and annoying to me." He and his mother generated a variety of solutions (e.g., he could have left the house and gone to the library when the noise upset him, he could have purchased earplugs, he could have listened to music). They selected a solution that involved speaking with the parents of the children and asking them to quiet their children or to ask them to move to another end of the play-lot. As preparation for implementing this solution, the client practiced the skills of expressing a negative feeling and making a positive request in role plays with his mother. The client and his mother reported that the solution was successfully implemented and further incidents did not occur.

The use of communication and problem-solving skills alone will not resolve the difficulties of most families in which anger is out of control and violence results. Members of these families usually benefit from supplemental work on these topics. In families where violence is an issue, we typically devote one or two sessions solely to this issue, in addition to monitoring levels of aggression in the initial assessment portion of each session. First, the family must be given the message that physical aggression is unacceptable and that every effort will be made to eliminate it so that the home can be a place of safety. All family members are encouraged to commit to a violence-free home. In our clinical experience, the vast majority of families have been willing to do so. Many family members have difficulty recognizing their own signs of provocation, however. In a discussion format, we spend time at the beginning of the special anger sessions discussing general signs of provocation and asking each family member to identify his or her unique signals (e.g., flushed face, tension in "gut," tight feeling in neck, etc.). Once these cues have been identified, they can be used to:

1. constructively express a negative feeling and suggest a compromise;

2. suggest the need for a problem-solving session and schedule a meeting time; or

3. request a time-out.

For less affectively charged topics, the immediate use of appropriate communication skills can frequently resolve the difficulty, while for more intensely emotional issues, the family member may require time alone to compose himself or herself prior to being able to engage in constructive problem solving. Using behavioral rehearsals of recent events, family members can practice these different options during the session.

In a family with a long history of violence, or when dealing with psychotic individuals, the above strategies may not be sufficient to eliminate the problem. For the former, the aggressor may benefit from participation in adjunctive treatment to learn better ways of coping with aggressive urges (Novaco, 1975; Deffenbacher & Stark, 1992). When domestic violence occurs between a husband and wife and there is some motivation to work on this issue, cognitive-behavioral strategies developed for this problem may be appropriate (Neidig & Friedman, 1984; Pence & Paymar, 1986), as well as referral of the offender to a spousal group for battering. Victims of domestic violence also need to be informed about the available resources in their community for dealing with the violence, such as emergency crisis telephone numbers, the police, and organizations such as Women Against Abuse and Women Organized Against Rape.

For many psychiatric clients, irritability, anger, and violence are related to either paranoid delusions or a hypomanic or manic state. For these individuals, an increase in anger or aggression may be a sign of an impending relapse that requires immediate evaluation for pharmacological stabilization and assessment of potential harm to others. A brief hospitalization and a medication adjustment may reduce the hostility.

In some families, a pattern of physical violence or destructive behavior by the client may be a problem that cannot be successfully resolved while the client continues living at home. Family members may need to be told that they have the right to live in a peaceful, secure home environment. These families may benefit from being encouraged to seek alternative living arrangements for the client, such as board-and-care homes and community rehabilitation residences. Relatives often feel guilty about asking the client to live somewhere else. The therapist can frame these changes in living arrangement as a positive step forward for the client toward greater independence. The therapist should also emphasize that the relatives are not abandoning the client and that their contact and support will continue to be beneficial. Furthermore, many clients recognize their own problems with violence and its imprint in their family members. These clients often welcome the exploration of alternative living arrangements, while experiencing the normal ambivalence that accompanies any major life change.

Anxiety Problems

Anxiety disorders, including social phobia, simple phobias, agoraphobia, panic disorder, post-traumatic stress disorder, obsessive-compulsive disorder, and generalized anxiety disorder, are the most common types of psychiatric disorders in the general population (Kessler et al., 1994; Robins & Regier, 1991). Furthermore, comorbidity of anxiety disorders is high in other major psychiatric illnesses, such as major affective disorders and schizophrenia-spectrum disorders (Akiskal, 1990; Argyle, 1990; Boyd et al., 1984; Eisen et al., 1997; Kessler et al., 1997; Penn et al., 1994). Therefore, even when the primary problem being addressed in the family involves schizophrenia or depression, BFT therapists are likely to encounter concurrent anxiety disorders in either the ill relative or in other family members.

The basic BFT structure, including the educational material, communication-skills training, and instruction in problem solving, can be utilized in the treatment of anxiety disorders. In fact, post-traumatic stress and obsessive-compulsive disorders can result in such significant impairments that they may be the primary diagnosis for the ill relative participating with his or her family, and educational materials for these disorders are included in Appendix 3. However, some family members (including the client) may have an anxiety disorder that is more peripheral to the primary psychiatric disorder in the family, and it is the issue of adjunctive treatment of an anxiety disorder that is being addressed in this section.

Reviewing with families educational handouts on anxiety disorders, either from the appendix of this book or from other sources, can be especially useful in helping families understand the nature of these disorders. However, research on the treatment of anxiety disorders suggests that traditional BFT must often be augmented with work dealing more specifically with the identification of and exposure to fear-eliciting stimuli. For some anxiety disorders, notably post-traumatic-stress disorder, the use of cognitive restructuring may provide an alternative to direct exposure-based intervention.

When feared stimuli are circumscribed, as in the case with agoraphobia, obsessive-compulsive disorder, and simple phobias, the bulk of exposure treatment can be conducted within the framework of BFT by extending therapy sessions to review and assign exposure homework with the relative acting as a support person. Using a relative as an exposure "coach" has been shown to be successful in couples-based treatment of both agoraphobia and obsessive-compulsive disorder (Baucom et al., 1998). It should be noted, however, that family treatment may not be the optimal choice for the treatment of a comorbid anxiety disorder. Circumstances that suggest that specific, individual treatment for anxiety may be preferred to treatment in the context of the family include:

1. high levels of negative affect in the family;

2. substantial chronicity and generalization of the fear;

3. a concurrent substance-use disorder; and

4. logistical constraints that preclude extending BFT sessions.

An important consideration for the BFT therapist when treating anxiety disorders is the issue of secondary gain for current avoidance behavior. That is, the avoidance behavior of one family member is frequently socially reinforced by other members, and such reinforcement may attenuate the commitment of the afflicted member to exposure work and recovery. For example, in persons with agoraphobia it is common for other family members to assume a wide range of household (and other) responsibilities in order to accommodate the person's fear of leaving the home. The spouse of someone with agoraphobia may increase the amount of time spent with the person so he or she does not have to be alone, which may be socially reinforcing. Similarly, in obsessive-compulsive disorder a relative may recruit other family members into performing elaborate cleaning or avoidance strategies, increasing the person's power over others while decreasing his or her personal responsibility for personal and shared tasks.

The therapist can respond to issues of secondary gain by prompting a problem-solving discussion. This discussion can focus on identifying ways of providing social reinforcement to the member with anxiety contingent upon participation in exposure and clinical improvement, rather than reinforcement for continued avoidance. In addition, it can also be useful to encourage family members to draw up a list of how the avoidance behavior has interfered with desired activities and goals. For example, forgoing family vacations, decrease in sexual relations, or financial strains often accompany anxiety disorders. Reviewing these "costs" of anxiety to all family members can increase motivation to change, in spite of a history of secondary gain from avoidance.

Special challenges for the BFT therapist are posed by the problem of comorbid post-traumatic-stress disorder (PTSD) in clients with another psychiatric disorder. Persons with severe mental illness have high rates of trauma over their lifetime (Goodman et al., 1997). These traumatic experiences take many forms but most commonly include physical or sexual assault either in childhood or adulthood, the sudden loss of a significant other, being threatened with violence, or witnessing violence to others. Accidents and natural disasters are also important traumatic events. Research on current PTSD in persons with severe mental illness indicates rates between 29 and 43 percent (Cascardi et al., 1996; Craine et al., 1988; Mueser et al., 1998), substantially higher than the 7 to 9 percent rate of lifetime PTSD in the general population (Breslau et al., 1991; Kessler et al., 1995).

Traumatic experiences in persons with severe mental illness usually need to be assessed in an individual rather than family context, although occasionally information concerning trauma will first appear in a family session. Eliciting traumatic experiences in clients with a psychosis can be difficult when there are questions as to the veracity of the verbal reports. Psychotic distortions can result in the false reporting of events that did not occur. Furthermore, most interpersonally traumatic events occur in the absence of innocent bystanders who can provide verification. However, most research suggests that people are more likely to underreport than overreport traumatic events due to fear of social rejection or the desire to protect the perpetrator(s) (Della Femina et al., 1990; Symonds, 1982). Therefore, we encourage therapists to assess traumatic experiences in clients participating in BFT.

PTSD can be diagnosed in individuals who have experienced a severe traumatic event that was life threatening or posed a grave danger to him or her or to others, in accordance with DSM-IV criteria. If PTSD is confirmed, in addition to reviewing the educational handout on PTSD (Appendix 3) with the family, the therapist has two main options concerning the treatment of this additional disorder. First, the therapist can use problem solving with the family to develop coping strategies for the management of common PTSD symptoms, such as frequent intrusive memories, difficulty sleeping, and avoidance of situations that remind the person of the trauma. Second, the therapist can treat the client individually (or refer the client to another clinician for treatment), while continuing to provide ongoing BFT. Treatment of PTSD in the general population indicates that both cognitive restructuring and exposure (imaginal and in vivo) are effective for reducing PTSD secondary to a variety of different traumas (Marks et al., 1998; Tarrier, Pilgrim et al., in press). Considering the sensitivity of clients with severe mental illness to stress, cognitive restructuring may be the preferred treatment approach.

Case Example

About five months into BFT with a forty-five-year-old man with bipolar disorder and his wife, the man reported that he was under extreme stress and was having problems sleeping due to repeated, nagging memories of some events that had happened many years ago. Subsequent assessment revealed that the client had experienced several traumatic events that continued to trouble him. First, over a period of four months when he was twelve years old, he was sexually abused by a foster mother in a new home placement. Second, at the age of nineteen, he returned to the apartment that he shared with his younger brother to discover his brother dead following a suicide by hanging. The therapist reviewed with the couple the educational handout on PTSD and then provided individual treatment for the client concurrent with BFT. Treatment included both cognitive restructuring, aimed at challenging dysfunctional thoughts arising from the traumatic experiences, imaginal exposure to the memories of the events, and in vivo exposure to feared situations. After nine individual sessions the client had demonstrated significant improvement in his symptoms, and he no longer met criteria for PTSD. At this point, individual treatment could be stopped. The client's PTSD remained in remission until the end of BFT six months later, and a one-year follow-up after termination of BFT indicated the disorder was still in remission.

In addition to the anxiety resulting from traumatic events such as experiencing and witnessing physical or sexual violence or the sudden loss of a family member, anxiety problems may also occur in clients and their relatives secondary to the experience of a psychotic episode. Many clients with remitted psychotic disorders are extremely fearful that they will experience another psychotic episode and again face the indignities of involuntary commitment, psychiatric hospitalization, and/or engaging in bizarre behavior that frightens or repulses family and friends. This anxiety can culminate in PTSD symptoms, including intrusive recollections of a psychotic experience, hypervigilance, and avoidance of events that remind them of the experience (Shaner & Eth, 1989; McGorrey et al., 1991). These reactions may be quite realistic and not reflect current psychotic symptoms. Similarly, many clients have traumatic memories about past events related to the treatment of the psychiatric illness, such as involuntary hospitalization, severe medication side effects, and use of seclusion and restraints in the hospital. These fears of subsequent episodes and the treatment they involve are often shared by the relatives of the client.

The anxiety experienced by clients and relatives due to past psychotic episodes can interfere with their willingness to pursue personal and shared goals. For example, family members may be afraid to work on the goals of the client getting a job or continuing his or her education for fear of upsetting the tenuous stabilization of the psychiatric disorder that has been achieved. As a consequence of this fear, there may be a lack of progress toward rehabilitation goals, and stagnation may ensue.

Families need a forum in which to discuss their concerns about past and future relapses. The educational sessions in BFT provide an opportunity to begin to address these topics by asking participants to discuss the impact of the disorder on their lives. The therapist continues to be alert to shame and fear issues as the therapy progresses and prompts the use of the communication skills (e.g., "I" statements, paraphrasing, active listening) when they are raised. Preparing a relapse-prevention plan often assuages the client's and relatives' concerns about the possibility of impending exacerbations.

Lingering concerns about the likelihood of a relapse often become evident during problem solving, when there may be conflict or reticence about working on certain goals. The therapist can explore possible fears family members may have about a future psychotic episode and provide additional information that may help them reevaluate their fears, as described in the case example below.

Case Example

A twenty-four-year-old young man with schizophrenia was enrolled in BFT with his mother and stepfather. In the individual interview at the beginning of BFT, the client stated that a goal of his was to pursue his college education, which had been interrupted four years earlier by his development of schizophrenia. However, when he asked for help addressing this goal during a problem-solving meeting, his mother objected. Specifically, the client wanted to resume his study of calculus, but the mother thought this would be too stressful and would precipitate a relapse, since he had first become ill when studying calculus in college. The therapist explained that, although calculus can be demanding, the nature of the client's program of study as a college student probably had little to do with his development of schizophrenia, and that the disorder usually becomes apparent around this time regardless of what the client is doing. With this in mind, the family worked on the client's goal in problem solving and agreed that it would be useful if the client first took a precalculus "refresher" course in order to get back into the routine of studying in a less demanding format and to review related mathematical concepts to see if it had any impact on his symptoms, now that he was receiving appropriate treatment.

Problems in Sexual Intimacy and Functioning

Problems with sexual intimacy and functioning are common in couples in which one person has a psychiatric disorder (Hafner, 1986). Persons with schizophrenia or affective disorders may lack the desire for sexual relations due to anhedonia, or clients with bipolar disorder may be overly demanding or promiscuous during a manic or hypomanic phase. People with chronic post-traumatic-stress disorder often experience a pervasive lack of trust in others, including their partners, which may inhibit their ability to initiate or respond to sexual advances. The extreme concerns about cleanliness, orderliness, and control characteristic of individuals with obsessive-compulsive disorder result in problems due to the naturally messy nature of sex. In addition to these disorder-related problems, tension, burden, and conflict in the marital relationship often dampen or eliminate positive feelings in the healthy partner, interfering with sexual expressiveness.

Problems with sex in a couple may become apparent during the initial assessment, but often it is later in the course of therapy that the therapist becomes aware of the difficulty. When there is evidence of a problem, the therapist first gathers more information from the couple in order to make a preliminary evaluation about whether the problem is related to a biological dysfunction (e.g., pain during intercourse, difficulty maintaining an erection, premature ejaculation), interpersonal factors (e.g., not enough time, disagreements), or possibly a combination of both (e.g., lack of desire).

If there is any evidence suggesting that the difficulty is related to a specific sexual dysfunction involving a person who is taking medication, that person or the couple are prompted to first discuss the concern with the prescribing physician in order to determine whether the medication is contributing to the problem. Common sexual side effects of prescribed psychiatric medications include difficulty maintaining erection, retrograde ejaculation, decreased sexual desire, and difficulty experiencing orgasm. If a determination is made that the problem is not due to medication, referral is made to a physician to evaluate the possible role of medical factors, and then (if recommended) to a sexual-dysfunction clinic or specialist.

Sexual difficulties are often related to intimacy problems that require long-term intervention. The primary goals of BFT (teaching the family how to manage the psychiatric disorder) are not incompatible with improving sexual intimacy, but usually both goals can not be addressed at the same time. It is best to first work on the core BFT material and to address sexual intimacy later when the couple has acquired the requisite skills for the management of the psychiatric disorder. However, the therapist can take some steps toward improving intimacy early in BFT. Goals can be set regarding the scheduling of pleasant time spent together, education can focus on the effects of some psychiatric disorders on sexual desire, and communication-skills training can emphasize the expression of positive feelings and empathic listening skills. Later in BFT, a problem-solving approach can be taken to address some of the conflicts that appear to contribute to a stressful environment (e.g., disagreements about child-rearing practices). Although these steps are often not sufficient to eliminate problems in intimacy, they frequently result in some improvement and set the stage for later work on sexual adjustment.

Parenting Difficulties

Many couples disagree about child-rearing practices and experience difficulties effectively parenting their children. These problems are often magnified when one of the parents has a psychiatric disorder. Similarly, parenting and child behavior problems are common in families in which a single parent with a psychiatric disorder and his or her children live with relatives. When problems with children become apparent to the therapist, a preliminary attempt is made to evaluate whether the problem reflects a childhood psychiatric disorder (e.g., attention-deficit hyperactivity disorder, conduct disorder) or a developmental disorder (e.g., mental retardation, autistic disorder), in which case a referral is made to a specialist. More often, problems with children are due to disagreements among the caregivers and/or inadequate parenting skills.

The communication and problem-solving training components of BFT are often helpful in addressing common problems in child rearing (e.g., temper tantrums, trouble at bedtime, regulation of television, rudeness, not doing homework). Although using the core BFT skills is often helpful, many families also benefit from recommended reading of self-help books for parents. A list of recommended self-help books for parents is provided at the end of the chapter. Two other books are useful for professionals and may be appropriate to recommend to some families: Blechman (1985) gives solutions to common childhood problems at home and at school; Robin and Foster (1989) provide a social-learning approach to teaching families how to resolve conflicts between parents and adolescents. In addition to or in place of these readings, caregivers may benefit from referral to parenting classes available in the community. Such classes typically meet weekly or biweekly for one to three months and may involve discussion and sharing of problems, use of demonstration video-tapes, role-playing, and self-monitoring. This combination of strategies allows the therapist to help family members address problems they experience with their children, while preventing those difficulties from becoming the center of BFT work.

CASE EXAMPLE OF DWAYNE AND TANIA

About eighteen months before initiating BFT, Dwayne had developed a phobia about driving on the freeway alone due to a panic attack. As a result, Dwayne rarely drove and used a bicycle as his primary means of transportation. Although this conferred obvious health benefits, it limited his activities to a radius of about five miles from his home. Dwayne recognized that this constraint curtailed his activities, but he accommodated it and did not consider it an urgent problem. His wife hoped he would begin driving again.

With Dwayne's consent, the therapist decided to implement a program of graduated exposure to driving. The therapist began by teaching Dwayne to monitor his comfort in the car. Homework assignments were developed to gradually expose Dwayne to driving, first by having him just sit in the car alone, then by taking brief driving trips with Tania near their home, and then taking brief trips alone. During problem solving Dwayne and Tania were encouraged to generate strategies that Dwayne could use to manage his fear when he drove on the freeway.

These steps were effective at slowly increasing Dwayne's ability to drive alone. Then, several months into therapy, Dwayne decided he wanted to visit his family and friends more frequently. They lived about forty miles away, but he believed he could comfortably manage the drive about once every two weeks. In a problem-solving meeting with Tania, he worked out a schedule that permitted him to make the drive when traffic would be minimal. Tania was encouraged to express positive feelings to Dwayne about this plan. Dwayne reported that he felt anxious during these drives, but he stuck to his schedule and eventually began to visit even more frequently. At follow-up, Dwayne was working odd jobs that required him to drive alone on the freeway several times per week. He had not experienced any panic attacks and reported feeling less nervous than before, but still a little concerned about driving.

Questions and Answers to Common Problems

Question: How does the therapist handle a situation in which the special problem of a family member is so great that it prevents teaching the basic BFT skills?

Answer: Occasionally the relative of a client experiences a very severe problem that greatly interferes with his or her participation in BFT (e.g., major depression, substance abuse). The therapist's first goal in such families is to refer (or treat) the problem while continuing to maintain that relative's involvement in BFT and altering expectations for the relative accordingly. If the relative is unable to participate, but other relatives are, BFT can be conducted without that family member, with an attempt made to engage the relative at a later time, when he or she has received appropriate treatment. If a problem prevents the client's only relative from participating in BFT (or a relative whose participation is clearly vital to achieving positive results), it may be best to postpone BFT until that person is able to participate. In such cases, it can be helpful for the therapist to maintain contact with the family in order to monitor progress toward resolution (or improvement) of the relative's problem.

Summary

The framework of BFT can be expanded to address many important issues facing the family of a client with serious psychiatric disorders. Common problems experienced by clients include depression and negative symptoms, persistent psychotic symptoms, disorganization, substance abuse, and social impairment. Common problems experienced by relatives include substance abuse and extreme levels of distress. Problems that occur in both clients or relative, or are shared among family members include intoxication in the BFT session, anger and violence, anxiety, intimacy and sexual functioning, and parenting problems. Although it is important that the integrity of the basic communication- and problem-solving skills training not be compromised, additional time and effort devoted to especially troubling topics can often greatly increase the adjustment of both the client and his or her family. Incorporating family members in the implementation of strategies for specific problems further increases the chances that these pressing needs will be successfully met.

Recommended Books on Parenting for Family Members

Children

Becker, W.C. (1971). *Parents Are Teachers: A Child Management Program*. Champaign, IL: Research Press.

Blechman, E.A. (1985). *Solving Child Behavior Problems at Home and at School*. Champaign, IL: Research Press.

Clarke, J.I., et al. (1993). *HELP! For Parents of Children from Birth to Five: Tried-and-True Solutions to Parents' Everyday Problems*. San Francisco, CA: Harper.

Elium, D. & J. Elium (1992). *Raising a Son and the Making of a Healthy Man*. Hillsboro, OR: Beyond Words Pub.

Faber, A., & E. Mazlish (1982). *How to Talk So Kids Will Listen and Listen So Kids Will Talk*. New York: Avon.

Faber, A., & E. Mazlish (1987). *Siblings without Rivalry*. New York: Norton.

Fraiberg, S. (1984). *The Magic Years: Understanding and Handling the Problems of Early Childhood*. New York: Charles Scribner.

Gottman, J., & J. Declaire (1997). *Raising an Emotionally Intelligent Child: The Heart of Parenting*. New York: Simon & Schuster.

Kurcinka, M.S. (1998). *Raising Your Spirited Child*. New York: HarperPerennial.

Mindel, J.A. (1997). *Sleeping Through the Night*. New York: HarperPerennial.

Schaefer, C.E., & H. Millman (1984). *How to Help Children with Common Problems*. New York: Van Nostrand Reinhold.

Adolescents

Forgatch, M., & G. Patterson (1989). *Parents and Adolescents Living Together: Part 2: Family Problem Solving*. Eugene, OR: Castalia Publishing Co.

Patterson, G., & M. Forgatch (1987). *Parents and Adolescents Living Together: Part 1: The Basics*. Eugene, OR: Castalia Publishing Co.

Robin, A.L. and Foster, S.L. (1989). *Negotiating Parent-Adolescent Conflict: A Behavioral Family Systems Approach*. New York: Guilford.

Children and Adolescents

Clark, J.I., et al. (1993). *HELP! For Parents of School-Age Children and Teenagers: Tried-and-True Solutions to Parents' Everyday Problems*. San Francisco, CA: Harper.

Nelsen, J. (1990). *Positive Discipline*. New York: Ballentine.

TERMINATION AND STRATEGIES FOR MAINTENANCE

CHAPTER 9

The goal of BFT is to help families master the skills needed to manage psychiatric illnesses and to achieve personal and shared goals through cooperative work. As families acquire the requisite knowledge and skills, their need for the therapist usually gradually decreases. Rather than teaching new skills, the therapist and family are confronted with the need to develop strategies to maintain the skills already gained. With adequate attention to maintenance, participation in formal BFT sessions is usually no longer necessary. In most cases, termination from BFT is appropriate.

In this chapter, we discuss issues related to the termination of BFT and techniques for maintenance. First, we outline the role of termination in the overall context of BFT; we then present issues informing decisions about readiness to terminate. Next, we outline strategies to support maintenance of BFT skills. We then describe the preparatory work in the final sessions prior to termination and detail a format suitable for the last BFT meeting. Finally, we discuss the parameters of decisions not to terminate.

The Place of Termination in BFT

The concept of termination is interwoven throughout BFT from the very beginning. During the initial engagement sessions, families are usually informed that BFT will be provided for a time-limited basis, and they are given an estimate of the duration of treatment or number of sessions to be held (e.g., ten to twelve months; twenty to twenty-five sessions). When embarking on each of the new skill areas, such as education, communication-skills training, or problem-solving instruction, the therapist places the upcoming activities within the context of the overall BFT program. For example, the therapist may begin the problem-solving training by saying, "We are now going to start our final skill area—problem solving. We'll be working on this skill each week for about the next six weeks, and then we'll begin to meet every other week for the following month. So, we have a total of about three more months of therapy together."

In many clinical settings, the exact duration of BFT is not established at the outset of treatment. Rather, the decision to terminate BFT is made jointly by the therapist and family members based on their progress in treatment and readiness for termination. When the duration of BFT has not been established in advance, the therapist still presents BFT throughout the course of treatment as a time-limited intervention designed to equip families with the skills they need to succeed without the therapist. This effectively prepares families for the fact that termination of family sessions will eventually take place.

Assessing Readiness for Termination

An overall treatment model for family intervention for serious psychiatric disorders was presented in Chapter 1. As depicted in that model, while BFT is progressing, the therapist is continually assessing the family members' understanding of the illness and their acquisition of communication and problem-solving skills. Over time, it may become clear that the family has not acquired high levels of mastery and that continued work is required. Often, this situation occurs in multiproblem families that seem to lurch from crisis to crisis. Under these circumstances, it is best if the therapist delays the termination of BFT and continues working with the family. Meetings should be scheduled at least twice a month (or more frequently, if possible). Meetings scheduled at longer than two-week intervals rarely provide the continuity required to shape new skills and reinforce their performance. The therapist may devote these sessions to reviewing the educational handouts again, or to previously taught communication skills, or to helping the family overcome obstacles to effective problem solving. The formal preparation for termination is deferred in these situations until a higher level of skill is attained and a transition to monthly booster sessions and/or participation in multiple-family groups is warranted.

Other families may have mastered the skills sufficiently well, but be anxious about termination because they feel uncertain about their ability to cope with new difficulties and challenges. For these families, after the formal termination session has been conducted, planned booster sessions (scheduled every four to six weeks) can be very helpful. During these sessions, the therapist briefly assesses the clinical status of the client, identifies any significant changes or obstacles the family is confronting, and then either reviews BFT material or provides information on a topic of interest to the family (e.g., the availability of a new medication, changes in services offered by the agency). In our experience, planned booster sessions can be invaluable in identifying difficulties and problems about which the family might be reluctant to contact the clinician spontaneously. Referral to a multiple-family support group can also be very useful in reducing this anxiety about termination. Note that when the family or therapist decides to end the planned booster sessions, then the format for the final few meetings (discussed below) is repeated.

Some families achieve high levels of skill relatively quickly and feel comfortable and prepared to terminate BFT. These families appear to have little need for subsequent intervention. Brief monthly telephone check-in calls initiated by the therapist have been successfully used to provide ongoing support and to assess how these families are managing. Given this consistent, albeit limited, contact, the family may feel more comfortable in requesting an occasional booster session with the therapist. Most often, this request is made when the family is facing a crisis and would like some consultation on how to resolve the problem. Examples of common topics for these "ad hoc" booster sessions include:

1. where the client should live;

2. if the client should marry;

3. should the client attempt to raise a child that he or she is having;

4. what will happen if the family moves away; and

5. unexpected serious illness in the family.

Typically, a course of two or three scheduled sessions permits the family to resolve these difficulties.

Strategies to Promote Maintenance of Skills

The primary mechanism for maintaining BFT skills is continuation of weekly family meetings at home. During the therapy, the therapist frequently reminds the family of termination in order to motivate them to conduct weekly problem-solving family meetings. The therapist emphasizes to the family that although therapy will end, the problems will not, and the time is ripe to establish a routine that will help members maintain their gains when they are no longer meeting with the therapist on a regular basis. Under ideal circumstances, these weekly meetings continue long after the end of BFT sessions and serve as a focal point for discussing goals and problems.

Participation in multiple-family support groups can also play an invaluable role in maintaining BFT gains. Such support groups may take many forms, including educational and/or problem-solving oriented groups run by mental health professionals or support groups conducted by advocacy organizations, such as local chapters of the National Alliance for the Mentally Ill (NAMI). Multiple-family groups can provide families with social validation for their concerns, encourage the sharing of coping strategies for dealing with common problems, and provide for continued and cost-effective contact with mental health professionals. Termination from BFT is greatly facilitated when the family has initiated participation in a multiple-family group that can provide ongoing support in a time- unlimited fashion.

While the individual-family format is preferable when the major goal of BFT is education and skills training, the multiple-family group format is useful when the major goal of intervention is the provision of social support and the maintenance of acquired skills. An integration of the two formats is optimal for many families. Individually based BFT can be provided to teach families basic information about the disorder, communication skills, and problem-solving skills. Subsequently, families can be engaged in a multiple-family group designed to maintain their learned skills and enhance social support.

The therapist introduces the concept of the benefits of participating in multiple-family groups as the family initiates training in communication skills. It is best if the therapist can provide information on local meetings and encourage families to attend them, on at least a trial basis, by the time problem-solving instruction commences. Attending meetings is an acquired habit, which may require shaping, prompting, and social reinforcement.

Multiple-family group meetings are usually scheduled on a biweekly or monthly basis. The typical format of a meeting might include opening with a brief opportunity for each participant to describe any issues or urgent topics requiring attention, followed by a twenty -to thirty-minute presentation on an educational topic (e.g., new medications, accessing benefits, etc.) or review of BFT skills. This is succeeded by general discussion, including problem solving, if necessary, and a wrap-up. At many agencies, BFT therapists who already know the family colead the multiple-family groups, allowing for a more comfortable transition from individual to group work.

The group format can facilitate good communication between clients and relatives in different families. The relatives in one family often are able to listen to the client from another family with an objectivity they lack when interacting with their own ill family member. Similarly, some clients may attend better to other clients' relatives than to their own. The multiple-family group format provides a greater range of role models to the participants. A final advantage of multiple-family groups is that they are often economical, although individual families often need additional consultations and crisis sessions.

Multiple-family groups are not without their limitations, however. These include the challenge of working on especially difficult problems raised by a single family, the possibility that some families may feel alienated due to their unique experiences (e.g., their ill family member lives at home while most others in the group live elsewhere), fewer opportunities for role-play practice and feedback for each participant, and the reluctance of some families to acknowledge openly a psychiatric disorder in the family, especially early in the course of the illness.

Preparing for BFT Termination

During the last several BFT sessions, more time is devoted to planning explicitly for termination. To encourage members to plan for the future, the family can be asked to conduct a problem solving on how to maintain the gains made in therapy during one of its at-home family meetings. In conjunction with this assignment, family members are asked to have a general discussion about what ending therapy will mean to them. In reporting the results of these meetings to the therapist, family members may display a wide range of attitudes toward terminating therapy. Some persons may be relieved that the burden of time-consuming meetings will be ending, while others may express concerns that the family will no longer make progress without the supervision and guidance of the therapist. The therapist is alert for any concerns raised by family members and helps them anticipate potential problems. Then, the therapist takes steps to help the family address potential termination problems that have been identified.

While the family is preparing for termination. the therapist also evaluates the progress achieved in therapy. Progress is evaluated both in terms of the original goals and in light of any additional problems that have arisen. Table 9.1 contains questions for the therapist to consider when preparing for termination of BFT. Often, the family has made gains in BFT, and yet other needs, not addressed fully by the therapy or work on special problems, continue to be apparent. In such circumstances, the therapist can be an invaluable resource to family members in determining what they need and how they can find it.

TABLE 9.1
QUESTIONS TO CONSIDER WHEN PREPARING TO
TERMINATE BFT

- Is the family sufficiently knowledgeable about the psychiatric illness?

- Has the family learned (or made significant progress toward learning) the requisite communication and problem-solving skills?

- What difficulties can the therapist or family members anticipate after BFT has ended?

- Does a referral for additional treatment need to be made?

- Are the other mental health providers involved in the client's treatment aware of when BFT will end?

- Will family stress or the severity of the client's illness prevent the family from coping effectively after termination?

- Should booster BFT sessions be scheduled?

Helping families access additional needed services can have an important impact on the family and its ability to manage the psychiatric disorder. When the therapist works for an agency that provides a broad array of services, such as a public community-mental-health center or a health maintenance organization, the referral to another service can be expedited by the direct involvement of the therapist. However, when the therapist is in independent practice, or a referral needs to be made to a different agency, special care must be taken to ensure that the family follows through and receives the required services. Factors that are likely to increase the likelihood that the referral is successful include:

1. having written information available on the agency, including its location, hours, the name of a specific contact person, and his or her phone number;

2. ensuring that the family can arrange transportation to the agency;

3. helping the family members plan (and rehearse, if necessary) what they will say at the agency; and

4. encouraging the family to anticipate and overcome obstacles that may impede following up on the referral.

It can often take families two or three weeks to pursue any referrals made to them. Therefore, it is useful to make referrals early enough in the termination process so that the therapist can prompt family members over several weeks to follow up the referral, or assist them if a difficulty is encountered with the referral.

The Final Session

Families often find BFT termination stressful. The therapist can help reduce the stress of the final meeting by carefully structuring opportunities for family members to review their progress and identify problem areas still to be addressed. He or she can begin by asking each participant to describe his or her own progress over the course of the therapy. The therapist can then ask each family member to express a positive feeling to another participant for a specific area of progress or change he or she has seen as a result of the therapy. After each person has given at least one other member positive feedback, the therapist can then note the areas in which he or she has seen progress, using a similar format. Finally, the therapist can ask each participant to identify one goal or problem on which he/she hopes to work over the next few months and can encourage family members to use their meetings to keep others abreast of their efforts and to seek consultation or aid in problem solving.

Providing Time-Unlimited BFT

BFT is generally conceptualized as a time-limited intervention designed to teach families the skills necessary to manage a serious, often persistent psychiatric disorder. Although it is desirable to provide a time-limited course of BFT, this may not always be a feasible goal. With some families, it may be preferable to provide BFT less intensively on an ongoing basis (e.g., sessions every two to four weeks) with no anticipated termination date. In these cases, simultaneous participation in multiple-family support groups is usually also valuable.

There are two clinical factors worth considering when evaluating whether a family will benefit from ongoing BFT. The first factor is the level of stress present in the family. Families facing severe stressors, such as extreme poverty, substance abuse, multiple ill family members, and violence, are often unable to marshal the psychological resources necessary to manage the psychiatric illness on their own. For these families, one member's psychiatric disorder is often not the greatest stressor in the family, and the management of the disorder can fall by the wayside when BFT is terminated. Ongoing BFT sessions can ensure that the psychiatric illness continues to be monitored by the family in conjunction with the therapist and that imminent or emergent psychiatric crises (e.g., medication noncompliance, substance abuse) are responded to in a timely fashion. In addition, continued BFT sessions with these families can provide a forum for members to discuss and problem solve about other stressors that they face, potentially resulting in a better quality of life for all family members.

The second factor contributing to the decision not to terminate is the severity or instability of the client's psychiatric illness. Some individuals receive only modest benefits from medications or may engage in uncontrolled substance abuse. Because of the unpredictable nature of psychiatric disorders under these conditions, even very competent families may be confronted with high levels of stress. For these families, the high stress can be mitigated by scheduling infrequent ongoing BFT booster sessions after the core BFT skills have been learned. For some of these families, the need for ongoing BFT sessions gradually decreases over time, and ultimately termination is possible. For other families, regular but infrequent sessions may be necessary in order to stabilize the family environment and psychiatric disorder.

CASE EXAMPLE OF DWAYNE AND TANIA

Dwayne and Tania participated in a total of twenty-one BFT sessions (including orientation and assessment meetings) over a seven-month period. While the two were concerned that they might not maintain the gains they had made in BFT after sessions stopped, the other demands in their lives made it increasingly difficult to attend sessions regularly, and they felt ready to terminate. A key component of termination involved finding other sources of support. Toward the end of the BFT treatment period, Tania had begun attending Narc Anon meetings (for relatives of persons with narcotics-use disorders) to learn how to cope more effectively with her sons' substance-abuse problems. She also began attending a veterans' wives support group. The therapist encouraged her to continue her involvement in both groups. In addition, the therapist provided a referral to Tania for treatment of her own PTSD.

Dwayne continued receiving treatment at the VA hospital and decided to pursue his auto technician certification more vigorously. Both Dwayne and Tania reported that their participation in BFT had been very beneficial, although they acknowledged they would need to continue trying to strengthen their relationship. Over the year following termination, Dwayne and Tania had occasional telephone contact with the therapist, but booster BFT sessions were not deemed necessary. At a one-year follow-up, the couple was still together, Dwayne and Tania were both working (Dwayne part-time), and they had taken a cruise together. Dwayne no longer experienced fear while driving. However, he continued to struggle with PTSD symptoms and had one brief (four-day) hospitalization. Both Dwayne and Tania indicated that they felt their relationship had improved significantly over the course of treatment and at follow-up, but that they had to struggle hard to maintain intimacy between them and avoid being "swallowed up" by their children's problems.

Questions and Answers to Common Problems

Question: What should be done when some family members are ready to terminate BFT, but others are not?

Answer: Termination of BFT need not be considered an "all or nothing" event; rather, the therapist and family members can agree on who should continue to participate in BFT and who should not. There are two types of situations in which it may be desirable for some family members to terminate BFT before others. First, families in which some members are closely involved with the client and others are only peripherally involved may benefit from staggered termination dates. In these families, the initial course of BFT serves to educate the entire family about the psychiatric disorder and to establish basic competence in the communication and problem-solving skills, while the later sessions that include only the client and relative who lives with him or her focus on the more day-to-day living problems and conflicts.

The second situation in which some family members may benefit from continued participation in BFT while others stop is when a discordant couple participates in therapy with other family members. In some of these cases, one member of the couple may have the psychiatric disorder, while in other cases someone else has the disorder (e.g., the offspring of the couple). Regardless of who has the psychiatric disorder, if the couple is interested in working on marital issues, a shift in the focus of BFT can be made when the core skills have been acquired, with other family members no longer participating in the therapy. Some couples prefer to continue working with the BFT therapist because they have already established a therapeutic alliance and much groundwork (e.g., assessment) has already been covered. When a decision is made to continue the BFT work with some family members but not others, the therapist and family members agree on a time frame for how long they will continue work together before reevaluation or termination.

Summary

Consistent with most approaches in behavior therapy, the concept of termination is integrated into BFT from its initiation. While many families need only infrequent contact with the therapist to maintain gains after termination, a subset of families may have not acquired high levels of skills by the planned termination date, and it is recommended that termination be deferred and skill training scheduled for at least biweekly sessions. Over the course of therapy, the therapist frequently refers to the time when he or she will no longer be working with the family and encourages members to learn the skills necessary to maintain their progress after the end of treatment. Maintenance strategies, such as ongoing weekly meetings and participation in multiple-family groups, are also supported. As termination approaches, the therapist prompts family members to use their problem-solving skills to anticipate and resolve impediments to successful termination. The last session includes formal evaluations of progress achieved in the therapy by each participant, as well as feedback on the same by the therapist. Finally, some families coping with severe stress or extremely impaired psychiatric clients living at home may benefit from continued BFT sessions provided on a time-unlimited basis. With these families, the frequency of sessions can be titrated based on family need, with sessions ranging from biweekly to once every six weeks for most families.

| CHAPTER 10 | RESEARCH ON BEHAVIORAL FAMILY THERAPY |

Research on the treatment of serious mental illness has a profound impact on determining the services available to clients and their families. Knowledge of which interventions enjoy the most empirical support, and what the specific effects of interventions are on the course and outcome of severe mental illness, can serve as a useful guide to clinicians in developing the most effective treatment programs for their clients. At the clinical level, clients and families depend on mental health treatment providers to be knowledgeable about the evidence supporting various treatment approaches. Adminstratively, awareness of the evidence supporting different treatments can be useful for determining which mental health services are most crucial to provide.

A wide variety of different models of family intervention have been developed for helping families manage psychiatric disorders. These models vary in theoretical orientation from behavioral to family systems to psychodynamic to broad-based psychoeducational and supportive. In this chapter we review evidence concerning the effectiveness of behaviorally based family intervention programs for psychiatric disorders (for research on marital discord, see Baucom et al., 1998). Because of the high comorbidity between severe psychiatric disorders and substance-use disorders (Regier et al., 1990), we also review behaviorally oriented intervention for substance-use disorders. The emphasis of this review is on examining the evidence supporting behavioral family interventions from well-controlled studies, usually involving random assignment of families to treatment or standard care.

For the purposes of this review, we include all family interventions that involve a specific skills-training component as "behavioral" or as reflective of the key features of BFT. The specific areas in which skills training is conducted in different behaviorally based family interventions vary somewhat from one application to the next. However, consistent with the basic BFT model explicated in this book, the most common areas of skills training in these reviewed studies have included communication and problem-solving skills. Thus, they can be informative about the utility of the BFT approach in improving outcomes for adult psychiatric disorders.

The primary goal of this review is to distill the critical findings concerning the effectiveness of behavioral family interventions in a simple and informative manner that will be easily digestible for clinicians, students, and administrators. Hence, this review is not comprehensive, and it focuses primarily on summarizing those findings that are supported by the most evidence. For more comprehensive reviews of family intervention for psychiatric disorders, see Baucom et al. (1998), Mueser and Glynn (1998), and Dixon and Lehman (1995).

This review is divided into sections according to psychiatric disorder. The primary focus of the review is on evaluating the effects of BFT on the psychiatric illness, with secondary attention to research on the effect of family treatment on relatives.

Schizophrenia

The effects family intervention for schizophrenia-spectrum disorders (including schizophrenia, schizoaffective disorder, and schizophreniform disorder) have been more extensively studied than for any other psychiatric disorder. Since the 1970s, a number of different family-intervention programs for schizophrenia have been developed and empirically evaluated. Both short-term (i.e., less than six months) and long-term family programs have been developed, including a variety of different theoretical orientations and formats. We briefly review the findings concerning short-term family treatment below, which has limited empirical support, followed by longer-term family treatments, which have received more empirical support.

Short-term Family Intervention

Many short-term family interventions have been developed for schizophrenia. These programs tend to improve relatives' knowledge of the illness and sense of mastery in coping with it and to decrease experience of burden (Abramowitz & Coursey, 1989; Birchwood et al., 1992; Glynn et al., 1993; Mills & Hansen, 1991; Posner et al., 1992; Sidley et al., 1991; Smith & Birchwood, 1987; Solomon et al., 1996a, 1997). However, the lack of evidence supporting the effectiveness of these programs for improving the long-term course of schizophrenia, including relapse and rehospitalizations, has tempered enthusiasm for these approaches (e.g., Glick et al., 1985; Solomon et al., 1996b; Vaughn et al., 1992).

The one exception to the limited benefits of short-term family intervention for schizophrenia appeared in a study by Goldstein et al. (1978), who reported reduced relapse rates at six months for a six-week crisis-oriented program conducted immediately following a hospitalization. The program was provided to clients who had experienced either a first or second episode of schizophrenia. Clients and relatives were engaged in six weekly sessions that were aimed at encouraging family members to accept that the client has had a psychosis, identifying probable precipitating stressors at the time of the psychosis, exploring possible stressors that the client might encounter in the future, and planning how to minimize or avoid exposure to such stressors. The control group received only standard treatment (e.g., medication, case management). Despite the positive findings, this study has not been replicated in over two decades, since it was conducted.

Long-term Family Intervention

In addition to BFT, several other long-term family-intervention programs have been developed in recent years. We briefly describe here some of those programs that have been the focus of controlled research. Anderson et al.'s (1986) approach involves combining psychoeducation about schizophrenia with techniques from family systems therapy (e.g., reinforcing generational boundaries). In Kuipers et al.'s (1992) model, families participate in individual and group educational sessions about schizophrenia and its management. McFarlane (1990) developed a program that is a variation of BFT in which families provide support to each other and problem solve about common problems in multiple-family group meetings. In a modification of this format, Schooler et al. (1997) developed an approach in which monthly group meetings are divided between education about schizophrenia and coping with common problems.

Different family programs vary according to how explicitly they incorporate a behavioral format and structure. Behavioral techniques are sometimes employed in the models developed by Anderson et al. (1986), Kuipers et al. (1992), and Schooler et al. (1997), but none are explicitly behavioral in their approach to assessment and intervention. Barrowclough and Tarrier (1992) developed a behavioral intervention program that clearly overlaps with BFT, as outlined in this book. Their program provides education combined with training in stress management, relapse prevention, and goal attainment, but explicit communication-skills training is not included.

Despite differences among the long-term family programs described here in terms of characteristics such as format (e.g., multiple vs. single family) and setting (home vs. clinic), they share many common features, as noted by Lam (1991), Glynn (1993), and Mueser (1996). All family treatment programs provide education about schizophrenia and avoid blaming family members or pathologizing their coping efforts. Effort is expended toward helping family members improve their communication and problem-solving skills, either through social-skills training or discussion. Family programs are focused on fostering the development of all family members, not just the client, while encouraging members to expand their social supports outside the family network. Finally, all of these programs take a long-term perspective to improving the ability of the family to manage the illness, including collaborating with the client's treatment team and endeavoring to instill hope that change is possible.

Effectiveness of Long-term Family Programs

Most controlled studies of long-term family intervention have examined cumulative relapse rates (i.e., either the reemergence of severe symptoms or the worsening of symptoms in a previously stabilized client) or rehospitalization as the main outcome measure. Table 10.1 summarizes all of the controlled (random assignment) studies comparing either a family-intervention program with routine care (no family treatment) or comparing two different family treatments and reporting outcomes for at least eighteen months following the initiation of treatment. For most of these studies, clients had recently been treated for an acute symptom exacerbation, were in regular contact with their families, and were living in the community. In all studies, clients received routine treatment for schizophrenia, including antipsychotic medication, case management, and access to other rehabilitation programs.

TABLE 10.1

CONTROLLED STUDIES OF LONG-TERM FAMILY THERAPY FOR THE TREATMENT OF SCHIZOPHRENIA

Theoretical Orientation	Reference	Sample (n)				Duration of Family Treatment (months)	Follow-up Period (months)	Relapse/Rehospitalization Rates (%)[1]			
		Single Family	Single + Multiple Family	Multiple Family	Routine Treatment			Single Family	Multiple Family	Single + Multiple Family	Routine Treatment
Behavioral	Falloon et al. (1984)	18	--	--	18	24	24	17	--	--	83
	Tarrier et al. (1989)	17[2]	--	--	27	9	24	33	--	--	59
	Xiong et al. (1994)	--	34	--	29	18	18	--	--	44[3]	64[3]
	Randolph et al. (1995)	21	--	--	20	12	24	10	--	--	40
	Schooler et al. (1997)	--	157	156	--	12/24[4]	24	--	35	29	--
	McFarlane et al. (1995a)[5]	18	--	16	--	24	24	27	16	--	--
	McFarlane et al. (1995b)	89	--	83	--	24	24	44	25	--	--

Supportive	Leff et al. (1985)	--	10	--	9	24	24	--	--	14	78
	Leff et al. (1990)	12	--	11	--	24	24	33	36	--	-
	Zhang et al. (1994)	--	42	--	41	18	18	--	--	15	-54
Family Systems	Hogarty et al. (1991)[6]	32	--	--	35	24	24	32	--	--	67
	Total/Mean (unweighted)	207	243	266	179	19.7	22.9	28.0%	28.0%	25.5%	63.6%

Footnotes

1. All group differences are different at p< .05 except Leff et al. (1990), Schooler et al. (1997), and Xiong et al. (1994).

2. Results combined from two treatment groups that received either a "symbolic" or "enactive" variant of the family intervention (which did not differ significantly).

3. Although these relapse rates were not significantly different, cumulative rehospitalization rates were significantly different: family treatment, 12.5%; routine treatment, 35.7%.

4. Single-family treatment, which was behavioral in orientation, lasted 12 months. Multiple family groups, which were supportive in orientation, lasted for 24 months.

5. A third family-treatment group, based on psychodynamic approaches (N=7), was initiated in this study, but randomization to this group was stopped because of high relapse rates. This study provided treatment and follow-up for four years; to compare with the other studies, only two-year relapse rates are summarized here.

6. This study also included a family treatment + social skills training group (N=20, 25% relapse rate over 24 months), and a group that received social-skills training but not family treatment (N=20, 50% relapse rate over 24 months).

Inspection of Table 10.1 reveals several noteworthy trends. Most important, the cumulative relapse or rehospitalization rates for clients who received any form of family intervention were lower than for clients who received routine care only. Specifically, the average cumulative relapse or rehospitalization rates over eighteen to twenty-four months for clients (and their families) who participated in either single-family treatment or multiple-family groups was 28 percent, and for clients who participated in both single- and multiple-family groups the rate was 25.5 percent. These rates are less than half the relapse and rehospitalization rate of 63.3 percent for clients who received routine care and participated in no family-treatment program. A second trend apparent from Table 10.1 is that different theoretical models of family-intervention were all equally effective, although the preponderance of research has focused on behavioral models. Overall, the results indicate that long-term family intervention programs are effective at reducing relapse and rehospitalization rates in schizophrenia.

Among the studies reviewed in Table 10.1, all but two (Randolph et al., 1995; Tarrier et al., 1989) provided family intervention until the end of the eighteen to twenty-four month follow-up period. These two studies provided twelve and nine months of family therapy, respectively, and then conducted follow-up evaluations at two years posttreatment initiation. Both studies reported that the cumulative relapse rates of clients who received family intervention were significantly lower at two years than control clients, suggesting that some beneficial effects of family treatment were maintained twelve to fifteen months after the end of therapy. In fact, Tarrier et al. (1994) have reported that clients who received their nine-month family program (Tarrier et al., 1989) continued to have significantly lower relapse rates five to eight years after the initiation of treatment compared to control clients.

Several other long-term family therapy studies have been attempted with shorter follow-ups than the eighteen to twenty-four months of those studies summarized in Table 10.1. Some of these studies reported mixed results. The findings from these studies are briefly described below, and interpretations for the negative results are offered.

Köttgen et al. (1984) failed to find beneficial effects on relapse rates of a family-intervention program over one year. In contrast to the studies reviewed in Table 10.1, Köttgen et al. employed an approach that involved the use of insight-oriented techniques and focusing on the past, such as exploring the origins of clients' and relatives' critical and hostile overinvolvement with each other. McFarlane et al. (1995) also reported negative outcomes with a group-psychodynamic family approach that led them to discontinue randomization to this group before completion of their study. These results, in line with the negative findings of research on individual psychodynamic treatment for schizophrenia (Mueser & Berenbaum, 1990), suggest that insight-oriented approaches are not useful with families of schizophrenic individuals. Linszen et al. (1996) evaluated the effects of (a) standard treatment plus intensive individual therapy with (b) standard treatment plus BFT for recent onset cases of schizophrenia. Nine-month cumulative relapse rates were quite low for both groups (15 percent and 16 percent, respectively). These findings either reflect low relapse rates due to the recent onset of the illness or indicate that both interventions were effective. This study is more unusual for the low relapse rate in the control group, which included intensive individual therapy, than for the lack of differences in the family-intervention group.

Telles et al. (1995) compared the effects of BFT with standard treatment in forty-two Latino clients with schizophrenia. In contrast to the studies reviewed in Table 10.1, there were no differences in relapse rates between the family-intervention and standard treatment groups at twelve months (50 percent and 41 percent, respectively; J. Mintz, personal communication, November 1996). As discussed in Chapter 5, cultural issues may play a role in interpreting the results here. Post hoc analyses indicated that poorly acculturated clients (i.e., clients with poor English-speaking skills and little involvement with Anglo culture outside of Latino culture) fared worse in the family-intervention program than when they received only standard treatment, whereas for well-acculturated clients the program had no effect. These negative findings suggests that the efficacy of family-intervention programs may interact with cultural factors. At a minimum, the findings indicate that family treatment models may need to be adapted for different cultures, as described by Xiong et al. (1994) in their modification of BFT to the Chinese population. The positive effects of family intervention in controlled studies from China (Xiong et al., 1994; Zhang et al., 1993, 1994) suggest that the benefits from this treatment are not limited to Western cultures.

These three studies raise some important questions about the effects of family intervention for schizophrenia and about the possible limitations of available models. The study by Linszen et al. (1996) is difficult to compare with the studies reviewed in Table 10.1 because the client populations differ significantly and the control group received intensive individual treatment. Köttgen et al. (1984) may have failed to find beneficial effects because their family treatment model was quite different from other models, given its emphasis on fostering insight and delving into the past. Telles et al.'s (1995) nonsignificant findings point to the need to adapt family models to different cultures. The methodological differences between these three studies and the studies reviewed in Table 10.1 are sufficiently great that the core findings supporting family intervention are not altered by these disparate findings.

In addition to the effects of family intervention on relapse and rehospitalization in schizophrenia, there is a need to examine its impact on other areas of functioning, such as the quality of social relationships, self-care, and vocational functioning. Although the findings are limited, several investigations have evaluated the effects of family treatment on other areas of functioning. Falloon et al. (1987) reported that BFT resulted in significant improvements in social relationships, household tasks, work activity, and leisure activities over the two-year treatment period compared to the standard treatment. These authors observed that many of the improvements in social functioning occurred during the second year and suggested that the emphasis in the first year on developing problem-solving skills may have contributed to the longer-term benefits.

Barrowclough and Tarrier (1990, 1998) reported that their nine-month behavioral family intervention resulted in significantly greater improvements at the two-year follow-up than standard treatment in social withdrawal, prosocial activities, and overall social adjustment. Both groups improved significantly in interpersonal functioning. Zhang et al. (1993) reported the benefits of family intervention over one year across a broad range of social-functioning variables, such as living ability, social role functioning, and work. Hogarty et al. (1991) also reported benefits from family intervention at two years on client social functioning. In a recent analysis of social functioning in clients who participated in the Treatment Strategies for Schizophrenia (TSS; Schooler et al., 1997), Mueser, Sengupta, Schooler, and Xie (unpublished data) found that clients in families who received BFT and monthly multiple-family groups, as well as clients who participated only in the multiple-family groups, improved at comparable rates in their social-leisure activities and romantic-sexual relationships. Furthermore, the clients in both groups reported significant improvements in their self-efficacy. Somewhat paradoxically, relatives in both groups reported that clients' self-care skills were worse at the end of the study.

Thus, several studies suggest that family intervention may improve social functioning in schizophrenia. Similarly, several studies have examined the effects of long-term family treatment on caregivers and have reported benefits in areas such as subjective and objective burden, coping, and knowledge of schizophrenia (Falloon & Pederson, 1985; Xiong et al., 1994; Zhang et al., 1993), in line with the findings of briefer family-intervention programs (e.g., Abramowitz & Coursey, 1989; Solomon et al., 1996a). In the TSS study previously described, Mueser et al. (unpublished data) found that the addition of BFT to monthly multiple-family support groups was associated with significantly greater reductions in family friction and in relatives' rejection of the client. These findings suggest that longer-term family intervention programs improve the overall functioning of the family, and that BFT in particular may be beneficial to the overall family atmosphere.

Finally, two studies suggest that family-intervention programs result in lower overall mental health costs compared to standard care (Cardin et al., 1985; Tarrier et al., 1991). Considering the high cost of inpatient psychiatric treatment, it is not surprising that the positive effects of family intervention on reducing relapse and rehospitalization also translate into economic benefits.

Quasi-experimental and Exploratory Studies

Several other unique studies of BFT for schizophrenia deserve brief mention. Hahlweg et al. (1994) compared the effects of standard neuroleptic dosage with targeted medication (i.e., provided only when symptoms worsen) combined with BFT. All clients received the family intervention. Cumulative relapse rates at eighteen months were significantly lower for the standard medication group (4 percent) than the targeted medication group (34 percent). Although family intervention was not directly studied, the low relapse rates of both groups in this study are consistent with the eighteen- to twenty-four-month relapse rates of other studies-family intervention (Table 10.1).

Brooker et al. (1994) conducted a quasi-experimental study in the context of a program designed to train community nurses in BFT. Using a within-subjects design, families were placed on a "waiting list" for six months, followed by twelve months of family intervention, or a "delayed-treatment group" for whom family treatment was initiated one year later. Families were assigned to either the waiting list or the delayed-treatment group based on when the community nurse received training in BFT (i.e., either early or late in the course of the study). Clients who received BFT experienced a range of positive outcomes compared to standard treatment, including reductions in positive and negative symptoms, improved social functioning, and improvements regarding relatives' distress and knowledge of medication.

Rund et al. (1994) reported the results of a study evaluating the effects of a long-term (two-year) family intervention program for clients with early-onset schizophrenia (ages thirteen to eighteen). Experimental clients were compared with matched clients who had been treated in the same clinic in previous years. Compared with standard treatment, family intervention both reduced relapses and was less costly. Interestingly, the authors reported that clients with poor premorbid social functioning benefited the most from the family intervention.

A final explorative study that hints at the potential preventative effects of BFT was reported by Falloon (1992). In an uncontrolled investigation, Falloon trained British family practitioners to detect prodromal signs of an initial psychotic disorder and refer clients for a more intensive psychiatric assessment if these symptoms were so identified. When the presence of these signs was confirmed, clients were prescribed minimal doses of antipsychotic medication, and clients and relatives were provided with education about schizophrenia and home-based stress management in a structured program. Participation in these interventions appeared to lower the documented first incidence rate of schizophrenia in the local catchment area.

Summary

There is very strong evidence that long-term family-intervention programs for schizophrenia have a significant effect on reducing cumulative relapse and rehospitalization rates. Across the eleven controlled studies summarized in Table 10.1, long-term family intervention reduced two-year relapse rates to under 30 percent, compared with over 60 percent for clients who received standard care. In addition to the effects of family treatment on relapse and rehospitalization, family programs also tend to improve client social functioning and to decrease burden and tension on relatives. Although behavioral models of family intervention have been most widely studied, other psychoeducational models that share much in common with BFT have also been found to be effective. The strength of evidence supporting the effectiveness of family intervention for schizophrenia has led to this treatment being included by the Patient Outcomes Research Team's (PORT) recommendation for the treatment of schizophrenia (Lehman and Steinwachs 1998).

Bipolar Disorder

In contrast to schizophrenia, less research has examined the effects of family intervention for bipolar disorder. However, several studies, including three controlled studies, provide preliminary evidence that family treatment may improve the course of bipolar disorder. We review these studies below.

In an early report, Davenport et al. (1977) compared the outcomes of married clients with bipolar disorder who participated in couples group therapy with clients who received routine care. Assignment to couples group therapy or routine care was "arbitrary" (based on the availability of a group where the couple lived), but not strictly "random." A total of sixty-five clients were included in the study, twelve of whom participated in weekly group couples therapy sessions. Clients were followed after hospital discharge for periods ranging between two and ten years. Results indicated that clients who participated in the couples group therapy were less like to relapse and be rehospitalized, were rated as functioning better socially and in their family interactions, and were more likely to continue to have an intact marriage.

Three controlled studies using random assignment to treatment groups have also examined family treatment for bipolar disorder. Clarkin et al. (1998) randomly assigned forty-two clients and their spouses to receive either marital therapy (including psychoeducation and problem-solving training) and medication or medication alone for eleven months. Results indicated that the clients who received marital therapy demonstrated better medication adherence and overall functioning at the end of the follow-up, whereas the groups did not differ in symptom severity.

Two studies of BFT for bipolar disorder using similar methods have recently been completed and only preliminary results are currently available. Rea et al. (1998) examined the effects of BFT in fifty-three bipolar-manic clients randomly assigned to either BFT or individual therapy for one year, with all clients receiving medication. Fifty-three percent of the clients lived in parental homes. Over the first year of treatment, the clients who received BFT demonstrated significantly fewer manic symptoms and less depression and were less likely to be hospitalized than the comparison group (20 percent vs. 40 percent). Over the one-year posttreatment follow-up, clients who had received BFT continued to be less likely to be hospitalized than the individually treated clients (20 percent vs. 48 percent).

Miklowitz (1998) compared the effects of one year of BFT in seventy-seven bipolar-manic clients randomly assigned to either BFT for nine months or standard care indefinately. Results of one- and two-year follow-up evaluations indicated that the clients in families who participated in BFT experienced significantly lower levels of symptoms than clients who received only standard care. In addition, analyses of family-interaction patterns indicated higher rates of positive behaviors at the follow-ups in the families who received BFT than in those who received standard care.

Summary

Research on family intervention for bipolar disorder provides strong encouragement for the effectiveness of working with families. Of the four studies conducted (three employing randomized designs), all reported strong effects favoring family intervention over standard care in terms of either client functioning or symptomatology. Two of the studies employed BFT (Miklowitz, 1998; Rea et al., 1998), whereas a third study used a variant of BFT (psychoeducation and problem-solving training; Clarkin et al., 1998). Thus, while there is a need for more research, the available evidence provides preliminary support for the effectiveness of family intervention, especially behavioral models of family treatment, for improving the course of bipolar disorder.

Other Adult Psychopathology: Depression, Anxiety Disorders, and Alcoholism

In contrast to the discussion of schizophrenia and bipolar disorder above, tests of the application of BFT, per se, in other adult psychiatric disorders are rare. With the exception of the Glynn et al. (in press) study on BFT for chronic combat-related PTSD discussed below, there are no published clinical trials of BFT for depression, anxiety disorders, or alcoholism. In spite of this lack of data supporting the efficacy of BFT, the available research on the influence of family factors on the course of these disorders, as well as the benefits accruing from participation in family-based behaviorally oriented programs that share many BFT features, suggests that the intervention could be successfully adapted for use with depression, anxiety disorders, and alcoholism.

As was discussed more fully in Chapter 1, the notion that family attitudes and behaviors can affect prognosis has been prevalent in psychiatric research for decades. The initial investigations on the predictive utility of Expressed Emotion on nine-month relapse rates included some clients with schizophrenia and some with depressive disorders (Brown et al., 1972; Vaughn & Leff, 1976). Family attitudes were predictive of outcome in both disorders, with depressed clients appearing to be even more sensitive to relative attitudes associated with critical comments than clients with schizophrenia. The importance of Expressed Emotion in predicting outcomes in depressive disorders has now been widely replicated (e.g. Hooley & Teasedale, 1989). There has been one study on the role of Expressed Emotion in predicting prognosis in anxiety disorders. Tarrier, Sommerfield, and Pilgrim (manuscript submitted for publication) found that relatives' Expressed Emotion predicted PTSD treatment outcome among participants in a controlled clinical trial comparing imaginal exposure with cognitive therapy. Clinical lore has long held that family attitudes can play a large role in helping maintain abstinence or promote a return to drinking among alcoholics. However, formal research on the influence of Expressed Emotion on outcome after alcohol treatment is only now being published. Again, the findings indicate that high levels of Expressed Emotion are at least modestly related to treatment outcome. Fichter et al. (1997) found that low levels of relatives' critical comments and high levels of warmth were predictive of six-month reduced relapse rates among individuals participating in an inpatient treatment program, though not of eighteen-month relapse rates. Interestingly, the initial number of critical comments was significantly predictive of time to relapse over the eighteen-month follow-up period. O'Farrell et al. (1998) found, among participants in an outpatient behavioral marital therapy (BMT) program for alcoholics, that compared to those with low Expressed-Emotion partners, clients with high EE partners were more likely to relapse, had a shorter time to relapse, and drank on a greater percentage of days in the twelve months after initiating the treatment.

Taken together, the consistency of the findings that family attitudes are related to outcome in depression, anxiety, and alcoholism highlights the potential utility of family-based interventions, and, in fact, a variety of different interventions, some behavioral and some not, have been investigated for each disorder. Behavioral-based interventions can use a wide array of techniques. As has been outlined by both Jacobson et al. (1989) and Baucom et al. (1998), behavioral interventions conducted within the family context typically use one of two approaches. The first model, often labeled "partner-assisted" or "partner as coach," basically integrates the family member into an individually based treatment intervention as a coach or cotherapist. Skills training, especially as related to communication and problem solving within the relationship, is kept to a minimum. Instead, the family member may be asked to prompt or model completion of a therapeutic task. For example, a caregiver might be called on to help a depressed relative keep to a schedule of potentially reinforcing activities, or may accompany an agoraphobic relative on assigned trips outside the home. Benefits accruing from treatments derived from this model have been reported, especially for anxiety disorders (Mehta, 1990), but the minimal attention paid to skills training would limit their relevance to BFT as presented in this book. These types of interventions pertain more to the special strategies described in Chapter 8.

The alternative family-based model incorporates the psychoeducation, communication instruction, and problem-solving skills training found in BFT, although they may be conducted in a less rigorous manner and augmented by other educational or behavioral interventions. Typically, relatively greater emphasis is given to communication-skills training in this model; less focus is placed on formal problem-solving instruction, although resolving problems associated with the disorder is always a core component of the intervention. This model is grounded in the tenet that improving communication and problem-solving skills will help families cope more effectively with stress and thus improve client functioning and reduce symptom exacerbations. In contrast to the work on schizophrenia discussed above, in depression, anxiety disorders, and alcoholism these interventions are most typically used with conjugal dyads, and thus attention is typically also directed at some issues unique to a partner relationship—commitment, intimacy, and relationship reciprocity—that are usually required to keep such pairings viable. These investigations are briefly reviewed below.

Depression

Three sets of investigators have published outcome studies on behaviorally based family interventions that include psychoeducation and formal communication and problem-solving skills training for depression. All three recruited conjugal pairs; in two (Jacobson et al., 1991; O'Leary & Beach, 1990), the depressed partners were women, in one set the depressed samples were mixed (Emanuels-Zuurveen & Emmelkamp, 1996, 1997). Depressed participants were not on medication. In addition to testing the overall impact of the interventions on resolving depression, a key objective in these studies has also been determining the role of initial baseline levels of marital satisfaction on predicting differential outcomes.

O'Leary and Beach (1990) randomly assigned forty-two depressed women in maritally dissatisfied ("discordant") relationships to fifteen to sixteen sessions of either individual cognitive therapy, BMT, or a waiting list control group; thirty-six completed treatment. In contrast to the control group, both active treatments were significantly effective in reducing depression at posttreatment and one-year follow-up. Wives' marital satisfaction improved significantly in the BMT, but not in the individual therapy. These authors argue that this pattern of results suggests that BMT is the treatment of choice for depressed women in discordant relationships in which the partners evidence at least some willingness to improve the relationship.

Jacobson et al. (1991) examined the role of relationship satisfaction on effectiveness of individual therapy and BMT in greater detail. They randomly assigned seventy-two depressed women in relationships to twenty sessions of either individual cognitive therapy for depression, BMT, or the combination; sixty participants completed treatment. Here, the cognitive-behavioral therapy included both changing nonreinforcing behavior patterns and dysfunctional attitudes and thoughts (Beck et al., 1979), and the BMT included behavioral exchange and reinforcement and communication and problem-solving training (Jacobson & Margolin, 1979). As expected, participants in all three groups had significant reductions in depression from pre- to posttreatment, which were maintained at six- and twelve-month follow-ups (Jacobson et al., 1993).

Interestingly, the investigators found that treatment benefits varied as a function of baseline levels of relationship satisfaction, as reflected in partners' averaged scores on the Dyadic Adjustment Scale (Spanier, 1976). In couples where the partners were satisfied or concordant, the BMT was less effective in reducing depression than the individual therapy; for couples in which the partners were maritally discordant, the treatments were equally effective. With regard to increases in intervention-related relationship satisfaction across the entire sample, all three treatment groups evidenced significant improvements from pre- to post-test; however, among the subset of distressed couples, only the BMT led to improved martial satisfaction. Contrary to prediction, the combination treatment did not reduce depression more than participation in the individual or marital components, but it was the only treatment yielding significant improvements in relationship satisfaction among nondiscordant couples. Overall, these results suggest that BMT may be particularly appropriate for couples in which one member is depressed and the relationship is marked by a high level of dissatisfaction, while individual cognitive-behavioral therapy may be more appropriate for depressed members of concordant couples.

Finally, in a series of two studies, Emanuels-Zuurveen and Emmelkamp (1996; 1997) have explored the role of specific types of family interventions on individuals with depression in relationships at varying levels of dissatisfaction. In their 1996 study, the investigators tested the impact of partner-assisted cognitive-behavioral treatment for depression in a mixed gender sample of nondiscordant partners. In line with the discussion on partner-assisted treatment above, the family intervention was not designed primarily to modify relationship communication or problem-solving skills, but instead to support the ill relative as he or she participated in a sixteen-session course of cognitive-behavioral therapy for depression incorporating work on reinforcement-increase strategies as detailed by Lewinsohn (1977) and modifications in cognitive distortions as discussed by Beck et al. (1979). (Nevertheless, it should be noted that four sessions were devoted to communication-skills training, in which both family members participated in role-plays.) Thirty-two depressed individuals were randomly assigned to either the individual or partner-assisted cognitive behavioral therapy; twenty-three completed treatment. Both treatments were significantly effective in reducing depression at posttreatment. As might be expected in a sample not marked by marital distress initially, no significant changes were found in either group on relationship satisfaction variables.

In 1997, Emanuels-Zuurveen and Emmelkamp reported on a trial of BMT (rather than partner-assisted treatment) for depressed individuals in discordant relationships. Thirty-six depressed individuals were randomly assigned to sixteen sessions of either individual cognitive-behavioral therapy as described in the 1996 study or BMT similar to that conducted in the O'Leary and Beach (1990) trial, but with a greater emphasis on formal communication-skills instruction. Both the individual and the marital interventions yielded similarly significant improvements in depression by posttreatment, while the BMT was more effective at improving partner satisfaction.

Summary

Taken together, the results from these four studies suggest that behavioral-based family interventions are particularly appropriate for depressed individuals in troubled relationships. Here, the improvements in depression and marital satisfaction accruing from conjoint behavioral therapy appear to outweigh any costs incurred in the scheduling constraints imposed by couples therapy. In nondiscordant relationships, family intervention may be relatively less critical.

Anxiety Disorders

The role of family-based treatment in anxiety disorders is complex. A key aspect of recovery from anxiety disorders is confronting a feared stimuli for a sufficient duration and frequency for the fear to be extinguished. Thus, exposure-based treatments, which formally incorporate this confrontation, are consistently found to be among the most effective for treatment of anxiety disorders. Not surprisingly, partner-assisted exposure has been well studied in anxiety disorders such as obsessive-compulsive disorder (Emmelkamp et al., 1990; Emmelkamp & de Lang, 1983) and agoraphobia (Hand et al., 1986). Results tend to indicate that partner-assisted exposure yields either the same or modestly greater improvements than individually based exposure for anxiety disorders.

In light of the prominence of exposure in the treatment of anxiety disorders, it is perhaps not surprising that only two sets of investigators have published family-based interventions using communication and problem-solving training to reduce anxiety disorder symptoms. Prior to the initiation of family communication and problem-solving intervention, both studies included exposure treatment. Arnow et al. (1985) randomly assigned twenty-five women with agoraphobia and their partners to either four weeks of partner-assisted exposure followed by eight weeks of group couples communication-skills and problem-solving training or four weeks of partner-assisted exposure, followed by eight weeks of group couples-relaxation training. One participant dropped out during the exposure treatment. Overall, participation in the exposure treatment yielded significant reductions in fear among all participants, and the subsequent communication skills condition yielded significantly more improvement in marital interactions and fear outcomes than the relaxation condition at post-test and eight-month follow-up.

In contrast to the positive results found by Arnow et al. (1985), Glynn et al. (in press) reported that BFT conferred no additional benefits over exposure therapy alone for combat-related PTSD. Forty-two Vietnam veterans with combat-related PTSD were randomly assigned to a wait-list control, eighteen sessions of exposure, or eighteen sessions of exposure followed by sixteen sessions of BFT as described in Glynn et al. (1995). Thirty-eight veterans participated with their partners, four with other family members (e.g., parent, sibling). All assigned veterans completed the exposure; seven veterans randomized to the combined treatment condition declined the subsequent BFT. Overall, participation in the exposure (whether or not followed by BFT) resulted in significant improvements in PTSD positive symptoms (e.g., reexperiencing and hyperarousal) at posttreatment and six-month follow-up; participation in BFT yielded no additional significant benefits.

This failure to find a substantial benefit of combined treatment modalities is reminiscent of the findings on depression reported by Jacobson et al. (1991) noted above, and consistent with other PTSD treatment studies (e.g., Marks et al., 1998). Limited statistical power to detect differences resulting from small sample size may be an issue in the Glynn et al. (in press) study, and the thirty years' chronicity of the disorder with the associated psychosocial dysfunction may have also reduced treatment effects. In contrast to many of the studies mentioned above, the clients here were male, and the wives' acceptance of realistic expectations of client role functioning, which is such a critical aspect of the BFT educational sessions, was often in stark contrast with their own normative role expectations for their husbands. BFT with more acute PTSD, where return to normative role functioning is a plausible outcome, is likely to be much more successful.

Summary

There is a dearth of research on behavioral family approaches in anxiety disorders, making it difficult to discern their overall probability of success. With one study on agoraphobia with positive outcomes and one on chronic PTSD with null effects, more research is clearly needed to clarify the utility of these approaches with anxiety disorders. Studies are particularly needed with other disorders, including panic, obsessive-compulsive, and acute PTSD

Substance-Use Disorders

Family involvement in the treatment of alcoholism has a long history, from participation in self-help groups such as Al-Anon, to unilateral family therapy, in which only the nondrinking partner participates (Thomas & Ager, 1993), to BMT for alcoholism (O"Farrell et al., 1985). Edwards and Steinglass (1995) have published a recent comprehensive review of family therapy treatment outcomes for alcoholism; O'Farrell (1993) has published clinical descriptions of the prominent models of family interventions extant today. Many of these models involve a comprehensive multifaceted intervention program in which family work is only one component; thus, it is difficult to discern what unique effect, if any, family treatment contributes to outcome. In this review, only the randomized studies in which the specific benefits of participation in behaviorally focused family-based treatment are tested are discussed.

Three groups of researchers have led the implementation and test of behavioral martial therapy for alcoholism. O'Farrell et al. (1985, 1992) present data on project CALM (Counseling for Alcoholics Marriages). The behavioral marital intervention here involves six to eight weekly conjoint meetings for orientation and developing a disulfirim (antabuse) use agreement, followed by ten weekly group meetings with other couples, involving education and monitoring of alcohol use, increasing positive family activities, communication-skills training, and negotiation of behavior-change agreements; periodic follow-ups are also scheduled. For most alcoholic participants, it is their only formal treatment during the time of participation. In the first trial, thirty-six male alcoholics and their partners were randomly assigned to either project CALM, a nonbehavioral couples interaction group, or an individual treatment control group; thirty-four participants completed treatment (O'Farrell et al., 1985). The behavioral marital intervention was significantly better than the other two groups on composite alcohol-related outcomes over the next two years. However, both the behavioral marital intervention and the individual treatment yielded more days actually abstinent, compared to the interactional treatment (O' Farrell et al., 1992). The behavioral marital intervention also yielded the greatest improvements in marital satisfaction, though there were changes also evidenced in the interactional comparison group.

In the second study, O'Farrell and colleagues extended the CALM behavioral marital intervention to include a subsequent year of couples relapse-prevention treatment on a declining contact basis. While some of this relapse-prevention work is oriented to maintenance of behavioral marital communication and behavior change skills, most is directed at identifying and planning for high risk of relapse situations (O'Farrell et al., 1993). Sixty-six participants completed the CALM program, and then half were randomly assigned to receive the additional relapse-prevention work, the others to measurement only; seven participants dropped out. Participation in the additional relapse prevention led to an increase in abstinence at six- and twelve-month follow-up, although there was no difference in adverse drinking consequences across the two groups. Important, sustained improvements in the skills targeted in the behavioral marital intervention seemed to account for some of the benefits of the subsequent relapse-prevention training.

Monti et al. (1990) also reported on a test of behavioral family involvement on alcohol outcomes. These investigators randomly assigned sixty-nine inpatient male alcoholics to one of three twelve-hour treatment conditions: (1) group communication- skills training; (2) group communication-skills training with a significant other also participating; and (3) group cognitive-behavioral alcohol treatment (e.g., relapse prevention, relaxation, etc.). The three groups did not differ on days abstinent or time to relapse at six- and eighteen-month follow-up; both groups receiving the communication-skills training had drunk less alcohol during the follow-up period, however. Family involvement did not accentuate the impact of the communication-skills training, but Monti et al. (1990) interpret this result as reflecting the fact that relative participation in the overall treatment program was so extensive that the addition of the communication-skills component might, in retrospect, be expected to have little effect.

McCrady and colleagues have also designed and implemented tests of family involvement for alcoholism. In contrast to the O'Farrell et al. (1985) work described above, these researchers have varied the level of family involvement in alcohol treatment (McCrady et al., 1986). They randomly assigned a mixed-gender sample of fifty-three alcoholics and their partners to one of three fifteen-session treatment conditions, which were conducted separately for each couple: (1) minimal spouse involvement—the partner attended all sessions, but treatment basically involved individual management of the alcohol problem; (2) alcohol-focused spouse involvement, in which the treatment was similar to the first group, but the spouse was specifically included in all activities; and (3) BMT, including communication skills and problem-solving training.

There were no group differences in total abstinence or abstinence days at posttreatment or six-month follow-up. However, participants in the BMT were more compliant and decreased their drinking more quickly than subjects in the alcohol-focused spouse involvement group and were more likely to remain in treatment and maintain their marital satisfaction than the minimal spouse-involvement group. At eighteen-month follow-up, participants in all groups still reported decreased alcohol consumption, with BMT participants actually improving over time, in contrast to the other two conditions (McCrady et al., 1991).

In contrast to research on alcoholism, less work has examined the effects of behaviorally based family intervention for drug use disorders, with only one controlled study published to date. In a natural extension of BMT work with couples for alcoholism, Fals-Stewart et al. (1996) examined the effects of behavioral couples therapy (BCT) on the substance-abuse outcomes of the male partner. Eighty clients, most of whom were referred from the criminal justice system, were randomly assigned to receive an individual- and group-based cognitive behavioral treatment program for substance abuse but no couples treatment, or that same program in combination with twelve weekly sessions of BCT. BCT addressed issues related to substance-abuse (e.g., dealing with cravings), crisis intervention for substance-abuse episodes, and communication-skills training. Over the twelve-month follow-up period, men who received BCT had fewer days of drug use, longer periods of abstinence, and fewer drug-related problems (e.g., arrests, hospitalizations) than the men who did not receive BCT. In addition, couples in the BCT treatment reported better relationship outcomes, including higher satisfaction and fewer separations.

This study provides good support for the benefits of behaviorally based family work for drug abusers, although more work is needed in this area. In line with the generally positive findings of Fals-Stewart et al. (1996), a recent meta-analytic review of family intervention for drug abuse, including 1571 cases, concluded that family treatment (usually including psychoeducational or family systems approaches) was an effective intervention modality for this disorder (Stanton & Shadish, 1997). Furthermore, Stanton and Shadish observed that family intervention for drug abuse was associated with lower levels of drop out than other treatment approaches.

Summary

In both all-male and mixed-gender samples, behavioral family interventions for alcoholism have been demonstrated to be effective for reducing problem drinking and alcohol-related consequences. They have also been shown to have a beneficial impact on marital satisfaction levels, rendering them an attractive treatment alternative for individuals in relationships with alcohol problems. Both individual or couple group formats appear feasible and effective. Although only one study has examined behavioral couples treatment for drug abuse, this study reported similarly positive results, including both reductions in drug abuse and improvements in relationships. Overall, the results provide support for the effects of behavioral family intervention for improving the outcome of substance-use disorders.

Conclusion

With the exception of schizophrenia, research on family-based interventions for serious psychiatric disorders is still limited. Nevertheless, the results available to date are encouraging. BFT has been shown to be effective in reducing relapse rates in schizophrenia and bipolar disorders. Similar types of interventions conducted with conjugal dyads have been shown to be effective in improving outcomes in depression and substance abuse, as well as in increasing marital satisfaction. Data on BFT for anxiety disorders are more mixed; here, further research is needed to ascertain whether it can be an effective intervention.

APPENDIX 1 ORIENTATION SHEETS

Orientation to Behavioral Family Therapy

Role of Therapist

- Coordinate, guide, and assist family members in learning new information and coping skills

Goals

- Reduce tension in family relationships
- Improve communications between family members
- Increase family's understanding and acceptance of the illness
- Assist the family in developing problem-solving strategies that are more satisfactory

Format

- Assessment of each individual family member
- Assessment of strengths and weaknesses of the family as a unit
- Education about the nature of the illness and its treatment
- Communication-skills training
- Problem-solving training
- Development of new strategies for specific problems

Expectations of Family Members

- Regular attendance
- A quiet working environment (if conducted at home)
- Active role-playing
- Completion of all homework assignments
- Cooperation with each other and the therapist

Family Can Expect the Therapist to Provide

- Regular attendance
- A comfortable working environment (if conducted in clinic)
- Thoughtful systematic intervention
- Strict confidentiality (except with treatment team)
- Homework materials
- Crisis counseling (if applicable)

Orientation to Goal Setting

This program will first focus on increasing your understanding of your (or your family member's) psychiatric disorder. Then, the focus will shift to improving the communication and problem-solving skills of family members. One important part of this program is to help each family member advance toward some goal that is valuable to him or her, because *everyone* in the family is important. To facilitate this, I would like each family member to choose a personal goal to work on during the next three or four months. By "personal," I mean some objective, problem, task, or interest each family member would like to make progress on for him or herself. Some examples of personal goals are: losing weight or improving your physical fitness level, developing a hobby or interest such as in sports or music or art, becoming more sociable if you are shy, or improving your working or financial status. Indeed, some goals can take years to accomplish, but you may set some short-term objectives for yourself to begin, and continue to work toward a long-term goal.

During the next few weeks, think about some things you would like to work on during the family treatment. Write some of your ideas down, and in an upcoming session, I will help you refine one or two of them to make them achievable over the next three or four months.

APPENDIX 2   FORMS

BFT Progress Notes

Date: _____Therapist: _____

Name: _____

Session #: _____   Duration: _____

Who Attended: _____

Assessment and Review

Progress on Individual Goals: _____

_____

_____

Completion/Progress on Homework Task Assigned: _____

_____

_____

Family Meeting

When: _____   Where: _____

Chaired by: _____   Duration: _____

Issues Discussed: _____

_____

Module Work in Sessions

Skills Taught/Reviewed: _____

_____

Homework Assigned: _____

_____

Issues Raised, Potential for Later Problem Solving: _____

_____

Couples Relationship Interview

History of Relationship

How did you meet? _____

_____

How did you get to know each other? _____

_____

How did you begin dating? _____

_____

What attracted you to one another? _____

_____

When you first began to see each other, what kinds of things did you do together? ___

_____

_____

Are there special things or times together that stand out in your memory (e.g., first date, first sexual encounter, weekend together)? _____

_____

Were there any problematic issues between you during the early part of your relationship? _____

_____

What led you to decide to marry or live together? _____

_____

Were there other factors in your decision to marry or live together (e.g., pregnancy, parental pressure)? _____

_____

What was your wedding like? _____

_____

Describe your living situation when you first moved in together. _____

_____

Did anyone else live with you? Stepchildren? Parents? _____

What conflicts did you have related to your living situation? _____

_____

What kinds of things did you do for enjoyment? _____

_____

How did you handle conflicts or disagreements? _____

_____

Were there any major areas of conflict between you? _____

_____

Current Relationship

How would each of you describe the problems in your relationship now? _____

Partner #1 _____

_____

Partner #2 _____

_____

How have you dealt with the problems or conflicts in your relationship? _____

_____

Arguments? Withdrawal? _____

_____

Name calling? Threats? Physical aggression (e.g., hitting)? _____

_____

Discussions aimed at problem solving? If so, what typically happens during these discussions? _____

_____

Do you enjoy spending time together?
Partner #1 _____
Partner #2 _____

What do you most enjoy doing together? _____

_____

Do you have any disagreements about time or activities spent together?_____

_____

What activities or interests do each of you like to pursue alone? _____

Partner #1 _____

_____

Partner #2 _____

_____

Does this lead to any conflict or disagreements?_____

Partner #1 _____

_____

Partner #2 _____

_____

Do you share the same religious beliefs?_____

If not, how have you handled the differences? _____

_____

Have you had any conflicts related to differences in religious beliefs or practices?

_____

How are finances handled? _____

Who is primarily responsible for finances? _____

Do you have any disagreements about how to handle financial matters? ____

_____

Tell me about how you have handled these disagreements? _____

_____

Who takes responsibility for managing the children?_____

Which responsibilities does each person assume? _____

_____

What disagreements do you have about children? _____

_____

Are you having any special problems with the children? _____

_____

How do you get along with your spouse's family? _____

Partner #1 _____

_____

Partner #2 _____

_____

Is there anyone you have clear disagreements with? _____

Partner #1 _____

_____

Partner #2 _____

_____

Is there anyone you feel particularly close to? _____

Partner #1 _____

_____

Partner #2 _____

_____

How are things between you sexually? _____

Is there anything regarding sex that is causing tension between the two of you?

_____

Individual Family Member Interview:
Summary Sheet

Background Information

Name of Family Member: _____

Relationship to Client:_____

Address: _____

Telephone Number: _____

Medical Treatment: _____

     Current: _____

     Past: _____

Psychiatric Treatment: _____

     Current: _____

     Past: _____

Knowledge of Client's Disorder

What do you understand about _____'s (your) problem?

     What is it called? _____

Causes

What do you think caused it? _____

_____

Beneficial Factors

Have you noticed anything you do that seems to make his or her (your) disorder
better? _____

_____

Detrimental Factors

Have you noticed anything you do that seems to make his or her (your) disorder
worse?_____

_____

Prognosis

What do you think will happen with his or her (your) disorder in the future?____

_____

Medications

What do you know about the medication he or she is (you are) currently receiving?

_____

Type & Dosage

_____

_____

What do you see as the benefits of this medication? _____

_____

What are the unpleasant effects of this medication? _____

_____

What does he or she (or do you) do to cope with these unpleasant side effects?

_____

Compliance with Medication

Has he or she (have you) been taking medications as the doctor instructed?_____

_____

What types of problems has he or she (have you) experienced regarding taking the medication (e.g., forgetting, troubling side effects)? _____

_____

Coping and Burden

What are the main difficulties you have experienced with the client (your relatives)?

_____

_____

How do you cope with these difficulties? _____

_____

Daily Routine

How do you spend a typical day (get details)? What activities do you spend time doing (e.g., work, chores, hobbies, doing nothing)? (Describe a typical day briefly.)

_____

_____

_____

_____

Leisure Activities

What are the things you like to do on a day off from work or a free day? (List several.)

_____

_____

_____

Do you have enough opportunity to do these things?_____

What prevents you from doing the things you like? _____

_____

Relationships

Current Relationships

What people do you spend most of your time with (e.g., workmates, friends, family, alone)? (Specify names, details.)

_____

_____

Desired Relationships

Is there anybody with whom you would like to spend more time?

_____

_____

Supportive Persons

Do you have someone you can discuss your problems with? (Specify who.)

_____

_____

_____

To whom else could you talk?

_____

_____

Privacy

Do you have enough privacy at home (e.g., do you have your own bedroom)?
(Describe.)

_____

_____

_____

Intimacy

Do you have an intimate relationship? (Choose appropriate wording.)

_____

If not, would you like to have one? _____

Friendship

Do you have at least one friend that you are close to? Are you satisfied with that
relationship?

_____

Unpleasant Activities, People, Places

What activities, people, or places do you find unpleasant (e.g., visiting in-laws, cleaning the house)?

_____

_____

_____

Does anyone in your family concern or irritate you? How much time do you spend
with them? How would you like them to be different (specify)?_____

_____

Problem Questions

What problems are you currently facing in your life (elicit specific examples)?____

_____

With what problems are other people in your family struggling? _____

_____

With what issues, situations, or problems do you feel you need the most help?___

_____

Include problems you have noted that may not have been identified by the family member as current limitations of functioning (e.g., marital conflict, medical or psychiatric symptoms, lack of friendship, social-skills deficits, substance abuse, financial stress, housing problems, work-related problems, cultural conflicts).

For the one or two most critical problems, use the following prompts to develop a functional analysis.

How does this specific problem handicap this person (and his or her family) in everyday life? _____

_____

What would happen if the problem were ignored? _____

_____

What would happen if this problem were reduced in frequency or intensity?_____

_____

What would this person (and his or her family) gain if the specific problem were resolved?_____

_____

Who reinforces the problem with attention, sympathy, or support? _____

_____

Under what circumstances is the problem reduced in intensity or frequency? Where? When? With whom? _____

_____

Under what circumstances is the problem increased in intensity or frequency? Where? When? With whom?_____

_____

Individual Life History Interview

Location and circumstances of birth:_____

_____

_____

Siblings:_____

Relationship with parents during childhood: _____

_____

_____

Progress in school during grade-school years: _____

_____

_____

Friendships: _____

_____

_____

Development of sexual interests: _____

_____

_____

Progress in high school:_____

_____

_____

Relationship with parents during high school:_____

_____

_____

Relationships with peers during high school:_____

_____

_____

Decisions about careers and training: _____

_____

_____

Marital history (unless discussed during marital interview above)_____

_____

_____

Problems in the relationship with the ill family member _____

_____

_____

Problems in the relationship with other family members _____

_____

_____

Children: ages, education, quality of relationship _____

_____

_____

Current occupation_____

_____

Experience with mental health services _____

_____

Legal difficulties _____

_____

Serious medical problems_____

_____

Case Formulation

Family: _____   Date: _____

Therapist: _____

Initial or Follow-up Formulation: _____

Assessment of BFT Skills

Communication Skill Excesses and Deficits

Family Member	Excesses	Deficits
_____	_____	_____
_____	_____	_____
_____	_____	_____
_____	_____	_____
_____	_____	_____

Problem-Solving Steps (record for the family as a unit)

Mastered: _____

_____

Therapist Goals to Guide BFT Intervention

_____

_____

_____

Family Member's Goals

Goal: _____

Current Status: _____

Family Member: _____

Goal: _____

Current Status: _____

Family Member: _____

Goal: _____

Current Status: _____

Family Member: _____

Goal: _____

Current Status: _____

Family Member: _____

Goal: _____

Current Status: _____

Family Member: _____

Problem-Solving Assessment Checklist

Date: _____

Family: _____

Problem Worked On: _____

Family Members Present: _____

Put a check in front of each step sucessfully completed:

____ Problem defined specifically and consensually

____ At least three possible solutions generated

____ Each solution evaluated at least briefly after all solutions generated

____ Family arrives at consensus on solution to be implemented

____ Family plans implementation of solution

____ Family implements solution (if applicable)[1]

____ Family evaluates whether solution was effective (if applicable)[1]

Notes: [1]Family may need to do out-of-session work to complete step

Relapse Prevention Worksheet

_____ has a risk of reexperiencing symptoms

of _____ (specify disorder)

The earliest OBSERVABLE signs that symptoms are flaring up are:

_____

_____

_____

The circumstances that tend to make symptoms worse include:

_____

_____

_____

Plan to be implemented when warning signs flare up:

_____

_____

_____

Doctor's Name: _____ Phone: _____

Therapist or Case Manager's Name: _____ Phone: _____

Decision Balance Matrix

Alternative A: _____

_____

Alternative B: _____

_____

Advantages of A   **Disadvantages of A**

_____   _____

_____   _____

_____   _____

_____   _____

Advantages of B   **Disadvantages of B**

_____   _____

_____   _____

_____   _____

_____   _____

Option that offers best combination of advantages and disadvantages _____

_____

APPENDIX 3

EDUCATIONAL HANDOUTS

Facts about Bipolar Disorder

What is Bipolar Disorder?

Bipolar disorder (also called *manic-depression*) is a major psychiatric disorder in which the person experiences occasional episodes of extremely elevated moods (*mania*). Most persons with this disorder also experience intermittent episodes of extremely low moods (*depression*). In between these extremes, the person's mood may be normal.

The symptoms of bipolar disorder can cause significant disruption to the person's ability to work, fulfill household responsibilities, and maintain interpersonal relationships. The experience of bipolar disorder, as well as having a close family member with the disorder, can be described as a roller-coaster ride that one cannot get off.

How Common Is Bipolar Disorder?

About one in every one hundred people (1 percent) develops bipolar disorder some time during his or her life.

How Is the Disorder Diagnosed?

Bipolar disorder can only be diagnosed with a clinical interview. The purpose of this interview is to determine whether the client has experienced specific "symptoms" of the disorder for a sufficiently long period of time (at least two weeks). In addition to conducting the interview, the diagnostician must make sure that other physical problems are not present that could produce symptoms similar to those found in bipolar disorder, such as a brain tumor, or alcohol or drug abuse. Bipolar disorder cannot be diagnosed with a blood test, an X ray, a CAT scan, or any other laboratory test.

The Characteristic Symptoms of Bipolar Disorder

There are two broad types of symptoms typically experienced by persons with bipolar disorder: *manic* symptoms and *depressive* symptoms. The diagnosis of bipolar disorder requires that the person has experienced a *manic syndrome*, that is, a period of at least two weeks in which manic symptoms have been present to a significant degree. If the person has only experienced a manic syndrome, he or she still qualifies for the diagnosis of bipolar disorder. However, most persons with this disorder also experience *depressive syndromes*, periods of at least two weeks in which symptoms of depression predominate. Usually, the symptoms of mania and depression occur at different times. However, it is possible for manic and depressive symptoms to be present at the same time (called a *mixed state*). If the person has experienced only symptoms of depression, but not mania, he or she is given a diagnosis of *major depression*, rather than bipolar disorder.

Symptoms of Mania

In general, the symptoms of mania involve an excess in behavioral activity, mood states (in particular, irritability or positive feelings), and self-esteem and confidence. At least some of these symptoms interfere with the client's day-to-day functioning. Not all symptoms must be present for the client to have had a manic syndrome.

Euphoric or Expansive Mood. The client's mood is abnormally elevated, such as extremely happy or excited (*euphoria*). The person may tend to talk more and with greater enthusiasm or emphasis on certain topics (*expansiveness*).

Irritability. The client is easily angered or persistently irritable, especially when others seem to interfere with his or her plans or goals, however unrealistic they may be.

Inflated Self-Esteem or Grandiosity. The client is extremely self-confidant and may be unrealistic about his or her abilities (*grandiosity*). For example, the client may believe he or she is a brilliant artist or inventor, a wealthy person, a shrewd business person, or a healer when he or she has no special competence in these areas.

Decreased Need for Sleep. Only a few hours of sleep are needed each night (such as less than four hours) for the client to feel rested.

Talkativeness. The client talks excessively and may be difficult to interrupt. The client may jump quickly from one topic to another (called *flight of ideas*), making it hard for others to understand.

Racing Thoughts. Thoughts come so rapidly that the client finds it hard to keep up with them or express them.

Distractibility. The client's attention is easily drawn to irrelevant stimuli, such as the sound of a car honking outside on the street.

Increased Goal-Directed Activity. A great deal of time is spent pursuing specific goals, at work, school, or sexually.

Excessive Involvement in Pleasurable Activities with High Potential for Negative Consequences. Common problem areas include spending sprees, sexual indiscretions, increased substance abuse, or making foolish business investments.

Symptoms of Depression

Depressive symptoms reflect the opposite end of the continuum of mood from manic symptoms, with a low mood and behavioral inactivity as the major features. Not all symptoms must be present for the client to have had a depressive syndrome.

Depressed Mood. Mood is low most of the time, according to the client or significant others.

Diminished Interest or Pleasure. The client has few interests and gets little pleasure from anything, including activities previously found enjoyable.

Change in Appetite and/or Weight. Loss of appetite (and weight), when not dieting, or increased appetite (and weight gain) are evident.

Change in Sleep Pattern. The client may have difficulty falling asleep or staying asleep, or may wake early in the morning and not be able to get back to sleep. Alternatively, the client may sleep excessively (such as over twelve hours per night), spending much of the day in bed.

Change in Activity Level. Decreased activity level is reflected by slowness and lethargy, in terms of both the client's behavior and his or her thought processes. Alternatively, the client may feel agitated, "on edge," and restless.

Fatigue or Loss of Energy. The client experiences fatigue throughout the day, or there is a chronic feeling of loss of energy.

Feelings of Worthlessness, Hopelessness, Helplessness. Clients may feel they are worthless as people, that there is no hope for improving their lives, or that they are helpless to improve their unhappy situation.

Inappropriate Guilt. Feelings of guilt may be present about events that the client did not even cause, such as catastrophe, a crime, or an illness.

Recurrent Thoughts about Death. The client thinks about death a great deal and may contemplate (or even attempt) suicide.

Decreased Concentration or Ability to Make Decisions. Significant decreases in the ability to concentrate make it difficult for the client to pay attention to others or complete rudimentary tasks. The client may be quite indecisive about even minor things.

Other Symptoms

Clients with bipolar disorder also have other psychiatric symptoms at the same time that they experience manic or depressive symptoms. Some of the most common other symptoms include *hallucinations* (false perceptions, such as hearing voices) and *delusions* (false beliefs, such as paranoid delusions). These symptoms disappear when manic or depressive symptoms have been controlled.

How Is Bipolar Disorder Distinguished from Schizophrenia and Schizoaffective Disorder?

Many persons with a diagnosis of bipolar disorder also have had, at some point, a diagnosis of schizophrenia or schizoaffective disorder. Diagnostic uncertainty results because during a symptom flare-up, a psychotic symptom such as delusional grandiosity (for example, a belief that a person is Jesus Christ) may reflect either mania, schizophrenia, or a schizoaffective disorder. However, over time, the symptoms of these three disorders tend to differ. Of particular importance, when their moods are stable, persons with bipolar disorder do not usually experience psychotic symptoms, while persons with schizophrenia or schizoaffective disorder often do.

What is the Course of Bipolar Disorder?

Bipolar disorder often develops in late adolescence or early adulthood, but it can also develop later in life, in an individual's 40s or even 50s. Bipolar disorder is a lifelong disorder, with symptoms varying over time in severity. In most cases, clients with the disorder are able to function between episodes; for instance, they can work, maintain household responsibilities, and raise children. Many famous people have struggled with bipolar disorder (such as Vincent Van Gogh, Patty Duke, Samuel Coleridge, Edgar Allan Poe, Carrie Fisher, and Robert Schumann), but have been able to make significant contributions to society.

What Causes Manic-Depression?

No one knows the cause of bipolar disorder. Theories suggest that the illness may be caused by an imbalance in chemicals in the brain, particularly the chemical called *norepinephrine*. It is believed that this imbalance is determined by genetic factors.

Are There Factors That Might Increase the Likelihood of Relapse?

Sleep deprivation and substance abuse tend to increase the possibility that a manic episode will develop. Depressive episodes often occur when the individual is confronting a loss or life change.

How Is Manic-Depression Treated?

Effective pharmacological treatments are available for bipolar disorder. These medications do not "cure" the disorder, but they reduce the symptoms and prevent relapses from occurring. Lithium is the most common drug used for bipolar disorder. Carbamazepine (Tegretol) and valproic acid are also effective medications. Some clients with psychotic symptoms also benefit from antipsychotic medications. A small subset of clients continue to have symptoms of the disorder, even when they are receiving excellent pharmacological treatment.

Dealing with episodes of bipolar disorder can be horribly disruptive and distressing. Many persons with the disorder can benefit from supportive counseling to learn how to manage the disorder, as well as deal with its impact on their lives. Some types of family therapy also can reduce stress and teach family members how to monitor the disorder.

> Consult a mental health professional (such as a psychiatrist, psychologist, social worker, or psychiatric nurse) about any questions you have concerning this handout.

Recommended Readings

Copeland, M.E. (1992), *The Depression Workbook: A Guide for Living with Depression and Manic Depression*, Oakland, CA: New Harbinger.

Duke, P. & Hochman, G. (1992), *A Brilliant Madness: Living with Manic-Depressive Illness.* New York: Bantam.

Goodwin, F.K. & Jamison, K.R. (1990), *Manic-Depressive Illness.* New York: Oxford University Press.

Papolos, D. & Papolos, J. (1992), *Overcoming Depression (Revised Edition).* New York: HarperPerennial.

Whybrow, P.C. (1997). *A Mood Apart.* New York: Basic Books.

Facts about Major Depression

What Is Major Depression?

Major depression (and the slightly less severe illness of *Dysthymic Disorder*) is a psychiatric disorder characterized by significant periods of time in which the person experiences a sad, "blue," or low mood. This depressed mood is often accompanied by other unpleasant changes, such as loss of appetite or trouble sleeping. In contrast to the normal "blues" that many people often experience, these problems are severe enough to interfere with day-to-day functioning, such as the ability to work, fulfill household responsibilities, and maintain interpersonal relationships.

The experience of depression varies considerably from one individual to the next. Some people describe depression as a loss in energy and interest in the world and a decreased ability to enjoy life. For others, depression is a unique, awful feeling of dread that is difficult to describe to someone who has not had the experience. Living with a person with depression can be difficult because the person may be difficult to engage and some of the depressed feelings may "rub off" on the other person.

How Common Is Major Depression?

Major depression is one of the most common psychiatric disorders. Between fifteen and twenty out of every one hundred people (15-20 percent) experience an episode of major depression some time during their life.

How Is the Disorder Diagnosed?

Depression can only be diagnosed with a clinical interview. The purpose of this interview is to determine whether the client has experienced specific "symptoms" of the disorder for a sufficiently long period of time. For a person to be diagnosed with *major depression*, severe symptoms must be present for at least a two-week period, although in most cases symptoms have been present for a longer period. If the symptoms are less severe but are present for long periods of time, the person has the diagnosis of *dysthymic disorder*.

In addition to conducting the interview, the diagnostician must make sure that other physical problems are not present that could produce symptoms similar to those found in depression, such as a brain tumor, a thyroid problem, or alcohol or drug abuse. Depression cannot be diagnosed with a blood test, an X ray, a CAT scan, or any other laboratory test.

The Characteristic Symptoms of Depression

The major symptoms of depression reflect both low mood and other disturbances in appetite, body weight, sleep, and activity level. Not all symptoms must be present for the person to be diagnosed with depression.

Depressed Mood. Mood is low most of the time, according to the client or significant others.

Diminished Interest or Pleasure. The client has few interests and gets little pleasure from anything, including activities previously found enjoyable.

Change in Appetite and/or Weight. Loss of appetite (and weight), when not dieting, or increased appetite (and weight gain) are evident.

Change in Sleep Pattern. The client may have difficulty falling asleep or staying asleep, or may wake early in the morning and not be able to get back to sleep. Alternatively, the client may sleep excessively (such as over twelve hours per night), spending much of the day in bed.

Change in Activity Level. Decreased activity level is reflected by slowness and lethargy, in terms of both the client's behavior and his or her thought processes. Alternatively, the client may feel agitated, "on edge," and restless.

Fatigue or Loss of Energy. The client experiences fatigue throughout the day, or there is a chronic feeling of loss of energy.

Feelings of Worthlessness, Hopelessness, Helplessness. Clients may feel they are worthless as people, that there is no hope for improving their lives, or that they are helpless to improve their unhappy situation.

Inappropriate Guilt. Feelings of guilt may be present about events that the client did not even cause, such as a catastrophe, a crime, or an illness.

Recurrent Thoughts about Death. The client thinks about death a great deal and may contemplate (or even attempt) suicide.

Decreased Concentration or Ability to Make Decisions. Significant decreases in the ability to concentrate make it difficult for the client to pay attention to others or complete rudimentary tasks. The client may be quite indecisive about even minor things.

Other Symptoms

Clients with depression (primarily major depression) also may have other psychiatric symptoms at the same time that they experience depressive symptoms. Some of the most common other symptoms include *hallucinations* (false perceptions, such as hearing voices) and *delusions* (false beliefs, such as paranoid delusions). These symptoms disappear when the symptoms of depression have been controlled.

How Is Major Depression Distinguished from Other Disorders?

Persons with major depression suffer episodes of depression interspersed with periods of normal mood. If the individual experiences both depression and the elevated, hyperenergized, expansive moods defined as mania, the individual is then diagnosed as having bipolar disorder (manic-depression). If the person experiences the psychotic symptoms discussed above when not depressed, he or she is typically given a diagnosis of schizoaffective disorder.

What Is the Course of Major Depression?

Major depression can develop at any time during adult life, starting during adolescence and extending up until old age. Some clients experience significant bouts of depression, ranging from weeks to months or even years, but fully recover from the disorder. For other individuals, however, depression is a lifelong disorder, with symptoms varying over time in severity. Many famous people have struggled with depression (such as Abraham Lincoln), but have been able to make significant contributions to society.

What Causes Depression?

No one knows the cause of depression, although many theories have been proposed. Many scientists believe that there is more than one cause of depression. Biochemical theories suggest that the disorder may be caused by an imbalance in chemicals in the brain, particularly the chemicals *norepinephrine* and *serotonin*. This imbalance may be determined partly by genetic factors and partly by early effects of the environment. There is evidence that the loss of a significant person early in life (such as a parent) increases an individual's vulnerability to develop depression at a later age.

Are There Factors That Might Increase the likelihood of Relapse?

For many people, depression is recurrent. Factors that tend to increase the likelihood of a recurrence include a life change or a loss, a seasonal change (especially the coming of winter), and excessive alcohol use.

How Is Depression Treated?

There are many effective treatments for depression. Medication is very helpful for some clients. Medications can reduce or eliminate the symptoms of depression and prevent relapses from occurring. Antidepressant medications are the most effective medications for depression, although some clients also benefit from antipsychotic medications. Some individuals with severe major depression benefit from electroconvulsive therapy (ECT), also referred to as "shock treatment."

Individual psychotherapy is quite effective in improving the symptoms of depression. The focus of therapy is usually on correcting common problems with thinking (such as a tendency to think in "black-and-white" terms), improving social skills and problem solving, or improving interpersonal relationships. Family or marital therapy can reduce stress in the family and teach the family how to monitor the disorder.

While there are many effective treatments for depression, it must also be noted that this tends to be an episodic disorder, and relapses often occur. In addition, a small subset of individuals with depression continue to suffer significant symptoms, in spite of the best pharmacologic and psychotherapeutic treatment.

Consult a mental health professional (such as a psychiatrist, psychologist, social worker, or psychiatric nurse) about any questions you have concerning this handout.

Recommended Readings

Burns, D. (1980), *Feeling Good: The New Mood Therapy.* New York: William Morrow and Company.

Copeland, M.E. (1992), *The Depression Workbook: A Guide for Living with Depression and Manic Depression.* Oakland, CA: New Harbinger.

Papolos, D. & Papolos, J. (1992), *Overcoming Depression (Revised Edition).* New York: Harper Perennial.

Yapko, M.D. (1997), *Breaking the Patterns of Depression.* New York: Doubleday.

Facts about Obsessive-Compulsive Disorder

What Is Obsessive-Compulsive Disorder?

Obsessive-compulsive disorder (OCD) is a major psychiatric disorder that can affect all aspects of a person's functioning, including his or her relationships with others, the ability to work, and recreational activities. Clients with OCD typically experience anxiety related to severe obsessions (repeated worries that are difficult to let go of) or compulsions (recurrent behaviors or thoughts that must be frequently repeated to reduce anxiety). Clients with OCD often understand that their obsessions are unrealistic or their compulsions are excessive, but they feel powerless to change. Some individuals with OCD lack insight into the senselessness of the obsessions and compulsions.

The experience of having OCD can be extremely frustrating. At times the disorder is like being a stuck record; the person feels forced to repeat thoughts or behaviors over and over, no matter how foolish they seem. Clients with OCD often feel as though life is passing them by, with all of their attention focused on their obsessions and compulsions, and little time spent enjoying themselves and their families.

How Common Is OCD?

OCD is a relatively common psychiatric disorder. Between two and three out of every one hundred persons (2-3 percent) develop OCD at some time during their life.

How Is the Disorder Diagnosed?

OCD can only be diagnosed by a clinical interview. The purpose of the interview is to determine whether the client has experienced specific "symptoms" of the disorder and whether these symptoms have been present long enough to merit the diagnosis. OCD cannot be diagnosed with a blood test, an X ray, a CAT scan, or any other laboratory test.

The Characteristic Symptoms of OCD

The symptoms of OCD can be broadly divided into three different categories: *obsessions, compulsions,* and *other symptoms.* Clients with OCD can have either severe obsessions or severe compulsions, although the majority of clients have both types of symptoms. Regardless of which symptoms the client has, they cause significant distress and disruption to his or her life. Specific symptoms of OCD are described below.

Obsessions. Obsessions are recurrent thoughts, impulses, or images that cause anxiety and are disturbing to the client, such as the impulse to kill a loved child or the thought that one has somehow been exposed to a fatal disease. The insight clients have into the true basis of their concerns varies from one client to the next, ranging from a recognition that the obsessions are unrealistic to fully believing that the obsessions are realistic. However, regardless of the client's insight, obsessions cause distress, which leads to efforts to avoid, suppress, or neutralize these thoughts. These efforts provide temporary relief, but then the obsessions return again.

Compulsions. Compulsions are the urge to engage repeatedly in behaviors or thoughts in order to reduce anxiety related to an obsession or because the person finds it difficult to resist the behavior. These stereotyped behavior patterns serve no useful purpose, except to fend off anxiety. The compulsions can be so pervasive that the person repeats them innumerable times throughout the day. Several types of specific compulsive symptoms include:

Washing and Cleaning. Fear of dirt, disease, and contamination are quite common among clients with OCD, and one natural consequence of this fear is compulsions about cleanliness. Hand washing is common, to the point where the client may wash more than fifty to one hundred times per day, with resulting chaffing, redness, and bleeding of skin. Vigorous body scrubbing, washing of clothes, and excessive use of disinfectants may occur. The person may spend hours in the bathroom washing, attending to dental hygiene, etc., making it difficult to live a "normal" life. The fear of contamination may also lead clients to avoid many situations or touching commonplace objects.

Checking. The client may repeatedly check on things, such as making sure the door is locked, windows are shut, electrical appliances are turned off, or a task has been done correctly. The person may check something many times in a row, just to make sure there is no safety risk or error. Even though the client knows he or she just checked something, the fear of possible catastrophe leads to checking again and again.

Ordering. An excessive level of order in the home or at work is maintained (such as requiring symmetry of objects, insisting on a particular organization of the house or workplace). The client spends a considerable amount of time keeping this order and may become anxious or angry if others upset the order.

Repeating. The client repeats specific actions over and over because of a "magical" belief that it will protect him or her in some way. For example, a client repeatedly dresses and undresses until a thought about her loved ones being hurt disappears. Unlike washing, cleaning, and checking rituals, repeating rituals are not "logically" related to the concerns the person has; rather, the behaviors are simply repeated until the undesired thought or feeling goes away, sometimes after numerous repetitions.

Hoarding. The client has difficulty throwing things away, forming idiosyncratic collections of no value (such as scraps of paper, old newspapers, etc.). The major reason given by clients for saving the objects is that they may need them sometime in the future, although the need never seems to arise.

Thinking Rituals. The client develops thinking rituals that stop the obsession and neutralize the anxiety associated with it. These rituals may need to be repeated many times before the obsession is stopped. For example, a religious person with recurrent blasphemous thoughts may develop an elaborate set of specific prayers that are repeated over and over until the thought has ceased.

Other Symptoms

In addition to *anxiety*, which is present in most clients with OCD, a variety of other symptoms may also occur. *Depression* is a common problem for many clients, as the obsessions and compulsions take control of their life. *Alcohol and drug abuse* problems may occur as clients try to escape the ever-present obsessions or compulsions. Sometimes clients with OCD have quite bizarre obsessions that seem quite real to the person, and are thus *delusions* (or "false beliefs"). For example, one client was genuinely terrified of carpets because he was afraid of getting tacked under the carpet.

What Is the Course of the Disorder?

The course of OCD varies from one client to the next. OCD often develops in late adolescence or early adulthood, although onset during childhood and later in adulthood also occurs. For some clients, OCD is a chronic and debilitating disorder that lasts throughout much of their lives. Many clients are capable of recovering substantially from OCD, especially when they have received appropriate treatments for the disorder.

What Causes OCD?

The precise causes of OCD are not understood at this time, although there are several theories. The most prominent theories of OCD involve learning and altered brain chemistry. According to learning theory, obsessions and compulsions develop gradually over a period of time. First, the person experiences a minor distressing thought, image, or impulse, which results in anxiety. The person tries to think about something different or engages in a particular behavior as a distraction from the thought, thereby lowering his or her anxiety. However, the thought or image is likely to occur again, since no method of distraction is permanent. Gradually, the person spends more and more time anticipating (and experiencing) these distressing thoughts (obsessions) and developing increasingly elaborate cognitive strategies (thinking rituals) and behaviors (compulsions) for lowering his or her anxiety. As a result, much of the person's time becomes occupied with these obsessions and compulsions, with his or her anxiety steadily worsening.

   Biological theories of OCD suggest that the disorder may result from differences in brain neurotransmitters (chemicals in the brain). One particular neurotransmitter has been linked to *OCD—serotonin*. However, the nature of the abnormality is not known. Both learning and biological factors may be involved in OCD.

Are There Factors That Might Increase the Likelihood of Relapse?

OCD symptoms often wax and wane over time, usually in response to life stress. Symptoms tend to worsen under periods of life change or stress, or when going off prescribed medication against the doctor's advice.

How Is OCD Treated?

Two primary treatments can improve or eliminate the symptoms of OCD: behavior therapy and medication. Two specific techniques of behavior therapy are especially effective at reducing obsessions and compulsions: *exposure* to the feared stimuli (such as situations, thoughts, etc.) and *response prevention* to stop behavior patterns that reduce anxiety. When clients permit themselves to confront feared thoughts, places, or objects for extended periods of time, their anxiety gradually subsides. Teaching clients to refrain from rituals and compulsions breaks the vicious cycle of repeated behaviors, providing relief. Most behavior therapy programs for OCD require several weeks of intensive treatment or longer periods of less intensive therapy. Family treatment can help lower the stress on clients with OCD and their relatives, improving the long-term outcome of the disorder.

Pharmacological treatment with antidepressant medications also improves the symptoms of OCD. There is evidence that antidepressants with a primary effect on serotonin (such as Anafranil, Prozac, Zoloft, or Paxil) have the most beneficial effect on OCD. Medication usually requires at least ten weeks to be effective. A combination of behavior therapy and medication may also be helpful.

> Consult a mental health professional (such as a psychiatrist, psychologist, social worker, or psychiatric nurse) about any questions you have concerning this handout.

Recommended Readings

Foa, E.B. & Wilson, R. (1991), *Stop Obsessing! How to Overcome Your Obsessions and Compulsions.* New York: Bantam.

Rapoport, J.L. (1989), *The Boy Who Couldn't Stop Washing: The Experience and Treatment of Obsessive-Compulsive Disorder.* New York: Dutton.

Steketee, G. & White, K. (1990), *When Once Is Not Enough: Help for Obsessive Compulsives.* Oakland, CA: New Harbinger.

Facts about Post-traumatic Stress Disorder

What Is Post-traumatic Stress Disorder?

Post-traumatic stress disorder (PTSD) is a major psychiatric disorder that develops in some individuals after experiencing a traumatic, often life-threatening event. Common events that can lead to PTSD include combat, assault or rape, accidents, and natural disasters. People with PTSD experience high levels of anxiety, arousal, and avoidance due to recurrent memories of the traumatic event. This severe anxiety often interferes with the client's interpersonal relationships, enjoyment of life, and ability to maintain a job or meet other role responsibilities (such as homemaker).

The experience of having PTSD (or living with someone who does) can feel like living in constant danger; the client constantly attempts to avoid situations that might remind him or her of the trauma, but no matter how hard he or she tries, the memories resurface when least expected.

How Common Is PTSD?

PTSD is quite common. About ten in every one hundred persons (10 percent) develop PTSD at some time during his or her life.

How Is the Disorder Diagnosed?

PTSD can only be diagnosed by a clinical interview. The purpose of the interview is to determine whether the client has experienced specific "symptoms" of the disorder and whether these symptoms have been present long enough to merit the diagnosis. PTSD cannot be diagnosed with a blood test, an X ray, a CAT scan, or any other laboratory test.

The Characteristic Symptoms of PTSD

The symptoms of PTSD can be broadly divided into four different categories: *reexperiencing of the trauma, avoidance of stimuli associated with the trauma, increased arousal,* and *other symptoms.* These symptoms are described below. Although every client with PTSD has at least some of the symptoms in each of these first three categories, clients do not need to have all of these symptoms in order to be diagnosed with PTSD. Each client's specific symptoms are unique to that individual.

Reexperiencing the Trauma

This can occur in various ways, such as:

Recurrent and Intrusive Memories of the Event. Memories of the trauma are often intrusive images that can happen at any time, any place. The memories may be triggered by something that reminds the client of the trauma, or by nothing in particular.

Recurrent Nightmares of the Event. Nightmares about the traumatic event often interfere with the client's ability to get a good night of sleep. Sometimes during sleep the person will experience the onset of sudden, violent, anxiety-provoking dreams that are not exactly a nightmare of the event but are very disturbing.

Sudden Acting or Feeling as if the Event Were Recurring. The client may have a flashback as though the event were happening again, or have illusions or hallucinations of the event.

Distress at Events That Remind the Client of the Trauma. Ordinary, everyday things may remind the client of the trauma, causing intense distress. Memories may recur and symptoms worsen at anniversaries of the trauma.

Avoidance of Stimuli Associated with the Trauma or Numbing of Responsiveness

Several different types of avoidance or numbing are common, including:

Efforts to Avoid Thoughts, Feelings, Situations, or Activities That Trigger Memories of the Trauma. The client may try to distract himself or herself from these unpleasant memories by using alcohol or drugs, or by maintaining a high level of activity. Some clients avoid so many different situations that their range of activity is quite restricted and they are socially withdrawn.

Inability to Recall an Important Aspect of the Trauma. The client is able to remember some but not other parts of the traumatic event.

Diminished Interest in Significant Activities. Activities that were formerly enjoyable are no longer pleasurable. The client may feel apathetic and not pursue leisure activities.

Feeling Detached or Estranged from Others. The client does not feel close to others or is not able to experience love, feeling numb instead.

A Sense of Foreshortened Future. It is difficult for the client to look into the future. He or she may sense that he or she may not have a long life, or he or she may not expect to marry, have children, or have a career.

Increased Arousal

Several different symptoms can be due to heightened arousal, including:

Increased Arousal in Situations that Remind Client of the Trauma. For example, a person who was assaulted in an elevator experiences increased heart rate and perspiration when entering any elevator.

Hypervigilance. The client feels "super-alert," constantly scanning his or her environment for possible threats or challenges. It may be difficult or impossible to relax, even when tired, because of the need to remain alert.

Exaggerated Startle Response. A sudden, unexpected loud noise or flash can jolt or startle the person in an exaggerated manner.

Difficulty Sleeping. Problems falling asleep or staying asleep are most common.

Irritability or Anger Outbursts. The client is often irritable and easily annoyed. Anger outbursts may occur over seemingly trivial matters.

Difficulty Concentrating. Problems with concentration may interfere with the ability to work, enjoy leisure activities, or pursue short- and long-term goals.

Other Symptoms

A variety of other symptoms are often present in clients with PTSD. *Depression* is a common problem for many persons with this disorder, and the recurrent, intrusive memories of the trauma lead some clients to contemplate or attempt suicide. *Alcohol and drug abuse* problems are quite common in PTSD, because clients use these substances to help them escape their unpleasant memories, to relax, or to sleep. Some clients with PTSD experience mild levels of hallucinations (such as hearing voices) or delusions (such as feeling paranoid).

What Is the Course of the Disorder?

The course of PTSD is highly variable, depending upon the individual, when the trauma occurred, how severe it was, and how long after the trauma the person received treatment. Most people who have been traumatized experience the symptoms of PTSD for several days or weeks after the trauma but do not actually have PTSD. While for some individuals these symptoms gradually disappear over weeks or months, for others the symptoms remain or worsen. Individuals who continue to experience symptoms for more than one month after the traumatic event have PTSD.

Many people who receive treatment soon after the traumatic event (within several weeks or months) recover completely. Some clients with PTSD who were traumatized but did not receive treatment until a long time later (such as after several years) are nevertheless able to recover fully from the disorder. However, for other clients with PTSD their disorder can be a more long-lasting one that continues, even after treatment, to affect their day-to-day lives.

What Causes PTSD?

It is not known why some persons develop PTSD after a trauma and others do not. However, theories about the causes of PTSD suggest that both *learning* and *biological factors* may play a role in the development of PTSD.

Some of the most common anxiety symptoms in PTSD (such as avoidance of stimuli that remind the person of the trauma) may be learned as the person tries to decrease his or her anxiety and cope with unpredictable reminders of the trauma. There is also evidence that exposure to traumatic events can lead to physiological changes in the nervous system, resulting in chronically high levels of arousal. This may be more likely to happen if the trauma occurred when the person was young and if they did not receive treatment for a long time. For most persons with PTSD, symptoms are probably caused by a combination of both learning and biological factors.

A final factor to be considered is multiple traumatization. Some individuals may have experienced a series of traumas in their life (e.g., intense childhood abuse, a sexual assault during adolescence, and a severe car accident during adulthood). In comparison with the person who did not have a history of prior traumas, the previously traumatized individual may appear to have an especially intense PTSD reaction to the later trauma (in this example, the car accident). In short, the effects of repeated traumas may accumulate over time and contribute to the increased severity of symptoms with subsequent traumatic events.

Are There Factors That Might Increase the Likelihood of Relapse?

PTSD symptoms tend to worsen when individuals have too much unstructured time, suffer a loss, or are retraumatized.

How Is PTSD Treated?

A number of different treatments can be helpful to persons with PTSD. Behavior therapy that focuses on reviewing the traumatic events with the encouragement of a caring therapist and teaching stress management techniques can substantially improve symptoms. Many people with PTSD find that supportive therapy (either individual or group) is also helpful. Family therapy can help reduce stress on all family members and help develop strategies for managing chronic symptoms.

Pharmacological treatments can also be useful in the treatment of PTSD. Antidepressant medications are often used to relieve depression. Antianxiety and sedative drugs are sometimes prescribed to reduce anxiety and agitation, and to facilitate sleep. Antipsychotic medications are occasionally used to treat less common symptoms, such as hallucinations or delusions.

> Consult a mental health professional (such as a psychiatrist, psychologist, social worker, or psychiatric nurse) about any questions you have concerning this handout.

Recommended Readings

Matsakis, A. (1996), *I Can't Get Over It: A Handbook for Trauma Survivors*, *(Second Edition)*. Oakland, CA: New Harbinger.

Sterns, A.K. (1988), *Coming Back: Rebuilding Lives after Crisis and Loss*. New York: Ballantine.

Veninga, R.L. (1985), *A Gift of Hope: How We Survive Our Tragedies*. New York: Ballantine.

Facts about Schizoaffective Disorder

What Is Schizoaffective Disorder?

Schizoaffective disorder is a major psychiatric disorder that is quite similar to schizophrenia. The disorder can affect all aspects of daily living, including work, social relationships, and self-care skills (such as grooming and hygiene). People with schizoaffective disorder can have a wide variety of symptoms, including problems with their contact with reality (hallucinations and delusions), mood (such as marked depression), low motivation, inability to experience pleasure, and poor attention. The serious nature of the symptoms of schizoaffective disorder sometimes requires clients to be hospitalized at times for treatment. The experience of schizoaffective disorder can be described as similar to "dreaming when you are wide awake"; that is, it can be hard for the person with the disorder to distinguish between reality and fantasy.

How Common Is Schizoaffective Disorder?

About one in every two hundred people (1/2 percent) develops schizoaffective disorder at some time during his or her life. Schizoaffective disorder, along with schizophrenia, is one of the most common serious psychiatric disorders.

How Is the Disorder Diagnosed?

Schizoaffective disorder can only be diagnosed by a clinical interview. The purpose of the interview is to determine whether the client has experienced specific "symptoms" of the disorder, and whether these symptoms have been present long enough to merit the diagnosis. In addition to conducting the interview, the diagnostician must also check to make sure the client is not experiencing any physical problems that could cause symptoms similar to schizoaffective disorder, such as a brain tumor or alcohol or drug abuse.

Schizoaffective disorder *cannot* be diagnosed with a blood test, an X ray, a CAT scan, or any other laboratory test. An interview is necessary to establish the diagnosis.

The Characteristic Symptoms of Schizoaffective Disorder

The diagnosis of schizoaffective disorder requires that the client experience some decline in social functioning for at least a six-month period, such as problems with school or work, social relationships, or self-care. In addition, some other symptoms are commonly present. The symptoms of schizoaffective disorder can be divided into five broad classes: *positive symptoms, negative symptoms, symptoms of mania, symptoms of depression,* and *other symptoms.* A person with schizoaffective disorder will have some (but not all) of the symptoms described below.

Positive Symptoms

Positive symptoms refer to thoughts, perceptions, and behaviors that are ordinarily *absent* in people in the general population, but are *present* in persons with schizoaffective disorder. These symptoms often vary over time in their severity, and may be absent for long periods in some clients.

Hallucinations. Hallucinations are "false perceptions"; that is, hearing, seeing, feeling, or smelling things that are not actually there. The most common type of hallucinations are *auditory hallucinations*. Clients sometimes report hearing voices talking to them or about them, often saying insulting things, such as calling them names. These voices are usually heard through the ears and sound like other human voices.

Delusions. Delusions are "false beliefs"; that is, a belief that the client holds, but that others can clearly see is not true. Some clients have *paranoid delusions*, believing that others want to hurt them. *Delusions of reference* are common, in which the client believes that something in the environment is referring to him or her when it is not (such as the television talking to the client). *Delusions of control* are beliefs that others can control one's actions. Clients hold these beliefs strongly and cannot usually be "talked out" of them.

Thinking Disturbances. The client talks in a manner that is difficult to follow, an indication that he or she has a disturbance in thinking. For example, the client may jump from one topic to the next, stop in the middle of the sentence, make up new words, or simply be difficult to understand.

Negative Symptoms

Negative symptoms are the opposite of positive symptoms. They are the *absence* of thoughts, perceptions, or behaviors that are ordinarily *present* in people in the general population. These symptoms are often stable throughout much of the client's life.

Blunted Affect. The expressiveness of the client's face, voice tone, and gestures is diminished or restricted. However, this does not mean that the person is not reacting to his or her environment or having feelings.

Apathy. The client does not feel motivated to pursue goals and activities. The client may feel lethargic or sleepy and have trouble following through on even simple plans. Clients with apathy often have little sense of purpose in their lives and have few interests.

Anhedonia. The client experiences little or no pleasure from activities that he or she used to enjoy or that others enjoy. For example, the person may not enjoy watching a sunset, going to the movies, or a close relationship with another person.

Poverty of Speech or Content of Speech. The client says very little, or when he or she talks, it does not amount to much. Sometimes conversing with the client can be unrewarding.

Inattention. The client has difficulty attending and is easily distracted. This can interfere with activities such as work, interacting with others, and personal care skills.

Symptoms of Mania

In general, the symptoms of mania involve an excess in behavioral activity, mood states (in particular, irritability or positive feelings), and self-esteem and confidence.

Euphoric or Expansive Mood. The client's mood is abnormally elevated; for example, he or she is extremely happy or excited (euphoria). The person may tend to talk more and with greater enthusiasm or emphasis on certain topics (expansiveness).

Irritability. The client is easily angered or persistently irritable, especially when others seem to interfere with his or her plans or goals, however unrealistic they may be.

Inflated Self-Esteem or Grandiosity. The client is extremely self-confident and may be unrealistic about his or her abilities (grandiosity). For example, the client may believe he or she is a brilliant artist or inventor, a wealthy person, a shrewd businessperson, or a healer when he or she has no special competence in these areas.

Decreased Need for Sleep. Only a few hours of sleep are needed each night (such as less than four hours) for the client to feel rested.

Talkativeness. The client talks excessively and may be difficult to interrupt. The client may jump quickly from one topic to another (called *flight of ideas*), making it hard for others to understand.

Racing Thoughts. Thoughts come so rapidly that the client finds it hard to keep up with them or express them.

Distractibility. The client's attention is easily drawn to irrelevant stimuli, such as the sound of a car honking outside on the street.

Increased Goal-Directed Activity. A great deal of time is spent pursuing specific goals, at work, school, or sexually.

Excessive Involvement in Pleasurable Activities with High Potential for Negative Consequences. Common problem areas include spending sprees, sexual indiscretions, increased substance abuse, or making foolish business investments.

Symptoms of Depression

Depressive symptoms reflect the opposite end of the continuum of mood from manic symptoms, with a low mood and behavioral inactivity as the major features.

Depressed Mood. Mood is low most of the time, according to the client or significant others.

Diminished Interest or Pleasure. The client has few interests and gets little pleasure from anything, including activities previously found enjoyable.

Change in Appetite and/or Weight. Loss of appetite (and weight), when not dieting, or increased appetite (and weight gain) are evident.

Change in Sleep Pattern. The client may have difficulty falling asleep or staying asleep, or may wake early in the morning and not be able to get back to sleep. Alternatively, the client may sleep excessively (such as over twelve hours per night), spending much of the day in bed.

Change in Activity Level. Decreased activity level is reflected by slowness and lethargy, in terms of both the client's behavior and his or her thought processes. Alternatively, the client may feel agitated, "on edge," and restless.

Fatigue or Loss of Energy. The client experiences fatigue throughout the day, or there is a chronic feeling of loss of energy.

Feelings of Worthlessness, Hopelessness, Helplessness. Clients may feel they are worthless as people, that there is no hope for improving their life, or that they are helpless to improve their unhappy situation.

Inappropriate Guilt. Feelings of guilt may be present about events that the client did not even cause, such as a catastrophe, a crime, or an illness.

Recurrent Thoughts about Death. The client thinks about death a great deal and may contemplate (or even attempt) suicide.

Decreased Concentration or Ability to Make Decisions. Significant decreases in the ability to concentrate make it difficult for the client to pay attention to others or complete rudimentary tasks. The client may be quite indecisive about even minor things.

Other Symptoms

Clients with schizoaffective disorder are prone to *alcohol or drug abuse.* Clients may use alcohol and drugs excessively either because of their disturbing symptoms, to experience pleasure, or when socializing with others.

How Is Schizoaffective Disorder Distinguished from Schizophrenia and Affective (Mood) Disorders?

Many persons with a diagnosis of schizoaffective disorder have had, at a prior time, diagnoses of schizophrenia or bipolar disorder. Frequently, this previous diagnosis is revised to schizoaffective disorder when it becomes clear, over time, that the person has sometimes experienced symptoms of mania or depression but on other occasions has experienced psychotic symptoms such as hallucinations or delusions even when his or her mood is stable.

What Is the Course of Schizoaffective Disorder?

The disorder usually begins in late adolescence or early adulthood, often between the ages of sixteen and thirty. The disorder is lifelong, although the symptoms tend to improve gradually over the person's life. The severity of symptoms usually varies over time, at times requiring hospitalization for treatment. However, most clients have at least some symptoms throughout their lives.

What Causes Schizoaffective Disorder?

The cause of schizoaffective disorder is not known, although many scientists believe it is a variant of the disorder of schizophrenia. Schizoaffective disorder (and schizophrenia) may actually be several disorders. Current theories suggest that an imbalance in brain chemicals (specifically, *dopamine)* may be at the root of these two disorders. Vulnerability to developing schizoaffective disorder appears to be partly determined by genetic factors and partly by early environmental factors (such as subtle insults to the brain of the baby in the womb during birth).

Are There Factors Which Might Increase the Likelihood of Relapse?

Factors that tend to increase the likelihood of a psychotic episode include a significant life change (good or bad), use of stimulant drugs such as amphetamines or cocaine, and stopping prescribed medications against the doctor's advice.

How Is Schizoaffective Disorder Treated?

Many of the same methods used to treat schizophrenia are also effective for schizoaffective disorder. Antipsychotic medications are an effective treatment for schizoaffective disorder for most, but not all, persons with the disorder. These drugs are not a "cure" for the disorder, but they can reduce symptoms and prevent relapses among the majority of people with the disorder. Antidepressant medications and mood stabilizing medications (such as lithium) are occasionally used to treat affective symptoms (depressive or manic symptoms) in schizoaffective disorder. Other important treatments include social-skills training, vocational rehabilitation and supported employment, and intensive case management. Family therapy helps reduce stress in the family and teaches family members how to monitor the disorder. In addition, individual supportive counseling can help the person with the disorder learn to manage the disorder more successfully and obtain emotional support in coping with the distress resulting from the disorder.

Consult a mental health professional (such as a psychiatrist, psychologist, social worker, or psychiatric nurse) about any questions you have concerning this handout.

Recommended Readings

Dearth, N., Labenski, B. J., Mott, M. F., & Pellegrini, L. M. (1986), *Families Helping Families: Living with Schizophrenia.* New York: Norton.

Gottesman, I. I. (1991), *Schizophrenia Genesis: The Origins of Madness.* New York: W.H. Freeman and Company.

Keefe, R. S. F. & Harvey, P. D. (1994), *Understanding Schizophrenia.* New York: Free Press.

Mueser, K.T. & Gingerich, S.L. (1994), *Coping with Schizophrenia: A Guide for Families.* Oakland, CA: New Harbinger.

Torrey, E.F. (1995), *Surviving Schizophrenia: A Manual for Families, Consumers, and Providers (Third Edition).* New York: Harper & Row.

Facts about Schizophrenia

What is Schizophrenia?

Schizophrenia is a major psychiatric disorder that can affect all aspects of daily living, including work, social relationships, and self-care skills (such as grooming and hygiene). People with the disorder can have a wide variety of symptoms, including problems with their contact with reality (hallucinations and delusions), low motivation, inability to experience pleasure, and poor attention. The serious nature of the symptoms of schizophrenia sometimes requires clients to be hospitalized at times for treatment. The experience of schizophrenia can be described as similar to "dreaming when you are wide awake"; that is, it can be hard for the person with the disorder to distinguish between reality and fantasy.

How Common is Schizophrenia?

About one in every one hundred people (1 percent) develops schizophrenia at some time during his or her life. Schizophrenia is one of the most common serious psychiatric disorders. More hospital beds are occupied by persons with this diagnosis than any other psychiatric disorder.

How Is the Disorder Diagnosed?

Schizophrenia can only be diagnosed by a clinical interview. The purpose of the interview is to determine whether the client has experienced specific "symptoms" of the disorder, and whether these symptoms have been present long enough to merit the diagnosis. In addition to conducting the interview, the diagnostician must also check to make sure that the client is not experiencing any physical problems that could cause symptoms similar to schizophrenia, such as a brain tumor or alcohol or drug abuse.

Schizophrenia can not be diagnosed with a blood test, an X ray, a CAT scan, or any other laboratory test. An interview is necessary to establish the diagnosis.

The Characteristic Symptoms of Schizophrenia

The diagnosis of schizophrenia requires that the client experience some decline in social functioning for at least a six-month period, such as problems with school or work, social relationships, or self-care. In addition, some other symptoms are commonly present. The symptoms of schizophrenia can be divided into three broad classes: *positive symptoms, negative symptoms*, and *other symptoms*. A person with schizophrenia has some (but not all) of the symptoms described below.

Positive Symptoms

Positive symptoms refer to thoughts, perceptions, and behaviors that are ordinarily *absent* in people in the general population, but are *present* in persons with schizophrenia. These symptoms often vary over time in their severity, and may be absent for long periods in some clients.

Hallucinations. Hallucinations are false perceptions; that is hearing, seeing, feeling, or smelling things that are not actually there. The most common type of hallucinations are *auditory hallucinations*. Clients sometimes report hearing voices talking to them or about them, often saying insulting things, such as calling them names. These voices are usually heard through the ears and sound like other human voices.

Delusions. Delusions are false beliefs; that is, a belief that the client holds but that others clearly see is not true. Some clients have *paranoid delusions*, believing that others want to hurt them. *Delusions of reference* are common, in which the client believes that something in the environment is referring to him or her when it is not (such as the television talking to the client). *Delusions of control* are beliefs that others can control one's actions. Clients hold these beliefs strongly and cannot usually be "talked out" of them.

Thinking Disturbances. The client talks in a manner that is difficult to follow, an indication that he or she has a disturbance in thinking. For example, the client may jump from one topic to the next, stop in the middle of the sentence, make up new words, or simply be difficult to understand.

Negative Symptoms

Negative symptoms are the opposite of positive symptoms. They are the absence of thoughts, perceptions, or behaviors that are ordinarily present in people in the general population. These symptoms are often stable throughout much of the client's life.

Blunted Affect. The expressiveness of the client's face, voice tone, and gestures is diminished or restricted. However, this does not mean that the person is not reacting to his or her environment or having feelings.

Apathy. The client does not feel motivated to pursue goals and activities. The client may feel lethargic or sleepy and have trouble following through on even simple plans. Clients with apathy often have little sense of purpose in their lives and have few interests.

Poverty of Speech or Content of Speech. The client says very little, or when he or she talks, it does not amount to much. Sometimes conversing with the client can be unrewarding.

Anhedonia. The client experiences little or no pleasure from activities that he or she used to enjoy or that others enjoy. For example, the person may not enjoy watching a sunset, going to the movies, or a close relationship with another person.

Inattention. The client has difficulty attending and is easily distracted. This can interfere with activities such as work, interacting with others, and personal-care skills.

Other Symptoms

Many other symptoms can also be present in schizophrenia, as described below.

Depression and suicidal thoughts. Depressed feelings are common for some clients, as are thoughts of suicide or even suicide attempts.

Labile Mood. The client's mood can shift from one extreme to another (such as from happiness to anger to depression) over short periods of time, for little or no understandable reason.

Anger and Hostility. The client is angry and unpleasant to others, often because of delusions the person has (such as persecutory delusions).

Alcohol and Drug Abuse. Clients with schizophrenia are prone to abusing alcohol or drugs, either because of their disturbing symptoms, to experience pleasure, or when socializing with others.

How Is Schizophrenia Distinguished from Bipolar Disorder and Schizoaffective Disorder?

Many persons with a diagnosis of schizophrenia also have had, at some point, a diagnosis of bipolar disorder or schizoaffective disorder. Diagnostic uncertainty results because during a symptom flare-up, a psychotic symptom such as delusional grandiosity (for example, a belief that a person is Jesus Christ) may reflect either schizophrenia, schizoaffective disorder, or mania. However, over time, the symptoms of these three disorders tend to differ. Of particular importance, when their moods are stable, persons with bipolar disorder do not usually experience symptoms, while persons with schizophrenia or schizoaffective disorder often do. Schizoaffective disorder differs from schizophrenia in that clients with the former disorder have very prominent symptoms of mood disturbance (either depression or mania) throughout much of the course of their disorder, whereas clients with the latter disorder do not.

What Is the Course of Schizophrenia?

The disorder usually begins in late adolescence or early adulthood, often between the ages of sixteen and thirty. The disorder is a lifelong one, although symptoms gradually tend to improve over the person's life. The severity of symptoms usually varies over time, at times requiring hospitalization for treatment. However, most clients have at least some symptoms throughout their lives.

What Causes Schizophrenia?

The cause of schizophrenia is not known. Schizophrenia may actually be several disorders. Scientists believe that an imbalance in brain chemicals (specifically, dopamine) may be at the root of the disorder. Vulnerability to developing the disorder appears to be partly determined by genetic factors and partly by early environmental factors (such as subtle insults to the brain of a baby while still in the womb or during birth).

Are There Factors That Might Increase the Likelihood of Relapse?

Factors that tend to increase the likelihood of a psychotic episode include a significant life change (good or bad), use of stimulant drugs such as amphetamines or cocaine, and stopping prescribed medications against the doctor's advice.

How is Schizophrenia Treated?

Antipsychotic medications are an effective treatment for schizophrenia for most persons with the disorder. These drugs are not a "cure" for the disorder, but they can reduce symptoms and prevent relapses among the majority of persons with the diagnosis. Other important treatments include social-skills training, vocational rehabilitation and supported employment, and intensive case management.

Dealing with episodes of schizophrenia can be very disruptive and distressing. Many persons with the disorder can benefit from supportive counseling to learn how to manage the disorder, as well as deal with its impact on their lives. Some types of family therapy also can reduce stress and teach family members how to monitor the disorder.

Consult a mental health professional (such as a psychiatrist, psychologist, social worker, or psychiatric nurse) about any questions you have concerning this handout.

Recommended Readings

Dearth, N., Labenski, B.J., Mott, M.F., & Pellegrini, L.M. (1986), *Families Helping Families: Living with Schizophrenia.* New York: Norton.

Gottesman, I.I. (1991), *Schizophrenia Genesis: The Origins of Madness.* New York: W.H. Freeman and Company.

Keefe, RSF. & Harvey, P.D. (1994), *Understanding Schizophrenia.* New York: Free Press.

Mueser, K.T., & Gingerich, S.L. (1994), *Coping with Schizophrenia: A Guide for Families.* Oakland, CA: New Harbinger.

Torrey, E.F. (1995), *Surviving Schizophrenia: A Manual for Families, Consumers, and Providers. (Third Edition),* New York: Harper & Row.

The Stress-Vulnerability Model of Psychiatric Disorders

Two important questions facing both mental health professionals and families in which one member has a psychiatric disorder are: What causes the disorder? What factors influence its course? At this time, scientists do not have a precise understanding of why some individuals develop a psychiatric disorder and others do not. However, scientists formed a general theory to explain the causes of these disorders and their course over time, the *stress-vulnerability model*. This model can serve as a guide to families and professionals to ensure that the client with the psychiatric disorder has the best possible outcome.

The Stress-Vulnerability Model

According to the model, three critical factors are responsible for the development of a psychiatric disorder and its course over time: *biological vulnerability, stress,* and *protective factors*. The interaction between these factors is illustrated in Figure 1 and is described below.

Biological Vulnerability

In order for a person to develop a psychiatric disorder, he or she must have some biological vulnerability to that disorder. The actual amount of vulnerability varies from one person to the next, as does the severity of the disorder. An individual's vulnerability is thought to be determined by *genetic factors* and early *biological factors* (such as exposure to viral infection when the baby is in the womb), although it may be worsened by *alcohol or drug abuse*. Biological vulnerabilities are not limited to psychiatric disorders; they may include other diseases as well, such as cancer, heart disease, and arthritis.

Stress

Stress has an impact on vulnerability that can either trigger the onset of the disorder or worsen its course. Stress can be thought of as a response to environmental challenges that require the individual to adapt in order to avoid negative effects. If the person is not capable of adapting to the stress, psychiatric symptoms will develop or worsen. Some examples of stressors include: *life events* (such as the death of a loved one, a major move), *tense relationships* (such as frequent arguments, strong feelings of anger and resentment among family members), and *lack of meaningful stimulation* (such as sitting around the house all day).

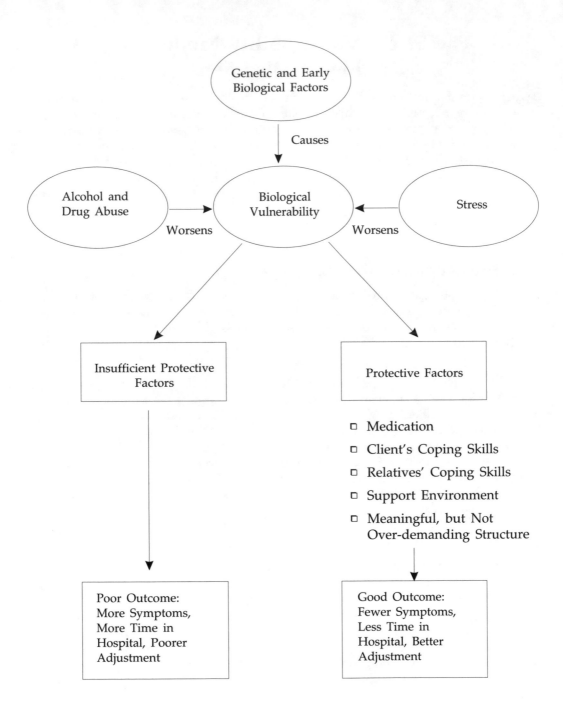

Adapted from Lazarus & Folkman, 1984; Lazarus, 1991; Nuechterlein and Dawson, 1984; Zubin and Spring, 1970.

FIGURE 1   THE STRESS VULNERABILITY MODEL

The Role of the Family

The stress-vulnerability model points to several areas in which the family can play an important role in improving the course of the disorder by bolstering protective factors:

1. Facilitate compliance with prescribed medications, and discourage alcohol abuse and drug use.

2. Develop good communication and problem-solving skills to prevent stress or to cope with unavoidable stress.

3. Strive to create a supportive family environment in which the client's efforts are recognized and small steps forward are encouraged.

4. Monitor symptoms of the disorder and alert the treatment team if changes are suspected, so that rapid treatment (if necessary) can be provided.

Conclusion

Psychiatric disorders have a biological basis, but environmental factors can influence their course over time. The stress-vulnerability model illustrates that a positive outcome of a psychiatric disorder is more likely if environmental stress is minimized or managed well, medication is taken as prescribed, and alcohol and drug abuse are avoided. Relatives and clients working together can improve the long-term course of psychiatric disorder, resulting in a better quality of life for all family members.

The Caregiver's Guide to Helping a Relative Who Has a Serious Psychiatric Illness

Caring for a relative with a serious psychiatric illness can be a daunting task. The potential for a relapse often weighs heavily on a caregiver's mind. Fortunately, a relapse is less likely to occur if a caregiver encourages a relative with a serious psychiatric illness to:

- take medication as prescribed;

- avoid drug and alcohol use;

- participate in a rehabilitation program and/or find something productive to do; and

- limit the amount of stress experienced within the family.

High Levels of Tension Are Common in Many Families with a Psychiatric Client

The caregiver can assume a positive role in managing stress in the family. Research conducted with caregivers has found that a positive family environment among caregivers and a relative with a serious psychiatric illness plays a very important role in minimizing the progression of symptoms. When interacting with a relative with a serious psychiatric illness, family members benefit from attempting to understand what the ill relative is experiencing. A relative with a serious psychiatric illness must cope with disturbing symptoms, side effects of prescribed medication, and the fact that he or she has a mental illness. These factors can seem like overwhelming challenges for both the ill relative and those who care for him or her. Levels of tension, anxiety, and confusion may be high for both the ill relative and family members.

Communication Patterns

A serious psychiatric illness can be a devastating disorder, and it is not surprising that loved ones of the person with a serious psychiatric illness may frequently feel irritable or "on edge." Sometimes, this stress causes the relative to prompt or nag the client to try to get things under control. However, these types of communication patterns have been related to higher rates of relapse. Criticism and extreme self-sacrificing behavior, even if done for the ill client's own good, usually have a bad effect. Repeated prompting, correcting, and fault finding may lead to an increase in relapse. Family members can become more aware of the behaviors they direct toward their relative with a serious psychiatric illness and try to reduce ineffective prompting or criticism. The goal of the caregiver is to become aware of the levels of criticism, nagging, and prompting within the family and to attempt to limit the intensity and frequency with which they occur. If the caregiver and family members focus on the reduction of these behavioral patterns, the stress level will lessen.

Behavioral Patterns

Many relatives are inclined to be extra watchful in caring for their ill relative. Caregivers may be reluctant to leave the client unsupervised and may decline work or social activities in order to increase the time they are available to assist the client. However, clients with a serious psychiatric illness are acutely sensitive to external pressure and may find this additional supervision to be stressful. It may even create guilt in the ill relative, who sees his or her family member refuse social, job, or leisure opportunities. Research shows that this self-sacrificing behavior may have the unintended impact of contributing to a worsening of symptoms.

Conclusion

It is clear that the relative with a serious psychiatric illness can reduce the frequency of relapses by taking his or her medication as prescribed and avoiding the use of drugs and alcohol. The manner in which family members interact with the relative with a serious psychiatric illness may also affect relapses. If family members become aware of and monitor the criticism, hostility, and extreme self-sacrificing behavior they exhibit, they can aid in the reduction of stress within the family. The frequency of relapse should be reduced, and the prognosis of the client will be improved. As the client improves, the caregiver will experience a positive impact as well!

Two good mottos to adopt:

- Don't sweat the small stuff!
- Choose your battles wisely!

Facts about Alcohol and Drug Use in Persons with a Psychiatric Disorder

Introduction

Using substances such as alcohol, marijuana, and cocaine is common, both in the general population and among persons with a serious psychiatric disorder. These and other substances can have a variety of effects. This educational handout reviews the different types of substances commonly used by people and their effects. The interactions between substance use and mental illness are discussed, as well as strategies for dealing with problems related to substance abuse.

Different Types of Substances

In addition to alcohol, there are many different types of substances that people use to change their mood or alter their thinking. The following table summarizes different categories of substances and provides examples of specific substances in each type. This table also gives examples of slang words for each substance, how each substance is taken ("route of administration"), and the effects of the substance.

EFFECTS OF DIFFERENT PSYCHOACTIVE SUBSTANCES

Substance Type	Specific Substance	Slang	Route	Effects
Alcohol	beer, wine, "hard liquor" (e.g. vodka, scotch, whiskey, gin, rum, tequila)	booze, brew (beer)	oral (drinking)	relaxation, sedation, slowed reaction time, impaired judgment, loss of inhibition
Cannabis	marijuana, hashish	pot, reefer, weed, joint (marijuana cigarette), dope, grass, buds, fatty	smoking (most common), ingestion (eating)	relaxation, mild euphoria, altered sensory experiences, fatigue, anxiety, panic, increased appetite, paranoia
Stimulants	cocaine, amphetamines (and related compounds)	cocaine: coke, crack, rock amphetamines: crank, speed, crystal meth	cocaine: intranasal (snorting), smoking (crack), injection amphetamines: oral (eating pills), intranasal, injection.	increased alertness and energy, decreased appetite, positive feelings, anxiety, tension, feeling jittery, heart racing, paranoia

Stimulants	cocaine, amphetamines (and related compounds)	cocaine: coke, crack, rock amphetamines: crank, speed, crystal meth	cocaine: intranasal (snorting), smoking (crack), injection amphetamines: oral (eating pills), intranasal, injection.	increased alertness and energy, decreased appetite, positive feelings, anxiety, tension, feeling jittery, heart racing, paranoia
Sedatives	anxiolytic (anxiety lowering) medications (e.g. Xanax, Klonopin, Ativan, Valium), barbituates	downers (barbituates)	oral	sleepiness, relaxation, loss of motor coordination, loss of inhibition, dulled sensory experiences
Hallucinogens	LDS, PCP, peyote, mescaline, MDMA	(LSD): acid, window pane (PCP): angel dust, ecstasy	LSD: oral, PCP: oral, smoking	enhanced or altered perceptions, hallucinations, disorientation, psychosis.
Narcotics	Heroin, morphine, opium, codeine	smack, horse, H	heroin: injection, intranasal, morphine, codeine, and related substances: oral	euphoria, pain relief, sedation, slowed reaction time, impaired judgment
Inhalants	glue, aerosols, nitrous oxide (laughing gas), freon		inhalation (includes sniffling)	altered perceptions, disorientation
Over-the-counter-medications	antihistamines and related compounds (e.g., benadryl, other cold tablets)		oral	sedation
Tobacco	cigarettes, pipe tobacco, chewing tobacco	snuff, cigs, butts	smoking, sublingual, under-the-tongue	alertness, relaxation
Caffeine	coffee, tea, chocolate		oral	increased alertness, anxiety
Anti-parkinsonian agents	cogentin, artane, symmetrel		oral	confusion, mild euphoria

Reasons for Using Substances

People who use substances describe a variety of different reasons for their use. Some people use substances primarily for social reasons; it is something that is done with friends, to relax around others, or because people feel they "fit in" more with others if they use alcohol or drugs. Sometimes people report that they use substances to enhance their coping; they may describe substances as helping them manage unpleasant feelings, such as anxiety or depression, sleeping problems, or other symptoms. Another common reason given by people for using substances is that it is a form of recreation; it is something to do when they are bored or just want to feel good, even if it is for only a short period of time.

There are many other reasons people give for using substances, and each person is unique. For some people, substance use simply becomes a habit that is difficult to break, because it is so familiar. Cravings for alcohol or drugs can also play a role in continuing the substance use. Although people give different reasons for using substances, the reasons are not always strictly accurate. For example, many people say that they drink alcohol excessively because they feel depressed, yet research has shown that alcohol actually worsens depression rather than improving it. Exploring their reasons for using substances can help individuals determine alternative ways of getting their needs met.

Interactions between Substance Use and Mental Illness

Substances such as alcohol, marijuana, and cocaine can have a wide range of effects on people. These and other substances often have even more potent effects on persons with a mental illness. In order to understand the interactions between substance use and mental illness, it is helpful to review the stress-vulnerability model of psychiatric disorders.

The stress-vulnerability model of psychiatric illnesses assumes that these disorders are caused by biological factors determined very early in life. Although this biological vulnerability must exist for the psychiatric illness to develop, the severity of the illness is influenced by current environmental, psychological, and biological factors as well. One factor that can worsen the severity of the disorder is stress in the environment. However, if a person has good coping skills, he or she will be less vulnerable to the negative effects of stress.

Biological factors that can have an effect on the severity of the psychiatric disorder include medications and substances. Prescribed medications can help correct some of the chemical imbalances in the brain believed to cause mental illnesses, lowering the severity of symptoms. On the other hand, even small amounts of substances such as alcohol, marijuana, or cocaine can worsen the psychiatric illness. These substances can have a negative effect on mental illness in two ways. First, alcohol and other substances can trigger the brain chemicals responsible for the illness, leading to more severe symptoms. Second, these substances can make prescribed medications less effective in controlling the psychiatric disorder. Thus, persons with a mental illness are highly sensitive to the effects of psychoactive substances.

Consequences of Substance Use in Mental Illness

Substance use can cause a variety of different negative effects in persons with a mental illness. Some of the most common consequences experienced by persons with a mental illness include:

- **Symptom relapses and rehospitalizations.** Very low amounts or alcohol and drugs can trigger relapses and rehospitalizations in persons with a serious psychiatric illness.

- **Depression and increased risk of suicide.** People often use substances when they feel depressed. Although they often feel some momentary relief, their substance use tends to worsen the longer-term severity of their depression.

- **Family conflict.** Conflict with family members is very common. Arguments may occur over substance use itself, or the consequences of substance use, such as not fulfilling a social role (worker, student, household chores), aggression, money problems, and worsening the psychiatric illness.

- **Housing instability and homelessness.** Substance use can interfere with the ability to maintain stable housing, either independently or with family members.

- **Anger and violence problems.** Substances can have disinhibiting effects, increasing problems with verbal or physical aggression.

- **Money difficulties.** The amount of money spent on substances can be a problem, leading to difficulty meeting other needs and financial obligations.

- **Legal problems.** Use of illegal substances, such as marijuana or cocaine, can lead to legal problems if the person is caught with procession of the substance. Use of alcohol and other substances can contribute to disorganized or aggressive behavior, resulting in legal consequences (such as being arrested for drunk and disorderly conduct).

- **Substance-Use Disorders.** A person who experiences negative consequences due to substance-use has a substance use disorder. Individuals whose substance use results in problems in the areas described above have a diagnosis of substance abuse.

For some individuals, in addition to experiencing these negative consequences, other problems may develop from substance use. *Psychological dependence* refers to when the person gives up important activities in order to use a substance, often uses more of the substance than intended, or repeatedly tries to cut down on substance use but is unsuccessful. *Physical dependence* refers to when a person develops tolerance to the effects of the substance, requiring greater amounts of it to achieve desired effects, or experiences withdrawal symptoms (such as stomach pain, sweats, tremor) when less of the substance is used. If a person experiences the symptoms of either psychological or physical dependence, he or she has a substance-use disorder.

Treatment of Substance-Use Disorders

A number of different strategies are available to help individuals recover from a substance use disorder.

- **Family problem solving.** Family support and problem solving can help individuals decrease (and stop) their substance use by working on problems such as finding alternative social outlets to substance-use situations, developing different leisure and recreational activities, and brainstorming effective coping strategies for dealing with persistent symptoms.

- **Group treatment.** Some clients with substance-use problems find group interventions helpful. Some group treatments are focused on social-skills training, both for dealing with substance use situations and other social situations. Other group approaches are based on exploring the effects of substances on clients' lives, and sharing different strategies for reducing substance-use or maintaining abstinence.

- **Individual counseling.** Cognitive-behavioral counseling focused on substance-use problems can be helpful. This counseling can work on addressing motivation to reduce substance abuse, ways of dealing with "high risk" situations for using substances, and relapse prevention.

- **Self-help groups.** Self-help groups such as Alcoholics Anonymous and Narcotic Anonymous can provide social support for individuals who understand the effects of substances on their lives and endorse abstinence from alcohol and drugs as an important personal goal.

- **Medication.** Certain medications have been developed to decrease substance abuse (mainly alcohol abuse), such as disulfirim (Antabuse) or naltrexone (Revia).

Facts about Antianxiety and Sedative Medications

Introduction

Antianxiety and sedative medications are drugs primarily used to reduce anxiety and chronic overarousal, and to facilitate sleep. These medications are widely prescribed, both to persons with a psychiatric disorder and to those in distress but without a specific psychiatric disorder. Antianxiety and sedative drugs are used with a variety of different psychiatric disorders, usually in combination with other medications.

Different Types of Medication

Antianxiety and sedative medications can be divided into two broad classes of drugs: *antianxiety medications* and *sedative-hypnotics* (the term *hypnotic* refers to sleep inducing). All of these drugs have clinical effects on both reducing anxiety and causing sedation, although antianxiety drugs have the most specific effect on anxiety. Unlike many other medications for psychiatric disorders, the effects of these drugs are quite rapid and require only one to two hours to take effect. These different types of medication are described below.

Antianxiety Medications

The most common type of antianxiety drugs are the chemical class of *benzodiazepines*. In addition to relieving severe symptoms of anxiety, these drugs also relax the muscles and cause mild sedation. Many different types of benzodiazepines exist. Another common antianxiety medication is *Buspar* (buspirone), which is in a different chemical class from the benzodiazepines. Antidepressant medications are sometimes also used for the treatment of anxiety, such as obsessive-compulsive disorder. Antidepressant medications are described in a separate handout.

The clinical effects of the different types of benzodiazepines on anxiety are the same. However, the drugs differ in how long they remain in the body (measured by how long it takes for the body to excrete half of the drug — the drug's *half-life*). Some benzodiazepines remain in the body for relatively brief periods of time (such as Xanax, with a half-life of twelve hours), while others remain much longer (such as Valium, with a half-life of sixty hours).

The most common (non-antidepressant) medications used for anxiety are summarized in the following charts.

ANTIANXIETY MEDICATIONS

Long-Acting Benzodiazepines
(more than 24-hour half-life)

Brand Name	Chemical	Average Daily Dosage (mg/day)
Valium	diazepam	2–60
Librium	chlordiazepoxide	15–100
Centrax	prazepam	20–60
Klonopin	clonazepam	0.5–20

Short-Acting Benzodiazepines
(less than 24-hour half-life)

Brand Name	Chemical	Average Daily Dosage (mg/day)
Serax	oxazepam	30–120
Ativan	lorazepam	0.5–10
Xanax	alprazolam	0.5–6

Other Antianxiety Medications

Brand Name	Chemical	Average Daily Dosage (mg/day)
Buspar	buspirone	20–60

Rebound Anxiety. Some individuals, as the benzodiazepine level in their body declines, begin to experience an increase in anxiety called *rebound anxiety*. In some cases this anxiety can be quite severe and frightening. This is more common for the short-acting than long-acting drugs. If the person taking the benzodiazepine notices an increase in anxiety before the next dosage, the physician should be consulted. Sometimes the person will be switched from a short-acting to a long-acting benzodiazepine (or buspirone) to prevent rebound anxiety.

Sedative-Hypnotic Medications

Sedative-hypnotic drugs are used in the treatment of agitation and to facilitate sleep. Similar to antianxiety drugs, the most commonly used sedative-hypnotic drugs are the *benzodiazepines*. A different type of sedative-hypnotic drug is *chloral hydrate*. *Antihistamines* are also used sometimes as sedative-hypnotic drugs. The most common types of these drugs are listed in the following chart.

SEDATIVE-HYPNOTIC MEDICATIONS

Benzodiazepines

Brand Name	Chemical	Average Daily Dosage (mg/day)
Dalmane	flurazepam	15–30
Restoril	temazepam	7.5–60
Halcion	triazolam	0.125–0.5

Other Sedative-Hypnotics

Brand Name	Chemical	Average Daily Dosage (mg/day)
Noctec	chloral hydrate	500–2000

Antihistamines

Brand Name	Chemical	Average Daily Dosage (mg/day)
Benadryl	diphenhydramine	25–300

Side Effects of Antianxiety and Sedative-Hypnotic Drugs

The most common side effect of these drugs is sedation and fatigue (except Buspar). With the long-acting benzodiazepines, the sedation can persist for more than a day after the drug has been taken. Because of the sedating effects, the intake of alcohol should be limited to not more than one drink per week, and appropriate cautions should be exercised when driving. The benzodiazepines can also effect memory and other cognitive abilities.

How Do These Drugs Work?

The different types of antianxiety and sedative-hypnotic medications operate by different mechanisms. In general, scientists believe these drugs influence *neurotransmitters* in the brain (chemicals in the nerve cells) that regulate arousal and anxiety.

Importance of Regular Medication

Taking medication on a regular basis can prevent fluctuations in symptoms that are due to changes over time in the amount of the drug in the body. It can be helpful to take medication at the same time each day so that it is part of the person's daily routine. It is also important for the person to meet regularly with his or her physician to have symptoms checked, discuss side effects, and have adjustments in medication made when necessary.

Common Questions about Antianxiety and Sedative-Hypnotic Medications

What If the Person Misses a Dose of Medication?

The client should consult with his or her physician to find out what to do if a dose of medication is missed.

Are Antianxiety or Sedative-Hypnotic Medications Addictive?

Benzodiazepines can be addictive, but the risk for dependence can be minimized by taking low doses and always staying within the prescribed dosage range. If a decision is made for the person to stop taking a benzodiazepine, the dose should be gradually tapered over a number of weeks to prevent withdrawal symptoms, rebound anxiety, or seizures.

How Long Should Antianxiety or Sedative-Hypnotic Medications Be Taken?

In many cases these drugs are given for a brief period of time (such as several weeks or months) to treat temporary increases of anxiety, agitation, or sleep problems. Sometimes these medications are given over long periods of time when the symptoms are more severe and long-lasting.

Consult the client's physician about any questions you have concerning this handout.

Facts about Antidepressant Medications

Introduction

Antidepressant medications are a class of drugs commonly used to treat depression. Some of these types of medication were discovered in the 1950s and have since been used extensively with a variety of psychiatric populations. Antidepressants are not a "cure" for psychiatric disorders, but they can provide significant relief from many symptoms of depression.

The Clinical Effects of Antidepressant Medications

Antidepressant medications are effective for treating the symptoms of depression, such as low mood, appetite disturbance, sleep problems, low energy, and poor concentration. Some of these drugs are also helpful for treating the sumptoms of obsessive-compulsive disorder. Antidepressants are most often used to treat clients with *major depression* or *obsessive-compulsive disorder* (OCD), although clients with other disorders (such as agoraphobia and panic disorder) may also benefit from them.

There are two major uses for antidepressant medications:

1. reducing or eliminating acute (severe) symptoms to a level where the symptoms are more manageable; and

2. preventing symptom relapses and rehospitalizations.

Reducing Acute Symptoms

When a client has moderate to severe symptoms of depression or OCD, antidepressants are given. If the client has already been receiving these drugs, the dosage may be changed or a different medication may be tried. Antidepressants must usually be taken for several weeks before significant clinical effects occur. Some clients respond to the first antidepressant they are given. Others may require multiple trials of different antidepressants to find the best medication.

Preventing Symptom Relapses

Some clients need to take antidepressants for only a limited period of time, such as a few months, and can then stop the medication with no negative effects. Others, however, may need to take these medications on a longer-term basis in order to prevent relapses and rehospitalizations.

Types of Antidepressant Medication

There are many different types of antidepressant medication. These drugs can be divided into four different groups: *serotonin selective reuptake inhibitors* (SSRIs), *tricyclics, monoamine oxidase* (MAO) *inhibitors,* and *other compounds*. The chart on the next page contains the brand names, chemical names, and average daily oral dosage for some of the most commonly prescribed antidepressant medications.

ANTIDEPRESSANT MEDICATIONS

Type of Drug	Brand Name	Chemical Name	Average Dosage Range (mg/day)
SSRIs	Paxil	paroxitine	20–50
	Prozac	fluoxetine	20–80
	Zoloft	sertraline	50–200
	Serzone	nefazadone	300–500
	Luvox	fluvoxamine	100–200
Tricyclics	Anafranil	clomipramine	25–250
	Elavil	amitriptyline	100–300
	Norpramin	desipramine	100–300
	Pamelor, Aventyl	nortriptyline	50–150
	Sinequan, Adapin	doxepin	75–300
	Tofranil	imipramine	100–300
	Vivactil	protriptyline	10–60
MAO Inhibitors	Marplan	isocarboxazid	10–50
	Nardil	phenelzine	45–90
Other Compounds	Desyrel	trazodone	150–600
	Wellbutrin	buproprion	75–450
	Ludiomil	maptrotiline	75–225
	Effexor	Venlafaxine	75–225

Side Effects

Antidepressant medications, like other drugs for treating disorders, can cause undesired side effects. The most common side effects are summarized in the chart below. Not all clients taking medication experience side effects. In many cases the side effects are temporary, although they may persist for some persons. Sometimes the medication dosage needs to be reduced because of side effects or a different type of medication must be given. When side effects are detected, the physician should be consulted as soon as possible.

SIDE EFFECTS OF ANTIDEPRESSANT MEDICATIONS

Drug Class	Side Effects
SSRIs	Nausea, vomiting, excitement, agitation, headache, sexual problems (delayed ejaculation, not experiencing orgasm)
Tricyclics	Dry mouth, dizziness, sedation/agitation, weight gain, constipation, heart palpitations, cardiac abnormalities
MAO Inhibitors	Insomnia, dizziness, weight gain, sexual difficulties, confusion/memory problems, overstimulation, hypertensive crisis
Other Compounds	Sedation/agitation

Hypomania and Mania after Antidepressant Treatment

One occasional side effect of antidepressants deserves special mention. A small percentage of clients who are prescribed these medications gradually develop the symptoms of *hypomania* or *mania* after a few weeks. The symptoms of hypomania include: irritability or argumentativeness, agitation, decreased need for sleep, and excessive talking. In addition to these symptoms, the symptoms of mania include: grandiosity, euphoria, hostility, extreme goal-directed behavior, and engagement in activities that are potentially harmful.

If these changes in mood and behavior are observed, the physician should be contacted immediately. In most cases, the dosage level of the antidepressant medication can be reduced and the symptoms will go away. Sometimes the medication must be stopped and other drugs used to control the hypomanic or manic symptoms.

Precautions When Taking MAO Inhibitors

Clients who are prescribed MAO inhibitors must take special precautions to avoid certain foods. Foods that are high in the chemical *tyramine* should be avoided, such as aged cheeses (not including cottage cheese, cream cheese, and processed cheese), aged meats (such as salami and pepperoni), and yeast extracts (except in baked products). The following beverages should also be avoided: beer, chianti wine, sherry wine, and vermouth. Certain drugs that have "adrenaline-like" effects (such as decongestants and stimulants) should also be avoided when taking an MAO inhibitor. For a more complete list of foods and beverages that should be avoided or taken in moderation when on an MAO inhibitor, consult the client's physician.

An unusual side effect of MAO inhibitors is the development of carpal tunnel syndrome, which is due to pyridoxine (B_6) deficiency. This can be corrected by appropriate vitamin supplements (B_6). Early symptoms of B_6 deficiency are numbness and tingling.

How Do Antidepressant Medications Work?

Scientists do not have a thorough understanding of how antidepressant medications work. There is evidence that these medications tend to increase the amount of certain *neurotransmitters* in the brain (chemicals in the nerve cells). Antidepressants appear to affect two neurotransmitters in particular, *serotonin* and *norepinephrine*. Some antidepressants tend to affect one neurotransmitter more than the other. Only those antidepressants that have a major effect on serotonin (such as the SSRIs and Anafranil) improve OCD symptoms. It is possible that the symptoms of depression or OCD (or other disorders that can be treated with antidepressants) are related to imbalances in these neurotransmitters in the brain.

Importance of Regular Medication

Taking medication on a regular basis can help prevent symptoms from returning or getting worse. It can be helpful to take medication at the same time each day so that it is part of the client's daily routine. It is also important for the client to meet regularly with his or her physician to have symptoms checked, discuss side effects, and have adjustments in medication made when necessary.

Common Questions about Antidepressant Medications

What if the Client Misses a Dose of Medications?

The client should consult with his or her physician to find out what to do with a dose of medication is missed.

Are Antidepressant Medications Addictive?

Antidepressant drugs are not addictive. People who take these medications do not develop tolerance to these drugs, requiring a higher dose to achieve the same effects. If a decision is made to stop antidepressant medication, the medication is usually tapered gradually. However, stopping antidepressant medications may increase the risk of relapse for people with major depression or OCD.

Do Antidepressants Interact with Other Drugs?

Certain drugs should be avoided when taking an MAO inhibitor: Tegretol, Dopar, Sinemet, Demerol, Aldomet, and Ritalin. MAO inhibitors can also increase the effects of other drugs, including stimulants, sedatives, appetite suppressants, and insulin. The physician should be consulted if any of these medications have been prescribed in addition to an MAO inhibitor. Tricyclic antidepressants can decrease the effectiveness of certain antihypertensive medications and increase the sedative effects of alcohol and sedative-hypnotic drugs.

Consult the client's physician about any questions you have concerning this handout.

Facts about Antipsychotic Medications

Introduction

Antipsychotic medications (also referred to as *major tranquilizers* or *neuroleptics*) are a class of drugs commonly used to treat serious psychiatric disorders. These drugs were discovered in the 1950s and have since been used extensively with a variety of psychiatric populations. Antipsychotics are especially useful in the treatment of schizophrenia, schizoafective disorder, and mania with psychosis. Antipsychotics are not a "cure" for psychiatric disorders. However, most clients who are prescribed these medications experience some relief from their symptoms.

The Clinical Effects of Antipyschotic Medications

Antipsychotic medications are used primarily for reducing psychotic (positive) symptoms of schizophrenia and schizoaffective disorder, such as hallucinations, delusions, and bizarre behavior. These medications sometimes also improve negative symptoms of these disorders, such as social withdrawal and poor attention. Antipsychotics are used most often for the treatment of *schizophrenia* and *schizoaffective disorder*, although clients with other disorders, such as bipolar disorder and major depression, may also benefit from them. When antipsychotics are used in the treatment of bipolar disorder or major depression, it is usually in combination with other medications (such as mood stabilizers or antidepressants).

There are two major uses for antipsychotic medications:

1. reducing acute (severe) symptoms to a level where the symptoms are more manageable; and

2. preventing symptom relapses and rehospitalizations.

Reducing Acute Symptoms

When a client has severe psychotic symptoms, such as during a relapse, antipsychotics are given. If the client has already been receiving these drugs, the dosage may be increased. Sometimes the clinical effects of antipsychotics are quite rapid, with improvements apparent in as little as one or two days. Usually, however, several weeks of antipsychotic treatment are needed to reduce symptoms significantly.

Preventing Symptom Relapses

Even after symptoms have been controlled by antipsychotics, the medication can prevent future relapses. For example, about seven in every ten people (70 percent) with schizophrenia or schizoaffective disorder who are *not* on antipsychotics relapse over a one-year period, but only three in ten people (30 percent) who are taking the medication relapse. Thus, antipsychotics can help many clients stay out of the hospital and improve their overall functioning.

How Are Medications Taken?

Antipsychotics are usually taken orally or with long-acting injections (taken every two to four weeks). In emergency situations, antipsychotics can also be given in higher doses by injections, although the advantage of this mode of administration is not clearly established.

Types of Antipsychotic Medication

There are many different types of antipsychotic medication. Most antipsychotic drugs have the same beneficial effects on symptoms and reducing relapse, although there is evidence that Clozaril has unique effects on treatment-refractory symptoms (see section below on Clozaril). While most antipsychotics have similar clinical effects, some medications are more potent than others. Thus, larger amounts of low-potency drugs are given than high-potency drugs. The chart below contains the brand names, chemical names, and daily oral dosage range for some of the most commonly prescribed antipsychotic medications.

Brand Name	Chemical Name	Estimated Dosage Ratio*	Average Daily Dosage (mg/day)
Clozaril	clozapine	**	200–900
Haldol***	haloperidol	1:50	1–40
Loxitane	loxapine	1:10	4–250
Mellaril	thioridazine	1:1	50–600
Moban	molindone	1:10	15–250
Navane	thiothixene	1:20	6–60
Prolixin***	fluphenazine	1:50	1–40
Risperdal	risperidone	**	1–8
Serentil	mesoridazine	1:2	25–300
Seroquel	quetiapine	**	300–600
Stelazine	trifluoperazine	1:20	4–60
Thorazine	chlorpromazine	1:1	50–1250
Trilafon	perphenazine	1:10	8–64
Zyprexa	zolanzapine	**	5–10

* Estimated dosage ratio in relation to Thorazine. For example, a dose of 10mg. of Prolixin is equivalent to 500 mg. of Thorazine, since Prolixin is fifty times as potent as Thorazine.

** These medications have different mechanisms of action than the other antipsychotic medications, and therefore their dosage range in not comparable.

*** Also available in long-acting injections.

Side Effects

Antipsychotic medications, like other drugs for treating other illnesses, can cause undesired side effects. Some side effects include: drowsiness, muscle stiffness, dizziness, dry mouth, mild tremors, restlessness, increased appetite, blurred vision, and sexual difficulties. Not all clients taking medication experience side effects. In many cases the side effects are temporary, especially if they are treated with side-effects medications. Sometimes the medication dosage needs to be reduced because of side effects or a different type of medication must be given. When side effects are detected, the physician should be consulted as soon as possible.

Medications for Side Effects

Two types of medications are commonly used to treat the "extrapyramidal" side effects of antipsychotics (such as muscle stiffness, mild tremors, and increased salivation): *anticholinergics* and *dopamine agonists*. The specific medications and daily-dose ranges are provided in the chart below.

MEDICATIONS FOR EXTRAPYRAMIDAL SIDE EFFECTS OF ANTIPSYCHOTICS

Type of Drug	Brand Name	Chemical Name	Average Daily Dosage (mg/day)
Anticholinergic Drugs	Artane	trihexyphenidyl	5–15
	Benedryl	disphenhydramin	50–300
	Cogentin	benztropine	0.5–8
	Kemadrin	procyclidine	5–20
Dopamine Agonists	Symmetrel	amatadine	40–100

One side effect of antipsychotics that can be especially disturbing is *akathisia*. This side effect is characterized by restlessness and difficulty sitting still and an uncomfortable feeling of agitation. Side-effect medications used to treat other side effects of antipsychotics are sometimes less effective for akathisia. One strategy for treating akathisia is to lower the dose of antipsychotic medication. Another strategy is to prescribe other medications, including beta blockers (such as Inderal, Tenormin, or Corgard) or benzodiazepines (such as Ativan or Valium). Side-effect medications can also cause mild side effects. The following chart summarizes the most common side effects associated with each of these medications.

POSSIBLE SIDE EFFECTS OF SIDE-EFFECT MEDICATIONS

Drug Class	Side Effects
Anticholinergics	Dry mouth, constipation, blurry vision, drowsiness, urinary retention, memory loss
Dopamine Agonists	Increase in psychotic symptoms
Beta-blockers	Fatigue, depression
Benzodiazepines	Drowsiness, psychological or physiological dependence, psychomotor impairment, memory loss

Tardive Dyskinesia

One side effect of special concern is *tardive dyskinesia* (TD). This is a neurological syndrome in which the person has involuntary muscle movements usually in the tongue, mouth, or lips, the trunk, or in the extremities, such as hands, fingers, or toes. In most cases, the movements associated with TD are mild. In some cases of more severe TD, some clients are distressed, while others are not.

The risk of developing TD is low during the first year of treatment with antipsychotics, but increases after this period. Most studies suggest that between one or two of every ten clients (10-20 percent) develops TD. The chances of developing TD increase with the amount of time the person is on antipsychotics and the dosage level.

TD seldom worsens when the client is maintained on the lowest effective dose of antipsychotic medication. Clozaril does not appear to cause TD and may even improve the condition in some clients. It is not known at this time whether Risperdal, Seroquel, or Zyprexa cause TD. Other than treating with the lowest effective dose or considering a switch to Clozaril, there are no established treatments for TD.

Clozaril

Clozaril (clozapine) is a unique antipsychotic drug that has recently become available in the United States (it has been used in Europe for more than twenty years). Some research has found that Clozaril is an especially effective medication for treatment-refractory symptoms, such as hearing voices or severe social withdrawal. Although Clozaril is most often prescribed for persons with schizophrenia or schizoaffective disorder, it can also be given for other psychiatric disorders.

Some of the side effects of Clozaril are different from other antipsychotic medications. Side effects of Clozaril include: drowsiness, increased salivation, dizziness, stiffness, a slight increase in body temperature (temperatures between 98.6 and 101 degrees Farenheit), changes in blood pressure, constipation, weight gain, headache, tachycardia (rapid heart rate), cataplexy (sudden loss of muscle tone), and seizures.

One important side effect of Clozaril that occurs in a small percentage of people is a reduction in number of white blood cells (a condition called *agranulocytosis*). If this side effect begins to develop, the person must be taken off of Clozaril (and switched to another antipsychotic), because white blood cells are necessary to fight diseases. Clients who develop agranulocytosis should not be given Clozaril again. In order to make sure that agranulocytosis is not developing, the client's blood must be checked weekly with a simple blood test.

Precautions When Taking Antipsychotics

Alcohol should be used in moderation (not more than two drinks per week), because higher levels can reduce the effectiveness of antipsychotics, leading to relapses. Antipsychotic medications can enhance the effects of certain other medications, including: anticoagulants, anticonvulsants, beta-blockers, and diuretics. The physician should be consulted if any of these medications are taken in combination with antipsychotics. Antipsychotics can also increase vulnerability to sunburn. Sun block should be used if the client will be exposed to the sun for several hours or more.

How Do Antipsychotic Medications Work?

Scientists do not have a full understanding of why antipsychotic medications are effective. However, all of these medications reduce the action of a particular neuro-transmitter (a chemical in the brain for communication between nerve cells) called *dopamine*. Unique antipsychotics (Clozaril, Risperdal, Zyprexa, and Seroquel) have effects both on dopamine and on another neurotransmitter, *serotonin*. It is possible that dopamine and serotonin are involved in the production of psychotic symptoms.

The Importance of Regular Medication

Taking medication on a regular basis can help prevent symptoms from returning or getting worse. It can be helpful to take medication at the same time each day so that it is part of the client's daily routine. It is also important for the client to meet regularly with his or her physician to have symptoms checked, discuss side effects, and have adjustments in medication made when necessary.

Common Questions about Antipsychotic Medications

What If the client Misses a Dose of Medication?

The client should consult with his or her physician to find out what to do if a dose of medication was missed.

Are Antipsychotic Medications Addictive?

Antipsychotic drugs are not addictive. People who take these medications do not develop tolerance to these drugs (do not require a higher dose to achieve the same effects). If a decision is made to stop taking antipsychotic medication, the medication is usually tapered gradually. However, stopping antipsychotic medications increases the risk of relapse for people with schizophrenia or schizoaffective disorder.

How Long Must Antipsychotic Medications Be Taken?

When antipsychotics are used in the treatment of schizophrenia and schizoaffective disorder, these medications must often be taken throughout much of the person's life. This is similar to diabetes, in which a person must take insulin daily.

Many clients with other psychiatric disorders (such as bipolar disorder and major depression) need to take antipsychotic medication for only a temporary period of time, such as several weeks or months.

Consult the client's physician about any questions you have concerning this handout.

Facts about Mood Stabilizers

Introduction

Mood stabilizing medications are a group of drugs used to treat disturbances in mood, including mania and depression. The most widely used mood stabilizing drug is *lithium*. The clinical effects of lithium were discovered in the 1940s, and it has since become a widely used medication. The clinical properties of other mood stabilizers (carbamazepine, valproic acid) were discovered in the 1970s and 1980s. These medications do not "cure" mood swings, but they often provide significant relief from many symptoms.

The Clinical Effects of Mood-Stabilizing Medications

Mood-stabilizing drugs are most often used to treat the symptoms of bipolar disorder (manic-depression), although clients with other disorders may also benefit from them. There are two major uses for mood-stabilizing medications:

1. reducing acute (severe) symptoms of mania or depression to a more manageable level; and

2. preventing symptom relapses and rehospitalizations.

Reducing Acute Symptoms

When a client has severe symptoms of mania or depression, mood-stabilizing medications can be given. The medications both stabilize mood and reduce associated symptoms, such as agitation, sleep problems, hallucinations, and delusions. If the client has already been receiving these drugs, the dosage may be increased. These medications must usually be taken for several weeks before significant clinical effects occur. Other medications (such as antipsychotics) are sometimes given in addition to mood stabilizers for a temporary period of time.

Preventing Symptom Relapses

Even after symptoms have been controlled by mood stabilizers, these medications can prevent future relapses and rehospitalizations for people with bipolar disorder.

Types of Mood Stabilizers

There are two broad types of mood stabilizing medication: lithium and *anticonvulsants* (medications originally developed for the treatment of seizure disorders). The specific medications and their dosage ranges are summarized in the chart below.

MOOD STABILIZERS: LITHIUM

Brand Name	Chemical	Average Daily Dosage (mg/day)
Eskalith, Eskalith Controlled Release	lithium carbonate	900–3600

MOOD STABILIZERS: ANTICONVULSANTS

Brand Name	Chemical	Average Daily Dosage (mg/day)
Tegretol	carbamazepine	100–2000
Depakene, Depakote	valproic acid	125–2000

Lithium

Lithium is one of many chemical elements, like oxygen or copper, that occurs in nature. Lithium is highly reactive and combines easily with other elements and compounds. For this reason, lithium is rarely found in its pure state, but exists in compounds with other elements. When lithium is given as medication, it is combined with oxygen and carbon to form *lithium carbonate.*

Side Effects of Lithium

Many people experience few or no side effects from lithium. Some side effects are temporary and go away after a period of several weeks or months. Some of these side effects include: nausea, stomach cramps, thirst, fatigue, headache, and mild tremor. If any of these side effects is severe, the client should consult his or her physician.

Other side effects may be more serious and should be reported to the physician immediately. These side effects include: vomiting, diarrhea, extreme thirst, muscle twitching, slurred speech, confusion, dizziness, or stupor.

Precautions When Taking Lithium

Lithium can be harmful to the kidneys and other organs if taken in too high a dosage. In order to prevent this, the physician must monitor the amount of lithium in the person's body by taking regular blood tests.

Other precautions are also necessary when taking lithium. The body requires sodium to effectively excrete lithium. If the amount of sodium in the body is too low, lithium can build up to a dangerously high level. Because sodium is contained in table salt, a low-salt diet should be avoided (unless prescribed and coordinated by a physician). In addition, prescription and over-the-counter diuretic medications (such as Fluidex with Pamabrom, Aqua-Ban, Tri-Aqua, Aqua-Rid) can lower sodium levels and should be taken only after consultation with a physician. Also, anti-inflammatory drugs (such as ibuprofen) should be taken only under a physician's recommendation. If these precautions are followed, lithium is a very safe medication.

Anticonvulsant Medications

Anticonvulsant medications were developed for the treatment of seizure disorders, such as epilepsy. However, some of these medications have also been found to be effective mood stabilizers. In general, these medications tend to act more rapidly on acute mood disturbances, especially mania. Like lithium, these drugs have some side effects and certain precautions must be exercised when taking them.

Side Effects of Anticonvulsants

These medications cause mild side effects in many people. Often these side effects are temporary, but sometimes they may continue for longer periods of time. Some of the most common side effects include: fatigue, muscle aching or weakness, dry mouth, constipation or diarrhea, loss of appetite, nausea, skin rash, headache, dizziness, decreased sexual interest, and temporary hair loss. If any of these side effects is severe, the person should consult the physician.

Other side effects may be more severe and should be reported to the physician immediately. These side effects include: confusion, fever, jaundice, abnormal bruising or bleeding, swelling of lymph glands, vomiting, and vision problems (such as double vision). Anticonvulsant medications can affect both blood cells and liver function. In order to determine whether this is occurring (and to take steps to prevent harm), routine laboratory tests need to be conducted on blood samples.

Precautions When Taking Anticonvulsants

These drugs cause sedation, and therefore appropriate precautions must be taken when driving or operating heavy machinery. Moderation in alcohol consumption (not more than one drink per day) is advised, because the effects of alcohol are greatly increased when a person is taking anticonvulsants. The effects of sedative drugs are also enhanced by anticonvulsants. People are usually not prescribed more than one type of anticonvulsant medication at a time.

Like lithium, the amount of anticonvulsant in the body must be monitored by taking blood tests. These anticonvulsant medications are not used for people with a liver disease or a blood-cell or bone-marrow disorder. If appropriate precautions are taken and side effects are monitored, these medications are very safe.

How Do Mood Stabilizers Work?

Scientists do not fully understand how mood-stabilizing medications work. It is believed that these drugs influence certain *neurotransmitters* in the brain (chemicals in the nerve cells) that may be involved in causing the mood disturbance. There is evidence that anticonvulsants reduce the "excitability" of nerve impulses in the brain.

Importance of Regular Medication

Taking medication on a regular basis can help prevent the symptoms of mania or depression from returning or getting worse. It can be helpful to take medication at the same time each day so that it is part of the person's daily routine. It is also important for the person to meet regularly with his or her physician to have symptoms checked, discuss side effects, and have adjustments in medication made when necessary.

Common Questions about Mood Stabilizing Medications

What If the Person Misses a Dose of Medication?

The person should consult with his or her physician to find out what to do if a dose of medication is missed.

Are Mood-Stabilizing Medications Addictive?

Mood-stabilizing drugs are not addictive. People who take these medications do not develop tolerance to these drugs, requiring a higher dose to achieve the same effects. If a person stops taking mood stabilizers, they do not experience *withdrawal effects* (such as nausea, stomach cramps, headache), unlike addictive drugs (such as alcohol, nicotine, sedatives). However, stopping these medications increases the person's risk of having a relapse.

How Long Must Mood-Stabilizing Medications Be Taken?

When mood stabilizers are used in the treatment of bipolar disorder, these medications must often be taken throughout much of the person's life. This is similar to diabetes, in which a person must take insulin daily. Clients with other psychiatric disorders may benefit from taking mood-stabilizing medications for only a limited period of time, such as several weeks or months.

Consult the client's physician about any questions you have concerning this handout.

KEYS TO GOOD COMMUNICATION

Effective communication is important to the functioning and well-being of every family. Families need to communicate about a wide range of topics. Some topics have to do with running the household, schedules, meals, recreation time, money, chores, transportation, shopping, bedtimes, etc. Other communications may focus more on the expression of feelings, including happiness, pride, anger, sadness, disappointment, etc. Sometimes family members need to communicate effectively in order to resolve conflicts between one another. The ability of family members to talk clearly, to express feelings to one another, and to communicate personal needs can help the family cope with everyday stresses and solve common problems.

Effective Communication Is Helpful to All Families

Communication and Serious Psychiatric Illness

When a person has a serious psychiatric illness, his or her ability to concentrate, to pay attention, to remember, and to process information may be impaired. Someone with a serious psychiatric illness once described the confused feeling as being like "too many tennis balls coming over the net at once. I don't know which one to hit. I don't even know if I have a racket."

Persons with Serious Psychiatric Illnesses Often Have Difficulty Following Conversations

When a family member has a serious psychiatric illness, effective communication is even more important than usual. The ill family member can experience stress when the person has difficulty understanding what is said or what is expected of him or her. It can also be stressful when there are many arguments or too much criticism in the household. Since serious psychiatric illnesses are made worse by stress, it is important to reduce stress whenever possible.

> *Improving Communication Can Reduce Stress for Persons with Serious Psychiatric Illnesses*

In this handout we provide some tips on how families can communicate together effectively. Some may be very familiar, while others make take some practice and feel awkward at first. Nevertheless, many skills feel uncomfortable at first (remember how it was to learn to ride a bike!) but are worthwhile in the end.

How to Improve Communication

Many familiy members are able to talk with one another effectively. Every family has arguments and disagreements, however, and almost everyone could benefit from improving the way he or she communicates. However, it is not easy to change communication patterns; it takes time and practice. It is important for each family member to see small improvements and to give each other encouragement whenever there is a positive change. Also, everyone in the family needs to participate in trying to improve.

> *Effective Communication Takes Time, Practice, and Cooperation*

Specific Suggestions for Improving Communication

The following are some specific suggestions that can help family members improve their communication.

Getting to the point. A person with a serious psychiatric illness often has difficulty concentrating. Short, clear, and specific statements are easier to understand and answer. For example:

- **Avoid saying:** "I was walking to the supermarket this morning after breakfast. Remember we ran out of that cereal you like—Wheaties, I think it is. As I was walking, a bus stopped at the corner, and who should get off but Johnny Westheimer. I hadn't seen him since your high school graduation. Anyway, he saw me and asked what I was doing. I told him I was going to the store for a few things. He asked how I was, then he told me what he was doing. He was in a rush, but he said to say 'hi' to you. I went to the market then and they were out of Wheaties, but . . ."

- **Instead, try saying:** "I saw Johnny Westheimer today. He asked me to say 'hello' to you."

Keep Communication Brief

Keeping Communications Focused. When people have difficulty concentrating, it is helpful to focus on one subject at a time. Although there may be several things to be discussed, communication will be more effective if only one topic is talked about at a time. Otherwise, it can be very confusing to follow the conversation, especially for someone with a serious psychiatric illness.

For example:

- **Avoid saying:** "Sandra, I'm so worried about you. You aren't going to your program or taking your medication. You sleep all day and you smoke cigarettes whenever you're awake. I just don't know what's to become of you."
- **Instead, try saying:** "Sandra, I'm concerned that you haven't taken your medication for the past three days."

Use "I" Statements and Talk about One Topic at a Time

Speaking Clearly. When someone is vague about what he or she is trying to say, it can be difficult to understand the message. The more specific the communication, the more likely it will be understood.

For example:

- **Avoid saying:** "You're so nice."
- **Instead, try saying:** "I like the way you smile at me and ask me about my day when I come home from work."

For example:

- **Avoid saying:** "You never do anything around here."
- **Instead, try saying:** "I was annoyed that you did not take out the garbage last night."

Be Specific

Focusing on Behavior. It is very difficulty to change personality, attitudes, or feelings. However, if specific behaviors are identified as desirable or undesirable, it is more likely that the person will be able to work on changing these behaviors. Also, people tend to be more open to changing when people express unpleasant feelings about their behavior, rather than their personality or character.

For example:

- **Avoid saying:** "You're just lazy."

- **Instead, try saying:** "I was upset when you stayed in bed until noon today."

For example,

- **Avoid saying:** "You're no good."

- **Instead, try saying:** "I feel irritated when you spend all your money before the end of the month and then ask me for some"

Focus on Behaviors Rather Than the Personality, Attitude, or
Feelings of the Other Person

Using "Feeling" Statements. When someone does something that you feel happy, sad, or angry about, let him or her know it in a calm, noncritical way. Do not assume that the other person will guess or that he or she "should" know how you feel without your saying something directly. Telling someone explicitly how you feel can foster good communication.

For example:

- **Avoid saying:** "You never pay attention to my feelings."

- **Instead, try saying:** "I appreciated your listening to me yesterday when I told you about my bad day."

For example:

- **Avoid saying:** "Your cooking is okay."

- **Instead, try saying:** "I really liked the way you baked the pork chops and potatoes tonight."

If Someone's Behavior Affects You, Tell Them How You Feel

Giving Positive Feedback

Family members often do pleasant things for each other (e.g., prepare meals, gas up the car, run errands, etc.), and it is important to recognize these positive actions when they occur. Even when activities are done routinely (or even daily), acknowledging the presence of these helpful actions or attitudes has two benefits: (1) it lets the family member know that the positive action has been noticed and appreciated and (2) it makes it more likely that the positive action will be done again. Both help-ing family members and acknowledging the help is like putting deposits in the family bank, which can be withdrawn during times of stress.

For example:

- **Avoid** ignoring other's positive actions
- **Instead, try saying:** "I am really relieved that you made dinner. I was so tired tonight."

Let People Know When They Please You

Making Requests. Making requests of other people is a part of everyday living. Requests that are made in a demanding or threatening manner can be ineffective and produce stress. Sometimes making demands works in the short run, but it can also lead to resentment and hurt feelings and can be ineffective in the long run. Naturally, people do not comply with every request that is made, no matter how polite. How-ever, making requests in a positive way can minimize stress and is more likely to result in the request being met. When asking for something, it is helpful to be brief and specific about what you would like the other person to do, and to use a calm, pleasant voice. It helps to start a request with phrases such as "I would like you to . . ." or "I would appreciate it if you would . . ." The word "please" can also be helpful.

For example:

- **Avoid saying:** "Mom, make something good for dessert for a change."
- **Instead, try saying:** "Mom, I would appreciate it if you would make apple pie for dessert sometime this week."

For example:

- **Avoid saying:** "Clean up your room."
- **Instead, try saying:** "I would like you to put your dirty clothes in the hamper and make your bed before dinner tonight."

Make Requests in a Nondemanding, Positive Manner

Dealing with Unpleasant Feelings. Sometimes a person has unpleasant or negative feelings about what another person has done. Examples of feelings that are unpleas-ant to experience include anger, annoyance, sadness, anxiety, and worry. When expressing these unpleasant feelings it is important to focus on what the person has done, rather than to criticize the person directly. It can be helpful to make a sugges-tion as to how the person might correct the situation or prevent it from happening in the future. When speaking, the tone of voice should be consistent with what you are feeling, but not unduly harsh or critical.

For example:

- **Avoid saying:** "You drive me crazy when you come home late."
- **Instead, try saying:** "I was very worried tonight when you came home after six. I would like you to call me when you're going to be late."

For example:

- **Avoid saying**: "You're such a slob."
- **Instead, try saying:** "I am angry that you didn't clean up after your snack last night. Next time please put the dishes of food away when you finish your snack."

> *When Expressing Unpleasant Feelings, Focus on Behavior and Suggest How to Improve the Situation*

Listening. It is often difficult for people to say what is really on their minds. Good listening can help the other person speak his or her mind clearly. A person can show that he or she is listening by looking at the person, making small comments like "uh-huh," or "okay," nodding, asking clarifying questions, and checking out what he or she has heard. One way to make sure you understand what was said is to summarize, and then ask if that was the intended message.

For example:

- **Avoid:** (1) looking away from the speaker; (2) being totally still, showing no facial expression; (3) assuming that you understand what is said; (4) saying nothing.
- **Instead, try:** (1) looking directly at the speaker; (2) nodding your head and saying, "uh-huh," or "I see," as the speaker continues; (3) asking questions; (4) summarizing what you heard.

> *Let the Other Person Know You Are Listening*

Nonverbal Behaviors. The *content* of what is said is important, as well as *how* it is said. Eye contact, tone of voice, and facial expression are important nonverbal behaviors that contribute to effective communication.

Eye Contact. When you look at people you are speaking with, they are more likely to know that you're really talking to them and more likely to pay attention. Also, when people have difficulty concentrating, looking directly at them helps them to focus their attention. If you are uncomfortable with maintaining eye contact, look at the other person's forehead or nose.

For example:

- **Avoid:** (1) calling out to a person in another room; (2) facing the television rather than the person to whom you're talking; (3) sitting beside the person, looking straight ahead as you're talking; (4) looking at the floor.

- **Instead, try to:** (1) make sure you have the other person's attention before speaking; (2) maintain eye contact during the conversation.

Look at the Person

Tone of Voice. In general, people are more receptive to a calm, pleasant tone. This tone is easier to hear and to comprehend. People with serious psychiatric illnesses are particularly sensitive to harsh and critical voice tones. If the tone of voice puts a person on the defensive, he or she is less likely to hear what is being said and less likely to try to do what you're asking.

For example:

- **Avoid these tones:** (1) high-pitched; (2) critical; (3) sarcastic; (4) demanding; (5) shouting; (6) excessively angry

- **Instead, try to remain:** (1) calm; (2) pleasant; (3) reasonable; (4) warm.

Use a Calm, Pleasant Voice Tone

Facial Expressions. It can be very confusing when someone is saying one thing but his or her facial expression is saying another. For example, if your words are praising someone but you have a scowl on your face, the other person will have difficulty knowing what you really mean. A contradiction between facial expression and content of speech is particularly disorienting if someone has difficulty with their thinking.

For example:

- **Avoid saying:** "I was very angry when you did not keep your appointment," while smiling.

- **Instead, try saying:** "I was very angry when you did not keep your appointment," with a serious, firm look on your face.

For example:

- **Avoid saying:** "I like the dress you're wearing," with a sad look on your face.

- **Instead, try saying:** "I like the dress you're wearing," with a smile.

Use a Facial Expression That Matches What You Are Saying

Summary

1. Effective communication is helpful in all families.

2. Persons with serious psychiatric illnesses often have difficulty following conversations.

3. Improving communication can reduce stress for persons with serious psychiatric illnesses.

4. Effective communication takes time, practice, and cooperation.

5. Keep communications brief.

6. Use "I" statements and talk about one topic at a time.

7. Be specific.

8. Focus on behaviors rather than the personality, attitudes, or feelings of the other person.

9. If someone's behavior affects you, tell them how you feel.

10. Let people know when they please you.

11. Make requests in a nondemanding, positive manner.

12. When expressing unpleasant feelings, focus on behavior and suggest how to improve the situation.

13. Let the person know you are listening.

14. Look at the person.

15. Use a calm, pleasant voice tone.

16. Use a facial expression that matches what you're saying.

Key Communication Elements

- Good eye contact
- Use "I" statements ("I feel _____ when you _____ ")
- Be specific about the event or behavior upon which you are commenting
- Make sure you are close enough to hear each other

Examples:

Expressing Positive Feelings

- "I feel happy that you cleaned the bathroom."
- "I felt relieved that you called the family meeting when you said you would."

Making a Positive Request

- "I would appreciate it if you would pick up your clothes off the floor. It would make me feel happier if we shared the responsibilities."
- "I would feel proud if you really tried to complete the school semester without any more absences."

Expressing Negative Feelings (usually combined with a positive request)

- "I am hurt that you criticized me in front of the kids. In the future, I would feel less upset if you would wait until we were alone."
- "I am frustrated that you forgot to pay the rent again. I would feel calmer if you would make sure you pay it a day or two before it's due."

Active Listening

- Look speaker in eye.
- Nod head.
- Ask clarifying questions.
- Paraphrase what you have heard.
- Wait until the speaker finishes before responding.

Compromise and Negotiation

- Look at the person.
- Explain your viewpoint.
- Listen to the other person's viewpoint.
- Repeat back what you heard.
- Suggest a compromise (more than one may be necessary).

Requesting a Time-out

- Indicate that the situation is stressful.
- Tell the person that it is interfering with constructive communication.
- Say that you must leave temporarily.
- State when you will return, and be willing to problem solve.

Expressing Positive Feelings Homework

Key elements:

- Look at the person who pleased you.

- Tell him or her exactly what he or she did to please you—be specific.

- Tell him or her the feeling it gave you—be precise

Example:

"I am really happy that you came home on time."

"I feel relieved that you paid the bills this weekend like you said you would."

Day	Person Who Pleased You	What He/She Did	What You Said
Monday			
Tuesday			
Wednesday			
Thursday			
Friday			
Saturday			
Sunday			

Making a Positive Request Homework

Key elements:

- Look at the person to whom you are making a request.

- Tell him or her exactly what you are requesting—be specific.

- Tell him or her how it would make you feel if the request were met—be precise.

Example:

"Would you please watch the baby for half an hour? I would really appreciate the break."

"I would feel less stressed if you would gas up the car. Would you be able to do that?"

Day	Person to Whom Request Was Made	What You Said	How He/She Responded
Monday			
Tuesday			
Wednesday			
Thursday			
Friday			
Saturday			
Sunday			

Expressing Negative Feelings Homework

Key elements:

- Look at the person who displeased you.
- Tell him or her exactly what he/she did to displease you—be specific.
- Tell him or her the feeling it gave you—be precise.
- Make a positive request for change, if possible.

Example:

"I felt irritated when I had to hold dinner for an extra hour. In the future, I would appreciate it if you would call me if you are going to be more than thirty minutes late."

"I felt hurt when you criticized my driving in front of your friends. In the future, I would like it if you would wait until we are alone if you are going to give me negative feedback."

Day	Person Who Displeased You	What He/She Did	What You Said
Monday			
Tuesday			
Wednesday			
Thursday			
Friday			
Saturday			
Sunday			

Family Meeting Active Listening Homework

Date of Meeting: _____

Person Listening	Skills Used	Person Speaking/Topic
1.		
2.		
3.		
4.		
5.		

Active Listening Skills

- Look speaker in eye.
- Nod head.
- Ask clarifying questions.
- Paraphrase what you have heard.
- Wait until the speaker finishes before responding.

Be sure each person is given positive feedback on his or her use of active listening skills immediately after his or her practice.

Compromise and Negotiation Homework

Date: _____

Topic: _____

Your suggestion:

Other person's suggestion:

Compromise to which you agreed:

Requesting a Time-out Homework

To be completed by person requesting time-out.

Date you requested time-out: _____

Reason you requested time-out: _____

_____

What did you say to request time-out? _____

_____

How long did time-out last? _____

How did you resolve the situation? _____

_____

STRUCTURED PROBLEM SOLVING AND GOAL ATTAINMENT

Many families find that working to solve problems in a systematic way can lead to better outcomes. In BFT, families are taught to use a particular set of strategies to resolve problems and meet goals effectively. In this handout, we first discuss how to use family meetings to work on solving problems and then present the steps of successful problem solving. Most families find it helpful to complete a "Problem-Solving/Goal-Setting Record" for each problem on which they work. These records can be filed in a notebook so that family members can remember what they decided to do at each meeting.

Structuring the Family Problem-Solving Meeting

Families find that following a specific structure for solving a problem can help to organize the members and keep them focused on the problem at hand. In order to solve problems using a clear structure, families need to first decide who will be the chair for the family discussion. The chair is responsible for guiding the family through the steps of solving the problem, but participates equally with other members in actively solving the problem. The same chair need not be chosen each time the family meets. In addition to selecting the chair, family members need to decide who will be the secretary responsible for keeping a written record of the problem-solving meeting. The chair can also be the secretary or a different person can be selected.

> *To Solve Problems Using a Structured Approach, First Select a Chair and a Secretary for the Meeting*

Steps of Problem Solving and Goal Attainment

One structured approach to solving problems is based on a model developed by Ian Falloon et al. (1984) and follows six steps. The chair keeps family members focused on one step at a time while the secretary keeps notes. Both the chair and secretary participate actively in the family discussion. The six steps are as follows:

1. *Discuss the problem or goal.* All the family members talk about the problem or goal and pay attention to what each person says. It is especially important for the people most involved to talk about how the problem affects them. When everyone has expressed opinions, family members try to arrive at a common definition of the problem or goal. This may require family members to compromise with each other. Wording the problem or goal positively in terms of how to change something can facilitate accomplishing this step. When family members agree on a specific definition, it is written down.

2. *Brainstorm at least three possible solutions.* At the beginning of this step, family members review previous attempts to solve the problem and the consequences of these attempts. This review helps to avoid repetition of unsuccessful efforts. Then, everyone identifies as many potential solutions to the problem as possible. Do not evaluate the solutions at this time. Even "fantasy solutions," outlandish ideas, and humorous responses are be acknowledged and recorded, regardless of their impracticality. Everyone should contribute at least one idea, and criticism is avoided at all costs.

3. *Briefly evaluate each solution.* List the advantages and disadvantages of each idea for solving the problem or achieving the goal. Some families like to make brief notes about each possible solution.

4. *Choose the best solution.* Try to pick the easiest solution that is likely to work. The chosen solution(s) should be agreed upon by the family members. Sometimes, one or two solutions are clearly favored by everyone. Other times, family members may differ as to which solutions they prefer. Solutions may need to be modified or compromises made in order for the family members to reach agreement.

5. *Plan the implementation.* When family members agree on how they want to solve the problem or achieve the goal, they need to formulate a plan to put their ideas into action. This plan addresses four key elements:
   A. **Time-frame.** When will different parts of the plan be accomplished?
   B. **Resources.** Are any special resources needed to carry out the plan (e.g., money, skills, information)?
   C. **Roles.** Who is responsible for doing what?
   D. **Possible obstacles.** What could possibly interfere with successfully implementing the plan? How could these obstacles be avoided or dealt with if they occur?

6. *Review implementation at the next family meeting.* After the family has agreed upon a plan, a date is set to meet again and evaluate whether the plan was successful. At this meeting, family members will discuss and praise efforts that have been made to implement the plan and evaluate whether further

effort is necessary to solve the problem or achieve the goal. The follow-up meeting can be just a few days away or a week away.

Summary of Steps to Solve Problems and Achieve Goals:

1. Define the problem.

2. Generate possible solutions.

3. Evaluate each possible solution.

4. Choose the best solution or combination of solutions.

5. Plan how to carry out the solution(s).

6. Review implementation of the plan and praise all efforts.

Example

Four members of a family, including the mother, two brothers (one with schizoaffective disorder), and a sister (with schizophrenia) all lived together in a small apartment. One day, the sister got into an argument with her boyfriend and threatened to throw a lamp at him. It appeared to the mother that her daughter was experiencing an increase in her symptoms and she interceded. A family meeting, including the daughter, was immediately called. The mother took the role of the chair and one of the brothers took the role of secretary. After several minutes of discussion about the problem, everyone agreed to define the problem as "our sister feels like she might hurt someone." The family identified six different possible solutions:

1. Take extra medication.

2. Go to the nearest hospital.

3. Leave the apartment.

4. Other family members leave the apartment.

5. Go to the hospital where the daughter was previously admitted.

6. Call the treatment team for an evaluation.

After considering the advantages and disadvantages of each possible solution, the family members agreed that the best solution was number 5, because the sister felt the situation was urgent, and she was most comfortable going to a hospital where she was familiar with the treatment staff. A plan was formulated to implement the solution that included the following steps:

1. Mother calls hospital to see if there are available beds for admission. (If no beds are available, the closest hospital is called.)

2. Mother calls cab for transportation to hospital.

3. Sister packs clothes and toiletries.

4. Brother accompanies sister to hospital.

The plan was followed successfully, and the sister was admitted to the hospital.

Common Hitches to Solving Problems and Achieving Goals

It is Difficult to Get People to Meet Together

This is a common problem for many families with busy schedules. First, choosing a time when everyone is together and it is convenient to meet is crucial (e.g., after a meal, on Saturday morning). Arranging for someone to remind family members about the meeting and to get everyone together at the appointed time can also be helpful. A reminder notice, such as a note posted on the refrigerator door on the morning of the meeting, may be useful. Finally, it is important to make family meetings as pleasant and rewarding as possible, even when difficult topics are discussed. Serving refreshments and praising family members for attending can encourage members to participate in family meetings.

One Person Does Not Want to Solve the Problem

In general, there are two strategies for dealing with the difficulty of one person not wanting to be involved in solving the problem. First, an attempt can be made to redefine the problem so the person becomes more interested in participating in the discussion. For example, parents who were upset about their son's refusal to bathe regularly were able to engage him in a discussion by changing their definition of the problem from "Joseph rarely bathes and smells unpleasant" to "Joseph doesn't like it when his parents nag him about bathing."

The second strategy to use when one person will not participate in solving the problem is to meet without that person. For example, two parents had a daughter who smoked incessantly in all rooms of the house, despite clear household rules. Since they were unable to enlist her cooperation in solving this problem, the parents chose to meet without their daughter to establish consequences for their daughter's breaking these rules. The consequences were shared with the daughter at the next scheduled family meeting.

Choosing among Multiple Problems

Families may be besieged by many problems. Decisions must be made regarding which problems should be addressed first, second, and so on. The most important consideration when prioritizing problems is the urgency of the problem. Crisis-oriented problems, such as suicidal thoughts, self-destructive behavior, violence or threats of violence toward others, or marked worsening in symptoms, must be addressed immediately. The next order of problems to be addressed are those related to a possible relapse of symptoms. For example, the abuse of drugs or alcohol, which can precipitate a relapse, is a high-priority problem. Similarly, if the person with schizophrenia has become noncompliant with his or her antipsychotic medication or has begun to have early warning signs of a relapse, it is important to have a problem solving discussion to try to prevent a relapse.

While urgent problems tend to get addressed more quickly than less pressing problems or goals, it is best to strike a balance between the needs of all the family members. Thus, when one family member is more needy or requires more help than other family members, family discussions should not neglect the less needy family members. In order to have the lowest possible stress in the family, each person's needs and goals must be met through the mutual effort of everyone involved.

The Problem or Goal Is Too Broad and It Is Unclear Where to Start

Some problems or goals may be so large they seem to be as insurmountable as a towering mountain. Breaking down a large problem into small, manageable chunks can aid the process of problem solving, just as a high mountain can be climbed by taking many small steps. To break the problem down into small steps, identify what needs to be changed first, then second, etc. Try to make each step small enough so that it can be solved, and work on only one step at a time. For example, the client in one family was interested in improving his personal hygiene without prompting from family members. The task of improving hygiene, including bathing regularly, washing hair, brushing teeth, combing hair, and deodorant use, was too great to solve in a single family meeting. However, family members were able to make headway on the problem when they worked on improving only one hygiene area (e.g., brushing teeth) at a time.

The Discussion Rapidly Degenerates into Arguments

Meeting when tension is low and avoiding blaming statements can reduce arguments. Defining the problem very specifically, rather than generally, can also help prevent arguments. Focusing on how to improve things for the future, instead of dredging up the past, facilitates constructive discussion. When there is a conflict among family members, it is usually because each person has a different viewpoint about the problem that is difficult to change.

For example, the wife of one couple believed that all viewing of TV was harmful to her school-age child, whereas the husband thought that TV was harmless entertainment. The couple argued when each tried to change the other's viewpoint. However, when they accepted the differences in perspective, they were able to come to agreement about the specific problem: both the husband and wife agreed it was a problem that their son insisted on watching TV rather than eating dinner with the family. Accepting different viewpoints, instead of attempting to change them, can avoid arguments and facilitate discussion.

People Don't Follow Through on Plans

There are three basic reasons why most family members do not follow through on a plan that has been agreed upon at a family meeting: (1) they forget; (2) they do not know exactly what they are supposed to do; (3) they do not believe the plan selected will lead to the best solution. Strategies for overcoming these obstacles are as follows:

1. Reminding people to follow through on their part of the plan can prevent forgetfulness. Reminders can be verbal or written. Some families post a list of all

family members' roles in solving a problem. It is helpful to post the list in a prominent spot such as on a bulletin board or the refrigerator.

2. When a plan is being discussed in a family meeting, effort should be made to clarify exactly what each person's role is and what he or she is expected to do. After the plan has been made, make sure that everyone understands his or her role correctly by asking each family member to describe what he or she will do.

3. Sometimes people do not do their part of a plan because they do not really believe that the plan will work or they disagree with the definitions of the problem itself. If someone repeatedly does not follow through on the plan, despite reminders, this possibility should be explored. If someone disagrees with the plan or their role in the plan, the family should attempt to resolve this difference, either through discussion, compromise, or negotiation. If this is unsuccessful, the family may elect to modify the plan so that its implementation does not depend upon the involvement of the family member who disagrees with it.

No Matter How Hard You Try, the Problem Can't Be Solved

Sometimes it is difficult to solve a problem or achieve a goal despite many attempts. When all reasonable efforts have been made, redefining the problem or goal can be a useful strategy. For example, one family tried repeatedly to help the son achieve his goal of getting a paying job. Unfortunately, his work rate was too slow and a suitable job could not be found. When the goal was modified to "participating in a constructive activity in the community," a volunteer job at a museum was found.

Summary

1. To solve problems using a structured approach, first select a chair and a secretary for the meeting.

2. Summary of steps to solve problems and achieve goals:
    A. Discuss the problem.
    B. Brainstorm three possible solutions.
    C. Briefly evaluate each solution.
    D. Choose the best solution(s).
    E. Plan the implementation.
    F. Review implementation at next family meeting.

3. Families may encounter difficulties in solving problems together, but there are strategies for overcoming the obstacles.

Problem-Solving/Goal-Setting Record

Discuss the problem or goal. Get everyone's opinion. Try to reach agreement on exactly what the problem/goal is. Write down *specifically* what the problem/goal is.

_____

_____

_____

Brainstorm at least three possible solutions (five is better). Do not evaluate them at this time—wait till step 3.

_____

_____

_____

_____

_____

Briefly evaluate each solution. List major advantages and disadvantages.

Advantages   **Disadvantages**

_____

_____

_____

_____

_____

Choose the best solution(s). Consider how easy it would be to implement each solution and how likely it is to be effective.

_____

Plan the implementation. When will it be implemented? _____

What resources are needed and how will they be obtained?_____

Who will do what to implement the solution? _____

List what might go wrong in the implementation and how to overcome it._____

_____

Practice any difficult parts of the plan. _____

Who will check that all the steps of the plan have been implemented?_____

Review implementation at next family meeting. (Date: _____) Revise as needed.

REFERENCES

Abramowitz I.A., & Coursey R.D. (1989). Impact of an educational support group on family participants who take care of their schizophrenic relatives. *Journal of Consulting and Clinical Psychology, 57*, 232-236.

Addington, J., & Duchak, V. (1997). Reasons for substance use in schizophrenia. *Acta Psychiatrica Scandinavica, 96*, 329-333.

Akiskal, H.S. (1990). Toward a clinical understanding of the relationship of anxiety and depressive disorders. In J.D. Maser & C.R. Cloninger (Eds.), *Comorbidity of Mood and Anxiety Disorders* (pp. 597-607). Washington, DC: American Psychiatric Press.

Anderson, C.M., Reiss, D.J., & Hogarty, G.E. (1986). *Schizophrenia and the Family*. New York: Guilford.

Anderson, E.A., & Lynch, M.M. (1984). A family impact analysis: The deinstitutionalization of the mentally ill. *Family Relations, 33*, 41-46.

Andersson, C., Chakos, M., Mailman, R., & Lieberman, J. (1998). Emerging roles for novel antipsychotic medications in the treatment of schizophrenia. *The Psychiatric Clinics of North America, 21*, 151-179.

Angermeyer, M.C., & Kuhn, L. (1988). Gender difference in age at onset of schizophrenia: An overview. *European Archives of Psychiatry and Neurological Sciences, 237*, 351-364.

Appleton, W.S. (1974). Mistreatment of patients' families by psychiatrists. *American Journal of Psychiatry, 131*, 655-657.

Argyle, N. (1990). Panic attacks in chronic schizophrenia. *British Journal of Psychiatry, 157*, 430-433.

Arnow, B.A., Taylor, C.R., Agras, W.S., & Telch, M.J. (1985). Enhancing agoraphobia treatment outcome by changing couple communication patterns. *Behavior Therapy, 16*, 452-467.

Ascher-Svanum, H., & Krause, A.A. (1991). *Psychoeducational Groups for Patients with Schizophrenia*. Gaithersburg, MD: Aspen Publishers.

Atkinson, J.M., & Coia, D.A. (1995). *Families Coping with Schizophrenia: A Practitioner's Guide to Family Groups*. New York: John Wiley & Sons.

Atkinson, S.D. (1994). Grieving and loss in parents with a schizophrenic child. *American Journal of Psychiatry, 151*, 1137-1139.

Backlar, P. (1994). *The Family Face of Schizophrenia: Practical Counsel from America's Leading Experts*. New York: Tarcher/Putnam.

Bandura, A. (1969). *Principles of Behavior Modification*. New York: Holt, Rinehart, and Winston.

Bandura, A., & Walters, R.H. (1963). *Social Learning and Personality Development*. New York: Holt, Rinehart & Winston.

Barlow, D.H. (1988). *Anxiety and Its Disorders: The Nature and Treatment of Anxiety and Panic*. New York: Guilford.

Barlow, D.H., Mavissakalin, M., & Hay, L.R. (1981). Couples treatment of agoraphobia: Changes in marital satisfaction. *Behaviour Research and Therapy, 19*, 245-256.

Barlow, D.H., O'Brien, G.T., & Last, C.G. (1984). Couples' treatment of agoraphobia. *Behavior Therapy, 15*, 41-48.

Barrowclough, C., & Parle, M. (1997). Appraisal, psychological adjustment and expressed emotion in relatives of patients suffering from schizophrenia. *British Journal of Psychiatry, 171*, 26-30.

Barrowclough, C., & Tarrier, N. (1990). Social functioning in schizophrenic patients: I. The effects of expressed emotion and family intervention. *Social Psychiatry and Psychiatric Epidemiology, 25*, 125-129.

Barrowclough, C., & Tarrier, N. (1992). *Families of Schizophrenic Patients: Cognitive Behavioural Intervention*. London: Chapman & Hall.

Barrowclough, C., & Tarrier, N. (1998). Social functioning and family interventions. In K.T. Mueser & N. Tarrier (Eds.), *Handbook of Social Functioning in Schizophrenia*, (pp. 327-341). Boston: Allyn & Bacon.

Bateson, G., Jackson, D.D., Haley, J., & Weakland, J. (1956). Toward a theory of schizophrenia. *Behavioral Science, 1*, 251-264.

Baucom, D.H., & Epstein, N. (1990). *Cognitive-Behavioral Marital Therapy*. New York: Brunner/Mazel.

Baucom, D.H., Sayers, S.L., & Sher, T.G. (1990). Supplementing behavioral marital therapy with cognitive restructuring and emotional expressiveness training: An outcome investigation. *Journal of Consulting and Clinical Psychology, 58*, 636-645.

Baucom, D.H., Shoham, V., Mueser, K.T., Daiuto, A.D., & Stickle, T.R. (1998). Empirically supported couple and family interventions for adult mental health problems. *Journal of Consulting and Clinical Psychology, 66*, 53-88.

Beach, S.R.H., Sandeen, E.E., & O'Leary, K.D. (1990). *Depression in Marriage*. New York: Guilford.

Beach, S.R.H., Winters, K.C., & Weintraub, S. (1986). Marital dissolution and distress in a psychiatric population: A longitudinal design. *Behavioral Residential Treatment, 1*, 217-229.

Beck, A.T., Epstein, N., Brown, G., & Steer, R.A. (1988). An inventory for measuring clinical anxiety: Psychometric properties. *Journal of Consulting and Clinical Psychology, 56*, 893-897.

Beck, A.T., Rush, A.J., Shaw, B.F., & Emery, G. (1979). *Cognitive Therapy of Depression*. New York: Guilford.

Beck, A.T., Ward, C.H., Mendelsohn, M., Mock, J., & Erbaugh, J. (1961). An inventory for measuring depression. *Archives of General Psychiatry, 4*, 561-571.

Bellack, A.S., & Hersen, M. (Eds.) (1998). *Comprehensive Clinical Psychology*. New York: Pergamon.

Bellack, A.S., Mueser, K.T., Gingerich, S., & Agresta, J. (1997). *Social Skills Training for Schizophrenia: A Step-by-Step Guide*. New York: Guilford.

Bennun, I. (1985). Two approaches to family therapy with alcoholics: Problem-solving and systemic therapy. *Journal of Substance Abuse Treatment, 2*, 19-26.

Berger, D., & Berger, L. (1991). *We Heard the Angels of Madness: A Family Guide to Coping with Manic Depression*. New York: Quill.

Bertelsen, A., Harvald, B., & Hauge, M. (1977). A Danish twin study of manic-depressive disorders. *British Journal of Psychiatry, 130*, 330-351.

Biglan, A., Hops, H., Sherman, L., Friedman, L.S., Arthur, J., & Osteen, V. (1985). Problem solving interactions of depressed women and their husbands. *Behavior Therapy, 16*, 431-451.

Birchwood M., Smith J., & Cochrane R. (1992). Specific and non-specific effects of educational intervention for families living with schizophrenia. *British Journal of Psychiatry, 160*, 806-814.

Bisbee, C.C. (1991). *Educating Patients and Families About Mental Illness: A Practical Guide*. Gaithersburg, MD: Aspen Publishers.

Blackwell, B. (1976). Treatment adherence. *British Journal of Psychiatry, 129*, 513-531.

Blanchard, E., Martin, J., & Dubbert, P. (1988). *Nondrug Treatments for Essential Hypertension*. New York: Pergamon.

Blanchard, E.P., Jones-Alexander, J., Buckley, T.C., & Forneris, C.A. (1996). Psychometric properties of the PTSD Checklist. *Behavior Therapy, 34*, 669-673.

Blechman, E.A. (1985). *Solving Child Behavior Problems at Home and at School*. Champaign, IL: Research Press.

Bongar, B., & Beutler, L.E. (Eds.)(1995). *Foundations of Psychotherapy: Theory, Research and Practice*. New York: Oxford University Press.

Bornstein, P.H., & Bornstein, M.T. (1986). *Marital Therapy: A Behavioral Communications Approach*. New York: Pergamon Press.

Bourne, E.J. (1996). *The Anxiety & Phobia Workbook (Second Edition)*. Oakland, CA: New Harbinger.

Bowen, M. (1961). The family as a unit of study and treatment. *American Journal of Orthopsychiatry, 31*, 40-60.

Boyd, J.H., Burke, J.D., Gruenberg, E., Holzer, C.E. III, Rae, D.S., George, L.K., Karno, M., Stoltzman, R., McEvoy, L., Nestadt, G. (1984). Exclusion criteria of DSM-III: A study of co-occurrence of hierarchy-free syndromes. *Archives of General Psychiatry, 41*, 983-959.

Breier, A., & Strauss, J.S. (1983). Self-control in psychotic disorders. *Archives of General Psychiatry, 40*, 1141-1145.

Breslau, N., Davis, G.C., Andreski, P., & Peterson, E. (1991). Traumatic events and post-traumatic stress disorder in an urban population of young adults. *Archives of General Psychiatry, 48*, 216-222.

Brewin, C.R., MacCarthy, B., Duda, K., & Vaughn, C.E. (1991). Attribution and expressed emotion in the relatives of patients with schizophrenia. *Journal of Abnormal Psychology, 100*, 546-554.

Brooker, C., Falloon, I., Butterworth, A., Goldberg, D., Graham-Hole, V., & Hillier, V. (1994). The outcome of training community psychiatric nurses to deliver psychosocial intervention. *British Journal of Psychiatry, 165*, 222-230.

Brown, G.W., Birley, J.L.T., & Wing, J.K. (1972). Influence of family life on the course of schizophrenic disorders: A replication. *British Journal of Psychiatry, 121*, 241-58.

Brown, G.W., Carstairs, G.M., & Topping, G. (1958). The post hospital adjustment of chronic mental patients. *Lancet, 2*, 685-689.

Brown, G.W., & Harris, T. (1978). *Social Origins of Depression: A Study of Psychiatric Disorders in Women*. New York: Free Press.

Brown, G.W., Monck, E.M., Carstairs, G.M., & Wing, J.K. (1962). Influence of family life on the course of schizophrenic illness. *British Journal of Preventive and Social Medicine, 16*, 55-68.

Brown, G.W., & Rutter, M. (1966). The measurement of family activities and relationships: A methodological study. *Human Relations, 19,* 241-263.

Brown, S., & Birtwistle, J. (1998). People with schizophrenia and their families: Fifteen-year outcome. *British Journal of Psychiatry, 173,* 139-144.

Bulger, M.W., Wandersman, A., & Goldman, C.R. (1993). Burdens and gratifications of caregiving: Appraisal of parental care of adults with schizophrenia. *American Journal of Orthopsychiatry, 63,* 255-265.

Bullock, R., Siegel, R., Weissman, M.M., & Paykel, E.S. (1972). The weeping wife: Marital relations of depressed women. *Journal of Marriage and the Family, 34,* 488-495.

Burland, J. (1993). *The Journey of Hope Family Education Course.* Baton Rouge, LA: Louisiana Alliance for the Mentally Ill.

Burland, J., & Mayeux, D. (1995). The Journey of Hope: A family to family self-help education and support group program. *The Journal of the California Alliance for the Mentally Ill, 6,* 3.

Busfield, J. (1982). Gender and mental illness. *International Journal of Mental Health, 11,* 46-66.

Butzlaff, R.L., & Hooley, J.M. (1998). Expressed emotion and psychiatric relapse. *Archives of General Psychiatry, 55,* 547-552.

Cardin V.A., McGill C.W., & Falloon I.R.H. (1986). An economic analysis: Costs, benefits and effectiveness. In Falloon I.R.H. (Ed.), *Family Management of Schizophrenia* (pp. 115-123). Baltimore: Johns Hopkins University Press.

Carey, K.B., & Carey, M.P. (1995). Reasons for drinking among psychiatric outpatients: Relationship to drinking patterns. *Psychology of Addictive Behaviors, 9,* 251-257.

Carpentier, N., Lesage, A., Goulet, I., Lalonde, P., & Renaud, M. (1992). Burden of care of families not living with a young schizophrenic relative. *Hospital and Community Psychiatry, 43,* 38-43.

Carter, D.M., MacKinnon, A., & Copolov, D.L. (1996). Patients' strategies for coping with auditory hallucinations. *Journal of Nervous and Mental Disease, 184,* 159-164.

Cascardi, M., Mueser, K.T., DeGirolomo, J., & Murrin, M. (1996). Physical aggression against psychiatric inpatients by family members and partners: A descriptive study. *Psychiatric Services, 47,* 531-533.

Cerny, J.A., Barlow, D.H., Craske, M.G., & Himaldi, W.G. (1988). Couple treatment of agoraphobia: A two year follow-up. *Behavior Therapy, 18,* 401-416.

Chadwick, P., Birchwood, M., & Trower, P. (1996). *Cognitive Therapy for Delusions, Voices and Paranoia.* Chichester, England: John Wiley & Sons.

Chambless, D.L., Caputo, G., Bright, P., & Gallagher, R. (1984). Assessment of fear in agoraphobics: The Body Sensations Questionnaire and the Agoraphobic Cognitions Questionnaire. *Journal of Consulting and Clinical Psychology, 52,* 1090-1097.

Clark, R.E. (1996). Family support for people with dual disorders. In R.E. Drake & K.T. Mueser (Eds.), *Dual Diagnosis of Major Mental Illness and Substance Abuse Disorder II: Recent Research and Clinical Implications. New Directions in Mental Health Services.* 65–77. San Francisco: Jossey-Bass.

Clark, R.E., & Drake, R.E. (1994). Expenditures of time and money by families of people with severe mental illness and substance use disorders. *Community Mental Health Journal, 30,* 145-163.

Clarkin, J.F., Carpenter, D., Hull, J., Wilner, P., & Glick, I. (1998). Effects of psychoeducational intervention for married patients with bipolar disorder and their spouses. *Psychiatric Services, 49,* 531-533.

Clausen, J.A. (1975). The impact of mental illness: A twenty-year follow-up. In R.D. Wirt, G. Winokur, & M. Roff (Eds.), *Life History Research in Psychopathology, Volume 4* (pp. 270-289). Minneapolis, MN: University of Minnesota Press.

Clausen, J.A., & Yarrow, M.R. (Eds.) (1955). The impact of mental illness on the family. *Journal of Social Issues, 11*.

Cloninger, C.R. (1987). Recent advances in the genetics of anxiety and somatoform disorders. In H.Y. Meltzer (Ed.), *Psychopharmacology: The Third Generation of Progress* (pp. 955-966). New York: Raven Press.

Coiro, M.J., & Gottesman, I.I. (1996). The diathesis and/or stressor role of expressed emotion in affective illness. *Clinical Psychology: Science and Practice, 3*, 310-322.

Cooper, M. (1996). Obsessive-compulsive disorder: Effects on family members. *American Journal of Orthopsychiatry, 66*, 296-304.

Copeland, M.E. (1994). *Living Without Depression & Manic Depression: A Workbook for Maintaining Mood Stability*. Oakland, CA: New Harbinger.

Corcoran, K., & Fisher, J. (1987). *Measures for Clinical Practice: A Sourcebook*. New York: Free Press.

Coryell, W., Solomon, D., Leon, A.C., Akiskal, H.S., Keller, M.B., Scheftner, W.A., & Mueller, T. (1998). Lithium discontinuation and subsequent effectiveness. *American Journal of Psychiatry, 155*, 895-898.

Costello, C.G. (1982). Social factors associated with depression: A retrospective community study. *Psychological Medicine, 12*, 329-339.

Coyne, J.C., Kessler, R.C., Tal, M., Turnbull, J., Wortman, C.B., & Greden, J.F. (1987). Living with a depressed person. *Journal of Consulting and Clinical Psychology, 55*, 347-352.

Craine, L.S., Henson, C.E., Colliver, J.A., & MacLean, D.G. (1988). Prevalence of a history of sexual abuse among female psychiatric patients in a state hospital system. *Hospital and Community Psychiatry, 39*, 300-304.

Creer, C., & Wing, J. (1974). *Schizophrenia at Home*. London: Institute of Psychiatry.

Cuffel, B.J. (1996). Comorbid substance use disorder: prevalence, patterns of use, and course. In: R.E. Drake & K.T. Mueser (Eds), *Dual Diagnosis of Major Mental Illness and Substance Disorder: Recent Research and Clinical Implications. New Directions for Mental Health Services*. San Francisco, Jossey-Bass.

Davenport, Y.B., Ebert, M.H., Adland, M.L., & Goodwin, F.K. (1977). Couples group therapy as an adjunct to lithium maintenance of the manic patient. *American Journal of Orthopsychiatry, 47*, 495-502.

Davis, J.M. (1976). Overview: Maintenance therapy in psychiatry: II. Affective disorders. *American Journal of Psychiatry, 133*, 1-13.

Deffenbacher, J.L., & Stark, R.S. (1992). Relaxation and cognitive-relaxation treatments of general anger. *Journal of Counseling Psychology, 39*, 158-167.

Della Femina, D., Yaeger, D., & Lewis, D. (1990). Child abuse: Adolescent records vs. adult recall. *Child Abuse and Neglect, 14*, 227-231.

Derogatis, L.R. (1993). *Brief Symptom Inventory (BSI) Administration, Scoring, and Procedures Manual. (Third Edition)*. Minneapolis: National Computer Systems.

Deveson, A. (1991). *Tell Me I'm Here: One Family's Experience of Schizophrenia*. New York: Penguin.

Dixon, L.B., & Lehman, A.F. (1995). Family Interventions for schizophrenia. *Schizophrenia Bulletin, 21*, 631-643.

Dixon, L., McNary, S., & Lehman, A. (1995). Substance abuse and family relationships of persons with severe mental illness. *American Journal of Psychiatry, 152*, 456-458.

Dobson, K.S., & Craig, K.D. (Eds.) (1998). *Best Practice: Developing and Promoting Empirically Supported Interventions*. Newbury Park, CA: Sage.

Douglas, M. S. & Mueser, K. T. (1990). Teaching conflict resolution skills to the chronically mentally ill: Social skills training groups for briefly hospitalized patients. *Behavior Modification, 14,* 519–547.

Drake, R.E., & Burnette, M.F. (1998). Complications of severe mental illness related to alcohol and drug use disorders. In M. Galanter (Ed.), *Recent Developments in Alcoholism, Vol 14: The Consequences of Alcohol,* (pp. 285-299). New York: Plenum Press.

Drake, R.E., McHugo, G.J., Clark, R.E., Teague, G.B., Xie, H., Miles, K., Ackerson, T.H. (1998). Assertive community treatment for patients with co-occurring severe mental illness and substance use disorder: A clinical trial. *American Journal of Orthopsychiatry, 68,* 201-215.

Drake, R.E., Wallach, M.A., Teague, G.B., Freeman, D.H., Paskus, T.S., & Clark, T.A. (1991). Housing instability and homelessness among rural schizophrenic patients. *American Journal of Psychiatry, 148,* 330-336.

Drury, V., Birchwood, M., Cochrane, R. & MacMillan, F. (1996) Cognitive therapy and recovery from acute psychosis: A controlled trial: I. Impact on psychotic symptoms. *British Journal of Psychiatry, 169,* 593–601.

Drury, V., Birchwood, M., Cochrane, R. & MacMillan, F. (1996) Cognitive therapy and recovery from acute psychosis: A controlled trial: II. Impact on recovery time. *British Journal of Psychiatry, 169,* 602–607.

D'Zurilla, T.J., & Goldfried, M.R. (1971). Problem solving and behavior modification. *Journal of Abnormal Psychology, 78,* 107-126.

D'Zurilla, T.J., & Nezu, A.M. (1999). *Problem-Solving Therapy, (Second Edition): A Social Competence Approach to Clinical Intervention.* New York: Springer.

Eckman, T.A., Wirshing, W.C., Marder, S.R., Liberman, R.P., Johnston-Cronk, K., Zimmermann, K., & Mintz, J. (1992). Technique for training schizophrenic patients in illness self-management: A controlled trial. *American Journal of Psychiatry, 149,* 1549-1555.

Edwards, M.E., & Steinglass, P. (1995). Family therapy treatment outcomes for alcoholism. *Journal of Marital and Family Therapy, 21,* 475-509.

Eisen, J.L., Beer, D.A., Pato, M.T., Venditto, T.A., & Rasmussen, S.A. (1997). Obsessive-compulsive disorder in patients with schizophrenia or schizoaffective disorder. *American Journal of Psychiatry, 154,* 271-273.

El-Islam, M.F. (1989). Collaboration with families for the rehabilitation of schizophrenic patients and the concept of expressed emotion. *Acta Psychiatrica Scandinavica, 79,* 303-307.

Emmanuels-Zuurveen, L., & Emmelkamp, P.M.G. (1996). Individual behavioural-cognitive therapy v. marital therapy for depression in maritally distressed couples. *British Journal of Psychiatry, 169,* 181-188.

Emmanuels-Zuurveen, L., & Emmelkamp, P.M.G. (1997). Spouse-aided therapy with depressed patients. *Behavior Modification, 21,* 62-77.

Emmelkamp, P. M. G., & de Lange, I. (1983). Spouse involvement in the treatment of obsessive-compulsive patients. *Behavioural Research and Therapy, 21,* 341-346.

Emmelkamp, P.M.G., & Gerlsma, C. (1994). Marital functioning and anxiety disorders. *Behavior Therapy, 25,* 407-429.

Emmelkamp, P.M.G., van Dyck, R., Bitter, M., Heins, R., Onstein, E.J., & Eisen, B. (1992). Spouse-aided therapy with agoraphobics. *British Journal of Psychiatry, 160,* 51-56.

Fadden, G., Bebbington, P., & Kuipers, L. (1987). Caring and its burdens: A study of the spouses of depressed patients. *British Journal of Psychiatry, 151,* 660-667.

Falloon, I.R.H. (1988). *Handbook of Behavioral Family Therapy.* New York: Guilford.

Falloon, I.R.H. (1992). Early intervention for first episodes of schizophrenia: A preliminary exploration. *Psychiatry, 55,* 4-15.

Falloon, I.R.H., Boyd, J.L., & McGill, C.W. (1984). *Family Care of Schizophrenia: A Problem-Solving Approach to the Treatment of Mental Illness*. New York: Guilford.

Falloon, I.R.H., Boyd, J.L., McGill, C.W., Williamson, M., Razani, J., Moss, H.B., Gilderman, A.M., & Simpson, G.M. (1985). Family management in the prevention of morbidity of schizophrenia: Clinical outcome of a two year longitudinal study. *Archives of General Psychiatry, 42*, 887-896.

Falloon IRH, Held T, Coverdale JH, Roncone R & Laidlaw TM (1999) Psychosocial interventions for schizophrenia: A review of long-term benefits of international studies. *Psychiatric Rehabilitation Skills* (in press).

Falloon, I.R.H., Laporta, M., Fadden, G., & Graham-Hole, V. (1993). *Managing Stress in Families: Cognitive and Behavioural Strategies for Enhancing Coping Skills*. New York & London: Routledge.

Falloon, I.R.H., & Lillie, F.J. (1988). Behavioral family therapy: An overview. In I.R.H. Falloon (Ed.), *Handbook of Behavioral Family Therapy* (pp. 3-26). New York: Guilford.

Falloon, I.R.H., McGill, C.W., Boyd, J.L., & Pederson, J. (1987). Family management in the prevention of morbidity of schizophrenia: Social outcome of a two-year longitudinal study. *Psychological Medicine, 17*, 59-66.

Falloon, I.R.H., Mueser, K.T., Gingerich, S., Rapaport, S., McGill, C., & Hole, V. (1988). *Workbook for Behavioural Family Therapy*. Buckingham, England: Buckingham Mental Health Service.

Falloon, I.R.H., & Pederson, J. (1985). Family management in the prevention of morbidity of schizophrenia: The adjustment of the family unit. *British Journal of Psychiatry, 147*, 156-163.

Fals-Stewart, W., Birchler, G.R., & O'Farrell, T.J. (1996). Behavioral couples therapy for male substance-abusing patients: Effects on relationship adjustment and drug using behavior. *Journal of Consulting and Clinical Psychology, 64*, 959-972.

Farina, A. (1981). Are women nicer people than men? Sex and the stigma of mental disorders. *Clinical Psychology Review, 1*, 223-243.

Farina, A., Garmezy, N., & Barry, H., III. (1963). Relationship of marital status to incidence and prognosis of schizophrenia. *Journal of Abnormal and Social Psychology, 67*, 624-630.

Fawzy, F.I., Cousins, N., Fawzy, N.W., Kemeny, M.E., Elashoff, R., & Morton, D. (1990). A structured intervention for cancer patients: I. Changes over time in methods of coping and affective disturbance. *Archives of General Psychiatry, 47*, 720-725.

Fenton, W.S., Blyler, C.R., & Heinssen, R.K. (1997). Determinants of medication compliance in schizophrenia: Empirical and clinical findings. *Schizophrenia Bulletin, 23*, 637-651.

Fichter, M.M., Glynn, S.M., Weyer, S., Liberman, R.P., Frick, U. (1997). Family climate and expressed emotion in the course of alcoholism. *Family Process, 36*, 203-221.

Foa, E. (1995). *Posttraumatic Stress Disorder Scale*. Minneapolis: National Computer Systems.

Foa, E.B, Riggs, D. S., Dancu, C. V, & Rothbaum, B. O. (1993). Reliability and validity of a brief instrument for assessing post-traumatic stress disorder. *Journal of Traumatic Stress, 6*, 459–473.

Foa, E.B., & Rothbaum, B.O. (1998). *Treating the Trauma of Rape: Cognitive-Behavioral Therapy for PTSD*. New York: Guilford.

Fowler, D., Garety, P., & Kuipers, E. (1995). *Cognitive Behaviour Therapy for Psychosis: Theory and Practice*. Chichester, England, John Wiley & Sons.

Fowler, I.L., Carr, V.J., Carter, N.T., & Lewin, T.J. (1998). Patterns of current and lifetime substance use in schizophrenia. *Schizophrenia Bulletin, 24*, 443-455.

Foy, D.W. (1992). *Treating PTSD: Cognitive-Behavioral Strategies*. New York: Guilford.

Franks, D.D. (1990). Economic contribution of families caring for persons with severe and persistent mental illness. *Administration and Policy in Mental Health, 18*, 9-18.

Franks, P., Campbell, T.L., & Shields, C.G. (1992). Social relationships and health: The relative roles of family functioning and social support. *Social Science & Medicine, 34*, 779-788.

Fromm-Reichmann, F. (1947). Notes on the development of treatment of schizophrenics by psychoanalytic psychotherapy. *Psychiatry, 11*, 263-273.

Garavan, J., Browne, S. Gervin, M., Lane, A., Larkin, C., & O'Callaghan, E. (1998). Compliance with neuroleptic medication in outpatients with schizophrenia; relationship to subjective response to neuroleptics; attitudes to medication and insight. *Comprehensive Psychiatry, 39*, 215-219.

Gerber, K.E., & Nehemkis, A.M. (Eds.) (1986). *Compliance: The Dilemma of the Chronically Ill.* New York: Springer Publishing Company.

Gershon, E.S., Bunney, W.E., Leckman, J.F., Van Eerdewegh, M., & Debauche, B.A. (1976). The inheritance of affective disorders: A review of data and of hypotheses. *Behavioral Genetics, 6*, 227-261.

Gibbons, J.S., Horn, S.H., Powell, J.M., & Gibbons, J.L. (1984). Schizophrenic patients and their families: A survey in a psychiatric service based on a DGH Unit. *British Journal of Psychiatry, 144*, 70-77.

Glick, I., Clarkin, J., Spencer, J., Haas, G., Lewis, A., Peyser, J., DeMane, N., Good-Ellis, M., Harris, E., & Lestelle, V. (1985). A controlled evaluation of inpatient family intervention: I. Preliminary results of a six-month follow-up. *Archives of General Psychiatry, 42*, 882-886.

Glynn, S.M. (1993). Family-based treatment for major mental illness: A new role for psychologists. *The California Psychologist, 25*, 22-23.

Glynn, S.M. (1998). Psychopathology and social functioning in schizophrenia. In K.T. Mueser & N. Tarrier (Eds.), *Handbook of Social Functioning in Schizophrenia* (pp. 66-78). Boston: Allyn & Bacon.

Glynn, S.M., Eth, S., Randolph, E.T., Foy, D.W., Leong, G.B., Paz, G.G., Salk, J.D., Firman, G., & Katzman, J.W. (1995). Behavioral family therapy for Vietnam combat veterans with posttraumatic stress disorder. *Journal of Psychotherapy Practice and Research, 4*, 214-223.

Glynn, S.M., Eth, S., Randolph, E.T., Foy, D.W., Urbaitis, M., Boxer, L., Paz, G.G., Leong, G.B., Firman, G., Salk, J.D., Katzman, J.W., & Crothers, J. (in press). A test of behavioral family therapy to augment exposure for combat-related PTSD. *Journal of Consulting and Clinical Psychology.*

Glynn, S., Pugh, R., & Rose, G. (1993). Benefits of attendance at a state hospital family education workshop. *Psychosocial Rehabilitation Journal, 16*, 95-101.

Glynn, S., Randolph, E., Eth, S., Paz, G., Leong, G., Shaner, A., & Strachan, A. (1990). Patient psychopathology and expressed emotion in schizophrenia. *British Journal of Psychiatry, 157*, 877-880.

Goering, P.N., Lancee, W.J., & Freeman, S.J.J. (1992). Marital support and recovery from depression. *British Journal of Psychiatry, 160*, 76-82.

Goldman, H.H. (1984). The chronically mentally ill: Who are they? Where are they? In M. Mirabi (Ed.), *The Chronically Mentally Ill: Research and Services* (pp. 33-44). New York: Spectrum Publications.

Goldstein, A.J., & Chambless, D.L. (1978). A reanalysis of agoraphobia. *Behavior Therapy, 9*, 47-59.

Goldstein, J.M. (1988). Gender differences in the course of schizophrenia. *American Journal of Psychiatry, 145*, 684-689.

Goldstein, J.M., & Kreisman, D. (1988). Gender, family environment and schizophrenia. *Psychological Medicine, 18,* 861-872.

Goldstein, M., Rodnick, E., Evans, J., May, P., & Steinberg, M. (1978). Drug and family therapy in the aftercare of acute schizophrenics. *Archives of General Psychiatry, 35,* 1169-1177.

Goodman, L.A., Corcoran, C., Turner, K., Yuan, N., & Green, B.L. (1998). Assessing traumatic event exposure: General issues and preliminary findings for the Stressful Life Events Screening Questionnaire. *Journal of Traumatic Stress, 11,* 521-542.

Goodman, L.A., Rosenberg, S.D., Mueser, K.T., & Drake, R.E. (1997). Physical and sexual assault history in women with serious mental illness: Prevalence, impact, treatment, and future directions. *Schizophrenia Bulletin, 23,* 685-696.

Goodwin, F.K., & Jamison, K.R. (1990). *Manic Depressive Illness.* New York, NY: Oxford University Press.

Gottesman, I.I. (1991). *Schizophrenia Genesis: The Origins of Madness.* New York: W.H. Freeman and Company.

Gottesman, I.I., & Shields, J. (1972). *Schizophrenia and Genetics: A Twin Study Vantage Point.* London: Academic Press.

Graham, H.L. (1998). The role of dysfunctional beliefs in individuals who experience psychosis and use substances: Implications for cognitive therapy and medication adherence. *Behavioural and Cognitive Psychotherapy, 26,* 193-208.

Green, B.L. (1996). Trauma History Questionnaire. In B.H. Stamm (Ed.), *Measurement of Stress, Self-Report Trauma, and Adaptation* (pp. 366-368). Lutherville, MD: Sidran Press.

Greenberg, J.S., Greenley, J.R., & Benedict P. (1994). Contributions of persons with serious mental illness to their families. *Hospital and Community Psychiatry, 45,* 475-480.

Greenley, J.R. (1986). Social control and expressed emotion. *Journal of Nervous and Mental Disease, 174,* 24-30.

Grob, G.N. (1994). *The Mad Among Us: A History of the Care of America's Mentally Ill.* Cambridge, MA: Harvard University Press.

Haas, G., Glick, I., Clarkin, J., Spencer, J., Lewis, A., Peyser, J., DeMane, N., Good-Ellis, M., Harris, E., & Lestelle, V. (1988). Inpatient family intervention: A randomized clinical trial: II. Results at hospital discharge. *Archives of General Psychiatry, 48,* 217-224.

Haas, G.L., & Garratt, L.S. (1998). Gender differences in social functioning. In K.T. Mueser & N. Tarrier (Eds.), *Handbook of Social Functioning in Schizophrenia* (pp. 149-180). Boston: Allyn & Bacon.

Hafner, R.J. (1986). *Marriage & Mental Illness: A Sex Roles Perspective.* New York: Guilford.

Häfner, H., & an der Heiden, W. (1989). Effectiveness and cost of community care for schizophrenic patients. *Hospital and Community Psychiatry, 40,* 59-63.

Hahlweg, K., Goldstein, M.J., Nuechterlein, K.H., Magana, A.B., Mintz, J., Doane, J.A., Miklowitz, D.J., & Snyder, K.S. (1989). Expressed emotion and patient-relative interaction in families of recent onset schizophrenics. *Journal of Consulting and Clinical Psychology, 57,* 11-18.

Hahlweg, K., Wiedemann, G., Müller, U., Feinstein, E., Hank, G., & Dose, M. (1994). Effectiveness of behavioral family management in combination with standard dose or targeted medication to prevent relapse in schizophrenia. Manuscript.

Hand, I., Angenendt, J., Fischer, M., and Wilke, C. (1986). Exposure in-vivo with panic management for agoraphobia: Treatment rationale and longterm outcome. In I. Hand & H.-U. Wittchen (Eds.), *Panic and Phobias: Empirical Evidence of Theoretical Models and Long-term Effects of Behavioral Treatments* (pp. 104-127). Berlin: Springer-Verlag.

Hatfield, A.B. (1990). *Family Education in Mental Illness.* New York: The Guilford Press.

Harding, C.M., & Keller, A.B. (1998). Long-term outcome of social functioning. In K.T. Mueser & N. Tarrier (Eds.), *Handbook of Social Functioning in Schizophrenia* (pp. 134-148). Boston: Allyn & Bacon.

Hatfield, A.B. (1978). Psychological costs of schizophrenia to the family. *Social Work, 23,* 355-359.

Hatfield, A.B. (1987). Social support and family coping. In A.B. Hatfield & H.P. Lefley (Eds.), *Families of the Mentally Ill: Coping and Adaptation* (pp. 191-207). New York: Guilford.

Hatfield, A.B. (1990). *Family Education in Mental Illness.* New York: Guilford.

Hatfield, A.B., & Lefley, H.P. (Eds.) (1987). *Families of the Mentally Ill: Coping and Adaptation.* New York: Guilford.

Hatfield, A.B., & Lefley, H.P. (Eds.) (1993). *Surviving Mental Illness: Stress, Coping, and Adaptation.* New York: Guilford.

Hatfield, A.B., Spanoil, L., & Zipple, A.M. (1987). Expressed emotion: A family perspective. *Schizophrenia Bulletin, 13,* 221-235.

Hersen, M., & Bellack, A.S. (1977). Assessment of social skills. In A.R. Ciminero, K.S. Calhoun, & Adams, H.E. (Eds.), *Handbook of Behavioral Assessment* (pp. 509-554). New York: Wiley and Sons.

Hersen, M., & Bellack, A.S. (Eds.) (1988). *Dictionary of Behavioral Assessment Techniques.* New York: Pergamon.

Hodgins, S., Mednick, S.A., Brennan, P.A., Schulsinger, F., & Engberg, M. (1996). Mental disorder and crime. *Archives of General Psychiatry, 53,* 489-496.

Hodgson, R.J., & Rachman, S. (1977). Obsessional-compulsive complaints. *Behaviour Research and Therapy, 15,* 389-395.

Hoenig, J., & Hamilton, M. (1966). The schizophrenic patient in the community and his effect on the household. *International Journal of Social Psychiatry, 12, 105-176.*

Hogarty, G.E., Anderson, C., Reiss, D., Kornblith, S., Greenwald, D., Ulrich, R., & Carter, M. (1991). Family psychoeducation, social skills training, and maintenance chemotherapy in the aftercare treatment of schizophrenia: II. Two year effects of a controlled study on relapse and adjustment. *Archives of General Psychiatry, 48,* 340-347.

Hooley, J.M. (1986). Expressed emotion and depression: Interactions between patients and high vs. low expressed emotion spouses. *Journal of Abnormal Psychology, 95,* 237-246.

Hooley, J.M., Richters, J.E. Weintraub, S., & Neale, J.M. (1987). Psychopathology and marital distress: The positive side of positive symptoms. *Journal of Abnormal Psychology, 96,* 27-33.

Hooley, J., & Teasdale, J.D. (1989). Predictors of relapse in unipolar depression: Expressed emotion, marital quality, and perceived criticism. *Journal of Abnormal Psychology, 98,* 229-235.

Horowitz, M., Wilner, N., & Alvarez, W. (1979). Impact of Event Scale: A measure of subjective stress. *Psychosomatic Medicine, 41,* 209-218.

Hoult, J., & Reynolds, I. (1984). Schizophrenia: A comparative trial of community-oriented and hospital-oriented psychiatric care. *Acta Psychiatrica Scandinavica, 69,* 359.

Isen, A.M., Daubman, K.A., & Nowicki, G.P. (1987). Positive affect facilitates creative problem solving. *Journal of Personality and Social Psychology, 52,* 1122-1131.

Jackson, H.J., Smith, N., & McGorry, P. (1990). Relationship between expressed emotion and family burden in psychotic disorders: An exploratory study. *Acta Psychiatrica Scandinavica, 82,* 243-249.

Jacob, M., Frank, E., Kupfer, D.J., & Carpenter, L.L. (1987). Recurrent depression: An assessment of family burden and family attitudes. *Journal of Clinical Psychiatry, 48,* 395-400.

Jacobson, A. (1989). Physical and sexual assault histories among psychiatric outpatients. *American Journal of Psychiatry, 146,* 755-758.

Jacobson, A., & Richardson, B. (1987). Assault experiences of 100 psychiatric inpatients: Evidence of the need for routine inquiry. *American Journal of Psychiatry, 144,* 508-513.

Jacobson, N.E., & Addis, M.E. (1993). Research on couples and couple therapy: What do we know? Where are we going? *Journal of Consulting and Clinical Psychology, 61,* 85-93.

Jacobson, N.E., Dobson, K., Fruzzetti, A.E., Schmaling, K.B., & Salusky, S. (1991). Marital therapy as a treatment for depression. *Journal of Consulting and Clinical Psychology, 59,* 547-557.

Jacobson, N.E., Holtzworth-Munroe, A., & Schmaling, K.B. (1989). Marital therapy and spouse involvement in the treatment of depression, agoraphobia, and alcoholism. *Journal of Consulting and Clinical Psychology, 57,* 5-10.

Jacobson, N.S., Fruzzetti, A.E., Dobson, K., Whisman, M., & Hops, H. (1993). Couples therapy as a treatment for depression II: The effects of relationship quality and therapy on depressive relapse. *Journal of Consulting and Clinical Psychology, 61,* 516-519.

Jacobson, N.S., & Margolin, G. (1979). *Marital Therapy: Strategies Based on Social Learning and Behavior Exchange Principles.* New York: Brunner/Mazel.

Jacobson, N.S., Schmaling, K.B., Holtzworth-Munroe, A., Katt, J.L., Wood, L.F., & Follette, V.M. (1988). Research-structured vs. clinically flexible versions of social learning-based marital therapy. *Behavior Research Therapy, 27,* 173-180.

Johnson, A.B. (1990). *Out of Bedlam: Myths of Deinstitutionalization.* New York: Basic Books.

Johnson, D.L. (1990). The family's experience of living with mental illness. In H.P. Lefley, & D.L. Johnson (Eds.), *Families as Allies in Treatment of the Mentally Ill: New Directions for Mental Health Professionals* (pp. 31-64). Washington, DC: American Psychiatric Press.

Jones, S.L., Roth, D., & Jones, P.K. (1995). Effect of demographic and behavioral variables on burden of caregivers of chronic mentally ill persons. *Psychiatric Services, 46,* 141-145.

Jordan, B.K., Schlenger, W.E., Fairbank, J.A., & Caddell, J.M. (1996). Prevalence of psychiatric disorders among incarcerated women: II. Convicted felons entering prison. *Archives of General Psychiatry, 53,* 513-519.

Judge, K. (1994). Serving children, siblings, and spouses: Understanding the needs of other family members. In H.P. Lefley & M. Wasow (Eds.), *Helping Families Cope with Mental Illness* (pp. 161-194). Newark, NJ: Harwood Academic.

Kahn, J., Coyne, J.C., & Margolin, G. (1985). Depression and marital disagreement: The social construction of despair. *Journal of Social and Personal Relationships, 2,* 447-461.

Kane, J.M. (1990). Psychopharmacologic treatment of schizophrenia. In A. Kales, C.N. Stefanis, & J. Talbott (Eds.), *Recent Advances in Schizophrenia* (pp. 257-276). New York: Springer-Verlag.

Kanter, J., Lamb, H.R., & Loeper, C. (1987). Expressed emotion in families: A critical review. *Hospital and Community Psychiatry, 38,* 374-380.

Keane, T.M., Malloy, P.F., & Fairbank, J.A. (1984). Empirical development of an MMPI subscale for the assessment of combat related post-traumatic stress disorder. *Journal of Consulting and Clinical Psychology, 52,* 888-891.

Keane, T.M., Zimering, R.T., & Caddell, J.M. (1985). A behavioral formulation of posttraumatic stress disorder in Vietnam veterans. *The Behavior Therapist, 8,* 9-12.

Kessler, R.C., McGonagle, K.A., Zhao, S., Nelson, C.B., Hughes, M., Eshleman, S., Wittchen, H.-U., & Kendler, K.S. (1994). Lifetime and 12-month prevalence of DSM-III-R psychiatric disorders in the United States. *Archives of General Psychiatry, 51,* 8-19.

Kessler, R.C., Rubinow, D.R., Holmes, C., Abelson, J.M., & Zhao, S. (1997). The epidemiology of DSM-III-R bipolar I disorder in a general population survey. *Psychological Medicine, 27,* 1079-1089.

Kessler, R.C., Sonnega, A., Bromet, E., Hughes, M., & Nelson, C.B. (1995). Posttraumatic stress disorder in the national comorbidity survey. *Archives of General Psychiatry, 52,* 1048-1060.

Kingdon, D.G., & Turkington, D. (1994). *Cognitive-Behavioral Therapy of Schizophrenia.* New York: Guilford.

Kirk, S.A., & Therrien, M.E. (1975). Community mental health myths and the fate of former hospitalized patients. *Psychiatry, 38,* 209-217.

Klein, D.F., & Wender, P.H. (1993). *Understanding Depression: A Complete Guide to its Diagnosis and Treatment.* New York: Oxford University Press.

Köttgen, C., Sönnichsen, I., Mollenhauer, K., & Jurth, R. (1984). Group therapy with the families of schizophrenic patients: Results of the Hamburg Camberwell-Family Interview study III. *International Journal of Family Psychiatry, 5,* 84-94.

Kuipers, E., Garety, P., Fowler, D., Dunn, G., Bebbington, P., Freeman, D., & Hadley, C. (1997). London-East Anglia randomised controlled trial of cognitive-behavioural therapy for psychosis: I. Effects of the treatment phase. *British Journal of Psychiatry, 171,* 319-327.

Kuipers, L., Leff, J., & Lam, D. (1992). *Family Work for Schizophrenia: A Practical Guide.* London: Gaskell.

Lam, D.H. (1991). Psychosocial family intervention in schizophrenia: A review of empirical studies. *Psychological Medicine, 21,* 423-441.

Lamb, H.R. (1990). Continuing problems between mental health professionals and families of the mentally ill. In H.P. Lefley & D.L. Johnson (Eds.), *Families as Allies in Treatment of the Mentally Ill: New Directions for Mental Health Professionals* (pp.23-30). Washington, D.C.: American Psychiatric Press.

Lamb, H.R., & Weinberger, L.E. (1998). Persons with severe mental illness in jails and prisons: A review. *Psychiatric Services, 49,* 483-492.

Lazarus, R.S. (1966). *Psychological Stress and the Coping Process.* New York: McGraw-Hill.

Lazarus, R.S. (1991). *Emotion and Adaptation.* New York: Oxford University Press.

Lazarus, R.S., & Folkman, S. (1984). *Stress, Appraisal and Coping.* New York: Springer.

Leff J.P., Berkowitz R., Shavit N., Strachan A., Glass I., & Vaughn C. (1990). A trial of family therapy versus a relatives' group for schizophrenia. Two-year follow-up. *British Journal of Psychiatry, 157,* 571-577.

Leff, J., & Vaughn, C. (1985). *Expressed Emotion in Families: Its Significance for Mental Illness.* New York: Guilford.

Leff, J., Kuipers, L., Berkowitz, R., Eberlein-Vries, R. & Sturgeon, D. (1982). A controlled trial of social intervention in the families of schizophrenic patients. *British Journal of Psychiatry, 141,* 121-134.

Leff, J.P., Kuipers, L., Berkowitz, R., & Sturgeon, D. (1985). A controlled trial of social intervention in the families of schizophrenia patients: Two-year follow-up. *British Journal of Psychiatry, 146,* 594-600.

Lefley, H.P. (1987). The family's response to mental illness in a relative. In A.B. Hatfield (Ed.), *Families of the Mentally Ill: Meeting the Challenges.* New Directions for Mental Health Services, 34 (pp. 3-21). San Francisco: Jossey-Bass.

Lefley, H.P. (1996). *Family Caregiving in Mental Illness.* Thousand Oaks, CA: Sage.

Lefley, H.P., & Johnson, D.L. (Eds.) (1990). *Families as Allies in Treatment of the Mentally Ill: New Directions for Mental Health Professionals.* Washington, DC: American Psychiatric Press.

Lehman, A.F., & Steinwachs, D.M. (1998). At issue: Translating research into practice: The Schizophrenia Patient Outcomes Research Team (PORT) treatment recommendations. *Schizophrenia Bulletin, 24,* 1-10.

Lester, G.W., Beckham, E., & Baucom, D.H. (1980). Implementation of behavioral marital therapy. *Journal of Marital and Family Therapy, April*, 189-199.

Liberman, R.P. (1970) Behavioral approaches to family and couple therapy. *American Journal of Orthopsychiatry, 40*, 106-118.

Liberman, R.P., DeRisi, W.R., & Mueser, K. (1989). *Social Skills Training for Psychiatric Patients*. Boston: Allyn & Bacon.

Liberman, R.P., Wheeler, E.G., deVisser, L.A.J.M., Kuehnel, J., & Kuehnel, T. (1980). *Handbook of Marital Therapy: A Positive Approach to Helping Troubled Relationships*. New York: Plenum Press.

Lin, N., Dean, A., & Ensel, W. (1986). *Social Support, Life Events, and Depression*. Orlando, FL: Academic Press.

Linszen, D., Dingemans, P., Van der Does, Nugter, A., Scholte, P., Lenior, R., & Goldstein, M.J. (1996). Treatment, expressed emotion and relapse in recent onset schizophrenic disorders. *Psychological Medicine, 26*, 333-342.

MacDonald, E.M., Pica, S., McDonald, S., Hayes, R.L., & Baglioni, A.J. Jr. (1998). Stress and coping in early psychosis: Role of symptoms, self-efficacy, and social support in coping with stress. *British Journal of Psychiatry, 172 Suppl 33*, 122-127.

Marks, I., Lovell, K., Noshirvani, H., Livanou, M., & Thrasher, S. (1998). Treatment of posttraumatic stress disorder by exposure and/or cognitive restructuring. *Archives of General Psychiatry, 55*, 317-325.

Marks, I.M., & Mathews, A.M. (1979). Brief standard self-rating for phobic patients. *Behaviour Research and Therapy, 17*, 263-267.

Marsh, D.T. (1992). *Families and Mental Illness: New Directions in Professional Practice*. New York: Greenwood Publishing Group.

Marsh, D.T. (1998). *Serious Mental Illness and the Family: The Practitioner's Guide*. New York: John Wiley & Sons.

Marsh, D.T., & Dickens, R.M. (1997). *Troubled Journey: Coming to Terms with the Mental Illness of a Sibling or a Parent*. New York: Tarcher/Putnam.

Marsh, D.T., & Magee, R.D.(Eds.) (1997). *Ethical and Legal Issues in Professional Practice with Families*. New York: John Wiley & Sons.

Massie, H.N., & Beels, C.C. (1972). The outcome of the family treatment of schizophrenia. *Schizophrenia Bulletin, 6*, 24-36.

Matsakis, A. (1996). *I Can't Get Over It: A Handbook for Trauma Survivors (Second Edition)*. Oakland, CA: New Harbinger.

Mayfield, D., McLeod, G., & Hall, P. (1974). The CAGE questionnaire: Validation of a new alcoholism screening questionnaire. *American Journal of Psychiatry, 131*, 1121-1123.

McCrady, B.S., Noel, N.E., Abrams, D.B., Stout, R.L., Nelson, H.F., & Hay, W.M. (1986). Comparative effectiveness of three types of spouse involvement in outpatient behavioral alcoholism treatment. *Journal of Studies on Alcohol, 47*, 459-467.

McCrady, B.S., Stout, R., Noel, N., Abrams, D., & Nelson, H. (1991). Effectiveness of three types of spouse-involved behavioral alcoholism treatment. *British Journal of Addiction, 86*, 1415-1424.

McElroy, E.M. (1987). The beat of a different drummer. In A.B. Hatfield & H.P. Lefley (Eds.), *Families of the Mentally Ill: Coping and Adaptation* (pp. 225-243). New York: Guilford.

McFarlane, W.R. (1990). Multiple family groups and the treatment of schizophrenia. In M.I. Herz, S.J. Keith, & J.P. Docherty (Eds.), *Handbook of Schizophrenia, Volume 4: Psychosocial Treatment of Schizophrenia* (pp. 167-189). Amsterdam, Netherlands: Elsevier Science Publishers.

McFarlane, W.R., Dunne, E., Lukens, E., Newmark, M., McLaughlin-Toran, J., Deakins, S., & Horen, B. (1993). From research to clinical practice: Dissemination of New York State's Family Psychoeducation Project. *Hospital & Community Psychiatry, 44,* 265-270.

McFarlane, W.R., Link, B., Dushay, R., Marchal, J., & Crilly, J. (1995). Psychoeducational multiple family groups: Four-year relapse outcome in schizophrenia. *Family Process, 34,* 127-144.

McFarlane, W.R., Lukens, E., Link, B., Dushay, R., Deakins, S.A., Newmark, M., Dunne, E.J., Horen, B., & Toran, J. (1995). Multiple-family groups and psychoeducation in the treatment of schizophrenia. *Archives of General Psychiatry, 52,* 679-687.

McGoldrick, M. (Ed.) (1998). *Revisioning Family Therapy.* New York: Guilford.

McGoldrick, M., Giordano, J., & Pearce, J. (Eds.) (1996). *Ethnicity and Family Therapy (Second Edition).* New York: Guilford.

McGorry, P.D., Chanen, A., McCarthy, E., Van Riel, R., McKenzie, D., & Singh, B.S. (1991). Posttraumatic stress disorder following recent-onset psychosis: An unrecognized postpsychotic syndrome. *Journal of Nervous and Mental Disease, 179,* 253-258.

Mehta, M. (1990). A comparative study of family-based and patient-based behavioral management in obsessive-compulsive disorder. *British Journal of Psychiatry, 157,* 133-135.

Meltzer, H.Y. (Ed.) (1987). *Psychopharmacology: The Third Generation of Progress.* New York: Raven Press.

Merikangas, K.R. (1984). Divorce and assortative mating among depressed patients. *American Journal of Psychiatry, 141,* 74-76.

Miklowitz, D.J. (1998). *Family-focused intervention for patients with bipolar disorders.* Presented at VI World Congress, World Association of Psychosocial Rehabilitation, Hamburg, Germany.

Miklowitz, D.J., & Goldstein, M.J. (1990). Behavioral family treatment for patients with bipolar affective disorder. *Behavior Modification, 14,* 457-489.

Miklowitz, D.J., & Goldstein, M.J. (1997). *Bipolar Disorder: A Family-Focused Treatment Approach.* New York: Guilford.

Miklowitz, D.J., Goldstein, M.J., Falloon, I.R.H., & Doane, J.A. (1984). Interactional correlates of expressed emotion in the families of schizophrenics. *British Journal of Psychiatry, 144,* 482-487.

Miller, F., Dworkin, J., Ward, M., & Barone, D. (1990). A preliminary study of unresolved grief in families of seriously mentally ill patients. *Hospital and Community Psychiatry, 41,* 1321-1325.

Miller, F.E. (1996). Grief therapy for relatives of persons with serious mental illness. *Psychiatric Services, 47633-637.*

Miller, W.R., & Rollnick, S. (1991). *Motivational Interviewing: Preparing People to Change Addictive Behavior.* New York: Guilford.

Mills, P.D., & Hansen, J.C. (1991). Short-term group interventions for mentally ill young adults living in a community residence and their families. *Hospital and Community Psychiatry, 42,* 1144-1149.

Mineka, S., Cook, M., & Miller, S. (1984). Fear conditioned with escapable and inescapable shock: Effects of a feedback stimulus. *Journal of Experimental Psychology: Animal Behavior Processes, 10,* 307-323.

Mintz, L.I., Liberman, R.P., Miklowitz, D.J., & Mintz, J. (1987). Expressed emotion: A call for partnership among relatives, patients, and professionals. *Schizophrenia Bulletin, 13,* 227-235.

Minuchin, S. (1974). *Families & Family Therapy.* Cambridge, MA: Harvard University Press.

Moncrieff, J. (1995). Lithium revisited: A re-examination of the placebo-controlled trials of lithium prophylaxis in manic-depressive disorder. *British Journal of Psychiatry, 167,* 569-574.

Monti, P.M.N., Abrams, D.B., Binkoff, J.A., Zwick, W.R., Liepman, M. R., Nirenberg, T.D., & Rohsenhow, D.J. (1990). Communication skills training, communication skills training with family and cognitive behavioral mood management training for alcoholics. *Journal of Studies on Alcohol, 51,* 263-270.

Moorman, M. (1992). *My Sister's Keeper.* New York: W.W. Norton.

Mors, O., Sorensen, L.V., & Therkildsen, M.L. (1992). Distress in the relatives of psychiatric patients admitted for the first time. *Acta Psychiatrica Scandinavica, 85,* 337-344.

Mueser, K.T. (1996). Helping families manage severe mental illness. *Psychiatric Rehabilitation Skills, 1,* 21-42.

Mueser, K.T. (1998). Social skill and problem solving. In A.S. Bellack & M. Hersen (Eds.), *Comprehensive Clinical Psychology (Vol. 6).* (pp. 183-201). New York: Pergamon.

Mueser, K.T., & Berenbaum, H. (1990). Psychodynamic treatment of schizophrenia: Is there a future? *Psychological Medicine, 20,* 253-262.

Mueser, K.T., & Gingerich, S.L. (1994). *Coping with Schizophrenia: A Guide for Families.* Oakland, CA: New Harbinger Publications.

Mueser, K.T., & Glynn, S. (1988). Behavioral family therapy for schizophrenia: The first educational session. *Social and Behavioral Sciences Documents, 18,* no. 2859.

Mueser, K.T., & Glynn, S.M. (1998). Family intervention for schizophrenia. In K.S. Dobson & K.D. Craig (Eds.), *Best Practice: Developing and Promoting Empirically Supported Interventions.* (pp. 157-186). Newbury Park, CA: Sage.

Mueser, K.T., & Noordsy, D.L. (1996). Group treatment for dually diagnosed clients. In R.E. Drake & K.T. Mueser (Eds.), *Dual Diagnosis of Major Mental Illness and Substance Abuse Disorder II: Recent Research and Clinical Implications. New Directions in Mental Health Services, 70.* (pp. 33-51). San Francisco: Jossey-Bass.

Mueser, K.T., Bellack, A.S., Morrison, R.L., & Wade, J.H. (1990). Gender, social competence, and symptomatology in schizophrenia. *Journal of Abnormal Psychology, 99,* 138-147.

Mueser, K.T., Bellack, A.S., Wade, J.H., Sayers, S.L., & Rosenthal, C.K. (1992). An assessment of the educational needs of chronic psychiatric patients and their relatives. *British Journal of Psychiatry, 160,* 674-680.

Mueser, K.T., Bellack, A.S., Wade, J.H., Sayers, S.L., Tierney, A., & Haas, G. (1993). Expressed emotion, social skill, and response to negative affect in schizophrenia. *Journal of Abnormal Psychology, 102,* 339-351.

Mueser, K.T., Bennett, M., & Kushner, M.G. (1995). Epidemiology of substance use disorders among persons with chronic mental illnesses. In A. Lehman & L. Dixon (Eds.), *Double Jeopardy: Chronic Mental Illness and Substance Abuse.* (pp. 9-25). Chur, Switzerland: Harwood Academic Publishers.

Mueser, K.T., Bond, G.R., Drake, R.E., & Resick, S.G. (1998). Models of community care for severe mental illness: A review of research on case management. *Schizophrenia Bulletin, 24,* 37-74.

Mueser, K.T., Douglas, M.S., Bellack, A.S., & Morrison, R.L. (1991). Assessment of enduring deficit and negative symptom subtypes in schizophrenia. *Schizophrenia Bulletin, 17,* 565-582.

Mueser, K.T., Drake, R.E., & Noordsy, D.L. (1998). Integrated mental health and substance abuse treatment for severe psychiatric disorders. *Practical Psychiatry and Behavioral Health, 4,* 129-139.

Mueser, K.T., Drake, R.E., & Wallach, M.A. (1998). Dual diagnosis: A review of etiological theories. *Addictive Behaviors, 23,* 717-734.

Mueser, K.T., Goodman, L.B., Trumbetta, S.L., Rosenberg, S.D., Osher, F.C., Vidaver, R., Auciello, P., & Foy, D.W. (1998). Trauma and posttraumatic stress disorder in severe mental illness. *Journal of Consulting and Clinical Psychology, 66,* 493-499.

Mueser, K.T., Yarnold, P.R., Rosenberg, S.D., Swett, C., Jr., Miles, K.M., & Hill, D. (in press). Substance use disorder in hospitalized severely mentally ill psychiatric patients: Prevalence, correlates, and subgroups. *Schizophrenia Bulletin.*

Mullen, P.E. (1992). Criminality, dangerousness and schizophrenia. In D.J. Kavanagh (Ed.), *Schizophrenia: An Overview and Practical Handbook* (pp. 145-158). London: Chapman & Hall.

Neidig, P.H., & Friedman, D.H. (1984). *Spouse Abuse: A Treatment Program for Couples.* Champaign, IL: The Research Press Company.

Nezu, A. M., Nezu, C. M., & Perri, M.G. (1990). Psychotherapy for adults within a problem-solving framework: Focus on depression. *Journal of Cognitive Psychotherapy, 4,* 247–256.

Noh, S., & Avison, W.R. (1988). Spouses of discharged psychiatric patients: Factors associated with their experience of burden. *Journal of Marriage and the Family, 50,* 377-389.

Noordsy, D.L., Drake, R.E., Teague, G.B., Osher, F.C., Hurlbut, S.C., Beaudett, M.S., & Paskus, T.S. (1991). Subjective experiences related to alcohol use among schizophrenics. *The Journal of Nervous and Mental Disease, 179,* 410-414.

Noordsy, D.L., Schwab, B., Fox, L., & Drake, R.E. (1996). The role of self-help programs in the rehabilitation of persons with severe mental illness and substance use disorders. *Community Mental Health Journal, 32,* 71-81.

Novaco, R.W. (1975). *Anger Control: the Development and Evaluation of an Experimental Treatment.* Lexington, Lexington, MA.

Nuechterlein, K.H., & Dawson, M.E. (1984). A heuristic vulnerability/stress model of schizophrenic episodes. *Schizophrenia Bulletin, 10,* 300-312.

Nuechterlein, K.H., & Dawson, M.E. (1984). Vulnerability and stress factors in the developmental course of schizophrenic disorders. *Schizophrenia Bulletin, 10,* 158–159.

O'Farrell,T.J., Chouquette, K.A., Cutter, H.S.G., Brown, E.D., & McCourt, W. (1993). Behavioral marital therapy with and without additional couples relapse prevention session for alcoholics and their wives. *Journal of Studies on Alcohol, 54,* 652-666.

O'Farrell, T.J., Cutter, H.S.G., Chouquette, K.S., Floyd, F.J., & Bayog, R.D. (1992). Behavioral marital therapy for male alcoholics: Marital and drinking adjustment during the two years after treatment. *Behavior Therapy, 23,* 529-549.

O'Farrell, T.J., Cutter, H.S., & Floyd, F.J. (1985). Evaluating behavioral marital therapy for male alcoholics: Effects on marital adjustment and communication from before to after treatment. *Behavior Therapy, 16,* 147-167.

O'Leary, K.D., & Beach, S.R.H. (1990). Marital therapy: A viable treatment for depression and marital discord. *American Journal of Psychiatry, 147,* 183-186.

Oldridge, M.L., & Hughes, I.C.T. (1992). Psychological well-being in families with a member suffering from schizophrenia. *British Journal of Psychiatry, 161,* 249-251.

Osher, F.C., & Kofoed, L.L. (1989). Treatment of patients with psychiatric and psychoactive substance abuse disorders. *Hospital and Community Psychiatry, 40,* 1025-1030.

Passamanick, B., Scarpitti, F.R., & Dinitz, S. (1967). *Schizophrenics in the Community.* New York: Appleton-Century-Crofts.

Patterson, G.R. (1971). *Families: Applications of Social Learning to Family Life.* Champaign, IL: Research Press.

Patterson, G.R., McNeal, S., Hawkins, N., & Phelps, R. (1967). Reprogramming the social environment. *Journal of Child Psychology and Psychiatry, 8*, 181-195.

Pearlin, L.I. (1983). Role strains and personal stress. In H.B. Kaplan (Ed.), *Psychosocial Stress: Trends in Theory and Research* (pp. 3-32). New York: Academic Press.

Pence, E., & Paymar, M. (1986). *Power and Control: Tactics of Men Who Batter. An Educational Curriculum.* Duluth, MN: Minnesota Program Development, Inc.

Penn, D.L., Hope, D.A., Spaulding, W., & Kucera, J. (1994). Social anxiety in schizophrenia. *Schizophrenia Research, 11*, 277-284.

Penn, D.L., Spaulding, W., Reed, D., Sullivan, M., Mueser, K.T., & Hope, D.A. (1997). Cognition and social functioning in schizophrenia. *Psychiatry: Interpersonal and Biological Processes, 60*, 281-291.

Pickett, S.A., Cook, J.A., Cohler, B.J., & Solomon, M.L. (1997). Positive parent/adult child relationships: Impact of severe mental illness and caregiving burden. *American Journal of Orthopsychiatry, 67*, 220-230.

Platt, S., Weyman, A., Hirsch, S., & Hewett, S. (1980). The Social Behaviour Assessment Schedule (SBAS): Rationale, contents, scoring and reliability of a new interview schedule. *Social Psychiatry, 15*, 43-55.

Posner, C.M., Wilson, K.G., Kral, M.J., Lander, S., & McIlwraith, R.D. (1992). Family psychoeducational support groups in schizophrenia. *American Journal of Orthopsychiatry, 62*, 206-218.

Potasznik, H., & Nelson, G. (1984). Stress and social support: The burden experienced by the family of a mentally ill person. *American Journal of Community Psychiatry, 12*, 589-607.

Prince, S.E., & Jacobson, N.S. (1995). A review and evaluation of marital and family therapies for affective disorders. *Journal of Marital and Family Therapy, 21*, 377-401.

Provencher, H.L., & Mueser, K.T. (1997). Positive and negative symptom behaviors and caregiver burden in the relatives of persons with schizophrenia. *Schizophrenia Research, 26*, 71-80.

Radloff, L.S., & Locke, B.Z. (1986). The Community Health Assessment Survey and the CES-D Scale. In M. Weissman, J. Meyers, & C. Ross (Eds.), *Community Surveys.* New Brunswick, NJ: Rutgers University Press.

Raj, L., Kulhara, P., & Avasthi, A. (1991). Social burden of positive and negative schizophrenia. *International Journal of Social Psychiatry, 37*, 242-250.

Randolph, E.T., Eth, S., Glynn, S., Paz, G.B., Leong, G.B., Shaner, A.L., Strachan, A., Van Vort, W., Escobar, J., & Liberman, R.P. (1994). Behavioural family management in schizophrenia: Outcome from a clinic-based intervention. *British Journal of Psychiatry, 144*, 501-506.

Randolph, E.T., Glynn, S.M., Eth, S., Paz, G.G., Leong, G.B., & Shaner, A.L. (1995). Family therapy for schizophrenia: Two year outcome. Paper presented at the Annual Meeting of American Psychiatric Association, Miami.

Rea, M.M., Goldstein, M.J., Tompson, M.C., & Miklowitz, D.J. (1998). Family and individual therapy in bipolar disorders: Outline and first results of the study. Presented at VI World Congress, World Association of Psychosocial Rehabilitation, Hamburg, Germany.

Regier, D.A., Farmer, M.E., Rae, D.S., Locke, B.Z., Keith, S.J., Judd, L.J., & Goodwin, F.K. (1990). Comorbidity of mental disorders with alcohol and other drug abuse: Results from the Epidemiologic Catchment Area (ECA) study. *Journal of the American Medical Association, 264*, 2511-2518.

Reinhard, S.C. (1994). Living with mental illness: Effects of professional contacts and personal control on caregiver burden. *Research in Nursing and Health, 17*, 79-88.

Riggs, D.S., & Foa, E.B. (1993). Obsessive compulsive disorder. In D.H. Barlow (Ed.), *Clinical Handbook of Psychological Disorders (2nd ed.)* (pp. 189-239). New York: Guilford.

Robin, A.L., & Foster, S.L. (1989). *Negotiating Parent-Adolescent Conflict: A Behavioral-Family Systems Approach.* New York: Guilford.

Robins, L.N., & Regier, D.A. (Eds.) (1991). *Psychiatric Disorders in America: The Epidemiologic Catchment Area Study.* New York: Free Press.

Robinson, E.A.R. (1996). Causal attributions about mental illness: Relationship to family functioning. *American Journal of Orthopsychiatry, 66,* 282-295.

Rosenberg, S.D., Drake, R.E., Wolford, G.L., Mueser, K.T., Oxman, T.E., Vidaver, R.M., Carrieri, K.L., & Luckoor, R. (1998). The Dartmouth Assessment of Lifestyle Instrument (DALI): A substance use disorder screen for people with severe mental illness. *American Journal of Psychiatry, 155,* 232-238.

Rosenheck, R., Leda, C., Frisman, L., & Gallup, P. (1997). Homeless mentally ill veterans: Race, service use, and treatment outcomes. *American Journal of Orthopsychiatry, 67,* 632-638.

Rosenthal, D. (1970). *Genetic Theory and Abnormal Behavior.* New York: McGraw-Hill.

Rosenthal, D., & Kety, S.S. (Eds.) (1968). *The Transmission of Schizophrenia: Proceedings of the Second Research Conference of the Foundation's Fund for Research in Psychiatry.* Oxford: Pergamon Press.

Roy, A. (Ed.) (1986). *Suicide.* Baltimore, MD: Williams & Wilkins.

Rund, B.R., Moe, L., Sollien, T., Fjell, A., Borchgrevink, T., Hallert, M., & Naess, P.O. (1994). The Psychosis Project: Outcome and cost-effectiveness of a psychoeducational treatment programme for schizophrenic adolescents. *Acta Psychiatrica Scandinavica, 89,* 211-218.

Runions, J., & Prudo, R. (1983). Problem behaviors encountered by families living with a schizophrenic member. *Canadian Journal of Psychiatry, 28,* 382-386.

Rutter, M., & Brown, G.W. (1966). The reliability and validity of measures of family life and relationships in families containing a psychiatric patient. *Social Psychiatry, 1,* 38-53.

Schooler, N.R., Keith, S.J., Severe, J.B., Matthews, S.M., Bellack, A.S., Glick, I.D., Hargreaves, W.A., Kane, J.M., Ninan, P.T., Frances, A., Jacobs, M., Lieberman, J.A., Mance, R., Simpson, G.M., & Woerner, M.G. (1997). Relapse and rehospitalization during maintenance treatment of schizophrenia: The effects of dose reduction and family treatment. *Archives of General Psychiatry, 54,* 453-463.

Schou, M. (1997). The combat of non-compliance during prophylactic lithium treatment. *Acta Psychiatric Scandinavica, 95,* 361-363.

Sederer, L.I., & Dickey, B. (Eds.) (1996). *Outcomes Assessment in Clinical Practice.* Baltimore, MD: Williams & Wilkins.

Selvini-Palazzoli, M., Cirillo, S., Selvini, M., & Sorrentino, A.M. (1989). *Family Games: General Models of Psychotic Processes in the Family.* New York: Norton.

Selzer, M.L. (1971). The Michigan Alcoholism Screening Test: The quest for a new diagnostic instrument. *American Journal of Psychiatry, 127,* 1653-1658.

Shaner, A. & Eth, S. (1989). Can schizophrenia cause posttraumatic stress disorder? *American Journal of Psychotherapy,* 1989 Oct, v43 (n4):588–597.

Sharfstein, S.S. (1984). Sociopolitical issues affecting patients with chronic schizophrenia. In A.S. Bellack (Ed.), *Schizophrenia: Treatment, Management, and Rehabilitation* (pp. 113-132). Orlando: Grune & Stratton.

Shea, M.T., Elkin, I., Imber, S.D., Sotsky, S.M., Watkins, J.T., Collins, J.F., Pilkonis, P.A., Beckham, E., Glass, D.R., Dolan, R.T., & Parloff, M.B. (1992). Course of depressive symptoms over follow-up: Findings from the National Institute of Mental Health treatment of depression collaborative research program. *Archives of General Psychiatry, 49,* 782-787.

Sidley G.L., Smith J., & Howells, K. (1991). Is it ever too late to learn? Information provision to relatives of long-term schizophrenia suffers. *Behavioural Psychotherapy, 19,* 305-320.

Skinner, H.A. (1982). The Drug Abuse Screening Test. *Addictive Behaviors, 7,* 363-371.

Smith, J. & Birchwood, M. (1987). Specific and non-specific effect of educational interventions with families of schizophrenic patients. *British Journal of Psychiatry, 150,* 645-652.

Sobell, M.B., & Sobell, L.C. (1993). *Problem Drinkers: Guided Self-Change Treatment.* New York: Guilford.

Solomon, P., & Draine, J. (1995). Subjective burden among family members of mentally ill adults: Relation to stress, coping, and adaptation. *American Journal of Orthopsychiatry, 65,* 419-427.

Solomon, P., Draine, J., Mannion, E., & Meisel, M. (1996a). Impact of brief family psycho-education on self-efficacy. *Schizophrenia Bulletin, 22,* 41-50.

Solomon, P., Draine, J., Mannion, E., & Meisel, M. (1996b). The impact of individualized consultation and group workshop family education interventions on ill relative outcomes. *Journal of Nervous and Mental Disease, 184,* 252-255.

Solomon, P., Draine, J., Mannion, E., & Meisel, M. (1997). Effectiveness of two models of brief family education: Retention of gains by family members of adults with serious mental illness. *American Journal of Orthopsychiatry, 67,* 177-186.

Song, L., Biegel, D.E., & Milligan, S.E. (1997). Predictors of depressive symptomatology among lower social class caregivers of persons with chronic mental illness. *Community Mental Health Journal, 33,* 269-286.

Spanier, G.B. (1976). Measuring dyadic adjustment: New scales for assessing the quality of marriage and similar dyads. *Journal of Marriage and the Family, 38,* 15-28.

Spaniol, L. (1987). Coping strategies of family caregivers. In A.B. Hatfield & H.P. Lefley (Eds.), *Families of the Mentally Ill: Coping and Adaptation* (pp. 208-222). New York: Guilford.

Spielberger, C.D., Jacobs, G., Russel, S., & Crane, R.S. (1983). Assessment of anger: The State-Trait Anger Scale. In J.N. Butcher & C.D. Spielberger (Eds.), *Advances in Personality Assessment, Volume 2* (pp. 159-187). Hillsdale, N.J.: Lawrence Erlbaum Associates.

Stanton, M.D., & Shadish, W.R. (1997). Outcome, attrition, and family—couples treatment for drug abuse: A meta-analysis and review of the controlled, comparative studies. *Psychological Bulletin, 122,* 170-191.

Stein, L.I., & Test, M.A. (1980). Alternatives to mental hospital treatment: I. Conceptual model, treatment program, and clinical evaluation. *Archives of General Psychiatry, 37,* 393-397.

Straus, M.A., Gelles, R.J., & Steinmetz, S.K. (1980). *Behind Closed Doors.* New York: Doubleday.

Straus, M.A., Hamby, S.L., Boney-McCoy, S., & Sugarman, D.B. (1995). *The Revised Conflict Tactics Scales (CTS2).* Durham, NH: Family Research Laboratory.

Straznickas, K.A., McNiel, D.E., & Binder, R.L. (1993). Violence toward family caregivers by mentally ill relatives. *Hospital and Community Psychiatry, 44,* 385-387.

Stuart, R.B. (1969). Operant-interpersonal treatment for marital discord. *Journal of Consulting and Clinical Psychology, 33,* 675-682.

Stueve, A., Vine, P., & Struening, E.L. (1997). Perceived burden among caregivers of adults with serious mental illness: Comparison of black, white, Hispanic, and white families. *American Journal of Orthopsychiatry, 67,* 199-209.

Sullivan, H.S. (1927). The onset of schizophrenia. *American Journal of Psychiatry, 7,* 105-134.

Surwit, R.S., & Feinglos, N.M. (1983). The effects of relaxation on glucose tolerance levels in non-insulin dependent diabetes. *Diabetes Care, 6,* 176-179.

Susser, E., Struening, E.L., & Conover, S. (1989). Psychiatric problems in homeless men: Lifetime psychosis, substance use, and current distress in new arrivals at New York City shelters. *Archives of General Psychiatry, 46*, 845-850.

Swados, E. (1991). *The Four of Us*. New York: Farrar, Straus, & Giroux.

Symonds, M. (1982). Victim responses to terror: Understanding and treatment. In F. Ochberg & D. Soskis (Eds.), *Victims of Terrorism*. 69–82. Boulder, CO: Westview Press.

Talbott, J.A. (1984). The chronic mental patient: A national perspective. In M. Mirabi (Ed.), *The Chronically Mentally Ill: Research and Services* (pp. 3-32). New York: Spectrum Publications.

Talbott, J.A. (1990). Current perspectives in the United States on the chronically mentally ill. In A. Kales, C.N. Stefanis, & J. Talbott (Eds.), *Recent Advances in Schizophrenia* (pp. 279-295). New York: Springer-Verlag.

Targum, S.D., Dibble, E.D., Davenport, Y.B., & Gershon, E.S. (1981). The family attitudes questionnaire: Patients' and spouses' views of bipolar illness. *Archives of General Psychiatry, 38*, 562-568.

Tarrier, N. (1992). Management and modification of residual positive psychotic symptoms. In M. Birchwood & N. Tarrier (Eds.), *Innovations in the Psychological Management of Schizophrenia* (pp. 147-169). Chichester, England: John Wiley & Sons.

Tarrier, N., Barrowclough, C., Vaughn, C., Bamrah, J., Porceddu, K., Watts, S., & Freeman, H. (1989). Community management of schizophrenia: A two-year follow-up of a behavioral intervention with families. *British Journal of Psychiatry, 154*, 625-628.

Tarrier, N., Beckett, R., Harwood, S., Baker, A., Yusopoff, L., Ugareburu, I. (1993). A trial of two cognitive-behavioural methods of treating drug-resistant residual psychotic symptoms in schizophrenic patients: I. Outcome. *British Journal of Psychiatry, 162*, 524-532.

Tarrier, N., Pilgrim, H., Sommerfield, C., Faragher, B., Reynolds, M., Graham, E., & Barrowclough, C. (in press). Cognitive and exposure therapy in the treatment of PTSD. *Journal of Consulting and Clinical Psychology*.

Tarrier, N., Sommerfield, C., & Pilgrim, H. (submitted manuscript). Relatives' expressed emotion (EE) and PTSD treatment outcomes.

Tarrier, N., Yusupoff, L., Kinney, C., McCarthy, E., Gledhill, A., Haddock, G., & Morris, J. (in press). A randomised controlled trial of intensive cognitive behaviour therapy for chronic schizophrenia. *British Medical Journal*.

Telles, C., Karno, M., Mintz, J., Paz, G., Arias, M., Tucker, D., & Lopez, S. (1995). Immigrant families coping with schizophrenia: Behavioral family intervention v. case management with a low-income Spanish-speaking population. *British Journal of Psychiatry, 167*, 473-479.

Teplin, L.A. (1984). Criminalizing mental disorder: The comparative arrest rate of the mentally ill. *American Psychologist, 39*, 794-803.

Terkelsen, K.G. (1983). Schizophrenia and the family: II. Adverse effects of family therapy. *Family Process, 22*, 191-200.

Thomas, E.J., & Ager, R.D. (1993). Unilateral family therapy with spouses of uncooperative alcohol abusers. In T.J. O'Farrell (Ed.), *Treating Alcohol Problems: Marital and Family Interventions* (pp. 3-33). New York: Guilford.

Thompson, E., & Doll, W. (1982). The burden of families coping with the mentally ill: An invisible crisis. *Family Relations, 31*, 379-388.

Torrey, E.F. (1995). *Surviving Schizophrenia: A Manual for Families, Consumers and Providers (Third Edition)*. New York: HarperPerennial.

Torrey, E.F., Stieber, J., Ezekiel, J., Wolfe, S.M., Sharfstein, J., Noble, J.H., & Flynn, L.M. (1992). *Criminalizing the Seriously Mentally Ill: The Abuse of Jails as Mental Hospitals*. Joint report of the National Alliance for the Mentally Ill, Arlington, VA, and Public Citizen's Health Research Group, Washington, DC.

Vargas, L.A., & Koss-Chioino, J.D. (1992). *Working with Culture: Psychotherapeutic Interventions with Ethnic Minority Children and Adolescents*. San Francisco: Jossey-Bass.

Vaughn, C.E., & Leff, J.P. (1976). The influence of family and social factors on the course of psychiatric illness: A comparison of schizophrenic and depressed neurotic patients. *British Journal of Psychiatry, 129*, 125-37.

Vaughn, K., Doyle, M., McConaghy, N., Blaszczynski, A., Fox, A., & Tarrier, N. (1992). The Sydney Intervention Trial: A controlled trial of relatives' counseling to reduce schizophrenic relapse. *Social Psychiatry and Psychiatric Epidemiology, 27*, 16-21.

Vine, P. (1982). *Families in Pain*. New York: Pantheon.

Wallace, C., Mullen, P., Burgess, P., Palmer, S., Ruschena, D., & Browne, C. (1998). Serious criminal offending and mental disorder. *British Journal of Psychiatry, 172*, 477-484.

Wallace, C.J., Liberman, R.P., MacKain, S.J., Blackwell, G., & Eckman, T.A. (1992). Effectiveness and replicability of modules for teaching social and instrumental skills to the severely mentally ill. *American Journal of Psychiatry, 149*, 654-658.

Warner, R., Taylor, D., Wright, J., Sloat, A., Springett, G., Arnold, S., & Weinberg, H. (1994). Substance use among the mentally ill: Prevalence, reasons for use, and effects on illness. *American Journal of Orthopsychiatry, 64*, 30-39.

Watson, D., & Friend, R. (1969). Measurement of social-evaluative anxiety. *Journal of Consulting and Clinical Psychology, 33*, 448-457.

Webb, C., Pfeiffer, M., Mueser, K.T., Mensch, E., DeGirolamo, J., & Levenson, D.F. (1998). Burden and well-being of caregivers for the severely mentally ill: The role of coping style and social support. *Schizophrenia Research, 34*, 169-180.

Weiss, R.L., Hops, H., & Patterson, G.R. (1973). A framework for conceptualizing marital conflict, technology for altering it, some data for evaluating it. In L.A. Hamerlynck, L.C. Handy, & E.J. Mash (Eds.), *Behavior Change: Methodology, Concepts, and Practice* (pp. 309-342). Champaign, IL: Research Press.

Whybrow, P.C. (1997). *A Mood Apart: Depression, Mania, and Other Afflictions of the Self*. New York: Basic Books.

Williams, C.D. (1959). The elimination of tantrum behaviour by extinction procedures. *Journal of Abnormal and Social Psychology, 59*, 269.

Wolpe, J. (1958). *Psychotherapy by Reciprocal Inhibition*. Stanford: Stanford University Press.

Wyatt, R.J. (1994). *Practical Psychiatric Practice: Forms and Protocols for Clinical Use*. Washington, DC: American Psychiatric Press.

Xiong, W., Phillips, M. R., Hu, X., Ruiwen, W., Dai, Q., Kleinman, J., & Kleinman, A. (1994). Family-based intervention for schizophrenic patients in China: A randomised controlled trial. *British Journal of Psychiatry, 165*, 239-247.

Zastowny, T.R., Lehman, A.F., Cole, R.E., & Kane, C. (1992). Family management of schizophrenia: A comparison of behavioral and supportive family treatment. *Psychiatric Quarterly, 63*, 159-186.

Zhang, M., Wang, M., Li, J., & Phillips, M.R. (1994). Randomised-control trial of family intervention for 78 first-episode male schizophrenic patients: An 18-month study in Suzhou, Jiangsu. *British Journal of Psychiatry, 165*, 96-102.

Zhang, M., Yan, H., Yao, C., Ye, J., Yu, Q., Chen, P., Guo, L., Yang, J., Qu, G., Zhen, W., Cai, J., Shen, M., Hou, J., Wang, L., Zhang, Y., Zhang, B., Orley, J., & Gittelman, M. (1993). Effectiveness of psychoeducation of relatives of schizophrenic patients: A prospective cohort study in five cities of China. *International Journal of Mental Health, 22*, 47-59.

Zubin, J., & Spring, B. (1977). Vulnerability: A new view of schizophrenia. *Journal of Abnormal Psychology, 86*, 103-126.

AUTHOR INDEX

SUBJECT INDEX

About the Authors

Kim T. Mueser, Ph.D. has had a strong commitment to working with individuals with serious psychiatric disorders and their families since the beginning of his professional career. After completing his Ph.D. at the University of Illinois at Chicago, he went to Camarillo State Hospital in California to complete his psychology internship training, where he also served as a postdoctoral fellow at the Mental Health and Clinical Research Center for the Study of Schizophrenia and Psychiatric Rehabilitation at UCLA. Following this, he joined the faculty at the Medical College of Pennsylvania in Philadelphia as an Assistant Professor of Psychiatry. There, Dr. Mueser later became an Associate Professor of Psychiatry and Director of the Psychology Internship Training Program. In 1994 Dr. Mueser joined the faculty at Dartmouth Medical School in Hanover, New Hampshire, where he is a Professor in the Departments of Psychiatry and Community and Family Medicine. In addition, Dr. Mueser is Scientific Director of the New Hampshire–Dartmouth Psychiatric Research Center.

Dr. Mueser has provided clinical training in family therapy and psychiatric rehabilitation to numerous professionals in workshops conducted nationally and internationally. He is the co-author of several books for professionals, including *Social Skills Training for Psychiatric Patients* (with R.P. Liberman and W.T. DeRisi; Allyn & Bacon, 1989), *The Dating Skills Program: Teaching Socio-Sexual Skills to Adults with Mental Retardation* (with D. Valenti-Hein; International Diagnostic Systems, 1990), and *Social Skills Training for Schizophrenia: A Step-by-Step Guide* (with A.S. Bellack, S. Gingerich, and J. Agresta; Guilford, 1997). He has also published a book for families, *Coping with Schizophrenia: A Guide for Families* (with S. Gingerich; New Harbinger, 1994).

In addition to Dr. Mueser's commitment to work with the seriously mentally ill and their families and in the training of professionals, he is active in research in this area and has published numerous articles and book chapters. Dr. Mueser is an active member of several organizations, including the American Psychological Association (APA), the Association for the Advancement of Behavior Therapy (AABT), the Association for Clinical Psychosocial Research (ACPR), the International Association of Psychosocial Rehabilitation Services (IAPRS), and the National Alliance for the Mentally Ill (NAMI).

Dr. Mueser is married and lives with his wife and three children in Henniker, New Hampshire.

Shirley M. Glynn became committed to the careful investigation of the effectiveness of psychotherapy treatments while completing her Ph.D. at the University of Illinois at Chicago in 1985. To further her training in working with persons with serious psychiatric disorders and their families, she completed her clinical psychology internship at the Mental Health Clinical Research Center (MHCRC) for the Study of Schizophrenia and Psychiatric Rehabilitation at Camarillo (CA) State Hospital. Dr. Glynn then accepted a position as the research psychologist on the MHCRC Clinical Research Unit at Camarillo (CA) State Hospital, where she tested the efficacy of behavioral therapy and pharmacotherapy with treatment-refractory psychiatric inpatients. In 1987, Dr. Glynn joined Research Service at the West Los Angeles Veterans Affairs Medical Center, where she has been involved in evaluating the benefits of behavioral family therapy for veterans with schizophrenia and for those with chronic and acute

PTSD. Dr. Glynn is also a Research Associate Psychologist in the UCLA Department of Psychiatry and Behavioral Science, where she conducts research on improving psychosocial treatments for serious psychiatric disorders.

Dr. Glynn is dedicated to improving services for families of persons with serious psychiatric disorders. She is a member of the National Alliance for the Mentally Ill (NAMI), the American Psychological Association (APA), the Association for Clinical Psychosocial Research (ACPR), the Association for the Advancement of Behavioral Therapy (AABT), and the International Society for Traumatic Stress Studies (ISTSS). She has published extensively on family treatment and has presented to many professional and family organizations. She is a licensed psychologist and has a private practice in Thousand Oaks and Camarillo, California.

Some Other New Harbinger Self-Help Titles

Claiming Your Creative Self: True Stories from the Everyday Lives of Women, $15.95
Six Keys to Creating the Life You Desire, $19.95
Taking Control of TMJ, $13.95
What You Need to Know About Alzheimer's, $15.95
Winning Against Relapse: A Workbook of Action Plans for Recurring Health and Emotional Problems, $14.95
Facing 30: Women Talk About Constructing a Real Life and Other Scary Rites of Passage, $12.95
The Worry Control Workbook, $15.95
Wanting What You Have: A Self-Discovery Workbook, $18.95
When Perfect Isn't Good Enough: Strategies for Coping with Perfectionism, $13.95
The Endometriosis Survival Guide, $13.95
Earning Your Own Respect: A Handbook of Personal Responsibility, $12.95
High on Stress: A Woman's Guide to Optimizing the Stress in Her Life, $13.95
Infidelity: A Survival Guide, $13.95
Stop Walking on Eggshells, $14.95
Consumer's Guide to Psychiatric Drugs, $16.95
The Fibromyalgia Advocate: Getting the Support You Need to Cope with Fibromyalgia and Myofascial Pain, $18.95
Healing Fear: New Approaches to Overcoming Anxiety, $16.95
Working Anger: Preventing and Resolving Conflict on the Job, $12.95
Sex Smart: How Your Childhood Shaped Your Sexual Life and What to Do About It, $14.95
You Can Free Yourself From Alcohol & Drugs, $13.95
Amongst Ourselves: A Self-Help Guide to Living with Dissociative Identity Disorder, $14.95
Healthy Living with Diabetes, $13.95
Dr. Carl Robinson's Basic Baby Care, $10.95
Better Boundries: Owning and Treasuring Your Life, $13.95
Goodbye Good Girl, $12.95
Being, Belonging, Doing, $10.95
Thoughts & Feelings, Second Edition, $18.95
Depression: How It Happens, How It's Healed, $14.95
Trust After Trauma, $15.95
The Chemotherapy & Radiation Survival Guide, Second Edition, $14.95
Surviving Childhood Cancer, $12.95
The Headache & Neck Pain Workbook, $14.95
Perimenopause, $16.95
The Self-Forgiveness Handbook, $12.95
A Woman's Guide to Overcoming Sexual Fear and Pain, $14.95
Don't Take It Personally, $12.95
Becoming a Wise Parent For Your Grown Child, $12.95
Clear Your Past, Change Your Future, $13.95
Preparing for Surgery, $17.95
The Power of Two, $15.95
It's Not OK Anymore, $13.95
The Daily Relaxer, $12.95
The Body Image Workbook, $17.95
Living with ADD, $17.95
When Anger Hurts Your Kids, $12.95
The Chronic Pain Control Workbook, Second Edition, $17.95
Fibromyalgia & Chronic Myofascial Pain Syndrome, $19.95
Kid Cooperation: How to Stop Yelling, Nagging & Pleading and Get Kids to Cooperate, $13.95
The Stop Smoking Workbook: Your Guide to Healthy Quitting, $17.95
Conquering Carpal Tunnel Syndrome and Other Repetitive Strain Injuries, $17.95
An End to Panic: Breakthrough Techniques for Overcoming Panic Disorder, Second Edition, $18.95
Letting Go of Anger: The 10 Most Common Anger Styles and What to Do About Them, $12.95
Messages: The Communication Skills Workbook, Second Edition, $15.95
Coping With Chronic Fatigue Syndrome: Nine Things You Can Do, $13.95
The Anxiety & Phobia Workbook, Second Edition, $18.95
The Relaxation & Stress Reduction Workbook, Fourth Edition, $17.95
Living Without Depression & Manic Depression: A Workbook for Maintaining Mood Stability, $18.95
Coping With Schizophrenia: A Guide For Families, $15.95
Visualization for Change, Second Edition, $15.95
Angry All the Time: An Emergency Guide to Anger Control, $12.95
Couple Skills: Making Your Relationship Work, $14.95
Self-Esteem, Second Edition, $13.95
I Can't Get Over It, A Handbook for Trauma Survivors, Second Edition, $16.95
Dying of Embarrassment: Help for Social Anxiety and Social Phobia, $13.95
The Depression Workbook: Living With Depression and Manic Depression, $17.95
Men & Grief: A Guide for Men Surviving the Death of a Loved One, $14.95
When Once Is Not Enough: Help for Obsessive Compulsives, $14.95
Beyond Grief: A Guide for Recovering from the Death of a Loved One, $14.95
Hypnosis for Change: A Manual of Proven Techniques, Third Edition, $15.95
When Anger Hurts, $13.95

Call **toll free, 1-800-748-6273,** to order. Have your Visa or Mastercard number ready. Or send a check for the titles you want to New Harbinger Publications, Inc., 5674 Shattuck Ave., Oakland, CA 94609. Include $3.80 for the first book and 75¢ for each additional book, to cover shipping and handling. (California residents please include appropriate sales tax.) Allow two to five weeks for delivery.

Prices subject to change without notice.